Debating Difference

'...*Debating Difference* [has] an exhaustiveness and depth that will likely make it the definitive work on its chosen topic...an extremely rich and subtle book.'

—*Osgoode Hall Law Journal*

'The uniqueness of [this] work [is in]...its reading of legislative debates to decipher the nature of political ideology...[and in]...its ability to link up the Indian debates on group rights to several key issues in liberal democratic theory.'

—*Studies in Indian Politics*

'Bajpai's penetrating and incisive analysis of Constituent Assembly debates [offers] a new tool kit to interpret group-differentiated rights...This work should form mandatory reading for those who seek to understand group rights, multiculturalism, and liberal democracy in India.'

—*South Asia Research*

'[Bajpai] seeks to demolish the myth that the resurgence of identity politics and the expansion of group-differentiated rights mark a break with the Nehruvian left-liberal consensus, although she admits that it involves a renegotiation of its terms.'

—*Frontline*

'...for Bajpai, group rights are not an attack on liberalism, but represent a central tenet of an alternative Indian liberalism that is still being articulated...'

—*The Caravan: A Journal of Politics and Culture*

'...Bajpai has tirelessly brought to our attention what so many members of the [Constituent] Assembly said with regard to group rights.'

—*The Book Review*

Debating Difference

Group Rights and
Liberal Democracy in India

ROCHANA BAJPAI

OXFORD
UNIVERSITY PRESS

OXFORD
UNIVERSITY PRESS

Oxford University Press is a department of the University of Oxford.
It furthers the University's objective of excellence in research, scholarship,
and education by publishing worldwide. Oxford is a registered trademark of
Oxford University Press in the UK and in certain other countries

Published in India by
Oxford University Press
22 Workspace, 2nd Floor, 1/22 Asaf Ali Road, New Delhi 110002, India

© Oxford University Press 2011

First Edition published in 2011
Oxford India Paperbacks 2016
4th impression 2023

ISBN-13: 978-0-19-945337-5
ISBN-10: 0-19-945337-3

Typeset in Adobe Jenson Pro 10.5/12.6
by Le Studio Graphique, Gurgaon 122 001
Printed in India by Replika Press Pvt. Ltd.

to my parents, to Prashant

Contents

Preface

This is a book about political arguments. It suggests, somewhat counter-intuitively, that the rhetoric of politicians merits close attention as reasoned argument. The primary interest of this book is in method, in exploring the possibilities of a political-theoretic reading of constitutional and legislative debates. Public reason, it suggests, is to be found not just in the thought of extraordinary individuals—an Ambedkar or a Nehru—but also in more routine practices of debate.

The debates that are the focus of this book involve policies of group-differentiated rights in India, mainly since independence in 1947. In the India that I grew up in, special treatment of Muslims and lower castes, in the Shah Bano and Mandal cases, posed urgent dilemmas and was the topic of intense debate. Could special treatment for particular groups be reconciled with liberal democratic commitments to equal individual rights? Would the greater recognition of religion and caste in public policy mean the end of the Nehruvian nationalist project of ultimately transcending ethnicity, of building political community across social difference? And finally, for tackling the difficult dilemmas of group rights, was politics a problem, or a part of the solution?

My interest in these questions coincided fortuitously with the emergence of liberal theories on group rights in the 1990s, which provided the initial intellectual shape to this inquiry. Two convictions animated my project. First, India's experience was of critical importance globally for addressing the dilemmas of group-differentiated rights in a liberal democratic framework. Second, India's own policies would benefit from locating the particularities of its debates on religion and caste in wider theoretical contexts. Embarking upon this subject as a graduate student in the mid-1990s, however, was challenging: no studies existed yet that located India's experience within political theory discussions of multiculturalism. Where to begin? In a bid to provide a historical background to the Shah Bano and Mandal cases, following a chance suggestion, I alighted upon the Indian Constituent Assembly debates. This was a crucial turning point. For those interested in public reasoning anywhere, the deliberations of the constituent Assembly of India are a treasure-trove. However, I was utterly unprepared for their intricacy, scale, and significance. The few studies of constitution-making in India were legal and historical analyses dating mainly to the 1950s and 1960s. While sophisticated in their own terms, these provided little detail on the structure of political arguments that was my interest, on the concepts and ideals invoked by the framers, their competing interpretations, and deployment in justifications for and against group rights. Arguments from the Constituent Assembly were not yet available to illuminate points of tension and convergence between liberal principles and group-differentiated rights. I had to first reconstruct these from reams of political rhetoric, a laborious task that extended from a term paper at Jawaharlal Nehru University (JNU) to a Masters thesis at Oxford in 1997. I soon ran into another difficulty: liberal arguments were not the most significant considerations in debates on special treatment for religious and caste minorities. Liberal concerns were often inseparable from nation-building. The strongest objection historically to minority rights in India and other postcolonial countries, where these are associated with a colonial divide and rule policy, has stemmed from nationalist concerns. Importantly, radical changes occurred to minority policies in the transition from British rule that were surprisingly little known: legislative representation for religious minorities came to be abolished and special treatment restricted mainly to the Scheduled Castes and Tribes during the drafting of the Constitution. My interest in pursuing these avenues led to a recasting of the initial frame of inquiry, from its location within normative liberal theory to the wider scope offered by approaches to political ideology. This allowed for a fuller examination of the range of arguments—liberal or otherwise—invoked in Indian debates. It also highlighted the relationship of norms and power, of the explanatory potential of political arguments.

Studies of political ideology, however, have traditionally focused on great individuals rather than policy debates. The rhetoric of political debate has suffered from the ennui evoked by familiarity. Moreover, analysts have, on the one hand, been preoccupied with the function of political ideologies rather than their internal structure, focusing on the motivations of actors and the purposes of their projects. On the other hand, those attentive to the details of concepts and moral reasoning have largely neglected their links to power. Clearing a space for this study thus required making a case for a particular method that combined close conceptual analysis of political rhetoric *with* an investigation of its relationship to power. This case, furthermore, had to remain detached from the two dominant frames for analysing political rhetoric, in terms of the motivations of individuals, and the interests of social classes, both of which have tended to diminish the argumentative or reasoning aspects of rhetoric. This book is an attempt to present the main findings of this continuing project. Based on detailed case studies of landmark debates, it develops a general conceptual model, in terms of which the particular forms of Indian arguments for and against group-differentiated rights in different historical periods can be understood. It shows that changes to arguments over time—between the Constituent Assembly debates (1946–49) and Mandal II (2005–6) for example—can be understood in terms of the changing relationship between the concepts of this frame. Further, changes to policies of special treatment over time—from the abolition of quotas for religious minorities in the late 1940s, to their renewed consideration by the national government in 2009—is better explained through changes to political arguments. The elaboration of the conceptual frame and its application to understanding key policy and power shifts in postcolonial India are the subject of this book.

During the writing of this book, I have benefitted greatly from the generosity and support of several individuals and institutions. I owe an immeasurable debt of gratitude to my doctoral supervisors, Michael Freeden and Nandini Gooptu for their guidance and support through many years. Michael encouraged me to think of the wider theoretical and methodological implications of my findings; his own path-breaking approach to the study of ideology forms the point of departure for this book. Nandini's intellectual rigour and acute engagement has greatly improved the quality of my arguments; her steadfast support and concern for my well-being have been vital throughout. For the initial suggestion to examine the Indian Constituent Assembly debates, in the mid-1990s when these were little studied, and for the example of her scholarship, I am indebted to Niraja Gopal Jayal. Thomas Blom Hansen and Marc Stears examined the doctoral thesis on which this book is based and offered important insights that helped to refine my arguments. For reading chapters of the manuscript, for their thoughtful comments and encouragement, I am deeply grateful to Graham Brown, Reidar Due, Brendan Fleming, Sudipta Kaviraj, James Manor, Bhikhu Parekh, and Tony Stewart. Matt Nelson and Samira Sheikh read the entire manuscript, offered invaluable suggestions, and urged me to lay it to rest, for which I am profoundly grateful.

This book has also benefitted from discussions with wonderful teachers and colleagues over the years. At Navrachna School, Baroda, my teachers and peers provided a remarkably stimulating intellectual environment. At the Maharaja Sayajirao University of Baroda, Thomas Pantham, Priyavadan Patel, AP Rana, and HS Shukul initially ignited my interest in theoretical questions, and gave generously of their books, knowledge, and time. At JNU, Delhi, Rajeev Bhargava, Zoya Hasan, Gurpreet Mahajan, and Majid Siddiqi were key interlocuters whose critical engagement and scholarship helped better define the questions that animate this study. At Oxford, the late Jerry Cohen supervised my Masters dissertation with his inimitable mix of a razor-sharp intellect and impish humour that are greatly missed. Nigel Bowles, Sudhir Hazareesingh, David Miller, Mark Philp, and Adam Swift, each an exceptional teacher and scholar, generously commented on my work, offering crucial suggestions and encouragement. The Department of Politics and International Relations at SOAS has been an unusually congenial academic home. For their advice about the book, I am particularly grateful to Arshin Adib-Moghaddam, Bhavna Dave, Laleh Khalili, Stephen Hopgood, Salwa Ismail, Tat Yan Kong, Lawrence Saez, and Charles Tripp.

This book has benefitted from the generous support of several institutions. I am very grateful to the Radhakrishnan-British Chevening Trust for allowing me to commence graduate studies at the University of Oxford. St Catherine's College and Nuffield College provided stimulating academic homes. A Nuffield studentship, a grant from the Harold Hyam Wingate Foundation and the Frere Exhibition in Indian Studies enabled the completion of doctoral research. The Beit Trust and the Radhakrishnan Bequest funded spells of fieldwork in India. I was very fortunate to be elected to Junior Research Fellowships at Wolfson College, St Anne's College, and Balliol College, which allowed me to push further the ideas that inform this study. I am deeply grateful to the Fellows and the staff of Wolfson, St Anne's and Balliol, for their generous encouragement, and many acts of solicitude and kindness.

For assisting with my research, I would like to thank the staff at the following institutions: Indian Institute Library, Oxford; the Nehru Memorial Museum and Library at Teen Murti, New Delhi; Parliament Library, New Delhi; the Minorities Commission, New Delhi; the Institute of Objective Studies, New Delhi; School of Oriental and African Studies, London. During fieldwork in Delhi, Rajeev Dhavan and Tahir Mahmood generously shared their personal libraries and vast knowledge with me. In the final stages of the manuscript, Sarah Holz and Jessica Steinmann provided valuable research assistance. I would also like to thank the team at Oxford University Press for their forbearance and support in seeing this manuscript through the various stages of the publication process.

Chapters from this book were presented at seminars in Boston, Cambridge, Oxford, London, Goa, Baroda, and Delhi. I would like to thank the organizers for inviting me, and the participants for helpful comments, in particular Chris Bayly, Sunil Khilnani, Pratap Mehta, and Sanjay Palshikar. Materials from Chapters 3–6 have appeared in *Economic and Political Weekly* (2000), 35(21–2): 1837–45; *Journal of Political Ideologies* (2002), 7(2): 179–97; *Journal of Contemporary Thought* (2009): 30: 57–87; *Modern Asian Studies* (2010), 44 (4): 675–708. I am grateful for permission to draw upon these here.

Friends and family have been an invaluable source of sustenance. For their support during the long writing of this book, I would like to mention in particular Nandini Bhattacharya, Elisabeth Bowes, Pratik Chakrabarti, Rajarshi Dasgupta, Susan George, Ewan Harrison, Gopa and Udai Joshi, Ruby Lal, Katherine Lunn-Rockliffe, Mallica and Matthew Landrus, Karma Nabulsi, Lavanya Rajamani, Rekha Rodwittiya and Ingeborg Robles. Kanti Bajpai, Gulammohammed, and Nilima Sheikh have been an inspiration in many ways. Samira Sheikh has been there from the beginning. Shalini Sharma and the Sharmas have been my family in London, as have the Chand-Bajpais, offering a home away from home. My extended family in Delhi, Hyderabad, and Bangalore—especially Chandra Chari, Sowmya Kidambi, Jaya Krishnamachari, Ira Misra, Shefali Misra, and Vasudhara Tiwari—has been a great support. My parents, Gita and Dhirendra Bajpai, have uncomplainingly endured my long absences, have lavished love, and constantly sought to ease my path. This book would not have been completed without their selfless support at critical moments. Prashant Kidambi has had to read and live with this manuscript for far too long. Without his critical insights, inimitable humour and gentle wisdom, this book, and much else besides, would not have been possible.

1

Introduction

Can group-differentiated rights be reconciled with liberal democratic principles? For the last three decades, this question has been at the centre of scholarly and political debate. Theory is still catching up with practice, as scholars come to grips with the variety of group rights along lines of culture, religion, language, race, and gender instituted by liberal democracies and the range of normative issues these raise.[1] In India the most important controversies in recent politics have centred around group rights. Do quotas for Other Backward Classes (OBCs) detract from equality of opportunity or realize social justice?[2] Do exemptions for

---

[1] Following current practice in this area, the terms 'group rights', 'minority rights', 'preferential provisions', and 'special treatment' are used interchangeably in this study, in a relatively loose and inclusive fashion. These refer broadly to group-differentiated provisions including 'public policies, legal rights and constitutional provisions' rather than narrowly to rights (Kymlicka and Norman 2000: 2). Such policies are distinguished by the fact that these go beyond common rights for all citizens, and in this study include both policies of cultural protection, as well as affirmative action. Minority rights and affirmative action have distinct histories in India that will be discussed in Chapters 2, 5, and 6. However, insofar as both involve state policies of differential treatment along ascriptive group lines that go beyond the equal rights of all individuals, these belong, for my purposes here, within the same frame.

[2] The term 'backward' is used to designate disadvantaged groups in Indian official usage and public debate. It includes mainly the ex-Untouchables (also referred to as Scheduled Castes, Harijans, Dalits, 'depressed classes'), tribal groups (the so-called Scheduled Tribes), as well as the category of intermediate low caste groups (the Other Backward Classes or OBCs). Religious minorities can be included among 'backward classes'; Muslim and Christian communities are so listed in a few Indian states. Official rankings of the 'backward' take into account a group's position in the traditional Hindu ritual hierarchy, and also other socio-economic

Muslim family law undermine equal citizenship rights for all individuals or enhance secularism?

Two kinds of answers have dominated public debate in India. The first laments the expansion of group-differentiated rights as reflecting the unprincipled compromises of electoral competition. Politicians have extended preferential policies to particular groups for electoral gain; the liberal principles of the founding fathers were doomed to failure in their confrontation with Indian realities. The second answer applauds the expansion of group rights as representing the ascendance to power of formerly excluded groups and the deepening of democracy in India. Criticisms of group rights as detracting from liberal ideals of equality of opportunity for individuals of all social backgrounds are dismissed here as little more than a mask for social privilege, weapons of upper castes and classes.

These conflicting assessments of group rights in India share some common assumptions. The first is a monochromatic understanding of liberal principles, which are seen largely to preclude the recognition of group-differentiated rights. At bottom, both perspectives reject the applicability of liberal principles to India. The second is the belief that the expansion of group rights since the late 1980s marks a fundamental break in Indian politics. Both critics and advocates agree that the resurgence of identity politics marked the end of the Nehruvian consensus, the left-liberal ideological framework fashioned by Constitution-makers. The third is a cynicism about ideas and ideals in politics. Both reduce arguments to the presumed motivations of their proponents—the pursuit of the spoils of power by the advocates of group rights and the preservation of social privilege by their critics. For both, the politics of group rights is to be understood in terms of power, not principles.

This book challenges each of these assumptions. It pursues three sets of claims. First, contrary to influential opinion that liberal values in India are ephemeral and restricted to a narrow, Westernized elite, I show that these have significantly informed public reasoning in India, that a range of liberal principles have been invoked in arguments both for and

---

indicators. For a useful tabulation of the varying usages of the category 'backward classes', see Galanter 1984: 155. The term 'minority' has had a long and varied career in Indian political discourse that is discussed in this study.

against group rights, by 'subaltern' as well as 'elite' politicians.[3] Further, against narratives of decline in liberal standards since Independence, this book argues that the *extent* of change in public reasoning between the 1950s and the present has been exaggerated. The rise of identity politics relating to religion and caste since the 1980s does not represent a fundamental break from the liberal democratic constitutional consensus, although it *does* represent a reinterpretation of its key terms. Second, contrary to the common view that political rhetoric is insignificant, little more than 'hot air', I argue that the principles professed by politicians matter. In the course of arguing for and against policies of group rights, Indian politicians have produced a rich and sophisticated body of public reasoning, close attention to which is crucial for an adequate grasp of policy and political outcomes. The Indian Constitution, unlike its counterparts in many other countries, did recognize minority rights and affirmative action. Nevertheless, constitution-making (1946–9) that marked the formal institution of a liberal democratic state, was a moment of containment in the long career of group rights in India. In contrast, the late 1980s represented a moment of crisis and renewed expansion of differentiated rights. Our understanding of the shifts that these moments embodied is incomplete without some knowledge of accompanying changes to public norms. Third, this book argues that in order properly to grasp the *form* of political rhetoric—not only in India but in general—macro-units of ideology, such as nationalism and liberalism, need to be unpacked into their conceptual elements, and questions of *function* that have dominated institutionalist as well as Marxisant analysis, subordinated to a renewed interest in form. Importantly, whereas accounts of public reasoning have overwhelmingly relied on the pronouncements of exceptional individuals, for instance,

---

[3] The terms 'principles', 'ideals', 'norms', 'values', are used relatively loosely and interchangeably in this study. These do, of course, denote distinct concepts in several debates—on the distinction between norms and values, see, for instance, Habermas 1998. However, for my purposes of examining the principles professed by politicians in a particular context, a strong categorical distinction between norms and values is not relevant, although a weak distinction is observed. 'Norms' denotes in most cases a subset of values that are shared across the polity, rather than those professed by particular parties; in other words values that are transcendental in an anthropological (Bourdieu 1977), rather than a philosophical sense (Habermas 1998).

Gandhi, Nehru, and Ambedkar in modern India, this book foregrounds
ordinary political thinking, demarcating legislative debates as a site for
mapping the range of public norms and the shifts in political power.

The story this book tells complicates the dichotomies of Western
and non-Western, elite and subaltern, ideals and political strategy, which
characterize scholarly as well as popular accounts. It is a story of the
constraints as well as the possibilities of liberal principles for policies
of group-differentiated rights; of the importance of liberal norms,
but also their insufficiency for comprehending justifications of group
rights in India. It is an account of the creative adaptation of liberal and
democratic values by Indian politicians, both elite and subaltern, and of
substantial ideological continuity amidst massive political change in post-
Independence India. And, ultimately, this is a book about how principles
matter in politics, and how an account of public reasoning can be told.

MULTICULTURALISM AND LIBERALISM:
LIBERAL AND POSTCOLONIAL THEORY

The problem of justifying minority group rights within a liberal framework
committed to equal individual rights has been a prominent preoccupation
in recent Anglo-American political theory. Normative theory on minority
rights has travelled some way since Kymlicka's *Liberalism, Community
and Culture* (1989) reopened the question of whether minority group
rights could be reconciled with liberal premises.[4] In Kymlicka's original
move, the rights of minority cultures were rendered compatible with the
key liberal concern for individual autonomy through an argument about
the value of cultural membership for individuals. Cultural structures, he
argued, provided the context within which the development of individual
capacities and the exercise of meaningful individual choice were possible
(Kymlicka 1989: 165). Minority rights were required to give effect to
principles of liberal justice in cases where the existence of the cultural
context of minority groups was threatened. For in such cases, members
of minority groups suffered from inequalities that were the product of
circumstance rather than choice.

While conceiving of culture as a context for choice for individuals
allowed for the derivation of minority rights from liberal individualist

---

[4] For an example of the earlier liberal position, see, for instance, Van Dyke 1995.

principles, it also set the limits to such reconciliation. The moral significance of cultural membership was established by construing cultures in a particular, liberal way—as enabling individuals to form, revise, and pursue their conceptions of the good. The implication was that minority cultures needed to be *liberal* in this crucial sense of valuing individual autonomy highly in order to qualify for protection (Kukathas 1992: 119–23; Parekh 2000: 99–109). While liberal principles could no longer be regarded as precluding minority rights at the outset, these would still only sanction such provisions when the latter did not come into conflict with liberal values of freedom and equality. In cases of conflict—and most of the real world hard cases pertained to such instances—the incompatibility would reassert itself. As such, Kymlicka's move refined, but did not transcend, the thesis regarding the incompatibility of liberalism and minority rights.

Liberalism, Community and Culture reset the terms of debate on group rights within a liberal framework. It came to be widely accepted that minority rights could cohabit with liberal principles, and the question for 'liberal culturalists' (Kymlicka 2001: 22) became how liberal principles could be interpreted as requiring such rights, and what limits these would set with regard to the recognition of group claims. Lines of argument in this debate have shifted somewhat as a result of subsequent development of multicultural theory. In Kymlicka's own later writings, minority rights are defended as a response, from a standpoint of liberal justice, to injustices of *nation-building* that unfairly disadvantage minority cultures. Other theorists have defended multiculturalism on liberal grounds such as individual autonomy (Raz 1994) and limitation of state power (Kukathas 1992); as well as from standpoints more critical of liberalism, such as radical egalitarianism (Young 1990); the recognition of difference (Taylor 1992); and respect for the value of cultures (Parekh 2000). However, the areas of tension between liberalism and group rights discernible in Kymlicka's original move remain. Liberals rarely oppose minority rights comprehensively now, but continue to resist such rights, where these come into conflict with liberal commitments to individual freedom as in the case of feminist critics (Okin 1999) and social justice, as with egalitarian liberals (Barry 2001).

While advancing our understanding of liberalism and the normative import of group rights, liberal multiculturalism has limitations as a framework for understanding group-differentiated rights. First,

multiculturalism and its relationship to liberal democracy are
understood and evaluated overwhelmingly in terms of the experience of
countries in Western Europe and North America. Engagement with the
experience of Asia and Africa is limited and often assumes the diffusion
of Western multiculturalism as its point of reference (Kymlicka 2007).
Some of the most long-standing and sophisticated traditions of cultural
diversity and group rights are to be found in the postcolonial states
of Asia and Africa. However, the experience of differential treatment
in postcolonial liberal democracies is yet to form the starting point
for theory-building on multiculturalism. Second, liberalism has been
the dominant frame for the evaluation of group-differentiated rights
in Anglo-American political theory. This has obscured normative
standpoints other than individual freedom and equality that are also
relevant for the assessment of special treatment—democratic goods
such as participation and deliberation; republican values such as civic
integration; and nationalist goals such as development, to take some
examples. Third, liberal multiculturalism puts culture and its protection
at the centre of arguments over group-differentiated rights. Yet most
real world debates on minority rights—those pertaining to African-
Americans in the United States, Dalits in India, Muslim immigrants
in Europe for example—are not about the protection of *cultures* as such
(Appiah 1997; Phillips 2007; Laborde 2008). Rather, cultural identity
serves to identify disadvantaged social groups that face unequal terms
when seeking participation in state and civil society institutions. Liberal
multiculturalism has also unintentionally reinforced highly reified
notions of culture and religion (Benhabib 2002), in which minority
cultures are construed in monochromatic terms, often defined by their
most conservative proponents.

These limitations form the first point of departure for this book.
To begin with, it proposes a comparative political theory approach
that takes as its starting point the experience of a non-Western liberal
democracy.[5] India is a paradigmatic example of deep diversity along

---

[5] The emerging field of comparative political thought is distinguished by an
interest in bringing non-European political thought to the attention of Western
audiences (Dallmayr 2004), as well as combining the tools of political theory
and comparative politics (Freeden 2007). This book pursues a methods-based
approach to comparative political thought. As such, 'comparative' here denotes
primarily joining up the methods of political theory and social science analysis,

lines of religion, language, caste, and tribe (for an overview, see Weiner 1997). More importantly, it possesses an extensive regime of group preference, which pre-dates the establishment of liberal democracy— group rights were thus in place prior to a system of equal individual rights. Second, instead of focusing on what liberalism can or cannot do for group-differentiated rights, this book seeks to bring to light the *range* of normative resources deployed for justifying such rights in the Indian context. It asks whether Indian debates are distinct from Western debates on differential treatment, which have focused on liberal principles. Have values other than individual freedom and equality been salient in the justification of group-differentiated rights in India? If so, might India's experience suggests respects in which arguments over special rights in postcolonial states might differ from Western liberal democracies? The main argument of this book in relation to liberal theory is interpretive rather than normative. Indian debates suggest that on its own, liberalism is inadequate as a framework for comprehending and evaluating postcolonial multiculturalism.[6] Liberal norms such as secularism, individual rights, and equality of opportunity have been inextricably intertwined with other considerations, notably nation-building, economic development, and democratic equality. Third, to probe the significance of culture for group-differentiated rights in India, this book *compares* debates in the case of two types of groups, religious minorities, and lower castes, involving policies both of cultural rights and affirmative

---

for the purposes discussed below, although of course, I also focus on non-Western political thinking. Comparison here does not have to explicitly involve more than one country or case.

[6] It might be wondered whether the concept of multiculturalism is adequate for comprehending the deep, multi-level diversity of the kind encountered in India and other countries of Asia and Africa. Doesn't multiculturalism flatten difference, reduce multiform diversity to a single level in a manner more suited to immigrant societies of North America and Western Europe? Perhaps multiculturalism is just *liberalism's* approach to diversity, inappropriate for contexts with other traditions for dealing with difference? These challenges undoubtedly have some merit. Nevertheless, multiculturalism remains a useful category for the analysis of *state* approaches to group-differentiated rights in liberal democracies, loosely defined, and is used as such in this study, sparingly, with cognizance of its possible limits. The category is also helpful for locating a particular state's approach to cultural diversity within a wider frame of reference and making it available for comparative purposes.

action. It takes the insights of historians and anthropologists on the role of the state in the construction of identities seriously, and traces the changing character of group claims over time in response to the evolving institutional framework. A key argument of this book pertains to the convergence over time, in normative terms, of arguments for preferential treatment for religious minorities and lower castes.

When this study commenced in the mid-1990s, there were no writings on group rights and liberal democracy in India. Works on minorities did exist: a literature dating from the pre-Independence period considered the problem of minorities from the standpoint of the Indian national movement (Krishna 1939; Sen 1940); legal-historical works traced the development of constitutional provisions pertaining to minorities in the post-Independence period (Imam 1972; Wadhwa 1975; Mahmood 1991). However, group rights in India had not yet been conceptualized as a problem in relation to a liberal democratic framework. Since the late 1990s, a sophisticated body of theoretical writing has emerged on minority rights in India, spurred by global interest in this area as well as local factors such as the rise of Hindu nationalism (see, for instance, Bajpai 1997; Bhargava 1998; Mahajan 1998; Chandhoke 1999; Jayal 1999). This book shares with this important literature the view that India is paradigmatic for evaluating the relationship of group rights and liberal democracy, and the need to pay attention to liberal ideals in the Indian context. This study differs, however, in its mode of engagement with postcolonial theory and its approach to political ideology.

While neglected in liberal theory, the experience of Asia and Africa does form the starting point for radical and postcolonial theory. Postcolonial theorists have importantly sought to highlight the *gaps* between ideal principles and real world circumstances typically neglected by contemporary liberal theorists. While the relationship of group rights and liberal democracy has rarely attracted analysis, postcolonial theory does have a distinct normative position on the subject. This might be described as a critique of liberalism and a defence of difference, usually from an unarticulated democratic standpoint. Liberal principles and indeed universal ideals in general usually appear as oppressive ideologies, sustained by asymmetrical relations of power, and necessarily antagonistic to difference. Viewed historically, liberalism is located within macro-social processes such as 'modernity', and associated with the development of capitalism in the modern West and colonialism in Asia and Africa. Seemingly universal, trans-group ideals such as equal citizenship serve the interest of particular groups, notably the metropolitan or native bourgeoisie's interest in the accumulation of state power. While providing unparalleled insights on the relationship of norms and power, postcolonial theory is characterized by over-generalized accounts of liberalism. An *a priori* assumption of postcolonial difference is also common, with Asia and Africa regarded as unsuited to the use of Western norms, incapable of adequate comprehension through Western categories. While the positing of cultural difference can be seen as an understandable attempt to resist Western domination, its effect has been to undermine the actual empirical investigation of meanings, the extent to which political practice across the West–East divide might address analogous problems and end up with similar solutions, even if these are arrived at through different routes. It has resulted in the reification of cultural difference not just along West and the rest lines, but also within postcolonial contexts, notably between the elite and the subaltern. Paradoxically, like liberal political theory, postcolonial theory too has ended up with the elevation and entrenchment of *culture*.[7]

These limitations of postcolonial theory form a second point of departure for this study. I problematize both liberal universalism and postcolonial narratives of difference and construct a framework that combines their insights for the analysis of Indian debates on group-differentiated rights. To begin with, as a way out of the problems of reification of culture and overstated contrasts between the West and the non-West (inadequate but unavoidable terms), I propose an empirical investigation of the meanings of liberal and democratic norms in non-Western contexts, India in this case.[8] This would provide the basis for more accurate, evidence-based assessments of the extent of

---

[7] Culture is, however, understood differently in postcolonial theory. I am grateful to Sudipta Kaviraj for highlighting this point. Of course, there are differences in the concept of culture *within* postcolonial theory and liberal theory, but my general point still applies. For a critique of liberal theory from a standpoint of cultural difference that arrives at similar conclusions to postcolonial theory, and shares many of its strengths and weaknesses, see Balagangadhara 1994.

[8] 'Empirical' is employed here in an interpretive sense (Geertz 1973) rather than a narrowly positivist one.

similarity and difference across the Western/non-Western divide. Postcolonial creativity, this study emphasizes, can be found in areas of *similarity* as well as difference from Western patterns: the historical origins of ideas are less important than their political career, the manner in which these are deployed in different, distant contexts. Second, liberalism in this study is not framed as a macro-ideology but rather unpacked into its conceptual elements. A more complex, differentiated picture of liberalism results, with the Indian case illustrating *both* areas of discord and concord between liberal principles and group rights. The relationship of liberal norms to group rights has, importantly, varied over time, depending upon how the requirements of national unity and development are construed. The argument of this study is not primarily normative: it does not explicitly prosecute a defence of liberalism or any other ideal. Nevertheless, in demonstrating that liberal principles have been interpreted, correctly, as consonant with some group-differentiated rights in the Indian context, it does show that liberal and other universal ideals are not *necessarily* hostile to difference, oppressive of the particular. This study does thereby seek to undermine a powerful objection to trans-cultural, trans-group ideals, and to suggest that postcolonial theorists have underestimated the resources that such ideals offer for the recognition of group-differentiated rights. Third, like in postcolonial theory, liberal democracy is considered in this book at a lower level of abstraction than in normative political theory, as an ideology rather than a philosophy. However, importantly, it is not tied to a social theory about capitalism, colonialism, and class hegemony. This is not to deny that capitalism played a role in the origins of liberalism and colonialism in its transmission, or to negate the invaluable insights about power offered by postcolonial theory. It is, however, to propose an alternative approach that involves some element of abstraction of ideas from their historical contexts. The central argument of this book is that such an approach offers a more nuanced account of the character of ideologies and their relationship to power.

IDEOLOGY, DISCOURSE AND HEGEMONY: AFTER COLONIAL DISCOURSE ANALYSIS

The subject of this book is legislative debates over group rights in independent India. Traditionally, the ideas expressed in everyday political thinking have been disregarded by political theorists as too crude in conceptual terms to merit serious attention, and by political scientists as insignificant for explanations of political outcomes. In recent times, there has been a revival of interest in the study of ideas and ideologies in political theory (Freeden 1996) as well as political science (for overviews, see Blyth 1997; Rueschemeyer 2006). However, accounts of ideology in the scholarship on India, as elsewhere, have remained in thrall to two powerful sources of reductionism: methodological individualism and Marxist social theory. In the sophisticated institutional literature that is emerging on Indian politics, ideas barely figure; when they do, these are framed in avowedly instrumental terms (e.g., Chandra 2004). Occasionally, a larger role for ideas in explanation is hinted at, in the form of elite beliefs informing policy, for instance, but this has remained untheorized.

The most sustained and sophisticated accounts of ideology and discourse in the Indian context have been influenced by Marxist social theory, notably those by scholars from the so-called Subaltern School (Chatterjee 1986; Kaviraj 1992). In contrast to the traditional Marxist view, subaltern scholars have striven to emphasize the importance of ideas and culture more broadly for political explanation. Chatterjee's seminal account of nationalist ideology seeks explicitly to avoid sociological determinism, to pay close attention to 'the content as well as the logical and theoretical forms of nationalist thought', for without this, it is not possible to adequately understand 'the true historical effectivity of nationalism itself' (1986: 40–1). Nevertheless, while its empirical focus is on nationalist thought, in *analytical* terms, ideas continue to occupy a subordinate position in Chatterjee's frame. Nationalist ideology is delineated overwhelmingly in terms of the strategic requirements of nationalism, understood as a bourgeois political movement for the capture of state power. Nationalist thought services the need of nationalism to build a broad-based alliance against colonial rule of dominant as well as subordinate classes such as the peasantry. Explicated in terms of its presumed function, the actual *justificatory structures* of nationalist thought remain elusive. For instance, social justice as an aspect of Nehru's thought is described as a political strategy whose objective was 'the establishment of a sovereign national state...[and] social and economic issues were necessary to mobilize the masses in the movement towards that goal'(1986: 130). Here we find little detail on the precise notion of equality deployed; the focus instead is on its *role* in facilitating the mobilization of masses. Nationalist thought serves to organize bourgeois hegemony, which is understood in explicitly Gramscian terms, involving domination of subordinate groups by the bourgeoisie, by presenting its class interest as the universal national interest (Chatterjee 1986: 44). As in the case of ideology, the functionalist frame for the analysis of hegemony pre-empts any detailed analysis of its ideational structure—what it actually looked like in conceptual terms, the different strands of opinion in the nationalist alliance, the points of ideological convergence and divergence.

This study pursues a different approach. Building upon Freeden's morphological analysis, it seeks to avoid the reductionism inherent in both instrumental institutionalist and functionalist Marxisant accounts of ideas by reframing the study of ideology along three related, dimensions. First, it dissociates analysis of the structure of ideology from that of its function. Ideologies possess a complex internal architecture and can serve a variety of purposes (Freeden 1996: 23, 48). In order to properly grasp the contours of ideologies—what these actually look like—we need to bracket off, at least temporarily, questions about function—what these do—and unpack macro-ideological blocks like nationalism into their conceptual elements. Of course, ideologies often serve purposes such as political mobilization, domination, manipulation, or integration. But *contra* colonial discourse analysis, an explication of function, unmasking of the purposes that ideologies serve, does not *suffice* as an account of meaning, for which conceptual disaggregation is a necessary first step. Second, the influence of Marxist social theory has meant that ideology and power are cast in colonial discourse analysis in largely *negative* terms, as regressive and repressive. By contrast, following Freeden, ideology is used in a more descriptive, neutral sense in this book. While ideologies can certainly be dissimulative, exploitative, or false, these are not their necessary, defining features.[9] Ideology, power, and hegemony can serve the interests of emancipation as of domination, of progressive change as of maintaining an unequal status quo. Indeed, *even* as instruments of domination, these might well retain a potential

---

[9] As Freeden notes, 'societies display ideological thinking in areas unrelated to domination', and the political ideas that constitute ideologies have other dimensions, including, for instance, the 'philosophical and fact-identifying' (1996: 136).

for progressive change. A third related difference from colonial discourse analysis in this book is that the account of ideologies offered here brackets off, and is agnostic about, their *social* origins. Instead of linking ideologies to social classes and their interests, it holds that it is possible and fruitful to examine these primarily in terms of the relationship between their component concepts. Whether ideologies serve the interests of dominant social groups and how exactly, should be treated as subsequent and distinct questions, in need of empirical investigation, and not as theoretical assumptions, as is the case in Marxisant approaches. In the analytical framework of colonial discourse analysis, the influence of Marxian social theory means that two different kinds of questions are conflated: why ideologies take the form that they do, and how ideologies help us better explain politics; both are elucidated in terms of the interests of dominant classes. By contrast, the analysis of political discourse pursued in this book separates these questions, and it does not seek to explain the *form* of ideologies. Instead, it explores what the shape of ideologies, however it might have come about, can tell us about politics, and it seeks to do so without recourse to assumptions regarding their social underpinnings.

But what, it might be asked, of the relationship of ideology and power that is at the heart of colonial discourse analysis and Marxian social theory more broadly? Can an approach to ideology that is agnostic about its social bases and functions illuminate relations of power?[10] This book extends Freeden's morphological approach to ideology to the domain of power and hegemony, drawing upon the insights of post-Marxist approaches and postcolonial studies. I argue that a conceptual analysis of political discourse offers not only a more accurate grasp of the intricacy of ideological form, but also a better understanding of political power.[11] That ideologies attempt to fix the contested meanings of political concepts (Freeden 1996) is an important neglected aspect

---

[10] For criticism along these lines, see, for instance, Bourdieu 1977: 188–9.

[11] 'Discourse' is used primarily in a narrow linguistic sense in this study, and not in the broad sense that characterizes post-structuralist and post-Marxist traditions where it encompasses subject formation and social structures (Foucault 1980; Laclau and Mouffe 1985). The epistemic value of discourse is in my view best examined by retaining a narrow conception of the term. Also, in contrast to Foucaultian and post-Marxist approaches, no categorical distinction between ideology and discourse obtains in this study.

of the struggle for power between contending political interests. Furthermore, the success and failure of attempts to recast the meaning of legitimating norms tells us about the construction and breakdown of *political* hegemony. Note the emphasis on political here: in my account, ideological content and contest provide information about the character and distribution of power in the polity, not necessarily about *social* relations of power as in colonial discourse analysis. The analysis of discourse and power offered here is compatible with many different accounts of social classes or groups and their relationship to the political domain. How the distribution of power in the polity relates to that in society is a separate question outside the scope of this study; the two are not fused together as is the case in accounts influenced by Marxian social theory.[12] The conceptual account of ideology and hegemony offered in this book thus does not provide a full theory of power: its explanatory ambitions are limited. What it does reveal are the *conceptual coordinates* of political interests and whether these are hegemonic or not in the sense of being able to establish a reigning set of political norms. Whereas scholars of ideology usually analyse power relations at the level of social forces seeking to realize particular goals, this study will show that the social and political interests behind ideologies can be observed in the very justificatory structures of ideologies, their internal conceptual configuration. We cannot understand political power sufficiently if we look upon ideology only as an instrument of power: ideologies are not simply dissimulative of power, these are also descriptive of it, in their conceptual contours.

The central hypothesis advanced by this book is that a legitimating vocabulary comprising a set of interlinked political concepts, chief

---

[12] Laclau and Mouffe have argued for reconceptualizing hegemony as a political relation. They seek explicitly to go beyond the Marxian notion that 'the ultimate core of a hegemonic force consists of a fundamental class', as well as Gramsci's formulation that 'every social formation structures itself around a single hegemonic centre', making a case for the 'openness and indeterminacy of the social' (Laclau and Mouffe 1985: 134, 138, 145). However, the elaboration of hegemony in their account relies upon a social theory of advanced capitalist societies and has a class core. Although social relations of its production are conceptualized differently from traditional Marxist accounts, hegemony is still understood in terms of its social bases, in contrast with the account offered in this study.

among which are those of secularism, democracy, social justice, and national unity and development, has framed political arguments on group rights in independent India. This conceptual constellation constitutes the defining *structural* features of public-political reasoning in India. All political arguments for and against different types of group preferential policies, advanced from conflicting ideological and political positions, and in distinct historical periods in independent India have invoked one or the other of the concepts from this vocabulary, although they have disagreed about their meanings and policy implications. Further, I argue that the particular and diverse historical forms of political arguments on group rights in India are best understood in terms of the *interlinkages* between these concepts and their relative *priority* in the legitimating vocabulary. So, for instance, when secularism and national unity were conjoined and dominant in the vocabulary, a particular set of arguments about group-differentiated rights ensued; when the dominant relationship was between social justice and democracy, a different set of arguments resulted.

Seen through the lens of this conceptual model, the historical trajectory of group rights and the Indian state appears in a new light. The founding of the postcolonial Indian state in the late 1940s marked a moment of containment of group rights (Bajpai 1997). The dominant nationalist construal of the legitimating vocabulary at this historical juncture was hostile to group preference. The nationalist vocabulary also expanded to become the new framework of political debate in India. In other words the Congress party was able to translate its dominance into hegemony, the establishment of a new ideological consensus. By contrast, the late 1980s were a moment of crisis, marking a reopening of the constitutional resolution of group rights. The dominant legitimating concepts, this book will show, were now reconfigured in forms more accommodating of group rights. These were, however, much more fiercely contested, and competing conceptions remained entrenched; this corresponded to the decline of Congress hegemony. However, even as the legitimating vocabulary came to be reinterpreted in important new ways, its broad structural features largely endured. In other words, the legacy of Congress hegemony persists even as group rights have expanded, although it has been remoulded to purposes distinct from, even opposed to those intended by its authors. That the ideational framework established at the founding of the postcolonial Indian state continues to endure is an important finding of this study, with implications for the important puzzle, only implicitly addressed here, of how democratic institutions survive in India.

POLITICAL RHETORIC AND LEGISLATIVE DEBATE: FROM A HISTORY OF IDEAS TO AN INTERPRETIVE SOCIAL SCIENCE

To map the conceptual contours of political discourse, this book focuses on reasons offered by politicians in policy debates. Philosophers have long emphasized the role of public reasoning and deliberative processes in a democracy (Rawls 1971; Cohen 1989). In the Indian context, Sen reminds us that democracy is 'intimately connected with public discussion and interactive reasoning' and India's long and well-developed tradition of public argument is an important, if neglected asset in the maintenance of its democratic institutions (2005: 13–14). Yet, empirical studies of public *debates* in India are rare. Public reasoning has mostly been examined as the thought of exemplary *individuals*—Ashoka and Akbar have represented India's ancient traditions, Nehru, Gandhi and to a lesser extent Tagore, Bankimchandra, and Ambedkar have served to define modern Indian political thought. Arguments professed in everyday public debate have rarely received close attention in their own right.

The reasons for this neglect are not hard to find. Political rhetoric falls foul of the traditional division of labour between political theory and political science. To political theorists, the principles professed by politicians are often muddled and indeterminate, designated incorrectly, and deployed in logically inconsistent ways, with little regard for clarity or precision in usage (Swift 2001). Indeterminacy and inaccuracy of political argument are often a deliberate political strategy, enabling politicians to reach out to disparate constituencies, or maximize their room for manoeuvre (Freeden 1996). But political rhetoric consequently seems too crude and commonplace to merit theoretical attention. To political scientists intent on explaining outcomes, political rhetoric usually appears as little more than a smokescreen for the pursuit of power, a distracting strategy deployed by politicians to disguise their real purposes (Skinner 1988). With politicians apparently tailoring their principles at will to fit the demands of political expediency, the arguments professed in policy debate seem to offer little additional explanatory leverage. Certainly, a detailed analysis of political rhetoric has not been considered germane to explanations of political outcomes.

This book challenges these assumptions. Of course the ideals professed by politicians are often ill-defined and insincerely held. But it does not follow from this that political arguments are necessarily unsophisticated or lacking explanatory efficacy. Probing underneath the surface of political rhetoric, using tools of political theorists in order to 'reconstruct and amplify' principles that are implicit or confused in pronouncements reveals an intricate, layered structure of public reasoning (Freeden 1996: 34). In the course of arguing for and against policies of group-differentiated rights, Indian politicians fashioned a sophisticated body of public norms. An analytical reconstruction of these norms sheds new light on gaps and tensions in political theory debates on group rights. It also advances explanation of how of certain policies of group preference came to be altered at particular historical moments and shifts in the distribution of power in the Indian polity.

Legislative debate provides a unique vantage point in this regard. Bringing as it does contending elements in public life onto a common stage, institutional policy debate offers an ideal site for mapping the different strands of public reasoning, as well as their internal variations.[13] Further, legislative debates provide a snapshot of the process whereby particular discourses seek to transform prevailing political norms, and the success and failure of such attempts. In other words, they offer an exceptional site for empirically grounding the analysis of ideological change and political hegemony. Finally, public debate, the give and take of reasons about what constitutes the right policy, is an important aspect of the life of a democracy, an indicator of its health and a mode whereby democracies renew their foundational ideals.

The case this study makes for taking rhetoric seriously does not require that politicians sincerely hold the principles that they profess. Political scientists, insofar as they have taken rhetoric into account in explanation, have emphasized the *beliefs* of agents (for example, Horowitz 1989). But as Skinner has famously pointed out, professing commitment

---

[13] Legislative debate serves in this study as a site for mapping the contest of ideas and the formation of public standards. How the institutional rules of the legislature, for instance, regarding procedures for raising questions, shape the form of arguments advanced, as these of course do, is outside the scope of this inquiry.

to a principle gives politicians a strong reason not to behave in ways that appear to contravene the principle, whether or not they genuinely believe in it. A rational agent claiming that 'his apparently untoward actions were in fact motivated by some accepted set of social or political principles' will be 'obliged to behave in such a way that his actions remain compatible with the claim that these principles genuinely motivated him' (1988: 116–17; see also 2002: ch. 8). Further, contrary to the common view that politicians freely tailor principles to fit their projects, Skinner suggests that individual agents cannot manipulate the norms they use to legitimate their conduct wholly according to their will, for the availability and applicability of these norms is limited by their prevailing social usage (2002: 156). Politicians do try to reinterpret prevailing norms in order to describe their actions as falling within accepted principles, but their capacity for manoeuvre is not infinite. For, if too many of the criteria of an accepted principle are dropped, it becomes apparent that the norm is not being used in the accepted way and the usage lacks legitimating capacity (Skinner 1988: 115–16).

This book's approach to the analysis of political rhetoric is distinct, however, from Skinner and other history of ideas accounts that dominate the study of ideologies. While sharing an interest with historians in the reconstruction of the meanings of ideas in particular contexts, my approach is in important respects more akin to interpretive social science (Geertz 1973; Taylor 1985; Rabinow and Sullivan 1987; Bevir and Rhodes 2002). First, whereas historians of ideas have typically sought to recuperate the theoretical and political creativity of key *individuals*, such individual actors remain largely faceless in this book. Nehru, Ambedkar and other important figures feature only as instances of more generally prevailing modes of argument, interchangeable sources that represent significant types of conceptual usage. The focus is on the *practice* of political debate. Political principles, this book suggests, are forged not only through unique deeds of 'innovating ideologists' (Skinner 2002), but also through more ordinary, iterated processes of collective discussion and debate in which reasons are put forward, negotiated and recast as a result of how they are received. The role of political debate in the process of ideological production and transmission merits greater attention.

Second, in contrast with histories of ideas, this study does not detail the wider intellectual, political, and social contexts in which political debate is located. Unlike the historian who typically seeks to tell the whole story of conceptual and political change, my approach is akin to the social scientist in isolating one portion of a complex story for close analysis. Most of the umbilical cords that connect ideas to the worlds from which these arise are cut off for analytical purposes, at least in the first instance. Instead, legislative debate is treated largely as a self-enclosed text; ideological continuity and change over time are established by examining 'multiple synchronic states' (Freeden 1996: 52). To do so is not to make the implausible ontological claim that political debate is in fact a creature independent of its context: of course a range of factors external to political arguments influence their shape. It is, however, to make the *epistemic* claim that our understanding of politics can be enhanced through a close study of the structure of political arguments. To avoid reductionist readings of politicians' pronouncements, and explore the possibilities (and limits) of a textual reading, information about agents and contexts is kept to a minimum.

Accordingly, the reconstruction of arguments undertaken in this study does not claim to offer a *full* account of meaning. Recent calls for greater attention to political rhetoric have emphasized aspects of rhetorical form such as situation, narrative, emotion, metaphor, affective and figurative forms of reasoning. By contrast, this study focuses on the *conceptual* structure of rhetoric, offering an analytical reconstruction of political arguments: its forays into the rhetorical aspects of political debate are deliberately minimal. I show that it is plausible and productive to cast political rhetoric as reasoned argument even against its grain; this is necessary for an adequate grasp of the conceptual dimensions of political power.

Third, the account of public reasoning constructed in this study is akin to social science as it is explicitly *explanatory* in intent: its purpose is not only to provide a better appreciation of the sophistication and diversity of everyday political thinking as is the case for most historical exercises in retrieval, but through this, to fashion an interpretive key that helps us better understand and explain political change.[14] The

---

[14] The model of explanation implicit here is distinct from positivist social science. As scholars have suggested, interpretive explanations are explanatory in at least the following ways. First, insofar as an explanation includes an account of the mechanisms or process whereby outcomes are produced, descriptions of the reasons given by agents can form part of causal explanations. This view challenges the *why-necessary* criterion for causal explanations of positivist social science, and

formulation of a legitimating vocabulary comprising inter-linked concepts of secularism, democracy, social justice, national unity and development, I argue, provide a better account not just of arguments about group rights, but also of policy shifts and political change in India. Its explanatory ambitions are limited: a textual analysis of political arguments does not claim to provide an account of necessary or sufficient conditions for political outcomes or to explain why arguments assume a particular form. Ideas might not be the most important factors in explanation, and the general limitations associated with establishing the role of ideas in explanation apply here as well: ideas are notoriously hard to separate from other factors, so it is often impossible to assign relative weight and assess their causal impact in relation to policy outcomes (Blyth 1997; Rueschemeyer 2006: 248–9). Nevertheless, this study does claim that without a conceptually detailed account of ideas, one that it is possible to construct through a largely textual reading of legislative debates, our explanations of political change are, necessarily, incomplete.

A conceptual analysis of political rhetoric can advance understanding and explanation in at least the following ways that are explored in this book. First, it brings to light the prevailing normative vocabulary that is an enabling or inhibiting condition for political action, and thereby provides an important bit of the story of *how* an outcome was brought about. Second, an analytical interpretation of political rhetoric illuminates the *conceptual coordinates* of political forces such as political parties, for instance, the precise notion of social justice or democracy espoused by the Congress party at a given moment, affording an additional dimension along which political change can be mapped and assessed (Farr 1989: 32; Wendt 1998: 86). Third, it

---

holds that the latter are also about *how* things—policies, institutions—came to be as they are (Wendt 1998: 83). Second, if we admit the possibility of non-causal explanations (a possibility accepted by most philosophers of social science and social theorists but rejected by positivist social scientists), interpretations explain by explicating how a phenomenon is put together, delineating the structures that make for its distinctive properties. Interpretations here are explanatory by providing answers to 'what' and 'how possible' questions, by telling us what a thing is, or how it is constituted so that it behaves as it does (*ibid.*: 112–13). For a critique of the causal/constitutive dichotomy and also of the dominant Humean model of causality, see Gofas and Hay 2008.

brings to light the shifts in *norms* that accompanies political *processes* of hegemony construction and breakdown. The ascendancy of Congress hegemony in India of the 1950s, and its final decline in the 1990s, are well documented in their institutional and sociological aspects. In a new departure, this book provides a conceptual-ideological account of the establishment and decline of political hegemony. It shows that this process can be traced in legislative debate, through mapping the shifts in legitimating norms. In the lineaments of political arguments, we can discern, in a crystallized form, the main lines of political change in post-Independence India.

This then constitutes the distinctive theoretical and methodological approach pursued in this book. It shares with the emerging literature on group rights in India an interest in liberal democratic ideals and political discourse. It differs in its detailed, *empirical* mapping of political ideals in legislative debates at key historical moments (e.g., Jayal 1999), its disaggregation of political discourse into semantic, conceptual and normative levels. Above all, whereas ideals such as secularism or democracy have hitherto been treated individually, this book proposes that these be examined as *interlocking* elements of a single legitimating vocabulary (Bajpai 1997, 2003). Such an approach, I argue, gives us a much more precise grasp of the layered structure of public norms in India. It provides a better grasp of continuities and shifts in the trajectories of political values, whose assessments have tended to be diffuse. Finally, as we shall see, the approach adopted here allows for more accurate evaluation of the extent to which Indian values are similar to, or different from Western discourses.

Three landmark legislative debates form the focus of the analysis of political arguments undertaken in this book. The Constituent Assembly Debates (1946–9) covered a wide range of preferential policies, most notably, political representation for minority groups, job quotas, and cultural rights. The debate over Muslim Women Protection of Rights on Divorce Act (1986) or the Shah Bano case as it is popularly known, centred on exemptions for Muslims from laws governing maintenance for divorced women. The 1990 Mandal debate concerned the extension of the Indian state's policy of quotas in government employment to a large new group, the so-called Other Backward Classes (OBCs), mainly comprising intermediate lower castes. A focus on legislative debate makes this a study of public reasoning in a particular, elite domain.

Overwhelmingly composed of social elites (upper caste and class urban professionals) in the late 1940s, the national parliament had become much more representative in caste and class terms by the time of the 1990 Mandal debate (although of course by definition, it is an institution of political elites).

STRUCTURE AND ARGUMENT OF THE BOOK

This book is divided into two parts. Each focuses on a defining moment in the career of the Indian state and recasts how this is commonly understood. Part I focuses on the founding moment of liberal democracy in India, the Constituent Assembly debates (1946–9), which marked a moment of containment in the career of group rights in India. Part II shifts to two key political debates of the late 1980s, the Shah Bano case (1986), and the Mandal debate (1990). These registered a moment of crisis and paradigm shift in the constitutional resolution of minority preference—group-differentiated rights at the national level have since steadily expanded.

Each part provides an analytical reconstruction of arguments of advocates and opponents of group rights, articulating implicit assumptions and tracing missing logical links (Laborde 2008: 26). I distinguish the different types of arguments for special rights for religious minorities and lower castes in these debates, teasing out competing conceptions of secularism, democracy social justice, national unity, and development. Recurrent normative terms are identified as components of the legitimating vocabulary through multiple studies of key debates across different policy areas. This reconstruction then becomes the basis for the book's argument about discursive changes between the debates on group rights of the late 1940s and the late 1980s and their implications for policy shifts and political change. The criteria followed for the selection and designation of political speeches are as follows. In line with the aims of this inquiry, utterances are chosen as illustrative of types of arguments about group rights: as such, these are not always representative of the range of parties or social groups. In the designation of an argument as characteristic of 'nationalist discourse' or 'Hindu right discourse', the most commonly expressed opinion in the party is taken as representative of its position in a debate. Such characterizations are qualified when necessary by indicating the relevant different strands of opinion within each party or group. A summary of the argument of each chapter is as follows.

Part One comprises three chapters. Chapter 2 offers a historical interpretation of the career of group preferential policies from the late nineteenth century through to close of the Constituent Assembly debates. I show that while group rights in the first half of the twentieth century saw steady expansion, as these entered independent India their colonial proportions came to be scaled back. Although unlike its counterparts elsewhere, the Indian Constitution did recognize group-differentiated rights, these nevertheless represented a cutting back on the regime of preferential provisions that existed before. I show that the dynamic of containment assumed different degrees and forms in different areas of group rights, with the most far-reaching changes occurring in political representation for religious minorities. While Partition is usually cited to account for attenuation in the rights of religious minorities during constitution-making, I argue that it does not constitute a sufficient explanation as is commonly believed. Instead, longer-term ideological features of Indian nationalism favoured the containment of differential treatment, features which are not adequately captured in existing formulations of 'nationalist modernity' or the beliefs of influential actors such as Nehru and Ambedkar.

Chapter 3 introduces the conceptual model proposed by the book. It argues that Indian nationalist discourse on group rights in the Constituent Assembly is best understood as comprising a set of interlinked concepts—secularism, democracy, social justice, national unity, and development.[15] In analytical terms, a legitimating vocabulary comprising a constellation of interdependent concepts was the frame for nationalist arguments on group rights. All arguments in nationalist opinion—for as well as against group rights, advanced from distinct ideological positions, in debates over different policies—invoked one or another of the key concepts of this vocabulary. National unity was the primary notion in this vocabulary, in relation to which the other concepts were construed. In historical terms, this chapter shows that the dominant interpretation of the nationalist vocabulary in this period was

[15] The term 'nationalist' is used in a heuristic sense in this study, to denote a position that accords normative primacy to the Indian nation. Parties and individuals who subscribe to this position have changed over time; for an elaboration, see Chapters 2, and 3 in this book.

opposed to special provisions for minority groups. As these were seen as
a threat to national unity, other concepts of the nationalist vocabulary
such as secularism and justice were also construed as antithetical to
group-differentiated rights. Nationalists of different ideological hues,
Hindu traditionalists, Gandhians as much as Nehruvian modernists,
professing distinct conceptions of secularism, social justice, national
identity, and development, *converged* in opposition to special treatment.
Indian nationalism spoke in a common, liberal voice against group-
differentiated rights in this period, with modernist ideas likely gaining
ground as these accorded with Hindu opinion on minority rights.
Finally, focusing on secularism, the chapter argues that the nationalist
vocabulary was substantially liberal democratic in character, even as it
was inflected by indigenous historical and cultural idioms.

Chapter 4 refines the formulation of the nationalist vocabulary
and explores its reach for understanding and explaining political
change. While group preference in general was problematic from liberal
nationalist standpoints, special treatment for cultural protection suffered
from a greater justificatory deficit than that for rectifying socio-economic
disadvantage. That legislative and employment quotas for religious
minorities were eventually withdrawn from the Indian Constitution, and
quotas for 'backward classes' retained, but in a weaker form, is entirely
consistent with the normative resources for group-differentiated rights in
nationalist discourse. The chapter shows further that as the deliberations
of the Constituent Assembly unfolded, the nationalist vocabulary
expanded to become the new legitimating framework of the polity,
the language in which all political argument was conducted. During
the Constituent Assembly debates, and in part through the process of
debating, both the institutional forms of group rights and the discursive
frame of the Indian polity came to be realigned: nationalists were able
to translate their dominance into hegemony. This is established through
an analytical reconstruction of positions in debates over three key
institutional mechanisms for group rights: legislative quotas, employment
quotas, cultural and educational rights.

Part Two comprises two chapters. Chapter 5 focusses on the
Shah Bano case and examines arguments for and against special
provisions for Muslim religious law through the prism of the concept
of secularism. It argues that discursive shifts can be observed in
conceptions of secularism in Congress discourse that were conducive

to stronger multicultural policies: policy change was accompanied by changes in political justifications regarding group rights. This discursive change, however, did not amount to a fundamental break in the normative vocabulary. Assertions of a radical shift rely among others, on an overstated contrast between a Western model pertaining to the separation of state and religion, and an Indian model of equal respect for all religions. With both equality and freedom-based arguments remaining under-developed in Congress discourse, preferential provisions for cultural protection continued to suffer from a justificatory deficit. This, together with the form of the discursive shift of the Congress, created a favourable ideological climate for the Hindu Right, which saw a surge of support in the aftermath of Shah Bano. Also, while the Congress was able to achieve the policy change it desired, in sharp contrast to the Constituent Assembly debates, it was unable to transform legitimating norms in the Shah Bano debate. This was an indicator of a *loss of hegemony*, observable in the shape of legislative debate, where conflicting conceptions of secularism remained entrenched and no single reigning set of norms emerged.

Chapter 6 reconstructs arguments for and against the extension of employment quotas to the OBCs in the 1990 Mandal debate, focussing on the concept of social justice. I show that in the discourse of the Janata Dal, the older nationalist ideal of equality was redefined, in terms of our formulation of the legitimating vocabulary, by linking equality closely to democracy, and distancing it from national unity. This strengthened the case for quotas: the expansion of the quota policy was thus accompanied by a discursive shift conducive to this outcome. At the same time, this discursive shift did not represent as radical a break with the constitutional vision as commentators have suggested. The Janata Dal's discourse of social justice involved a creative reinterpretation of the 'high ideological spectrum', rather than the triumph of indigenous, vernacular, subaltern values (Yadav 1999). In normative terms, arguments for OBC quotas were substantially social justice claims, relying largely on egalitarian liberal norms of fair equality of opportunity rather than identity as such. The shift in the normative basis of group preference inaugurated by the Constitution-makers, towards ameliorating *disadvantage* rather than maintaining *distinctness*, survived. With the emphasis on social justice as a legitimating norm in its own right, and the redefinition of equality in terms of empowerment of the disadvantaged, a distinctive ideological space was fashioned for lower caste politics in the 1990 Mandal debate. At the same time, this discourse of social justice relied to a large extent on notions of fair equality of opportunity, and as such remained vulnerable to criticisms on distributive grounds, to pressures for class-based refinements to the policy, as illustrated in subsequent debates on the exclusion of the 'creamy layer'. In contrast with the Constituent Assembly debates, competing conceptions of social justice remained entrenched in political debate, an indicator that no single party was now hegemonic. Finally, an examination of the 2005–6 parliamentary debates on OBC quotas in higher education (Mandal II) suggests that the broad picture is one of consolidation of the trends identified in the 1990 debate, but with a greater emphasis on the links between social justice on the one hand, and national unity and development, on the other, in keeping with Congress ideology.

The concluding chapter draws together the main findings of the study and suggests some implications for debates on multiculturalism, democracy, and the study of ideology. How might group-differentiated rights be better defended in India? Does the Indian case suggest a distinct pattern of debate on differential treatment in postcolonial liberal democracies? Can the findings for the legitimating vocabulary shed new light on the enduring puzzle of the survival of democratic institutions in India, and conditions conducive to democracy more generally? Finally, what does the approach to ideology elaborated in this study, the conceptual analysis of political rhetoric, suggest for the emerging field of comparative political thought? While not offering comprehensive answers to these questions, the conclusion seeks to suggest some possibilities, and limits, of the answers arrived at in this book and thereby indicate avenues for future research.

Part One

The Moment of Containment

The Constituent Assembly Debates, 1946–9

Minority rights in India pre-date liberal democratic institutions. From the late nineteenth century onwards, a range of special provisions were introduced by the British colonial state as well as native Princely states,[1] chiefly for groups designated as minorities or 'backward'. These included Muslims, Christians, Sikhs, Anglo-Indians, Untouchables, and Tribals. The Indian Constituent Assembly debates (1946–9) marked an important turning point in the trajectory of group rights: both the form and the basis of state policies of minority rights came to be fundamentally recast. Chapter 2 argues that as group preferential policies entered independent India, their colonial proportions came to be scaled back. Chapter 3 proposes a conceptual model for the analysis of Indian nationalist discourse. Five key concepts—secularism, democracy, justice, national unity, and development—constituted the frame within which nationalist argument over group rights was conducted. Chapter 4 analyses debates on minority rights in three policy areas: political representation, employment quotas and cultural rights. It shows how both the institutional forms of group rights, as well as normative discourses came to be recast in accordance with the nationalist vocabulary.

---

[1] These were territories governed by Indian princes, outside the direct control of the British colonial state.

2

Minority Rights in Colonial India and the Constituent Assembly

A Historical Background

INTRODUCTION

When minority rights came before the Constituent Assembly, these already had a controversial career of more than half a century behind them. This chapter offers an interpretation of the trajectory of minority policies from their origins in the Indian sub-continent up until the close of the Constituent Assembly debates. Whereas the career of special provisions for minority groups in the first half of the century can be seen as one of expansion, constitution-making marked a moment of containment. Containment would assume different degrees and forms in different policy areas of group rights. Evident in the alterations that minority provisions underwent during the framing of the Constitution, containment was part of wider political changes of the period.

GROUP RIGHTS IN COLONIAL INDIA AND THE CONSTITUENT ASSEMBLY

An Arc of Expansion

The period from the late nineteenth century to the middle of the twentieth century saw a steady expansion of group rights. Group representation in legislatures dates back to the first hesitant steps taken by the colonial state for the inclusion of Indians in the governing institutions of the colony. At the national level, minority representation can be traced to the 1909

Morley-Minto constitutional reforms, which instituted separate Muslim electorates. In local government bodies in provinces such as the Punjab, however, separate electorates had been in use since the 1880s (Barrier 1968: 537–8; Sarkar 1983: 21; Bose and Jalal 1999: 168). Impelled by a cautious liberalism, and the need for better information and more personnel after the Great Uprising of 1857, the late nineteenth century colonial state sought to include more Indians in government (Seal 1968: 156; Brown 1990: 142). As more Indians were incorporated into the representative institutions of the Raj through carefully measured doses of nomination and election, the question before the British was: how were Indians to be represented? The colonial answer to this was as groups; 'the interests of Indians, the British had decided, could not be individual' (Khilnani 1997: 24; Rudolph and Rudolph 2001: 45). The representation of 'important' and 'distinctive' interests became the hallmark of colonial constitutionalism. Minorities defined in religious terms, and later, caste and racial terms were the most prominent groups recognized for purposes of representation. But groups defined in terms of social and economic criteria—landholders, universities, and trade associations— were also accorded representation in legislative bodies (Brown 1990: 142; McMillan 2005: 20). By the early twentieth century, the main principles governing colonial representation were in place: 'that legitimate interests should be voiced, and that minority groups should have representation in proportion to their proportion of the population' (Brown 1990: 145).

The minority groups in question, as historians and anthropologists have richly documented, were shaped in important respects by colonial policies of enumeration and representation (Cohn 1987; Appadurai 1993; Dirks 2001). The first census of 1872 classified Indians according to their religious identity. Successive censuses amalgamated the myriad caste groups subject to the practice of untouchability into a single all-India category of Depressed Classes, creating the basis for their subsequent political mobilization as Untouchables (Mendelsohn and Vicziany 1998: 29; Gupta 1985: ch. 2).[1] Political representation policies also served to consolidate minority identities; for instance, the Montagu-Chelmsford reforms spurred the convening of political organizations representing

---

[1] In the early twentieth century, concerns about Hindu numbers in the context of the census awakened an interest among caste Hindu leaders in Untouchables (Galanter 1984: 25–6; Gupta 1985: 38–9; Gooptu 2001: 157).

the Depressed Classes (Patankar and Omvedt 1979: 415).[2] Group identities were not a product of colonial policy in any simple sense: wider economic, social, and political processes, including Indian elite and non-elite responses to the opportunities created by colonial policy, inevitably played a role. Whether colonial policies of group representation are best described as 'divide and rule' remains contentious. Against the view that the British sought to divide and rule (Sarkar 1983: 20; Kumar 1987: xxiii), scholars have emphasized governmental imperatives of maintaining peace (Barrier 1968), a general British tendency to perceive Indians through compartmental units (Brown 1990: 145), and the often dissonant motivations of colonial officials (McMillan 2005: 20–1, 52). Intentions, however, are elusive and need not detain us here. What remains indisputable is that the cumulative *effect* of colonial policy was the channelling of political competition along religious and caste group lines. By the mid-twentieth century, official group identities had acquired a vigorous life of their own and demanded recognition in the arenas of power created by the British.

Broadly coeval with the introduction of modern representative institutions in India, group representation expanded as colonial institutions gradually became more democratic (Coupland 1968).[3] Each step of constitutional reform that extended the Indian and elected element of colonial legislatures, and devolved more powers to colonial legislatures was accompanied by the extension of special representation provisions to more groups.[4] Different mechanisms of group representation came

---

[2] Most Depressed Class movements were regional organizations that drew their support from particular Untouchable castes. Dr Ambedkar's movement was dominated by Mahars, the Bengal movement by Namasudras, and the United Provinces movement by Chamars (Patankar and Omvedt 1979: 415; McMillan 2005: 37).

[3] The distinction between representative and democratic institutions, often elided in the literature, is important here. Group representation originated in India in a context of limited democracy in institutional and popular arenas. Democratization—of colonial institutions, in terms of franchise, powers, and 'Indianization', as well as of popular movements, in terms of their mass base—fuelled demands for more group representation and accentuated group political identities.

[4] On attitudes towards communal representation, see Coupland 1968; on British qualms about communal representation, see McMillan 2005: 24–6, 38–40, 48–51.

to be instituted in colonial legislatures, including separate electorates, reserved seats, weightage (guaranteed representation for minorities in excess of their enumerated demographic share), nomination, and various combinations of these provisions. Thus, the 1919 Montagu-Chelmsford reforms, which expanded the provincial and central legislative councils and transferred more powers to the provinces, also granted separate electorates and reserved seats to more groups. In addition to Muslims, these now included Sikhs, Indian Christians, Anglo-Indians, and Europeans (Brown 1990: 199).[5] Reserved seats were provided for 'non-Brahmins' among the Hindus in the provincial legislatures, and a provision was made for the nomination of members of the Depressed Classes (Chaube 1973: 8). The question of minority representation was central in the next round of constitutional negotiations, which began a decade later. The Simon Commission of 1928 recommended the continuation of separate electorates and the institution of reserved seats in legislatures for the Depressed Classes.[6] The Commission's report noted that the separate representation of communities and interests was 'the most noticeable feature of the Indian electoral system' (q. Chaube 1973: 8).[7] Following the failure of the Round Table Conferences (1930–2) to secure an agreement among Indian leaders on minority representation, the colonial government proposed the Communal Award.[8] Representation through

---

[5] Special electorates and reserved seats were also provided for some socio-economic interest groups such as landowners, businessmen, and university graduates. And in accordance with the 1916 Congress-League Lucknow Pact, provincial minorities—Muslim, Hindu, and Sikh—were overrepresented in the assemblies constituted after the 1919 reforms. For example, in Bombay, the 20 per cent Muslim minority had 33 per cent seats (Wilkinson 2004: 104).

[6] The Simon Commission was boycotted by the Congress as 'all-white', and by Jinnah's supporters in the Muslim League, but was met enthusiastically by leaders of Depressed Class organizations (McMillan 2005: 64).

[7] The Commission's report noted the overriding importance of questions of minority political representation to Indian opinion. It also granted reserved seats to Depressed classes, but rejected nomination and separate electorates (McMillan 2005: 38–9, 69). The only category for which the report suggested the withdrawal of special treatment were the non-Brahmins of Madras.

[8] At the Second Round Table Conference, Muslim, Untouchable, Christian, Anglo-Indian and European leaders put forward a joint memorandum, demanding, among others, representation through separate electorates for these groups (Indian Round Table Conference 1931: 68–70).

separate electorates was awarded to Muslims, Sikhs, Anglo-Indians, and in a new departure, to the Depressed Classes (Coupland 1968: 128). The Award's proposals for separate electorates for the Depressed Classes came to be abandoned as a result of the Gandhi-Ambedkar Poona Pact, which doubled the number of seats reserved for Untouchables in provincial assemblies, albeit under joint electorates.[9] Austin notes that the Government of India Act 1935, the last major colonial constitutional exercise, provided reserved seats in provincial legislatures for a total of thirteen communal and socio-economic categories: the central legislative assembly was to be constituted through indirect election, and 'in all cases on the basis of communal or functional electorates' (1966: 144). This included, for the first time, significant electoral representation for the Untouchables (as per the Poona Pact), and some representation for Backward Tribes.[10] Reserved seats in legislatures for religious and caste minorities were also instituted in some princely states such as Mysore (Wilkinson 2004:105). Legislative representation was augmented by

[9] For the background and details of the Poona Pact, see Galanter 1984: 32–3; Brown 1990: 280–2; Kumar 1985. While Ambedkar is usually seen to have driven a 'hard bargain' (Brown 1990: 280), as McMillan argues, Gandhi may have been a 'shrewder negotiator' than appears (2005: 59, 65, 107). Although securing double the number of seats, Ambedkar was unable to secure the influence for Untouchable voters that he thought necessary for their effective representation. A result of the representation mechanisms favoured by Gandhi was that 'arrangements that would foster an independent political movement' among Untouchables strong enough to challenge the Congress were prevented (Galanter 1984: 32–3). After the Poona Pact was implemented through the Government of India Act 1935, the Congress dominated elections for reserved seats. In the lead up to Independence, Ambedkar rejected the Poona Pact and returned to the demand of separate electorates.

[10] As per the 1935 Act, a few seats were reserved for 'backward tribes' in the provincial legislatures, but none in the Central Legislative Assembly (Chaube 1973: 9). The Act proposed representation of tribal groups through a mixture of reserved seats, in areas where tribal groups were considered sufficiently advanced to represent their own interests, and nomination for more 'backward' areas (McMillan 2005: 117–22). Although 'backward' tribal areas were granted some legislative representation following the 1918 Montagu Chelmsford reforms, this representation was largely token (Shiva Rao 1968: 570). Ambedkar opposed political representation of tribal groups in 1945, holding that their political consciousness was under-developed and could damage the cause of minorities (McMillan 2005: 130).

group representation in the executive level. A convention emerged of minority representation in cabinets in the provinces (Retzlaff 1963: 58). Under the Government of India Acts of 1919 and 1935, provincial governors 'were advised to select those leaders and parties most likely to form ethnically inclusive administrations' (Wilkinson 2004: 108).

The late colonial period also saw the expansion of group quotas in government employment. Some of the earliest instances of this policy were to be found in caste-based reservation schemes proposed by some Princely States in the late nineteenth century to counter Brahmin predominance in the public services.[11] In British India, the Punjab government introduced in the 1880s a policy of balancing Hindu and Muslim numbers in the administration (Barrier 1968: 535). In 1925, the Indian government declared it would reserve a portion of civil service jobs for the redress of communal inequalities. Twenty-five per cent of the posts to be filled by the direct recruitment of Indians were earmarked for Muslims and 8.3 per cent for other minority communities (Gwyer and Appadorai 1957: 117).[12] In 1937, Governors of several British provinces were issued with directions under the Government of India Act of 1935, to 'secure a due proportion of appointments in Our Services to the several communities', but proportions were not specified (*ibid.*: 379–80). Quotas of 8.3 per cent were instituted in the Government of India public services for the Depressed Classes, now termed the Scheduled Castes, in 1943 (Galanter 1984: 86).[13] By 1947, at the state-level, local

---

[11] Mysore accepted reservation for backward classes in 1874. Backward Classes were defined to include all castes and communities other than Brahmins who were not adequately represented in the public services, including Muslims. Kolhapur decreed in 1902 that half of all administrative posts were to be reserved for 'non-Brahmin' groups. Group quotas in the public services were also instituted by the governments of Travancore and Cochin, Madras, and Kerala in response to non-Brahmin movements (Singh 1982: 80–1; Kooiman 1997; Mendelsohn and Vicziany 1998: 130–1; Bayly 2000: 242).

[12] The 'other communities' mentioned were the Anglo-Indians and the domiciled Europeans.

[13] This percentage was raised to 12.5 per cent in 1946, to correspond to the Scheduled Caste proportion of the population. The Congress governments that assumed power in the provinces after elections in 1937 continued and extended employment quotas. With regard to tribal groups, instructions were issued in 1947 regarding the desirability of recruiting suitable candidates to the public services, but proportions were not specified (Galanter 1984: 36, 86).

religious minorities, and some caste and linguistic minorities were 'proportionately represented, often over-represented, in national and provincial government employment' (Wilkinson 2004: 106).

Progressive entrenchment and expansion of group-differentiated rights can also be observed in other policy areas in the later colonial period. Notable among these, although outside the scope of the present study, was the policy of protection of tribal lands: areas with a concentration of populations with 'tribal characteristics' were placed 'outside of ordinary administration to permit a policy of insulating them from...contact with more sophisticated outsiders' (Galanter 1984:147). The Scheduled Districts Act of 1874 empowered the executive to exclude areas from the operations of ordinary law. The Government of India Act of 1919 divided 'backward areas' into those within the writ of provincial legislation, and those excluded from it, a policy that was extended further by the 1935 Government of India Act (Shiva Rao 1968: 569–72). British policy was based on an assumption of tribal difference, a stance that was shared to an extent by the nationalist elite (Corbridge 2000; McMillan 2005: 116).

Changing Contours of the 'Minority Question'

In contemporary scholarly accounts of the period, the set of issues pertaining to minority rights came to be referred to as the 'minority question' or the 'problem of minorities' (Krishna 1939; Sen 1940; Shiva Rao 1968). The 'minority question' in colonial India was shaped, on the one hand, by processes of gradual democratic reform of colonial legislatures, and on the other, by a growing national movement for Indian independence. As institutional reform and popular mobilization developed over the first half of the twentieth century, the contours of the 'minority question' shifted accordingly. Broadly speaking, three phases can be discerned in the career of the 'minority question' in colonial India. It emerged onto the national stage in the first decade of the twentieth century as colonial legislatures were being enlarged to act as better sounding boards for Indian opinion. The powers of these legislatures were limited, as was the franchise: minority representation emerged within highly constrained democratic institutions (Coupland 1968; McMillan 2005). The Congress-led national movement was still modest in its demands, petitioning for better terms for Indians as British subjects, as well as its reach, limited largely to an English-speaking professional elite. In this context, the

'minority question' was primarily about the recognition of an entitlement
to representation of communities such as Muslims that were deemed to
be an important distinct element of Indian society. Communities were
represented by their elite and colonial institutional reform involved
balancing of contending social interests through elite consultation.

In the 1920s, the profile of the 'minority question' changed. Numbers
became important in the face of democratic pressures of different kinds.
Colonial representative institutions saw some democratic reform: the
franchise was extended, and more powers devolved to legislatures,
especially at the provincial level. The Congress-led national movement
expanded in scale and ambition. Under Gandhi, it acquired a mass base
and demanded self-government for Indians, albeit for the time-being
within the British Empire. In a context of increasing democratization of
institutional and popular arenas, the 'minority question' became primarily
one of 'safeguards' against Congress or Hindu numerical dominance.
Safeguards included mechanisms of minority representation that
sought to qualify Congress/Hindu preponderance in legislatures and
executives. These also comprised decision-making conventions such as
the minority veto against majority rule. Apart from Muslims, the pre-
eminent Indian minority, new contenders emerged, notably the Depressed
Classes, who also sought safeguards against the domination by higher
castes of the increased Indian places in colonial institutions.[14] With
Congress attempts to address minority concerns sporadic and equivocal,[15]
and colonial reform offering incentives to minority leaders, by the end of
the 1920s, the principal organizations of Muslims and Depressed Classes
had become antagonistic to nationalist politics.

[14] The term Depressed Classes was used from the 1870s, with Untouchables
becoming more popular in the early 1900s. Depressed Class organizations
tended to be concentrated in British Indian territories and to represent
Untouchable castes whose members had achieved some measure of economic
and social progress (McMillan 2005: 28, 30). Fears about Brahmin and
upper-caste domination of the national movement were also voiced by leaders
of non-Brahmin movements notably, Jyotirao Phule's Satyashodhak Samaj
(O'Hanlon 1985).

[15] For instance, the Congress only began to address the issue of Untouchability
in the 1920s, and then the Gandhian approach to 'Harijan uplift' was usually
paternalistic, offering little space in the organizations to the Untouchables
themselves (Zelliot 1988; Parekh 1989: 232–9; Gooptu 2001: 176; McMillan
2005: 34, 44).

In the 1940s, the 'minority question' took a new turn. The Congress-led national movement was by now pushing for a specific timetable for Indian independence, and the British became increasingly amenable to relinquishing power in the sub-continent.[16] In this context, the Muslim League, which had hitherto struggled to marry its principal concern for safeguards for Muslim minorities at the Centre with the demands of Muslim majority provinces for greater provincial autonomy, was now able to do so for a brief period. The Pakistan demand has been reappraised persuasively in recent years by Jalal (1985) and others. It is now seen less as a concrete territorial claim for a separate state than a bargaining ploy for extracting greater constitutional concessions for Muslims within an all-India confederation.[17] For our purposes, it suffices to note that in the prelude to Independence, the 'minority question' came to be dominated by Congress-League polarization over Muslim separatism. All other questions of safeguards, including those for the Depressed Classes, were subordinated to a resolution of the demand for Pakistan. It was an association that would indelibly mark the discourse on group rights in the Constituent Assembly.

The positions of the principal political actors on minority rights changed over time and were internally varied. Summarizing broadly, the colonial state positioned itself as the guardian and guarantor of the interests of important distinct communities, minorities, and 'weaker sections', a stance that served to legitimate British rule in India. Colonial constitutional proposals offered special safeguards and assurances that minorities would be protected, through continued British presence if necessary.[18] The British administration did have serious reservations about the effects of the system of communal representation. The historical record suggests that the authors of the Montagu-Chelmsford reforms, the Simon Commission report, and the Communal Award all voiced concerns that were in fact very similar to those of the Congress

---

[16] For reviews of the literature on the transfer of power in the Indian sub-continent, see Brasted and Bridge 1994; Kumar 1987.

[17] Jalal argues that even in electoral terms, this strategy was only successful in uniting divergent strands of Muslim politics behind the Muslim League during the 1945–6 elections (1985: 171–2).

[18] For instance, the Cabinet Mission Plan noted that the 'cession of sovereignty to the Indian people...would be conditional on adequate provisions being made for the protection of minorities' (Shiva Rao 1968: 746).

(McMillan 2005: 48–51).[19] However, for all the misgivings, differences, and shifts over time in the stance of the colonial state, the avowed position on minority safeguards remained consistent: a constitutional settlement in India, or the transfer of more power into Indian hands, required the agreement of important minorities.[20]

The party leading the demand for Indian independence, the Indian National Congress, was wary of minority safeguards, regarding these as a colonial device to divide the Indian nation and perpetuate British rule. The Congress insisted that the minority question could only be resolved by Indians once power had been transferred fully into Indian hands: far from being a necessary condition for a solution to the 'minority problem', British presence was the basic impediment to its resolution. The Congress position changed over time, and at various points it endorsed aspects of the colonial regime of minority safeguards. So, for instance, the 1916 Congress League Pact accepted separate Muslim electorates,[21] the Nehru Report of 1928 offered reserved seats in proportion to the population.[22] The Congress had also recognized some form of minority veto, notably in the 1916 Lucknow Pact (Adeney 2007).[23] However, Congress pre-independence resolutions and plans offered at best equivocal support

[19] Before announcing the Communal Award, the Prime Minister noted in private: 'A general survey of the papers shows what a terrible system this Communal Representation is. It really frightens one at the prospect of self-government working upon such a basis...' (q. McMillan 2005: 48).

[20] In effect, this meant that Muslims, the most significant minority, 'had a veto over important constitutional reforms at the centre...' (Wilkinson 2004: 107). With minority veto and also minority proportionality in legislatures, Cabinets, and government employment, the late colonial state was consociational in character (Wilkinson 2004).

[21] Congress leaders supported separate Muslim electorates in 1909 and 1916 in a bid to reach out to Muslims (Owen 1972), but Congress support remained ambivalent and would soon change to hostility (McMillan 2005: 23). To some extent, pre-independence plans should be seen as bargaining counters (Brown 1990; Adeney 2007).

[22] This was reiterated in the Congress Scheme for a Communal Settlement presented to the Second Round Table Conference in October 1931. See Note B (reportedly added by Gandhi) in Indian Round Table Conference 1931: 64.

[23] See also Congress resolution in its fourth session in 1888, and the Lahore resolution of 1929, reprinted in Zaidi 1984: 17, 89.

for minority political safeguards.[24] Its claim to represent all sections of the Indian nation meant that the Congress was intrinsically antagonistic to separate or special representation mechanisms for minorities.[25]

While demands for safeguards were put forward by a variety of groups, the most influential claimants of minority safeguards were the parties representing Muslims and the Depressed Classes. Minority parties and the British administration shared a concern about the Congress-led national movement and thus had 'a mutual self-interest in cooperation'. As constitutional reform was determined through a process of consultation with leaders, the leaders of minority organizations were well-placed 'to influence the decision-making process' (McMillan 2005: 31, 52). The Muslim League was the strongest advocate of special representation policies. Separate electorates, reserved seats, and veto rights in the central executive 'appear in all the plans that the League signed up for or advocated' (Adeney 2007: 47).[26] From the late 1920s, the Muslim League also demanded greater provincial autonomy for Muslim majority provinces (Jalal 1985: 10).[27] In the famous Lahore resolution of 1940, this took the form of a claim for independent sovereign states of Pakistan. With the Congress broadly in favour of a strong centre and the Muslim League insisting on a weak centre with extensive residual powers in the

[24] The Nehru report 1928, one of the most important Congress documents on constitutional reform, denounced special representation as spoon-feeding, required only because 'logic and sense have little to do with communal feeling'. It made no provision for special representation for the Depressed Classes, holding that constitutional rights against discrimination, together with adult suffrage and education meant that the Depressed Classes will 'rapidly disappear' (q. McMillan 2005: 41). This report is thought to mark a 'parting of ways' between the Congress and minority parties.

[25] Gandhi as the Congress delegate to the Second Round Table Conference in 1931 dismissed delegates of minority groups: 'All the other parties at this meeting represent sectional interests, the Congress alone claims to represent the whole of India, all interests...all...minorities' (Indian Round Table Conference 1931: 390).

[26] Although as Adeney points out, the League had been willing to compromise on separate electorates in the 1920s.

[27] Jinnah's programme of Fourteen Points sought a federal system with residual powers exercised by the provinces, in addition to guaranteed Muslim representation based on separate electorates (Phillips 1962: 235–7). On the ideological bases of the Muslim League's demand for parity, see Shaikh 1989.

provinces and rights to opt out of the Indian Union, the nature of the
Indian federation came to dominate constitutional negotiations in the
lead up to transfer of power. Differences between the Congress and the
League over the interpretation of the federal provisions of the Cabinet
Mission Plan would eventually culminate in the partition of the country.

After the Muslim League, the most significant actors in negotiations for minority safeguards were Depressed Class organizations.
Dr B.R. Ambedkar was their pre-eminent spokesman.[28] With regard to
the mechanisms for Untouchable representation, Dr Ambedkar's views
changed over time, alternating between support for separate electorates
and advocacy of reserved seats with universal adult franchise (removal of
the educational, property, income restrictions on franchise that excluded
most Untouchables).[29] Nevertheless, his general position on safeguards
was consistent, and distinct from the Congress. The disabilities of
Untouchability meant that the interests of Untouchables were different
from the rest of the population; this difference had to be recognised
institutionally, in terms of separate representation in government
institutions. A share in power for Untouchables was essential, 'the basis
for achieving any other kind of gain' (Patankar and Omvedt 1979:
417). The Depressed Classes, Dr Ambedkar's memorandum to the
First Round Table Conference noted, 'must be given sufficient political
power to influence legislative and executive action for the purposes of
securing their welfare' (q. McMillan 2005: 52). Dr Ambedkar's claim
that Untouchables alone could speak for Untouchables was famously
challenged by Gandhi at the Second Round Table Conference: 'I claim
in my own person to represent the vast mass of the Untouchables.'[30]

---

[28] On differences within the Untouchable movement, and the role of leaders
such as M.C. Rajah, G.A. Gavai, R. Srinivasan, P. Baloo, see Omvedt 1994; on
Dr Ambedkar's considerable influence on British policy on representation of the
Depressed Classes, see McMillan 2005: 43, 52.

[29] In his testimony to the Southborough Committee in 1919, during the second
Round Table Conference in 1931, and then again in 1947, Dr Ambedkar called
for separate electorates. At other times, however, notably the Simon Commission
in 1928 and the Nagpur Conference of the Depressed Classes in 1930, he
favoured reserved seats in legislatures for Untouchables so long as adult suffrage
obtained (Zelliot 1988: 190; Patankar and Omvedt 1979: 419).

[30] At the Second Round Table Conference, Gandhi accepted, reluctantly, the
representative claims of religious minority parties but remained adamant in his
opposition to Untouchable spokesmen.

Fundamental differences existed between Gandhi's approach to tackling the disabilities of Untouchables, with its emphasis on social reform, voluntary work, and changing attitudes of upper castes, and Ambedker's emphasis on political power for Untouchables and state programmes in education, employment, and welfare.

The 'Minorities Question' and the Demand for a Constituent Assembly

Like all constitutional proposals in late colonial India, the demand for a Constituent Assembly was disputed within Indian opinion. The proposal for a Constituent Assembly was formally put forward by the Congress party in 1934. Rejecting the British Government's 1933 White Paper, the Congress Working Committee declared that the only satisfactory alternative was

> a constitution drawn up by a Constituent Assembly elected on the basis of adult suffrage, or as near it as possible, with the power, if necessary, to the important minorities to have their representatives elected exclusively by the electors belonging to such minorities... (reprinted in Zaidi 1984: 98).[31]

This demand for a Constituent Assembly, it is important to note, both emphasized its election by universal suffrage and conceded separate electorates to important minorities. To the Congress, this offered a way of cutting through the communal deadlock that was frustrating progress towards its goal of Indian independence, a route that would preserve Congress dominance in constitutional negotiations.[32] Understandably, the proposal for a Constituent Assembly did not elicit similar enthusiasm from minority parties. Jinnah declared that a Constituent Assembly 'in the present condition of India, will mean a second and larger edition of the Congress', a vehicle for Hindu domination (q. Chaube 1973: 24–5). Dr B.R. Ambedkar was also unenthusiastic, holding that a Constituent Assembly was not necessary (q. Austin 1966: 3). The demand for a Constituent Assembly thus itself became a partaker in the 'minority

---

[31] From this point onwards, the demand for a Constituent Assembly was regularly reiterated in Congress resolutions. Adult franchise was endorsed by the Congress earlier, in the Nehru report of 1928.

[32] Even Gandhi, not usually enthusiastic about institutional solutions, offered strong endorsement—see Chaube 1973: 24–5.

problem', a point of contention in negotiations between the Congress, the minority parties, and the British.

From the 1940s onwards, for reasons largely to do with the changed situation resulting from the Second World War, the colonial administration became increasingly amenable to the idea of a Constituent Assembly (Brasted and Bridge 1994; Kumar 1987). An Indian Constituent Assembly was endorsed implicitly in the Viceroy's statement of 8 August 1940 (the so-called August Offer), and explicitly in the Cripps Mission declaration of 1942 (Chaube 1973: 26). After the failure of these initiatives to secure an agreement between the Congress and the Muslim League, the Cabinet Mission came to India in spring 1946 with the express purpose of setting up 'the machinery by which Indians can devise their own constitution' (Lord Pethwick-Lawrence, q. Austin 1966: 3). By this stage, the demission of colonial power was imminent, and the Plan, in addition to outlining a process for the creation of a Constituent Assembly, also put forward a last-ditch proposal for Indian unity. To address the concerns of the Muslim League, the Cabinet Mission Plan proposed a federation with a weak centre—an Indian Union that would deal with foreign affairs, communications, and defence, with all residual powers vested in the provinces.[33]

The formation of the Constituent Assembly was governed by the principles that had guided colonial representation for half a century: restricted franchise, separate electorates, and minority representation at least proportional to their demographic share. Elections based on adult suffrage were rejected as involving too much delay; instead the provincial legislative assemblies recently constituted in the elections of 1945–6 were to act as electoral bodies. Austin reckons that only around 28.5 per cent of the adult population had the vote, on account of restrictions based on tax, educational and property qualifications (1966: 10).[34] Each province was allotted seats in proportion to its population, and this provincial allocation of seats was to be divided between the main communities (Muslim, Sikh, and 'general', with the 'general' community including all who

---

[33] For details of the provision for regional groupings, see Austin 1966: 5. Differences between the Muslim League and the Congress in the interpretation of the grouping clause would be crucial in the eventual withdrawal of League support for the Plan.

[34] This figure represents an average; proportions varied from one province to another.

were not Muslims or Sikhs) in proportion to their population. Elections to these seats were to be held on the basis of separate electorates: members of legislatures belonging to Muslim, Sikh, and General categories elected separately their proportion of the provincial delegation (Austin 1966: 5). Representation of minorities other than Muslim and Sikh was sought to be ensured through the provision of an Advisory Committee on the 'rights of citizens, minorities, and tribal and excluded areas' that was to contain 'full representation of the interests affected' (Cabinet Mission Plan, q. Chaube 1973: 32). Untouchable and Tribal representatives, as well as Christians, Anglo-Indians, Europeans, and other numerically small minority communities who had not been given guaranteed places in the Assembly under the Plan, were thereby sought to be brought into the Constituent Assembly.

Elections were held to the Constituent Assembly in mid-July 1946, in the brief window of opportunity that existed while the Plan enjoyed the conditional support of both the Congress and the League. The Congress obtained 202, and the Muslim League 73, out of the 296 seats allotted to the provinces, with both parties winning an overwhelming proportion of General and Muslim places, respectively (Austin 1966: 9–10; Chiriyankandath 2000: 4–5).[35] The Congress majority in the Assembly rose to 82 per cent after the partition of the country, when the number of Muslim League representatives fell to 28. The Princely States were allotted 93 representatives in the Assembly according to the Plan. These were eventually selected by a mix of election and nomination, and augmented the Congress majority. Representatives of Parsis, Anglo-Indians, Indian Christians, the Scheduled Castes and Tribes were brought into the Assembly under the General category, in most cases, at the behest of the Congress leadership (Austin 1966: 12–13). The representation of minorities in the Assembly after Partition was as follows: Muslim: 31; Scheduled Caste: 33; Nepali: 1; Sikh: 5; Parsi: 3; Christian: 7; Tribal: 5 Anglo-Indian: 3—a total of 88 out of the 235 provincial seats, approximately 37 per cent of the provincial membership (*ibid.*: 13), roughly proportionate to their demographic share (Chiriyankandath 2000: 5).

[35] Small parties accounted for the remaining sixteen places. These were the Panthik Akali (3 seats), Unionists (3 seats), Communists (1 seat), and the Scheduled Caste Federation (1 seat—Dr Ambedkar). Of the Congress seats, 4 went to Muslims and 1 to a Sikh.

The representativeness of the Constituent Assembly, or lack thereof, has been a matter of debate (Corbridge and Harris 2000: 23–4).
Unquestionably, in caste, class, and gender terms, the Assembly was
not representative of Indian society. Upper castes, men, graduates, and
professionals were heavily over-represented: Chiriyankandath reckons that
Brahmins who formed 5 per cent of the population, constituted around
25 per cent of the Assembly's membership; professionals constituted over
60 per cent of membership, with lawyers almost a third—when more
than 80 per cent of the population was in the agricultural sector; and
only 15 women ever sat in the Assembly (2000: 5). In terms of religious
composition, and shades of political opinion, the Assembly was more
representative. Approximately 37.8 per cent of the population were non-
Hindu, Scheduled Castes and Tribes, and 37.5 per cent of the Constituent
Assembly excluding the Princely States comprised minorities (*ibid.*:
4–5). Austin notes that non-Congress experts with administrative and
legal experience were elected through Congress support, and important
political organisations such as the Socialist Party and the Hindu
Mahasabha, although not officially represented, had their views heard in
the Assembly (1966: 13–14). Given the limited franchise through which
it was constituted, the Assembly was reasonably representative of its
electorate, although it was obviously not representative in the democratic
terms that inform contemporary assessments.

After its election, the fortunes of the Constituent Assembly continued
to be tied to the 'minority question'. The Congress and the Muslim League
were unable to agree on the interpretation of the federal ('grouping')
provisions of the Cabinet Mission Plan. By end July 1946, Jinnah
had instructed the League representatives to boycott the Constituent
Assembly. With the British now eager to depart, the Congress pressing for
an early meeting of the Assembly, and no breakthrough in the Congress-
League deadlock in sight, the Constituent Assembly was convened on
9 December 1946. The Constituent Assembly had in a sense served the
Congress' purpose, that of loosening the stranglehold of the 'minority
question' on constitutional advance. However, it had done so at the cost
of setting the country on the road to Partition: the British government
had made clear, and the Congress had agreed that any Constitution made
by the Assembly would not apply to parts of the country unwilling to
accept this (Chaube 1973). With the British advancing their date of
departure from the subcontinent, Partition moved rapidly from being

a possibility to a reality. The Muslim League never lifted its boycott of the Constituent Assembly; League representatives who would remain in India after Partition began participating in the work of the Assembly from July 1947, after the decision to partition the country had been announced. With the India Independence Act that came into effect on 15 August 1947, the Constituent Assembly became legally sovereign, and would function henceforth also as the national legislature. While Hindu-Muslim violence raged as the country first lurched towards Partition and then reeled from its aftermath, the Assembly would remain for the next three years 'an island of calm deliberation amidst the historical currents that swirled through the country' (Khilnani 1997: 33).

MINORITY RIGHTS IN THE CONSTITUENT ASSEMBLY: A CASE OF RETRENCHMENT

In the three momentous years in Indian politics during which the Constitution was written, constitutional provisions for minorities were revised several times over in ways significant and small. When viewed against the colonial regime of group preference, constitution-making marked a moment of containment; further, minority provisions were progressively cut-back during the course of the Assembly's career. Constitutional curtailment of group rights was part of a broader political process in this period, wherein minority proportionality in legislatures and government jobs were dismantled by Congress-led central and provincial governments (Wilkinson 2004: 108–23). As we shall see, the main lines of this political process are visible in the changes to the draft constitution itself.

While an overall dynamic of containment can be discerned during constitution-making, this assumed different degrees and forms in different areas of group rights. Broadly speaking, minority provisions were of two types: political safeguards comprising mainly representation in legislatures, executives, and government employment; and cultural safeguards, concerning religious, cultural, and educational rights. The most far-reaching changes occurred with respect to political safeguards for religious minorities, which were abolished. However, attenuation can also be discerned in other areas of minority policy, although the changes here were less drastic. Analysing state strategies for regulating diversity, Adeney distinguishes between assimilationist, integrationist, multicultural, and segregationist categories (2007: 86–90). Adapting this typology for policy positions on group rights in the Constituent Assembly, it is helpful to distinguish three main positions at the outset. The first position, that of opposition to all group rights, might be characterized as assimilationist/integrationist; the second position of support for maximal group rights, as multinational; and a third intermediate position of support for some safeguards, as limited multiculturalism.[36] On political safeguards for religious minorities, the assimilationist/integrationist 'no safeguards' position won. On political safeguards for 'backward classes', and cultural safeguards for minorities, a limited multicultural position would be embodied in the Constitution.[37]

The location of the principal political parties in the Constituent Assembly on this classification scheme was as follows. At the start of the Assembly's deliberations, the Congress occupied a limited multicultural position on minority safeguards. By the end, on political safeguards for religious minorities, it had shifted to an assimilationist/integrationist position. Initially, non-Congress minority parties such as the Muslim League, the Akalis, and the Scheduled Caste Federation, favoured multinational policies of maximal safeguards. By the end, most had moved to limited multicultural policies.[38]

The task of drafting constitutional articles for minorities was entrusted to the Advisory Committee on Fundamental Rights, Minorities,

[36] In my classification, unlike Adeney's, these categories refer to positions on national identity, rather than state strategies to regulate ethnic diversity; also a new category of 'multinational' is included. It is important to underline that this is a heuristic classification: individuals frequently moved from one position to another, and sometimes occupied different positions in distinct policy areas (so, for instance, K.M. Munshi was integrationist in the matter of political safeguards, and more multicultural with respect to cultural rights).

[37] As Adeney notes, the Indian Constitution embodies a weak multicultural stance towards Muslims and Christians, but not in relation to Sikhs, Jains, or Buddhists who are treated in a more assimilationist fashion as part of the 'Hindu family' (2007: 97).

[38] Representatives from minority groups were to be found among all three positions. Some of the most vocal supporters of the hard line no-safeguards position were Muslim, Christian, Sikh, Parsi, and Scheduled Caste. Most women representatives in the Constituent Assembly espoused a no-safeguards position, for minorities and women. For the social background of representatives, see Austin 1966: 337–53; Chiriyankandath 2000: 5.

Tribal and Excluded Areas. Draft articles on minority provisions were approved in the first instance at the committee level: the Sub-Committees for Minorities, Fundamental Rights, Tribal and Excluded Areas received representations from various individuals and organizations and decided the initial wording of articles on minorities. The Advisory Committee adjudicated on unresolved differences and its reports were then placed before the Constituent Assembly, where final amendments were proposed and voted upon for inclusion in the Constitution. Much of the drafting and decision-making on constitutional provisions was done behind the scenes, by the Constitutional Advisor Sir B.N. Rau and in fora such as the Congress Assembly party.[39] Contentious proposals that were outvoted in the committees were usually raised again by their proponents on the floor of the Constituent Assembly.

The Assembly's deliberations can be divided into two main phases. During the first, report stage, from December 1946 until August 1947, committees were constituted. These prepared reports on constitutional provisions that were discussed, amended and adopted by the Constituent Assembly. The Assembly adjourned between the fall of 1947 and 1948, during which period the Drafting Committee completed a draft of the Constitution that was published in February 1948. The second phase in the Assembly's deliberations, the draft stage, covered the period from November 1948 when the Assembly reconvened, until December 1949, when the Constitution was finally passed, and comprised detailed readings of the Draft Constitution. Several minority policies adopted in the report stage of the Constituent Assembly's deliberations came to be withdrawn during the draft stage.

Retrenchment was most clear-cut in the area of political safeguards for religious minorities. The key developments here were as follows. Upon its formation in February 1947, the Minorities Sub-Committee circulated a questionnaire soliciting views on the nature and scope of political, economic, religious, educational, and cultural safeguards for minorities.[40] During March–July 1947, the Minorities Sub-Committee

---

[39] Austin holds that 'it was essentially the government wing of the Congress, not the mass party, that wrote the Constitution' and that Nehru, Patel, Prasad, and Azad 'constituted an oligarchy within the Assembly', controlling its affairs (1966: 17–18, 21).

[40] The Minority Rights Sub-Committee was chaired by Dr H.C. Mookerji, a Bengali Christian, and initially comprised 26 members (for membership, see

received several notes and memoranda in response to this questionnaire. Prominent among these representations were demands for separate electorates for Untouchables (Dr B.R. Ambedkar, All India Adi-Hindu Depressed Classes Association); for the protection of Parsi family laws (R.K. Sidhwa); for preferential treatment for Anglo-Indians in appointments to railways, Customs, Posts and Telegraphs (Frank Anthony and S.H. Prater).[41] These were considered in the Minorities Sub-Committee in July 1946, which then put forward proposals to the Advisory Committee, chaired by Sardar Patel.[42] Most minority members of the Sub-Committee, both Congress and non-Congress, favoured political safeguards.[43] K.M. Munshi ruefully noted in his memoirs: '... eventually all the minorities, including even the tiny but highly advanced Parsi community, claimed safeguards over and above the Fundamental Rights, which, as citizens, they would enjoy' (1967: 200).

The first draft of minority safeguards put forward before the Constituent Assembly, the Advisory Committee's Report on Minority Rights of August 1947, proposed the following. First, there was to be a system of joint electorates with representation for communities in proportion to their population for a period of ten years. Second,

---

Austin 1966: 334–5). In its first sitting on 28 February 1947, the Sub-Committee decided against a detailed questionnaire and endorsed K.M. Munshi's draft. This included the question: 'How is it proposed that the safeguards should be eliminated, in what time and under what circumstances?' (for minutes, see Shiva Rao 1967 II: 391).

[41] For more details and other demands including representation in legislatures and executives for Parsis (Homi Modi), Scheduled Castes (H.J. Khandekar, Jagjivan Ram), Sikhs (Ujjal Singh and Harnam Singh), tribal groups (R.N. Brahma), Jains... special status for Anglo-Indian schools (Frank Antony, S.H. Prater), Muslim Kazis (Maulana Hifzur Rahman and Abdul Qaiyum Ansari), see Shiva Rao II 1967: 309–81; for Ambedkar's memorandum, see Shiva Rao 1967 II: 84–114.

[42] For its membership, see Austin 1966: 333–4; Chiriyankandath 2000: 7.

[43] An exception was Rajkumari Amrit Kaur, 'a Protestant Christian from the Sikh royal house of Kapurthala' (Chiriyankandath 2000: 9), one of the handful of women in the Assembly, whose dissenting voice runs through the deliberations of the Sub-Committee. Congress Untouchable representatives such as Jagjivan Ram and H.J. Khandekar pressed for reserved seats. The Chairman of the Minorities Sub-Committee and leader of the Indian Christians H.C. Mookerjee, and Parsi leader Homi Modi, later renounced reservations (Austin 1966: 149).

an Instrument of Instructions to the President and Governor recommended the 'desirability of including members of important minority communities in Cabinets as far as practicable' along lines of the 1935 Act (*CAD* V: 246). Third, a general declaration was included to the effect that 'in the all-India and Provincial Services, the claims of all the minorities shall be kept in view in making appointments to these services consistently with the consideration of efficiency of administration' (*ibid.*: 249). Fourth, a provision was made for a Special Minority Officer at the central and provincial levels, to report to the legislatures regarding the working of various safeguards for minorities. The report also recommended the continuation of special provisions for Anglo Indians in Railways, Customs and Posts and Telegraphs Services and educational institutions for a temporary period.

The minority rights report of August 1947 is regarded as a 'high watermark in Congress concessions to the minorities' (Retzlaff 1963: 64). Nevertheless, several key elements of the British system of minority safeguards had already been discarded by the time of this report. These included separate electorates and weighted representation, long-standing features of the colonial regime of political representation.[44] Reserved seats in legislatures were admitted for a limited period of ten years, after which the policy was to be reconsidered. The demand for minority quotas in Cabinets was rejected, as were fixed quotas in government employment.[45] The Report stated that the Committee had had to reject some proposals 'partly because, as in the case of reservation of seats in Cabinets, we felt that a rigid constitutional provision would have made parliamentary democracy unworkable and partly because, as in the case of electoral arrangements, we considered it necessary to harmonize the special claims of minorities with the development of a healthy national life' (Shiva Rao 1967 II: 416). In terms of the classification outlined earlier, the first

[44] Demands for separate electorates were made on behalf of Muslims (Chaudhari Khaliquzzaman and Mohammed Saadulla) and Scheduled Castes (Dr Ambedkar, All-India Adi Hindu Depressed Classes Association), and weightage on behalf of Anglo-Indians (Frank Anthony). The Minorities Sub-Committee rejected separate electorates by 26 votes to 3, and the Advisory Committee, by 58 votes to 3 (Austin 1966: 150).

[45] The memoranda of Untouchable leaders Jagjivan Ram, H.J. Khandekar had recommended reserved seats in Cabinets. These were rejected by a narrow margin of 8 votes to 7 (Austin 1966: 125).

minority report of August 1947 rejected multinational demands for maximal safeguards and instead fashioned an intermediate position of limited multicultural safeguards.

The Minority Rights report was adopted by the Constituent Assembly in August 1947, a time when Austin notes that the mood of the Assembly was in favour of reserved seats for minorities in legislatures but against separate electorates (1966: 149). Its proposals were substantially accepted by the Drafting Committee in February 1948 and incorporated in the Draft Constitution published that year, in a section comprising ten articles, entitled 'Special Provisions relating to Minorities' (Shiva Rao 1967 III: 630–4). In a comprehensive reversal, however, during deliberations on the draft constitution in 1949, religious minorities were removed from the purview of each of these articles. The most contentious provision involved reserved seats in legislatures. The main developments here took place in and around meetings of the Advisory Committee, where amendments were adopted on 11 May 1949, following tense negotiations and key defections among minority representatives, to abolish reserved seats in legislatures for minority groups while maintaining reserved seats in the case of the Scheduled Castes and Tribes.[46] Moving the Advisory Committee's report in the Constituent Assembly on 25 May 1949, Chairman Patel observed that the issue had been reopened as some members felt that 'conditions having vastly changed since the Advisory Committee made their recommendations in 1947, it was no longer appropriate in the context of free India and of present conditions that there should be any reservation of seats for Muslims, Christians, Sikhs, or any other religious minority' (Shiva Rao 1968: 770). The Advisory Committee's proposal to restrict reserved seats

[46] At the Advisory Committee meeting of 30 December 1948, resolutions for the abolition of reserved seats in legislatures were proposed among others by H.C. Mookerjee, Tajamul Husain, L.K. Maitra, Govind Das, and Thakur Das Bhargava. Patel postponed a decision, saying that each minority should decide the matter for itself. When the Advisory Committee reconvened in May 1949, H.C. Mookerjee's resolution for the abolition of reservations was carried, with Begum Aizaz Rasul pressured to speak for the Muslim community. Of the four Muslim members present, one opposed the resolution (Jafar Imam), and the two Congress Muslim members (Abul Kalam Azad and Hafizur Rahman) remained silent (see Austin 1966: 154; Chaube 1973: 174–5; Munshi 1967: 207–8).

in legislatures to Scheduled Castes and Scheduled Tribes was adopted by the Constituent Assembly.

The abolition of reserved seats in legislatures for religious minorities was pivotal. Once secured, it had a snowballing effect. The removal of all other political safeguards for religious minorities followed almost as a matter of consequential adjustment in wording, with barely any prior discussion in the Advisory Committee. On 14 October 1949, after an acrimonious debate, the Constituent Assembly adopted an amendment confining special consideration for minorities in the public services, to the Scheduled Castes and Scheduled Tribes. The same day, the provision of a Special Officer to investigate and report on safeguards for minorities came to be restricted to the 'backward classes' and Anglo-Indians. Replying to objections, K.M. Munshi stated that the work of the Special Officer pertained to political safeguards, and since these were now restricted to 'backward' groups and Anglo-Indians, only these groups would be covered by the Special Officer, and not all minorities as originally envisaged (ibid.: 779). On 16 November 1949, T.T. Krishnamachari's amendment was adopted, replacing the word 'minorities' with 'special classes' in the section dealing with political safeguards: the heading now read 'Special Provisions relating to certain classes' (ibid.: 780).

While the retraction of provisions was portrayed at each stage as a demand of the minority communities, with Advisory Committee Chairman, Patel claiming that 'the vast majority of the minority communities have themselves realized after great reflection the evil effects in the past of such reservations on the minorities themselves' (CAD VIII: 270), it is nonetheless clear that each step of the dismantling of special representation provisions had been contested. Negotiations preceding the first report on minority rights of 1947 abolishing separate electorates and weightage had been fractious and the desired consensus, elusive. Accounts of the crucial Advisory Committee meetings in December 1948 and May 1949 suggest that several Muslim members, including Congress leaders such as Maulana Azad who had for long advocated reserved seats, were not reconciled to their abolition (Munshi 1967: 207–8; Ansari 1999: 119–20). Substantial sections of Muslims and Sikhs 'still demanded a wide range of...safeguards' (Retzlaff 1963: 71; see also Wilkinson 2004: 121). The withdrawal of special consideration in government jobs, and the removal of religious minorities from the remit of the oversight of the Special Officer, encountered vehement opposition on the floor of the Constituent Assembly from Sikh representatives in particular who accused the Congress of reneging on promises (CAD X: 253–60).

Nevertheless, significant portions of minority opinion did concur with their revocation in the later stages of constitution-making. Deals, disarray, and direct and indirect pressure from the Congress leadership, all appear to have played a role. Thus, representatives of the Indian Christian community appear to have given up their claim to political safeguards in return for the inclusion of the right to propagate religion as a fundamental right.[47] The Christian Chairman of the Minorities Sub-Committee, Dr H.C. Mookerjee, proposed the resolution for the abolition of legislative quotas for religious minorities and several Christian representatives urged the withdrawal of political safeguards in later debates. A few Sikh representatives also seem to have ceased to press for reserved seats in legislatures in return for the inclusion of some 'backward' Sikh groups in the list of Scheduled Castes.[48] Also, the disarray in minority parties after Partition meant that the discontent with the retraction of safeguards remained a scattering of dissonant voices without a unified position to defend (Retzlaff 1963: 68–9). Faced with the retraction of reserved seats in legislatures, some Muslim representatives persevered with the demand for separate electorates; others urged some form of proportional representation; and some pleaded for the retention of reserved seats. A few former Muslim League representatives supported the abolition of reserved seats in legislatures for religious minorities, on grounds that this was an ineffectual safeguard without separate electorates. Finally, as Austin

---

[47] In response to opposition from Congress Hindu opinion to the right to propagate religion, K.M. Munshi said: 'I was a party from the very beginning to the compromise with the minorities...it was on this word [propagate] that the Indian Christian community laid the greatest emphasis...because... "propagate" was a fundamental part of their tenet. We ought to respect the compromise' (CAD VII: 837).

[48] Sikh members of the East Punjab Assembly pressed for placing Sikh 'backward classes' such as Mazhabis, Kabirpanthis, Ramdasias, Sikligars on par with Hindu Scheduled Castes in the matter of political rights. This would form the basis of the controversial compromise whereby all other political safeguards for Sikhs were withdrawn (Shiva Rao 1968: 767–72, 777–9).

notes, there is little doubt that the Advisory Committee Chairman Patel 'quietly and privately put a great deal of pressure on the minorities to relinquish special privileges' (1966: 151). While avowing that decisions regarding safeguards must be made by the minority group concerned, behind the scenes Patel worked through allies such as K.M. Munshi to bring minority opinion towards his favoured position (Chiriyankandath 2000: 13). Dissenting voices were overridden through majority vote where necessary (Chaube 1973: 175–7). Patel was supported by wider Congress opinion: Congress Muslims remained silent on the abolition of legislative quotas for religious minorities perhaps on account of Nehru's support for the measure (Wilkinson 2004: 121).

Thus, one notable trend in the process of retraction of political safeguards for religious minorities was the fragmentation among its proponents. A second important trend was the separation of the question of safeguards for minorities from that of 'backward classes'. From the early stages of constitution-making, the question of special provisions for 'backward classes' was sought to be distinguished from, and emphasized over, that of minorities. For instance, the first minority rights report of 1947, while stating that the general approach of the Advisory Committee to minority safeguards was that the 'State should be so run that they should stop feeling oppressed by the mere fact that they are minorities', noted that it was a 'fundamental duty of the State to take special steps to bring up those minorities which are backward to the level of the general community' (Shiva Rao 1967 II: 416). It recommended special provisions for 'backward sections' in addition to those envisaged for minorities, such as the setting up of a Commission to investigate the conditions of 'socially and educationally backward classes'. The uncoupling of 'backward classes' from minorities was underscored in several ways during constitution-making, for instance, through specifying that Scheduled Castes were not a minority (*CAD* V: 227–8). It enabled the shift in the focus of state solicitude from 'minorities' to the 'backward classes', and the progressive narrowing of political safeguards to the latter.

Accounts of the attenuation of special rights during constitution-making have tended to focus on religious minorities (Retzlaff 1963; Ansari 1999; Wilkinson 2004). However, closer examination reveals that the containment of political safeguards also occurred in the case of the 'backward classes', albeit in a much more muted form. The August

1947 minority report, for instance, rejected several demands for political safeguards for Scheduled Castes put forward in representations to the Minorities Sub-Committee such as separate electorates, weightage and guaranteed representation in the Executive. While the report's intermediate position of limited safeguards was not abandoned in the case of the 'backward classes' as it was in the case of religious minorities, it did weaken in some respects. On 11 October 1949, the Constituent Assembly voted to delete the Instrument of Instruction to the President and Provincial Governors regarding the desirability of representation of minorities in the Cabinet (Retzlaff 1963: 72; Austin 1966: 126), a key concern of Scheduled Caste representatives.[49] On 14 October 1949, while reversing its earlier decisions on religious minorities, the Constituent Assembly also adopted an amendment dropping the provision for a Special Officer to supervise safeguards in the provinces: there would be only one Special Officer for the 'backward classes' at the Centre (Shiva Rao 1968: 779).

Thus far, I have focussed on the case of political safeguards and argued that there was overall trend towards containment during constitution-making. The Indian Constitution does, however, guarantee minorities rights in religious, cultural, and educational matters. These are enshrined as justiciable fundamental rights, and assume the form of individual as well as group rights.[50] Several minority representatives supported the abolition of political safeguards in later stages, explicitly on grounds that cultural rights of religious minorities had been secured. For instance, the Chairman of the Minorities Sub-Committee, H.C. Mookerjee (Indian Christian), argued: 'when we have passed the different Fundamental Rights which guarantee religious, cultural and educational safeguards...which are justiciable...the presence of people

---

[49] According to Austin, the deletion of this protection for minorities was part of a broader move from written to tacit conventions as the preferred means of limiting Executive authority (1966: 138–9).

[50] All individuals have the freedom to 'profess, practice, and propagate' religion (Article 25); every religious group or denomination, including a minority group, has the right to 'establish and maintain institutions for religious and charitable purposes', to 'manage its own affairs in matters of religion', to own, acquire, and administer property 'in accordance with law' (Article 26). Groups have the right to preserve their 'distinct language, script, and culture' (Article 29.1) and minorities have the right to 'establish and administer educational institutions of their choice' (Article 30.1).

belonging to certain groups is not necessary' (*CAD* VIII: 299; see also Jerome D' Souza, Tajamul Husain). Were only political safeguards abridged during constitution-making, as is sometimes suggested (see Mahajan 1998: 101, 103; Chiriyankandath 2000: 15)? In other words, did constitution-making represent not so much the containment of group preference, as a shift from political safeguards to other kinds of minority rights? Closer examination suggests that key cultural rights too came to be attenuated, albeit much less drastically than political safeguards.

The history of Articles 29 and 30 of the Indian Constitution is instructive. In August 1947, the Assembly had adopted a draft provision which read 'No *minority* whether based on religion, community, or language shall be discriminated against in regard to admission into State educational institutions, nor shall any religious instruction be compulsorily imposed on them'. Patel described this as 'a simple non-discriminatory clause' against minorities in admission to schools maintained by the state (*CAD* V: 366, 370). In December 1948, this was amended to read 'No *citizen* shall be denied admission into any educational institution maintained by the State or receiving aid out of State funds on grounds only of religion, race, caste, language, or any of them' (*CAD* VII: 925). As Ansari notes, however, the effect of the change was to build an ambiguity into the cultural and educational rights of minorities (1999:130). For it meant that if minority educational institutions were to argue, for instance, that the preservation of their language and culture or the educational advancement of the community required giving preference in admission to students from their community, this could be declared unconstitutional under the new phrasing. Another important change of wording in cultural rights between the report and the draft stage of constitution-making occurred in the article pertaining to the language and script of minorities. The original article adopted by the Constituent Assembly in May 1947 read: '*Minorities* in every unit shall be *protected* in respect of their languages, script, and culture, and no laws or regulations may be enacted that may operate oppressively or prejudicially in this respect' (*CAD* III: 503).[51] The Drafting Committee changed the wording to 'Any *section*

---

[51] A perusal of committee proceedings suggests that the Advisory Committee dropped some of the rights recommended by the Minorities Sub-Committee.

of citizens residing in the territory of India or any part thereof having a distinct language, script, and culture of its own shall have the *right* to conserve the same' (Shiva Rao 1967 III: 525). The change was defended by Dr Ambedkar as providing wider protection to cover linguistic minorities, and also more robust protection, for whereas earlier this had 'depended upon the goodwill of the State', now there was a fundamental right which meant that any state law that was inconsistent would be invalid (*CAD* VII: 923). That the new phrasing was not universally regarded as an improvement is evident from the debate that ensued in the Constituent Assembly. Z.H. Lari pressed for a restoration of the earlier wording and the addition of a provision that would entitle minorities to receive primary education in their mother tongue at the state's expense (*ibid.*: 900–3). This, however, was rejected. Under the new article, the state had no *obligation* to undertake measures to protect the language and script of minorities: protection would be a matter for community initiative. In contrast to the 'backward classes', where duties on the part of the state were written into the Constitution, the Constitution-makers declined to stipulate any obligation upon the state with regard to the preservation of the language, script, and culture of minorities.[52]

The cultural and educational rights eventually adopted thus represented some attenuation from the proposals initially accepted by the Constituent Assembly. But unlike in the case of political safeguards, opponents of special rights for religious minorities also did not get their way. Pandit G.B. Pant's proposal that cultural and educational rights of minorities be relegated from fundamental rights to directive principles that were not enforceable by courts, was rejected (Shiva Rao 1967 II: 279), as were amendments to confine cultural and educational rights to linguistic minorities proposed by Jayaprakash Narayan, Damodar Swarup Sheth, and Thakur Das Bhargava (Shiva Rao 1967 IV: 45–7). Constitution-makers would institute religious, cultural, and educational rights for minorities, in many cases in a form that was in keeping with the demands of minority representatives, against the wishes of Hindu

---

See, for instance, the exchange between Alladi Krishnaswamy Ayyar and K.M. Munshi on the clause that all citizens be entitled to use their mother tongue and its script, Shiva Rao 1967 II: 209, 278–9.

[52] See Chapter 4.

nationalists. Patel agreed to omit a clause outlawing conversion, in keeping with the demands of Christian members, and against the objections of majoritarian Hindu Congressmen (Chiriyankandath 2000: 14). Cultural rights of religious minorities thus did not suffer from the *same* fate as political safeguards as has been suggested (Ansari 1999). In terms of our classification, on cultural and educational rights, an intermediate position of limited multicultural safeguards eventually prevailed in the Constitution; these were protected as fundamental rights, but in forms that were weaker than those initially endorsed by the Assembly.

In the case of religious freedom provisions too, which extended to all citizens but were of particular consequence to religious minorities, an intermediate limited multicultural position would be embodied in the Constitution.[53] Many concerns of religious minorities were accommodated. After undergoing several permutations during its passage through the Sub-Committees on Fundamental Rights and Minorities and the Constituent Assembly, a broad definition of the right to freedom of religion was adopted, encompassing the right to 'practice' and 'propagate' religion as well as to 'profess' religion (Shiva Rao 1967 II: 140, 165, 173, 208; Jha 2002: 3177–8). Rajkumari Amrit Kaur, Hansa Mehta, and others who pressed for a narrower version of the right that would permit only the freedom of religious *worship*, against a broader definition encompassing the *practise* of religion, did not get their way.[54] Neither did those opposed to the propagation of religion. The Minorities Sub-Committee recommended the addition of a right to propagate religion on 19 April 1947.[55] The Advisory Committee qualified this

---

[53] In some respects, the length of the Constituent Assembly's deliberations—stretching over three years—gave time for positions to be modified and compromises to be worked out.

[54] Among the supporters of the narrower interpretation of the right to freedom of religion were Minoo Masani, Alladi Krishnaswamy Ayyar, Jagjivan Ram, Dr B.R. Ambedkar, Tajamul Husain. The broader view was supported among others by K.M. Munshi, K.M. Pannikar, Ujjal Singh. Harnam Singh's demand that the wearing and carrying of kirpans be recognized as part of Sikh religion was accepted. The right to profess and practice religion was extended to all persons, not just citizens. See Shiva Rao 1967 II: 76, 122–3 143, 146–7, 161–2, 187, 213, 265–7.

[55] During the Sub-Committee's deliberations, M. Ruthnaswamy had recommended the inclusion of an explicit provision permitting propagation

right by laying down that conversion brought about by coercion or
undue influence would not be recognized by law. However, eventually,
this was dropped and the right to propagate religion retained in the
teeth of strong opposition.[56] This was in keeping with the demands of
religious minorities, in particular, Christian representatives such as the
Anglo-Indian leader Frank Antony, who argued that propagation was
fundamental to the Christian faith. The concerns of religious minorities
were also accommodated in the fashioning of other provisions relating
to religious freedom. Overriding the objections of those seeking to
restrict the domain of religion, religious denominations were permitted
by right to hold property (Shiva Rao 1967 II: 269–70). On the
controversial issue of whether state could aid educational institutions that
imparted religious instruction, after extensive debate, the Constituent
Assembly eventually decided that it could do so, a position that was
in keeping with the wishes of several minority representatives.[57] With
regard to religious freedom, the recommendations of the Minorities Sub-
Committee, which were most shaped by minority concerns, prevailed to
a large extent.

These did not, however, prevail in their entirety: the rights to religious
freedom would be limited in important respects. The suggestions made
by the Fundamental Rights Sub-Committee in April 1947 that religious
freedom be subject to other fundamental rights provisions were accepted.
On 21 April 1947, in response to the concerns expressed by Alladi
Krishnaswamy Ayyar and others, the Advisory Committee decided to
add a clause stating that freedom of religious practice would not debar
the state from enacting laws for social welfare and reform. The eventual
wording of this clause reflected a 'Hindu assimilationist perspective

---

on grounds that some religions such as Christianity and Islam were essentially
proselytizing faiths (Shiva Rao 1967 II: 201, 208).

[56] Opponents in the Advisory Committee included Alladi Krishnawamy
Ayyar, G.B. Pant (Shiva Rao 1967 II: 268). See also Loknath Misra and Tajamul
Husain (CAD VII: 817–19 and 822–4). The right to propagate religion was
supported among others by K.M. Munshi, L.K. Maitra, K. Santhanam (ibid.:
831–8).

[57] Opponents of state aid for denominational educational institutions included
Rajkumari Amrit Kaur, Alladi Krishnaswamy Ayyar, K.T. Shah; supporters
included K.M. Munshi, Frank Antony, Mohammed Ismail, M.V. Kamath (Shiva
Rao 1967 II: 221, 281).

towards Sikhs, Jains and Buddhists' (Singh 2006: 916). Rajagopalachari's suggestion that the right of religious denominations to hold property be subject to the general law, was accepted (Shiva Rao 1967 II: 267, 270). In response to concerns expressed during the debate in the Constituent Assembly on 30 August 1947, an explicit provision was added to the effect that no religious instruction would be provided in schools wholly maintained by the state.[58] This was in addition to a clause that stipulated that no individual attending an educational institution recognized or aided by the state would be compelled to take part in religious instruction or worship conducted in such an institution against their will (Shiva Rao 1968: 264).

The form that rights to religious freedom eventually assumed thus represented a compromise with those seeking to restrict the domain of religion. This in turn meant that many of the freedoms that minorities had enjoyed in religious affairs under the colonial state could no longer be taken for granted. While the colonial state had largely followed a policy of non-intervention in the religious affairs of its subjects, the right to freedom of religion under the Indian Constitution would permit state intervention in the interests of public order, morality, and health; for upholding other fundamental rights provisions; for the purpose of social welfare and reform, and for the regulation and restriction of any economic, financial, political, or secular activity associated with religious practice (Article 25).

The case of personal law offers a good example of the intermediate compromise position that ultimately prevailed in the Constitution on religious freedom. On the one hand, demands that the different religious laws that governed 'personal' matters such as marriage and divorce in colonial India be supplanted by a uniform civil code were rejected. Despite the strong urging of members such as Rajkumari Amrit Kaur, Hansa Mehta, Minoo Masani, Alladi Krishnaswamy Ayyar, and K.M. Munshi, there would be no justiciable provision regarding a uniform civil code in the Constitution (Shiva Rao 1967 II: 162, 177; *CAD*

---

[58] This provision in effect represented a compromise between those who favoured religious instruction in educational institutions and those who sought to ban religious instruction also in educational institutions partially aided by the state. Minority representatives were to be found on both sides of this debate-see *CAD* VII, 866–86.

VII: 546–50).[59] On the other hand, despite earlier Congress assurances notably in the Nehru Report of 1928 and the Congress Scheme for a Communal Settlement at the Second Round Table Conference of October 1931 that personal laws would be protected by specific provisions in the future Constitution, no guarantees were provided for personal laws.[60] Demands put forward by Muslim representatives Mahboob Ali Baig Sahib Bahadur and Mohamed Ismail Sahib for explicit guarantees in the Constitution against state intervention in personal laws, were rejected (CAD VII: 540–4, 723). The inclusion in the Constitution of a provision for a uniform civil code, albeit only in a non-justiciable form, meant that the continued existence of religious laws could no longer be taken for granted.[61] With regard to religious freedom provisions then, an intermediate limited multicultural position was embodied in the Constitution, with some minority demands acceded to, but other freedoms no longer enjoying the immunity from state intervention that they had had in the colonial period.[62]

[59] Ansari's conclusion that the Constituent Assembly opted for 'pure and homogenous nationalism' after Partition, abandoning its commitment to cultural freedom of minorities, is thus overstated (1999: 133).

[60] At the Second Round Table Conference, the Congress scheme for a communal settlement had stated that 'Personal laws shall be protected by specific provisions to be embodied in the Constitution' (Indian Round Table Conference 1931: 64).

[61] Proponents of personal law were however reassured that the State would not impose a uniform code on unwilling communities. See, for instance, M. Ananthasayanam Ayyangar: 'Without the consent of the minority that is affected, no such law will be framed' (CAD VII: 778; also B.R. Ambedkar, CAD VII: 781–2).

[62] See also Wilkinson 2004: 106. Although the case of tribals is outside the scope of this study, here too, moderate attenuation can be discerned between the report and the draft stage of constitution-making. Tribal policies were considered separately from other minorities, in Sub-Committees on Excluded and Partially Excluded Areas in Assam and outside Assam (Shiva Rao 1968: 575). The main line of tension in debates was between a protectionist approach, which sought to preserve traditional tribal practices and an integrationist approach, which focussed on the remedy of economic and educational backwardness. Several protectionist provisions from Sub-Committee reports of 1947 and the 1948 Draft Constitution pertaining to regional autonomy and powers of tribal councils, were pared down during August–September 1949. At the same time, enthusiasts of greater assimilation of tribals also did not get their way (Shiva Rao 1968: 573–89). An intermediate, limited multicultural position was embodied in

To sum up, our examination of the career of minority provisions in the Constituent Assembly discloses a dynamic of attenuation with regard to most group rights, although this trend was more pronounced in the case of political safeguards than cultural rights, and in the case of some groups, notably religious minorities, than others such as the 'backward classes'. The containment was accomplished in different ways in different areas of group rights. In the case of religious minorities, it occurred through a series of steps involving a *narrowing* of the focus of political safeguards to the 'backward classes', and a *broadening* of cultural rights that pertained specifically to minorities, to all citizens.

The process of containment was encapsulated in the fortunes of the term 'minority', whose incidence and scope in constitutional provisions came to be abridged during constitution-making. As noted, in the cultural rights of minorities, the term 'minority' came to be replaced by 'any section of citizens' in important clauses. Similarly in the section on political safeguards, the word 'minorities' came to be replaced with 'special classes'. The Scheduled Castes were excluded from the ambit of the term 'minorities', which would eventually find mention in two articles (29 and 30) of the Constitution (Ansari 1999: 125). The Constitution does not specify which groups are to be regarded as 'minorities' (Wadhwa 1975: 4–5).

Explaining Minority Rights in the Constitution: Partition and Beyond

The curtailment of minority rights during the framing of the Indian Constitution has been noted in studies of the period but rarely analysed.[63] Partition and ensuing changes are usually considered sufficient to account for attenuation in the rights of religious minorities during constitution-making. Closer examination of the small literature on this subject suggests that Partition serves as shorthand for a range of factors. Prominent among these is the weakened bargaining position of religious minorities, particularly Muslims post-Partition. Partition is thought to

---

the Constitution, one that offered significant protections for cultural difference, but that was also tempered with more integrative mechanisms than had obtained in British India and early constitutional drafts.

[63] Notable exceptions include Retzlaff 1963; Ansari 1999; Bajpai 1997, 2000.

have reduced the bargaining power of minorities for safeguards in several respects.[64] Strategically, with Partition conceded, minorities lost their best bargaining card as well as their most powerful advocate, the Muslim League. Retzlaff notes that whereas prior to Partition, the Congress had been forced to tread extremely carefully on the issue of minority safeguards 'for fear of taking an action which the Muslim League might be able to seize upon as a "pretext" for refusing to join the Constituent Assembly...now...there was no further need to be extremely cautious in order to conciliate the League' (1963: 61). According to Wilkinson, once Partition was imminent, 'Congress governments had no compelling political reason to preserve job reservations for religious minorities' (2004: 110).

Organizationally, following Partition, the main political parties pressing for safeguards for religious minorities, the Muslim League and the Sikh Panthic Party disintegrated. Several Muslim League leaders decided to disband the party in February–March 1948, although some splinter groups such as the Madras Muslim League resisted. At the same time, the Akali Dal called for the Sikh Panthic Party to be dissolved, urging its members to unconditionally join the Congress party. Splinter groups such as those led by Master Tara Singh refused to disband (Retzlaff 1963: 67). The disarray in the Muslim League and the Sikh Panthic party meant that during key deliberations on political safeguards in 1949, several former advocates of safeguards now urged their revocation. Those who did not could not agree on a joint set of demands, thereby rendering their opposition ineffectual (Retzlaff 1963: 71; Austin 1966: 151). With prominent Muslim League proponents of safeguards moving to Pakistan during Partition, there were few powerful minority spokesmen to contend with, unlike in the case of the 'backward classes' (McMillan 2004). Numerically, as well, minorities were weakened by Partition. Adeney argues that reserved seats for Muslims were omitted from the Indian Constitution 'because the diminished proportion of Muslims within the state decreased their bargaining power....' (2007: 66).

Partition is also thought to have changed attitudes towards minority safeguards—in the wider public, the Congress party, as well as among

---

[64] These factors are indicative rather than exhaustive, and are not mutually exclusive.

minority representatives. Retzlaff notes that Partition contributed to a growing public mood against communal groupings, and hardened opinion within the Congress against political safeguards for religious minorities, which were thought to perpetuate communalism (1963: 66). Wilkinson concurs, holding that 'the general feeling among most Congress politicians' was that 'consociational policies were divisive and had led to Partition'. This 'combined with antipathy towards Muslims over Partition' led to the 'rapid dismantling of minority proportionality in politics and government employment, the non-fulfilment of previous Congress pledges to protect minority languages, and the overruling of the minority veto when minorities such as Muslims and Sikhs protested over their treatment at the hand of the majority' (2004: 108).[65] Significant sections of Hindu opinion became more vocal after Partition, accusing the Congress of 'discriminating against Hindus' (*ibid.*: 110). Partition is also thought to have changed minority attitudes towards political safeguards as a consequence of their weakened bargaining position. Austin notes that Partition made Muslims a smaller and highly suspect group, who would ultimately decide 'to forgo even reservation in the Legislature, hoping by its sacrifice to ensure fair treatment from the Hindu majority' (1966: 151). There was a reluctant recognition that the protection of minority interests could now be best achieved by not antagonizing Congress and Hindu opinion. Many Muslims were afraid 'to oppose openly a measure that was supported by Nehru, whose support they needed to protect their community from even more extreme policies being advocated by militant Hindus in Congress' (Wilkinson 2004: 121; see also Ansari 1999: 121).

Partition and the changed circumstances that ensued are undoubtedly crucial for explaining the curtailment in the rights of religious minorities during constitution-making. Nevertheless, these do not constitute an obvious or sufficient explanation as is commonly believed. While Partition weakened the bargaining position of minorities, it also put the Congress to test. It was now called upon to make good its claim that it was not just a Hindu party, but represented all sections of India, and that the Indian nation it had fought for was not a Hindu counterpart to Pakistan, but embodied a distinct ideal of nationhood. The Congress could hardly afford to be seen as simply using

---

[65] For an account of the motivations and behaviour of state governments with regard to the dismantling of job quotas, see Wilkinson 2004: 110.

its brute majority to force through a narrow party or Hindu agenda, on a question that had for so long and so bitterly divided Indians. Precisely *because* the Congress was overwhelmingly dominant in the Assembly, it could not be seen to be coercing the minorities. Also, it had a long-standing commitment to non-majoritarian decision making on minority questions, which it continued to profess throughout constitution-making, seeking to portray each step of withdrawal of political safeguards as a demand of the minorities themselves. Importantly, the retraction of reserved seats for religious minorities involved a reversal of the Congress's own earlier policy commitments. The Congress had signed up to legislative quotas in the Nehru Report of 1928, at the Round Table Conference in 1931 and more recently in the Report on Minority Rights of August 1947.[66] It should also be recalled that political safeguards were endorsed by the Constituent Assembly *after* the decision to Partition the country had been announced. These would remain in the draft constitution until 1949, when they were abolished through a narrow vote in the Advisory Committee in which key Congress Muslims abstained (Chaube 1973: 174–5; Ansari 1999: 120). As Retzlaff notes, 'had the initial timetable which called for the completion of the drafting of the Constitution by the fall of 1947 been adhered to...the Constitution would have included specific political safeguards for the minorities' (1963: 66). If the retraction of safeguards for religious minorities appears a foregone conclusion with hindsight, at the time, the question was much more open-ended.

One important condition that enabled the Congress effect this radical shift, this study contends, was the availability of a normative vocabulary in which political safeguards for minorities were illegitimate. For the Congress to dismantle long-standing colonial safeguards and break its own earlier policy commitments, *while* plausibly claiming to carry all sections with it, on this most divisive of political questions,

---

[66] The extent to which the minority safeguards in the 1947 report were consistent with long-standing Congress policy is disputed. Retzlaff holds that the report represented 'very considerable movements from the Congress's previous position of supporting only...a list of fundamental rights applicable to all citizens' (1963: 60, 64–5). By contrast, Ansari notes that the minority rights provided in the 1947 report 'were consistent with the Congress's policy on minorities evolved since the late twenties' (1999: 117). Both views are correct, for reasons elaborated in Chapters 3 and 4.

the availability of such a normative vocabulary was crucial. Of course Partition and the reduced bargaining power of minority parties post-Partition very likely played a role. However, it is only through a closer analysis of political ideals of Indian nationalism that the dynamic of containment of minority policies at work during constitution-making can be adequately grasped.

Nationalist ideas do figure, albeit not prominently, in some accounts of changes to minority safeguards during constitution-making (see Austin 1966: 144–5). Ansari, for instance, has argued that 'the leading lights of the Indian National Congress were inspired by a vision of a homogenized, unitary cultural nationalism' (1999: 134), and this, together with the circumstances of Partition, sealed their fate. While nationalist ideas are indeed important for understanding the revocation of safeguards for religious minorities, these did not always take the form 'homogenous nationalism' after Partition. As we shall see, Indian nationalism remained ideologically diverse: there was no sudden conversion of civic to ethnic nationalists post-Partition. It is difficult otherwise to explain the retention of cultural safeguards for religious minorities in the Indian Constitution, for instance. The diversity of institutional outcomes with respect to the rights of religious minorities—retraction in some cases, retention in an attenuated form in others—can only be properly understood in the light of the complex strands of Indian nationalist thought. These ideals were long-standing: Partition added ballast but was not the source.

In the case of the 'backward classes', the presence in the Constitution of political safeguards has been attributed to the role of leaders and institutional legacies. For example, according to McMillan, the retention of electoral reservation for the Scheduled Castes was due to the presence of a powerful spokesman at the centre of negotiations: Dr Ambedkar, who chaired the drafting committee, and was member of key committees which discussed special representation for the Scheduled Castes. This, together with the adoption of a policy process largely based on the British system of decision by committees in which minority representatives predominated, accounts for the presence of political safeguards for Scheduled Castes in the Indian Constitution (McMillan 2005: 63, 64; see also Adeney 2007: 75). But as we saw earlier, the demands for separate electorates and other mechanisms for giving Scheduled Caste electors greater influence were not met; institutional legacies such as the minority veto were not always observed. Instead, as we shall see, the institutional forms of Scheduled Caste representation eventually adopted closely corresponded to their normative bases in nationalist opinion.

CONCLUSION

For all the continuities between colonial constitutions such as the 1935 Government of India Act and the Indian Constitution highlighted by scholars (Washbrook 1999: 37; Bose and Jalal 1999: 206–7), with regard to group rights, 1947 marked an important departure.[67] India might have been 'one of the first countries to give constitutional recognition to the rights of minority communities' (Mahajan 1998: 83), but these rights still marked a cut-back upon what had obtained prior to Independence. Whereas existing explanations have focussed on the effects of Partition on the bargaining power of minorities, these are not sufficient to account for the containment of minority rights during constitution-making. Instead, longer-term ideological forces within Indian nationalism favoured containment and need to be understood in order to adequately account for the institutional forms of group rights under the Indian Constitution.

The role of nationalist ideology is acknowledged in some discussions of changes to minority policies during constitution-making (e.g., Ansari 1999; Adeney 2007: 81, 91). Historical and social science accounts, however, have only accorded cursory attention to ideas, mostly in the form of the beliefs of influential actors, such as Nehru and Ambedkar. This is inadequate for our grasp of the character of nationalist ideas and their significance for the fate minority provisions in the Constitution. Indian nationalism was ideologically diverse and complex: Nehru's views, as is well known, were not representative of opinion within the Congress. More importantly, belief-systems or world-views of individual actors are not the only form in which ideas have efficacy in politics. As political ethnographers have reminded us, ideas also work to produce political power in more material incarnations—symbolic actions, performances of support or

---

[67] There were also other departures from colonial constitutionalism, notably the adoption of democracy based on universal franchise (Sarkar 2001: 28).

dissent, patterns of political discourse—that go beyond the cognitive frames of individuals (Hansen 1999; Roy 2007). It is to an examination of nationalist ideas as discourses on group rights in the Constituent Assembly that we now turn.

3

Nationalist Discourse and Group Rights

A Conceptual Approach

INTRODUCTION

What did nationalist ideas on special provisions for minority groups look like? Building on Freeden's (1996) approach to the study of ideologies, this chapter elaborates a conceptual framework for the analysis of Indian nationalist discourse. All nationalist arguments in the Constituent Assembly debates invoked one or other of the following concepts: secularism, democracy, justice and equality, national unity, and development. Further, each concept was elaborated in relation to the other elements of the vocabulary. National unity was the primary concept in this vocabulary, in relation to which the other concepts were construed. Secularism, democracy, social justice, and development were elaborated in nationalist opinion in different ways, but predominantly in keeping with the requirements of national unity. At the risk of reification, for heuristic purposes, the nationalist vocabulary can be seen as a grid of interlocking normative concepts in which national unity had priority.

In contrast to dominant approaches to the study of nationalist thought in the postcolonial world, the account of the nationalist vocabulary elaborated here detaches ideas from macro-social processes such as the rise of the bourgeois nation-state or modernity.[1]

---

[1] For Chatterjee, mature nationalist thought recognized a 'central, autonomous and directing role of the state' and reflected a 'rationalist thematic' (1986: 132, 157). Kaviraj's pathbreaking analysis delineates the structure of nationalist discourse in terms of the triumvirate of the state, modernity, and rationality: nationalism is the legitimizing ideology of a new nation-state (1994: 300), and

Instead, nationalist thought is detailed in terms of its internal, conceptual structure. Methodologically, whereas scholars have focused overwhelmingly on great figures, for this period usually Nehru, nationalist thinking is mapped here through a close textual reading of the Constituent Assembly debates. The term 'nationalist opinion' in my account is used as a heuristic category, to designate a position that accorded primacy to national unity considerations. Agents who occupied this position—individuals and parties—changed over time during the course of the Assembly's deliberations. Also, individuals sometimes espoused 'nationalist' opinions on one issue, and not on another. Typically, 'nationalist opinion' in group rights debates comprised most Congress party members, some representatives on the margins of the Congress (Socialist, Communist, Hindu Mahasabha, Independent), and a sprinkling of non-Congress minority representatives (Muslim League, Akali). Several minority representatives were vocal 'nationalists'.[2] As we shall see, more and more non-Congress advocates of minority rights espoused nationalist opinion as the deliberations of the Assembly progressed, including key figures such as Dr Ambedkar. 'Minority opinion' designates a position that accorded primacy to minority rights. It was voiced mainly but not exclusively by representatives from minority groups, from both within and outside the Congress party.

My argument about the character and effects of the nationalist vocabulary unfolds over two chapters. This chapter focuses on the defining elements of nationalist discourse. The first section elaborates the notion of a nationalist vocabulary as a conceptual schema. A set of normative concepts recurred in nationalist arguments, chief among which were those of secularism, democracy, social justice, national unity, and development. The second section argues that national unity was the primary concept in the vocabulary to which all the other concepts were linked. As group rights were seen as a threat to national unity in this period, other concepts such as secularism and justice were also construed as antithetical to group rights in dominant nationalist

---

there is a 'fundamental relation' between 'nationalist thinking and the rationalist discourse of modernity' (1992: 30).

[2] These included Christians Rajkumari Amrit Kaur and Dr H.C. Mookerjee (Congress); Parsis Minoo Masani and R.K. Sidhwa (Congress); Jain Prof. K.T. Shah (Congress); Shia Muslim Tajamul Husain (Muslim League). See Chiriyankandath 2000: 9.

opinion. Focusing on the concept of secularism, the third section assesses some of the respects in which the nationalist vocabulary was Western or indigenous in character, and in doing so, argues against certain variants of Indian exceptionalism. The final section introduces group claims to preferential treatment. These, it argues, were caught in the midst of change. On the one hand, these continued to be cast in an earlier colonial framework of group entitlement, on the other, group claims increasingly sought to adapt to the nationalist vocabulary. The normative language in which contenders for legitimacy on the Indian political scene had to speak was shifting.

The Nationalist Vocabulary on Group Rights: A Conceptual Schema

Chatterjee states that nationalist discourse in its mature phase is conducted 'in a single consistent, unambiguous voice' (1986: 51). At first glance, nationalist arguments on group rights in the Constituent Assembly debates appear to confirm this view. The recurrence of a set of normative terms is striking. Again and again, secularism, democracy, justice and equal opportunity, national unity, and development were invoked by nationalists, in a range of debates on group rights, to support a variety of proposals for and against special treatment. There appears to be a common legitimating vocabulary framing nationalist arguments on group rights in the Constituent Assembly.

Closer examination reveals, however, that the similarity is deceptive. Each term referred to several interrelated concepts and idea-units. The term 'national unity', for instance, denoted, variously, the political integrity of the country; the stability of the state and the maintenance of civil peace; a sense of national solidarity; a national identity. So an assertion that group rights undermined national unity could embody different claims: that such rights threatened the integrity of the country; that these undermined loyalty to the nation; that these were incompatible with the kind of nation that was sought to be fashioned; and, of course, some combination of these claims.

Not only did each of secularism, democracy, justice, and national unity refer to a range of concepts, different *conceptions* of these concepts were invoked in political debate. Let us take the concept of a secular state, for example, which was one of the referents of secularism (others included a secular society; secular attitudes and identities; and the process of secularization). In some instances, this connoted a state that had no official religion; in others, a state that did not favour any particular religion; and in yet others, the exclusion of religion from the political domain. These different conceptions were to be found among those on the *same* side of a debate, so those who agreed that safeguards for minorities were incompatible with a secular state often disagreed about *why* exactly this was so.

Further, there were different norms underpinning each of the conceptions of the key legitimating concepts. For example, the conception of secularism as the exclusion of religion from politics was defended by some, but not all nationalists, in terms of the ideal of equal citizenship for all individuals. Even within a conception of a secular state defended in terms of equal citizenship rights for all individuals, there could be further variations, depending on whether the ultimate appeal was to another value, such as modernity. So when group rights were opposed as incompatible with a secular state, the appeal could be to different values. Coming to grips adequately with these values requires us to distinguish between semantic, conceptual and normative levels: between the key normative terms of debate on group rights, the conceptions denoted by these terms, and the norms underpinning these conceptions.

How do we make sense of the variety of conceptions encountered in nationalist discourse from the standpoint of a conceptual approach to ideology? Conceptions of secularism, democracy, justice, national unity, and development were mutually dependent. They were so in at least two respects. Connotations of each concept drew upon a common pool or 'idea-environment' comprising all the concepts of this vocabulary (Freeden 1996: 67). Further, differences in conceptions derived from variations in the arrangement of these concepts, that is, from the relationships that obtained between the key concepts of the vocabulary. The nationalist vocabulary can thus be seen as a grid of sorts that imparted meaning to each of its individual elements and ordered differences between them.[3]

The relationships between the component elements of the nationalist vocabulary were of different kinds. Miller's (1978) distinction between

---

[3] The idea of a grid is meant to capture here simply a set of elements held together, and not 'the deep configurations that make these possible' (Kaviraj 1994: 299).

instrumental, constitutive, and analogical relationships between concepts is useful here. One kind of relationship was *instrumental*. Let us take the example of secularism and national unity. A wide cross-section of nationalists agreed that religion had to be kept separate from the state for the sake of the political integrity of the country: the recent violent partition of the country on religious lines was regarded as a direct consequence of a colonial policy of mixing religion and politics. A secular state was considered instrumental for national unity in a negative sense, in that political unity would be endangered if the state were not secular. For a smaller section of nationalists, a secular state was also to be the means for consolidating national unity in a positive sense. The state was to be the agency for welding together diverse and conflicting religious groups into a nation, and it was felt that the state could only fulfil this role if it abstained from identification with any religion. A second kind of relationship between components of the nationalist vocabulary was *constitutive*. Some nationalists subscribed to a secular view of the national identity, where Indian-ness was defined primarily in political terms, in terms of membership of a state where religion was irrelevant for purposes of citizenship. A third kind of relationship between the key concepts in nationalist opinion was *analogical*. Some nationalists held that the Indian state had to be secular because this was the only kind of nation-state appropriate for the modern era—a country that aspired to join the ranks of the advanced industrialized nations of the world could not be otherwise. Nehru declared that 'no modern, civilized State can be other than a secular State.'(q. Smith 1958: 154). Here, the relationship between secularism and the nation-state was analogical: the claim was that one kind of idea—a nation-state—brought with it another—that of secularism.

I have so far claimed that nationalist argument on group rights was conducted within the terms of a vocabulary comprising notions of secularism, democracy, justice, national unity and development, and that each of these terms was elaborated through interlinkages with the other elements of the vocabulary. This, however, still leaves us with a very large range of possible conceptions. Does this imply that what nationalists shared was simply a set of normative *terms*, and that this all that is meant by the claim that a common vocabulary framed nationalist arguments over group rights? I now want to take the argument a step further. In the nationalist vocabulary, national unity was the core concept in relation to which all the concepts were construed, the axis around which the other elements were organized. In nationalist opinion, secularism, democracy, and social justice were construed in ways that furthered national unity.

THE ROLE OF NATIONAL UNITY IN THE NATIONALIST VOCABULARY

Thus far, our characterization of the nationalist vocabulary has been abstract and schematic. It is time to put more historical detail into the picture. While in analytical terms, the nationalist vocabulary can be seen as grid of interlocking political concepts, in historical terms, this ideological formation was associated with the ascendance of Indian nationalism. Components of the ideational repertoire of Indian nationalism can be discerned in their modern forms in public cultural arenas since at least the late nineteenth century, although their origins can be traced to earlier periods (Bayly 1996). By the 1920s–1930s, notions of secularism, democracy, justice, national unity, and development appear in their current forms with increasing frequency in Congress resolutions and pamphlets.[4] Apart from the Congress-led national movement, several other political movements based on class, caste, religion, and gender contributed to the development of these ideas. As Sarkar notes, grouping these diverse trends under nationalism or even the broader category of anti-colonialism is problematic: lower caste protests and movements for women rights 'often utilized aspects of colonial policies and Western ideologies as resources' and even on occasion were 'loyalist' or 'anti-national' (1997: 359; 2001: 24).[5] In the late colonial period, however, the Congress-led national movement

---

[4] In Congress resolutions from the 1930s onwards, for instance, the terms 'democracy', 'equal rights', 'justice', and 'national unity' start to appear with increasing regularity. The concept of 'secularism' can also be discerned in resolutions from this period (with terms like 'state neutrality' and 'state equidistance' with regard to religion being used), although the term 'secularism' comes into general currency around the time of independence. Several historical studies date the emergence of a new nationalist language to the 1930s. See, for instance, Pandey 1990: chs. 6, 7; Sarkar 2001: 29.

[5] On the antagonism of lower-caste movements and the national movement, see, for instance, Patankar and Omvedt 1979; Aloysius 1997. Untouchable leaders often emphasized the benefits of British rule, especially with regard to

sought to incorporate the key demands of contending political movements under its umbrella (Chatterjee 1986). Or, in the terms of my proposal, Congress nationalism of the mid-twentieth century stitched together secularism, democracy, social justice, and development into a single fabric using the thread of national unity.

The Constituent Assembly debates marked a key moment in the crystallization of this constellation of ideas into a normative framework for political debate. These brought to culmination an influential tendency in nationalist opinion, that of the construing the requirements of national unity, and by extension of secularism, democracy, and justice, as largely hostile to minority safeguards. Two qualifications are necessary here. First, nationalist opinion comprised distinct ideological strands, and therefore encompassed multiple conceptions of secularism, democracy, social justice, and even national unity. While minority safeguards were opposed on grounds of national unity in every case, these were not always the *same* grounds. Second, nationalists were not uniformly opposed to *all* minority safeguards: as we shall see, protections in the form of rights to non-discrimination, religious and cultural freedoms did find support in nationalist opinion. Nationalist opposition largely pertained to political safeguards: special representation in legislatures and public services. Nationalists of different ideological hues, however, *converged* on the view that political safeguards detracted from national unity, and thus also from secularism, justice, and democracy. This ideological convergence is important for understanding the fate of minority safeguards during constitution-making.

Dimensions of National Unity and Development

The most common nationalist opposition to political safeguards stemmed from concerns of national unity. Adapting Kymlicka and Norman's distinctions (2000) for our purposes, appeals to national unity in nationalist discourse encapsulated four main types of concerns. First, minority safeguards were regarded as a threat to the political integrity of the country and the maintenance of civil peace. The policy of minority safeguards, it was argued, had destroyed the physical integrity of the country and brought civil war; it would do so again if continued.

---

education and jobs in the lower administration (Gooptu 2001: 170). See also Chapter 2 above.

Religion-based separate electorates in particular were regarded as the direct cause of Partition. Purushottamdas Tandon declaimed:

> In politics [the Congress party] refuses to recognize any differences on account of religion...We ask Sir Stafford and other British leaders: 'If a hundred years or for that matter twenty years ago, the right of separate elections were given to different sects of your country, what sort of government you would have had today?...Would you not have had continuous civil wars?'[6] (CAD I: 68)

The impact of minority safeguards on political integrity was the dominant concern in this period, through which all other concerns about minority safeguards were mediated.

A second national unity concern pertained to a sense of common nation-hood. Nationalists were keenly aware that an overriding sense of belonging to the same nation, cutting across differences of community attachment, was still weak among Indians. Minority safeguards, it was felt, would promote particular group affiliations among citizens at the cost of wider national ones.[7] While religion was an obvious threat, linguistic, caste, and other ascriptive groups were also viewed with suspicion in this period, as competing loci for citizens' affections, and detracting from a common nationality in proportion to their strength. Whereas prior to the 1920s, the nation had been conceived as a composite of different religious, regional, and caste communities (Pandey 1990), this was not the case for dominant nationalist opinion in the Constituent Assembly. While nationalists of different ideological persuasions differed over how exactly minority safeguards undermined national belonging, they nevertheless agreed that the strengthening of attachment to minority groups took place at the *cost* of loyalty to the nation. Characteristically of nationalist doctrines, minorities, and groups more generally were described as 'part' of the 'larger whole' that was the nation, so the well-being of the

---

[6] R.V. Dhulekar lamented: 'In 1916 the Indian National Congress conceded to the Muslims their demand for separate electorates and reservation of seats. Within the last thirty years, this vicious system has brought the country to the verge of civil war and Partition...' (CAD II: 303).

[7] A sense of common nation-hood was regarded as a prerequisite both for the political integrity of the nation, and for the successful functioning of a democracy. Pandit G.B. Pant noted: 'If in a democracy, you create rival loyalties, or...a system in which any individual or group, instead of suppressing his extravagance, cares nought for larger or other interests, then democracy is doomed' (CAD V: 224).

nation was a necessary condition for the flourishing of individuals and the communities to which they belonged. For representatives to press for group advantages such as minority safeguards, which damaged the nation, was misguided and self-defeating. Jawaharlal Nehru admonished: '...there is no group in India, no party, no religious community which can prosper if India does not prosper. If India goes down, we go down, all of us, whether we have a few seats more or less, whether we get a slight advantage or we do not' (CAD II: 323). Those pressing for safeguards were exhorted not to be selfish and short-sighted, to raise their sights above their 'petty' group concerns and look to the 'larger' interest of the nation for 'if the larger interest suffers, there can be no question of real safeguarding of the interest of any minority' (Vijayalakshmi Pandit CAD II: 278). Such statements reflected nationalist apprehensions that minorities would withhold commitment to the nation or look to outside powers for the fulfilment of their interests—a sense that was a part of distrust of minorities as disloyal to the nation.

A third set of concerns implicit in the claim that minority safeguards undermined national unity pertained to national identity. Two main conceptions of India's national identity can be distinguished in this period: secular nationalist and Hindu nationalist (Varshney 1993: 235). Hindu nationalist versions of India's national identity were articulated by a substantial section of Congressmen in the Constituent Assembly debates.[8] Indian identity was defined here in cultural terms, based typically on Hindi as the national language, descent from Indian religions such as Hinduism and Sikhism, and other broadly Hindu cultural themes.[9] Minorities played no part in the definition of the national

[8] See, for example, Loknath Misra, CAD VII: 892–3. Seth Govind Das wanted Hindi to be the sole national language: 'For thousands of years one and the same culture has all along been obtaining here...It is in order to maintain this tradition that we want one language and one script for the whole country' (CAD IX:1328). Chiriyankandath notes that the majority of those expressing Hindu nationalist sentiments (notably Purushottamdas Tandon, Seth Govind Das, Shibban Lal Saksena, Algurai Shastri, and Mahavir Tyagi) were Hindi-speaking Congressmen from UP, Bihar, current day MP, and Punjab (2000: 10–11).

[9] Their proposals included the recognition of Hindi as the sole national language, descent from 'Indian' religions as a basis of citizenship, the naming of India as Bharat to reflect its Hindu past, and a strong centralized state (Chiriyankandath 2000: 16–18; Singh 2006: 911–15). While proposals for Hindi as the sole national language and citizenship based on descent from Indian religions were

identity, being either assimilated or excluded from it. From a Hindu nationalist standpoint, minority safeguards promoted identities that were at variance with the nation's cultural identity, and as such detracted from national unity. For secular nationalists, on the other hand, political safeguards required the recognition of religion, caste, and tribe in public policy and thereby detracted from the desired national identity, which sought to steer clear of ethno-cultural criteria in the political domain (Sheth 1999). The reigning European models of nationalism based on language and descent were rejected: commonalities of language, religion, or any other cultural attribute would not serve as the basis of national identity in India's case. Instead, the nation was conceived in political terms, as a community united by its commitment to common political ideals, those of secularism, democracy, and social justice. Nationality, then, was to consist in secular democratic citizenship. Secularism was constitutively tied to national unity here. Further, as we shall presently see, these ideals were construed as precluding the recognition of ethno-cultural criteria, particularly religious criteria, in the political domain. It is significant that Hindu nationalists and secular nationalists concurred that minority political safeguards were inconsistent with the national identity. Scholars have noted the prevalence of secular, non-ethnic articulations of Indian identity in this period (Chatterjee 1995: 203).[10] At least one reason for

---

rejected, the Constitution contains some Hindu nationalist elements. These include the prohibition on cow slaughter (Article 48, non-justiciable) and the subsuming of Sikhs, Jains, and Buddhists in the category Hindu for social welfare and reform (Article 25.2b)—see Singh 2006.

[10] As Sarkar notes, the distinction between secular and Hindu nationalism 'can at best claim a certain precision in logic, far less so in practice', which saw 'enormous overlaps in personnel, assumptions, and symbols' that would be accentuated after 1947 (1997: 360, 363). Even paradigmatic secular nationalists such as Nehru at times exhibited a tendency to assume 'some kind of cultural or civilizational integration as the ultimate foundation of nationalism'. That Indian unity was conceived of in Hindu, upper caste, often North Indian terms' was made easier by the undeniable fact that the bulk of the leading cadres of the nationalist and even Left movements have come from Hindu upper-caste backgrounds' (ibid.: 363). Nevertheless, the distinction between secular and Hindu nationalism is relevant. Secular nationalists as Sarkar notes, typically sought to unite people of all religions living on the territory of India, unlike Hindu nationalists who held that only 'Hindus could be true patriots' and encouraged 'hatred or violence' towards other religions (ibid.: 361–2).

this appears to have been their convergence with Hindu nationalists on the question of political safeguards for minorities.

One further type of claim needs consideration. In some cases, the main thrust of the opposition to minority safeguards on grounds of national unity came from the claim that these were inconsistent with a *modern* nation-state. This was a version of the objection to minority safeguards on grounds of secular democratic citizenship; only here, the links of secularism and national unity were constitutive as well as analogical. Renuka Ray, Congresswoman from West Bengal argued thus against separate electorates:

> After all...it is not a question of minorities and majorities on a religious basis that we should consider in a democratic secular State...we have stood aside helplessly while artificially this problem of religious differences—an echo of medieval times, has been fostered...by the method of political devices such as separate electorates in order to serve the interests of our alien rulers. (*CAD* V: 268)

Minority safeguards required the recognition of religious group identities in the political domain, and this was considered as a mark of 'backwardness' that signalled India's underdevelopment. It did not befit a country aspiring to join the ranks of advanced industrialized countries to recognize pre-modern forms such as religion and caste in politics. To be 'modern' was what was desired: as Baird notes, modernity constituted the norm, the un-argued for standpoint on the basis of which all other claims, such as the desirability of the nation and the undesirability of minority safeguards, were established (1978: 84). The nation was the appropriate locus for identity in the modern era, not religion or caste. S. Radhakrishnan declared: 'The present tendency is for larger and larger aggregations...nationalism, not religion is the basis of modern life' (*CAD* II: 272).[11] The self-evident legitimacy of the nation in this period derived partly from a sense of its historical necessity. Such views were based on a particular understanding of the history of the West, believed to be 'the movement of universal history' (Khilnani 1997: 33), where processes of modernization were seen to be eroding religious and other ascriptive affiliations. Religious and ethno-cultural identities

---

[11] Pandit G.B. Pant admonished advocates of separate electorates: 'Apart from other things it is an obsolete anachronism today. In a free country, nobody has ever heard of separate electorates' (*CAD* V: 224).

more broadly, it was held, had only acquired importance in the Indian context on account of poverty, illiteracy, and other features of socio-economic underdevelopment and because these had been propped up by the British for their own ends. Conflicts over safeguards, and those based on religious and other ascriptive identities more generally, would fade away once processes of modernization, arrested under colonial rule, got underway. Until then, claims for safeguards were regarded as reminders of India's backwardness', out of step with the times, and distractions from the real problems which were economic (Chatterjee 1986: 140–3). Significantly, while this line of opposition to minority safeguards was most prominent in the speeches of Nehru and other modernists in the Constituent Assembly, such views were also voiced outside modernist circles. Why did quite so many nationalists adopt a modernist language in the 1940s and 1950s? Our analysis suggests that the fact that the rhetoric of modernization and development offered a way to validate the nation and delegitimize minority safeguards likely played a role. In this and other debates, the rhetoric of historical necessity served to blur the political conflict of interests.

Scholars have commented extensively upon development as an element in the ideological repertoire of Indian nationalism. Colonial rule had relied for its justification on the underdevelopment of the subject people. By contrast, nationalists held that colonial rule was the main cause of India's underdevelopment (Chatterjee 1995: 203, 215; Zachariach 2005: 298). Given the difficulties of defining Indian identity in ethnic terms, this economic critique of colonialism, as Chatterjee notes, was crucial for supplying a positive content to Indian nationalism not available from other sources. The discourse of development was thus central to articulations of Indian national identity (Chatterjee 1995: 203; Zachariah 2005: 211).

But what did development imply? In our period, development was construed primarily in economic terms, with aspects of both growth and redistribution: a 'developed' country had a high standard of living and low levels of poverty characteristic of advanced industrialized countries of the West. Development meant trying to 'catch up' with the West: as Nehru put it, 'We are trying to catch up...with the Industrial Revolution that occurred long ago in Western countries' (q. Chatterjee 1995: 202). The principal strategy for development in Indian nationalism, from the 1940s, was industrialization (Chatterjee 1986: 144), with the modern sector as the key element: development involved the superseding of the 'traditional' by the 'modern' (Chatterjee 1995: 210). Construing underdevelopment in economic terms was liberating: India's lack of modernity 'had nothing to do with any essential cultural failings of Indian civilization' but could in principle be overcome (Chatterjee 1986: 137). The belief was 'that progress, as represented by the historical trajectory of development in the West, could at once be telescoped and replicated' (Jayal 1999: 151). Development as progress evoked a wide array of related political, social, and moral questions, pertaining to uplift, regeneration, science, technology, expertise, rationality, and socialism (Zachariah 2005: 4–6, 46, 253).[12] The identification of 'modern', 'industrialized', 'science', 'technologically advanced' with the West meant that 'Western' itself had positive connotations and was not a pejorative term (ibid.: 239), at least for an influential strand of nationalists.

Historians have focussed on the conservative and authoritarian aspects of nationalist discourses of development, in terms of continuities with the late colonial state, as facilitating the accumulation of state power in the hands of the bourgeoisie and the already privileged (Chatterjee 1995; Washbrook 1999: 37, 48–9). For our purposes, the following features are of note. First, within the discourse of development, minority demands could be cast as 'particular interests', which 'needed to be subsumed within the whole and made consistent with the general interest'. Conflicts involving particular interests had to be assessed and resolved in a manner consistent with their priority within the overall constraints of the whole (Chatterjee 1995: 204, 214–15). Identifying the nation with the good of society 'as a whole' and the 'public purpose' established its pre-eminence (Jayal 1999: 226–7). From minorities, construed as 'sections' of the whole, development could demand self-restraint, even self-sacrifice for the common good. Second, development was linked to nation-building, as the process through which over time an Indian people would be created. Material betterment, science and education, it was thought, would diminish 'pre-modern forms of social life and behaviour' (Zachariah 2005: 11, 242, 295); communal attachments that divided Indians were a function of 'backwardness'. Through the process of development, the

---

[12] On the centrality of science in this notion of development, and the primacy of the economic sphere, see Chatterjee 1986: 139; on the scientific optimism or the belief that science would cure most ills in Nehru and other socialists, see Zachariah 2005: 236–8.

traditional would be supplanted by the modern not just in the economy but also thereby in the polity and the society more broadly. In terms of our constellation of ideas, a developed state was also a secular democratic nation-state. Finally, development implied the reduction of poverty and 'backwardness' not just of the nation as a whole, but of 'backward' sections within it: nationalist notions of development carried connotations both of growth and social justice. Just as the underdevelopment of the nation was not fundamentally cultural but economic and so in principle surmountable, the 'backwardness' of particular groups was not inherent but could be overcome. This required the removal of barriers such as those erected by the caste system that had denied equality of opportunity to sections of the population. Equality of opportunity, in turn, would contribute to national development. Reflecting on equality and its link to development in the *Discovery of India*, Nehru wrote:

> [Equality]...does not... mean that everybody is physically or intellectually or spiritually equal or can be made so. But it does mean equal opportunities for all and no political, economic or social barrier in the way of any individual or group....It means a realization of the fact that the backwardness or degradation of any group is not due to inherent failings in it but principally to lack of opportunities and long suppression by other groups...Any such attempt to open the doors of opportunity to all in India will release enormous energy and ability and transform the country with amazing speed. (q. Chatterjee 1986: 159)

Development thus required justice in the sense of equality of opportunity, 'the removal of barriers' which prevented some groups from participating in the economy and polity (Chatterjee 1986: 159). Beyond equality of opportunity, development as social justice was also seen to imply a more equitable distribution of resources, although how much equality, and how this would be achieved was not specified in the lofty generalizations of nationalist rhetoric.[13] It was clear, however, that tackling material deprivation and a measure of redistribution was involved, through some sharing of the proceeds of growth and reallocation of existing assets. Development implied not just growth, but also (a measure of) social justice.

[13] Social justice in Nehru's pronouncements had connotations of welfare, encompassing policies of land reform and social reform (Chatterjee 1986: 154–5).

To recapitulate, the nationalist criticism of minority safeguards as
undermining the nation referred to at least four related sets of claims:
that these endangered the political integrity of the nation; that these
inhibited the emergence of national loyalties; that minority safeguards
were incongruent with the national identity conceived in cultural
or political terms; and that these were incompatible with a modern
developed nation-state. In its critique of the modernizing nation-state,
colonial discourse analysis has tended to conflate distinct national unity
concerns. Chatterjee's influential accounts of nationalist thought (1986:
132; 1995) characterize it as a state ideology, with the pursuit of social
justice through development as its legitimizing principle. Our analysis of
nationalist arguments through the lens of minority rights suggests that
while state-led development was undoubtedly an important element,
the *identification* of nationalist discourse with Nehruvian statism is
mistaken. Not all nationalists were statists, not 'all the way down', and
not in the same way. While all nationalists accorded pre-eminence to
national unity, the form and extent to which the modern national state
was central to this unity varied greatly. For most, the modern nation-state
was instrumental for securing the integrity of the nation and fostering
a sense of common nationality. It had a strong role in national unity,
providing the constitutive basis for national identity, only for a relatively
small section of modernists. As Sen notes in a different context, it is
mistaken to give

> ...an inescapably 'statist' orientation to the very conception of any
> political unity across religious communities and other social divisions...
> in the...consolidation of that unity, the nation-state may well have an
> important instrumental role, but the state need not be central to the
> conceptual foundation of this unity or provide its constructive genesis.
> (Sen 1998: 468–9)

How then do we make sense of the dominance of modernist ideas
that, as Chatterjee correctly notes, was a feature of nationalist discourse
of this period? Our analysis suggests that modernist ideas gained ground
from their *convergence* with other strands of nationalism, notably Hindu
opinion, on key questions such as minority rights.[14] This stemmed from

---

[14] On similarities in the positions of secular modernists and Hindu nationalists
in the context of the Constituent Assembly debates, see Bajpai 1997; Jaffrelot
2004; Singh 2006; and more broadly Chatterjee 1995; Hansen 1999; Roy 2007.

a shared overriding concern with *national unity*, and not necessarily from a common belief in the 'nation-state' (1995: 94, 110). Moreover, convergence is *not* identity: important differences remained between secular and Hindu nationalism with respect to ideology as well as policy.[15] Indian nationalism remained internally diverse after Partition: there was no sudden conversion of civic nationalists to ethno-cultural nationalism. Because nationalists of different ideological persuasions converged on the primacy of national unity and its incompatibility with minority safeguards, Hindu and other nationalists could use a modernist *language* of secularism, democracy, development, and social justice to legitimize their positions, even if they did not subscribe to these ideals 'all the way down'. Such congruence in the legitimating vocabulary is sufficient for my argument regarding its role in explaining the fate of minority safeguards: identity of *belief*, whether in the modern state or in Hindu culture, is not necessary as is commonly held to be the case.

National Unity and the Uses of the Past

Group rights, it can be argued, do not undermine national unity. Safeguards for minorities can strengthen the stability of the nation-state and national loyalties by encouraging minorities to feel part of the nation. Not all forms of group rights are inconsistent with secular democratic citizenship (Kymlicka and Norman 2000). As we shall see, arguments along these lines were put forward by supporters of group rights in the Constituent Assembly. Nationalist claims of our period that minority safeguards necessarily damaged national unity relied on a particular interpretation of the Indian past and of the history of minority safeguards. Partition entered this story as a key event that demonstrated, catastrophically, that nationalist fears about the dangers of minority safeguards were justified.

The broad outlines of the nationalist narrative are familiar. India, for all its manifold diversities, was essentially one. In the 'mythology of nationalism' (Kaviraj 1992: 14), the fundamental unity of India stretched back to antiquity and was a product of India's unique capacities of

---

[15] For example, unlike Hindu nationalists, secular nationalists largely supported cultural rights for minorities. For criticism of the anti-modernist conflation of Nehruvian secularism and Hindu nationalism, see, for instance, Sarkar 1997: 361–2; Bilgrami 1998: 382–4.

accommodation and synthesis of the diverse cultures that had made it their home.[16] The national unity that was so inadequately achieved in the present was here realized 'in the past, through a judicious reconstruction of Indian history' (Pandey 1990: 247), which focused selectively on instances of synthesis and peaceful coexistence. Such a reconstruction of the Indian past sought to counter the colonial view that India was less a nation than a congeries of antagonistic nationalities, which were only kept together by the exercise of imperial power. Rejecting colonial claims that communal discord was inherent and endemic to India, the nationalist story asserted that communal discord was the product of a deliberate colonial 'divide and rule' strategy. Congress leader Purushottamdas Tandon's speech was typical: '[T]he history of our relations with the British show that Hindu-Muslim differences are purely a British creation...They were not in existence before their advent. Hindus and Muslims had a common civilization and lived amicably' (CAD I: 68). In nationalist accounts, 'divide and rule' was depicted as originating in the lessons the British drew from the 1857 war of Independence, when all major communities made common cause against the British.

The principal instrument of the colonial strategy was the policy of minority safeguards. According to nationalists, these were deliberately fashioned by the British to set one community against another, and thereby to create roadblocks on the way to India's independence. R.V. Dhulekar voiced the typical nationalist position on safeguards:

> no doubt our country or community stands guilty for creating social barriers and divisions but the Britishers aggravated these evils in order to establish and consolidate their imperialistic hold on us... With their duplicity, they created a gulf between the Brahmins and non-Brahmins, between touchables and untouchables, between the Hindus and the Muslims...to continue the safeguards and perpetuate the division is not a wise course... . (CAD II: 303)[17]

[16] As Sarkar notes, in 'even the most secular of Indian nationalists', a Nehru writing the Discovery of India, there has remained a strong tendency to 'assume some kind of cultural or civilizational integration as the ultimate foundation of nationalism', a unity, that is 'primarily Hindu (and upper caste, often north-Indian at that)' (1997: 363).

[17] See also Pandit G.B. Pant, CAD II: 331. Several advocates of minority safeguards also echoed these sentiments. See, for instance, S. Nagappa, CAD V: 205–6.

Minority safeguards, it was argued, had bred community consciousness and rivalry, and thereby served to legitimize and prolong colonial presence in India, as the colonial state could portray itself as the guarantor of peace and of the interests of weaker groups—the minorities. Once instituted, safeguards necessarily followed an escalating and separatist logic, leading to an ever-increasing number of groups demanding special measures, and ever-larger and more antagonistic claims, a process that culminated in Partition. In this narrative, the British were viewed as the chief culprits and the architects of this policy, and the minorities, as pawns in the colonial game, obstructing progress towards the national goal of liberation from colonial rule, culpable in allowing themselves to be misled.[18] Partition provided decisive proof, if any were needed, of the destructive effect of minority safeguards for national unity. Henceforth, Partition would serve as shorthand for the 'lessons from experience' (Horowtiz 1989) of the ill effects of minority safeguards.

In this narrative, the precedence of the nation over minorities was frequently established through the employment of organic analogies. Sometimes a contrast was drawn between the minorities described as an 'artificial' construct, and the nation, typically of nationalist doctrines, as a given, 'natural' entity (Pandey 1990: 255). In other cases, the priority of the nation was established by depicting it as the physical whole—an 'organic whole', a 'body politic'; in contrast to minorities, who were characterized as a part, often as one that was distorted. Minority safeguards were often alluded to as 'disfigurements', 'cancerous', 'poisonous' for the body politic, or as 'crutches', their presence, a symptom of an 'unhealthy' polity.[19] A variation on the naturalistic theme was to be found

---

[18] Several early writings on the Indian Constituent Assembly reflect this nationalist perspective. The chapter on minorities in Shiva Rao's now classic study opens thus: 'The problem of minorities...was in fact the one single factor, above all others, that held up the progress of the country towards freedom and independence' (Shiva Rao 1968: 741).

[19] For instance, Parsi representative R.K. Sidhwa held: '...It has been our cherished desire for the last fifty years to see that this evil, that has played such havoc and which has been a kind of cancerous and poisonous element in our political life should be done away with...' (CAD VIII: 317). Col B.H. Zaidi supported the withdrawal of safeguards for Muslims thus: 'For nearly forty years, the Muslims were used to props and crutches provided to them by the British...' (CAD VIII: 347). See also Giani Gurmukh Singh Musafir, CAD VII: 1256.

in the modernist characterization of 'minorities' and communities more generally, as 'backward' and 'primitive' in the evolutionary chain of history, with the 'nation' as the most sophisticated form of human association hitherto realized. In general terms, such characterizations were instances of the usage of the standard ideological device of depicting the preferred object as normal and natural, whereas the disfavoured object is cast as abnormal or denatured. In Indian nationalist discourse, the employment of organic analogies can also be seen as a response to the following problem. Nationalists had to establish the precedence of the nation over minority safeguards, which were a long-standing and accepted feature of the political landscape, at a time when the very existence of an Indian nation was not yet beyond question. They had to do so without getting too drawn into the details of what India's nation-ness consisted in, given that one definition—in terms of the glue provided by Hindu culture and civilization—was too narrow to be acceptable all sections, and the other—in terms of secular, democratic citizenship—too abstract at the time to command popular allegiance. Appeals to India's essential and timeless unity, and characterizations of the nation and minorities in terms of organic analogies, were crucial in enabling nationalists to sidestep the *national* problem.

While in the nationalist narrative, minority safeguards appear as anti-national in their very essence and therefore since inception, historically speaking, the nationalist opposition to minority safeguards was more recent. Until the 1930s, the Congress had endorsed political safeguards for minorities. Nationalist opposition probably dates back to what historians have termed the 'new nationalism' of the 1930s. Minority safeguards appear to have been aligned very quickly into the history of separatism from this point onwards. What is clear is that by the time of the Constituent Assembly debates, in nationalist opinion of every persuasion, it had become an article of faith that the institution had led to separatism: 'history' had shown that minority safeguards destroyed national unity. Partition, seen as conclusive evidence for nationalist apprehensions, was seamlessly absorbed into this nationalist narrative.

The Primacy of National Unity in the Nationalist Vocabulary

Apart from national unity, nationalist arguments against minority safeguards also invoked justice, democracy, and secularism. Like in the case of national unity, there were different conceptions of these concepts in nationalist opinion, reflecting its ideological diversity. The priority of national unity in the nationalist vocabulary meant, however, that justice, secularism, and democracy were largely construed in ways conducive to the requirements of national unity.

One important line of opposition to minority safeguards was that these involved departures from justice. In demanding safeguards, Biswanath Das held, minorities were asking for more than what was due to them: '...it is very very unfortunate that the minority communities do not demand mere justice, equity, and fair-play but claim safeguards and weightages' (CAD II: 345). Women representatives in particular sought to distance themselves from minority claims: '[We have]...never asked for reserved seats, for quotas or for separate electorates. What we have asked for is social justice, economic justice, and political justice...'[20]

The sense that minority safeguards went beyond what justice required was reflected in their common characterization as 'privileges' or 'concessions'. It derived from an identification of justice with a system of equal individual rights. Two assumptions were crucial here. First, individuals were regarded as the primary subjects of justice and rights rather than groups. This marked a new departure: the colonial regime of minority safeguards had relied on notions of justice as giving each *group* its due share. A conception of justice that accorded primacy to the individual was considered insufficiently established, as evident in Pandit G.B. Pant's exhortation:

> There is the unwholesome and to some extent a degrading habit of thinking always in terms of communities and never in terms of citizens. But it is after all citizens who form communities and the individual as such is essentially the core of all mechanisms...that are adopted for securing progress and advancement. So let us remember that it is the citizen that must count...It is the citizen that forms the base as well as the summit of the social pyramid.... (CAD II: 332)

Second, equal individual rights were thought to imply that all individuals would have the *same* rights. Safeguards implied differences in the political rights of individuals deriving from their cultural group membership and were thus seen to contravene the state's commitment to treat all its citizens as equals. Such criticisms echoed familiar liberal objections to group preference, although the appellation 'liberal' was rarely used—the

---

[20] Hansa Mehta, CAD I: 138. See also Renuka Ray, CAD IV: 668–9.

opposition to minority safeguards on liberal grounds in this period
was cast in terms of justice, equality, and fair play. Mahavir Tyagi, a
Congressman with Hindu nationalist leanings, asserted:

> These minorities cannot be recognized because in a country whose
> administration is supposed to be run on the basis of justice alone,
> there is no question of minority or majority. All individuals are at
> par...We cannot recognize religion as far as the State is concerned....
> (CAD V: 219)

Group rights are not necessarily incompatible with a regime of equal
individual rights (Kymlicka 1989, 1995). For Indian constitution-
makers, recent historical precedent had emphasized groups as units of
justice calculation. In the Constituent Assembly debates, group rights
were often construed as unjust through a particular liberal interpretation
of justice, which insisted on the centrality of the individual as well as
the uniformity of her rights. Crucially, the requirements of justice so
construed converged with those of national unity. The emphasis on the
individual over the group and the same rights for individuals from all
groups provided a means for welding together a people divided by their
group membership into a nation. It also provided the basis for a common
national identity in a situation in which ethnic criteria were divisive:
as noted earlier, India's national identity was articulated in this period
largely in civic terms, as consisting in citizenship of a state where the
group membership of individuals was irrelevant from the standpoint of
rights and justice. Justice construed in terms of equal individual rights
was thus linked both instrumentally and constitutively to national unity.
The proximity of justice and national unity can be discerned in several
speeches against minority safeguards. Mahavir Tyagi queried:

> Why should we introduce this separatist tendency into our politics?...
> We are one nation which stands for justice. We will legislate in a
> manner that will be a guarantee against all injustice, and we shall not
> recognize any sections. (CAD V: 219)

Quoting Jinnah, he said:

> ...even in that State he says religions will not be taken notice of by the
> State. Every individual will be an individual and Hindus will lose their
> Hinduship as far as their political rights and privileges are concerned.
> ...even they are believers of one-ness of their people.... (CAD V: 219)

The Constituent Assembly debates are replete with instances of Hindu
conservatives speaking in an ideologically unfamiliar idiom of individual

rights and justice (Bajpai 2000; Jaffrelot 2004: 129–36). Contrary to the common view that liberal values in Indian political culture have been restricted to a narrow Westernized elite, liberal individualist norms were espoused in the Constituent Assembly by nationalists of diverse ideological and social moorings. It was perhaps its close links to national unity, and shared hostility to minority safeguards, that accounts for the widespread use of a liberal language in this period.

The close association of individual rights and national unity is also striking in arguments put forward by proponents of a uniform civil code in the Constituent Assembly. Grounds of equal rights and national unity were employed virtually interchangeably against the continuation of religious laws, with representatives moving seamlessly between the two. National unity considerations were usually more prominent. In their note of April 1947, Rajkumari Amrit Kaur, Hansa Mehta, and Minoo Masani, the strongest supporters of a uniform civil code in the Constituent Assembly, advocated it thus: '...one of the factors that has kept India back from advancing to nation-hood has been the existence of personal laws based on religion which keep the nation divided into watertight compartments in many aspects of life' (Shiva Rao 1967 II: 162). It was assumed that *equality* for individuals required *uniformity* in their rights across communities, with women from different communities having the same rights with respect to marriage, divorce, and maintenance. Rights to equality were construed here in a particular way: solely in terms of individuals, rather than also, for instance, in terms of the equal rights of each *group* to follow its religious practices; and as incompatible with any differences in the rights of individuals across communities. This was conducive to the requirements of national unity in nationalist opinion, for which common laws for citizens belonging to different religious communities were thought necessary.

Close links with national unity can also be observed in the case of the other key concepts of the nationalist vocabulary, those of democracy and secularism. In debates over minority representation that we shall look at in more detail in the next chapter, democracy was construed in individualist terms and identified with institutions of territorial representation. Rejecting separate electorates as detracting from 'true democracy', Mahavir Tyagi stated:

> ...unadulterated democracy...means a true representation of the people; true without any weightage, without any favour; without any disregard

of the rightful privileges of any section of the people or any individual...
If we put obstacles in the way of any...or give privilege to others, that
will mean that the democracy or the representation of the people will
not be as true and pure as it ought to be in an unadulterated democracy.
(*CAD* V: 218)

The democratic norm appealed to here was that of political
equality. This was construed in terms of equal representation for all
individuals, and identified with the equally weighted vote (one person
one vote), embodying a 'proceduralist and individualist' ideal of fair
representation (Williams 1998: 10). Territory rather than religious
group was regarded as the appropriate unit for aggregating citizens for
purposes of representation, with territorial constituencies equated with
the representation of individuals rather than groups. Once democracy
was identified with 'one person, one vote' secured through territorial
constituencies, the representation of religious minorities through devices
such as separate electorates appeared as biases in the procedure in favour
of certain groups, and as such, as undemocratic.

It is important to note that this was a particular interpretation
of democracy that involved a rejection of alternative forms of
representation. As is well known, democratic principles are
compatible with a range of mechanisms for representation, including
group-differentiated political rights (Beitz 1989; Phillips 1995;
Williams 1998). Consociational type of arrangements of guaranteed
representation for minorities had been prominent in colonial policy
and were advocated by minority representatives during the Constituent
Assembly debates (see, for instance Ambedkar's Note on Minorities
of March 1947, in Shiva Rao 1967 II: 112–13). However, democracy
conceived in individualist terms and secured through joint electorates
and territorial constituencies suited the requirements of national unity.
Scholars have noted that Indian nationalists were democrats (Bhargava
2000; Sarkar 2001: 29–30). It is important, however, to recall that in
the context of the colonial system of group representation considered
divisive, democratic procedures of universal adult suffrage, one-person-
one-vote *also* served the cause of nation-building.

Apart from national unity, justice, and democracy, nationalist
arguments against minority safeguards also invoked secularism. Different
conceptions of secularism can be discerned in nationalist opinion that
will be examined presently. Here, I want to consider some implications

of its close association with national unity. In most nationalist pronouncements, secularism was elaborated in terms of equal citizenship rights for all individuals. Renuka Ray, Congresswoman and one of the staunchest advocates of a secular state in the Assembly was concerned 'that the instruction that is given to the citizens of the future shall be such that the idea of a Secular State in which all citizens are equal comes into being...that they do not learn to realize the distinctions which separate man from man' (CAD VII: 879). While the idea of religious freedom was also invoked in nationalist articulations of a secular state, it was less prominent than equal rights for all individuals irrespective of religion. By contrast, in conceptions of secularism put forward by Muslim League proponents of Muslim personal law, religious freedom was central; in fact, secularism was identified with religious freedom. A secular order, it was argued, was one in which citizens had full religious freedom, including the freedom to live by the tenets of their religious family laws. Mahboob Ali Baig Sahib Bahadur explained:

> People seem to think that under a secular State, there must be a common law observed by its citizens in all matters, including matters of their daily life, their language, their culture, their personal laws. That is not a correct way to look at this secular State. In a secular State, citizens belonging to different communities must have the freedom to practise their own religion, observe their own life and their personal laws should be applied to them. (CAD VII: 544)

In nationalist opinion, however, full religious freedom for groups was seen as inconsistent with national unity. Arguing that religion not be construed expansively to include personal law, K.M. Munshi stated:

> Religion must be restricted to spheres which legitimately appertain to religion, and the rest of life must be regulated, unified and modified in such a manner that we may evolve, as early as possible, a strong and consolidated nation. Our first problem and the most important problem is to produce national unity in this country. (CAD VII: 548)[21]

The close links between secularism and national unity, clearly evident in the debates on personal law, meant that secularism was construed

---

[21] See also Alladi Krishnaswami Ayyar, CAD VII: 549, 550; and in a different context, Smith's seminal analysis of Indian secularism, which links, as Nehru did, a secular state to 'the emotional integration of the nation' (1963: 496; see also Galanter 1998a: 251).

largely in terms of equal citizenship rights for individuals. It was seen as requiring state intervention to curtail the domain of religion. Rights to religious freedom of groups had subordinate status; while recognized, these would be restricted to the extent that these conflicted with rights to equality of individuals.[22]

The language of secularism was ubiquitous in the Constituent Assembly debates, used by ideologically disparate nationalists, uncompromising modernists, majoritarian Hindus, and Gandhian advocates alike.[23] That so many Hindu nationalists, Gandhians and the religious-minded spoke in support of secularism *at all* is significant. It was its close links with national unity that extended the appeal of secularism to 'very many who would not be "secularist" in the sense of unbelief or religious indifference' (Sarkar 2001: 33). Chatterjee attributes the convergence of Nehruvians and Hindu nationalists on secularism to a shared belief in the modern nation-state. Our analysis, however, suggests that secularism was endorsed as a means of nation-building by nationalists who were *not* statists or secularists all the way down. For Gandhians and Hindu nationalists, secularism was instrumentally desirable for national unity.

Several connotations of secularism in nationalist opinion only make sense in the light of the close links between secularism and national unity. Secularism did not pertain to religion alone, but to *all* group affiliations. A secular state was defined as a state where a citizen's rights were unaffected by her caste, linguistic, or racial background, as much as her religious membership. The recognition in public policy of any cultural identity was considered anti-secular. Safeguards for Untouchables and Tribals as well as those for religious minorities were seen as detracting from secularism. Further, the term 'secular' in the Constituent Assembly debates referred not just to the stance of the state towards religious and other groups, but also to people's attitudes and identities. A truly secular state required the creation of a new secular ethos and identities, where

---

[22] The Constituent Assembly inherited from the colonial state a situation in which there was a common criminal law for all Indians, but in family or 'personal' law matters such as marriage, divorce, succession, and maintenance, members of the major religious communities (Hindu, Muslim, and Christian) were governed by their respective religious laws. For more details, see Chapter 5 below.

[23] Chiriyankandath distinguishes dogmatic secularists, 'unity in diversity' advocates', majoritarian Hindus, and Gandhian critics (2000: 9–12).

individuals would cease to regard themselves and others as members of this or that community and see themselves as Indians 'first and last', where religious, caste and other communal distinctions would be eradicated from the 'minds and hearts' of individuals, as much as from the political arena. Among modernist nationalists, a secular society was thought to be both an aspect of, and a pre-requisite for, a secular state. Again, secularism here did not pertain to religion alone, but to cultural affiliations more broadly. A caste-ridden society, Nehru claimed on several occasions, was not 'properly secular' (q. Smith 1963: 292). As Galanter notes, the national goal of a secular society implied more than the separation of religion and state, referring 'to the elimination (or minimization) of caste and religious groups as categories of public policy and as actors in public life' (1984: 559).

At least one of the reasons for the expansiveness of connotations of secularism in nationalist opinion—encompassing religion as well as caste and tribe, the state as well as social attitudes and identities—was its close association with national unity. While religious differences had been the chief culprits, caste, tribe, language, and other forms of diversity were also regarded as competing sources of belonging and as impediments to national cohesion. Secularism in the nationalist scheme was the answer to problem of the creation of an integrated nation-state and a common national identity out of competing allegiances not only of religion, but also of race, caste, tribe, and language (Embree 1990; Jayal 1999).

Because the term 'secular' described a stance of the state and individuals not so much towards religion, as towards religious and other ethno-cultural *groups*, proposals pressing for a greater role for religion in the Constitution were often, without any sense of incongruity, described as 'secular' (see Chiriyankandath 2000). The term 'secular' was most often contrasted not with 'religious', but with the pejorative term 'communal' which was opposed to both 'secular' and 'national' in nationalist discourse (Pantham 1997: 525). To be communal connoted, simultaneously, an inability to separate group affiliation from politics (a failure on the liberal secular front), as well as an inability to rise above loyalty to one's narrow group and identify with the nation at large (a failure on the national front). Minority safeguards were 'communal' on several counts for nationalists—because these required the recognition of a person's religion or caste in public policy; encouraged identification with religious and caste communities; and thereby detracted from national unity. Scholars have noted that it is from this period onwards that the term 'secular' comes to be used as the antithesis of 'communal'—prior to Independence, the antithesis of the pejorative term 'communalism' was nationalism (Pandey 1990: 145). Henceforth, to be 'anti-secular' was also 'anti-national'.

A Liberal Vocabulary? The Case of Secularism

I have so far argued that a vocabulary comprising a set of interlocking political concepts, those of secularism, democracy, justice, national unity, and development framed nationalist arguments on group rights in the Constituent Assembly. A wide and ideologically diverse cross-section of nationalist opinion spoke this language. National unity was the core concept in this vocabulary, in relation to which the other concepts were largely elaborated in nationalist opinion. The requirements of national unity were mostly aligned antithetically to minority safeguards in this period, as accordingly were dominant conceptions of secularism, democracy and justice.

Were the meanings of secularism, democracy, social justice in the Constituent Assembly debates similar to their Western connotations? To what extent did these invoke liberal values? An influential strand of scholarly opinion holds that liberal and democratic *values* (as distinct from liberal democratic institutions) have had a weak and insignificant presence in India. Western concepts such as secularism, democracy, rights, insofar as these exist in India, have had radically different meanings. Chatterjee, for instance, notes that 'there are serious difficulties in applying the standard meaning of the word [secularism]...to the Indian circumstances. The 'original' concept...will not easily admit the Indian case within its range of referents' (1998: 350). Since the 1980s, anti-modern critiques of the nation-state and secularism have been influential. Focusing on secularism, I shall now probe further the extent to which meanings of the key concepts of the nationalist vocabulary were similar to their Western connotations.[24] A cautionary note is necessary here. As Kaviraj reminds us, accounts of discourses in the colonial world 'must guard

---

[24] A sophisticated body of scholarship has challenged the validity of the contrast between Western and Indian secularism. See, in particular, chapters by Bhargava, Bilgrami, Chatterjee, Sen in Bhargava 1998.

against the mistake of...translating its concepts into its nearest European equivalents' (Kaviraj 1992: 37). This is important; however, it does not follow that Indian discourses are wholly dissimilar in their conceptual-normative lineaments to Western discourses as is sometimes suggested. Context-sensitivity requires an empirical investigation of meanings, not an *apriori* assertion of radical difference.

Secularism and Religion

Critics of secularism in India contend that it seeks to 'foster a modern scientific temper' and 'fails to recognize the immense importance of religion' in the lives of the peoples of South Asia (Madan 1998: 299). Is this borne out by nationalist opinion in the Constituent Assembly debates? Although the term secularism was not often used, there were frequent references to a 'secular state'. The first feature of note is that in terms of the state's stance towards religion, most advocates of a secular state emphasized that it did not imply that the state was hostile to religious belief.[25] Moreover, a secular state was not a state that was incognizant of the importance of religious faith in Indian society; nor was it zealous in inculcating scepticism towards religious belief among its citizens. Speeches in this vein argued simultaneously that a secular state did not imply this, as well as that a secular state could not assume such a stance in a country such as India, where religious beliefs were deep-rooted. Supporting an amendment giving the President the option of taking his oath of office in the name of God, a proposal that was supported by representatives of religious minorities and incorporated into the Constitution, K.M. Munshi asserted:

> A secular state is not a Godless state. It is not a state which is pledged to eradicate or ignore religion...We must take cognizance of the fact that India is a religious minded country. Even while we are talking of a secular state, our mode of thought and life is largely coloured by a religious attitude to life...the state in India cannot be secular in the sense of being anti-religious. (*CAD* VII: 1057)[26]

[25] While the inclusion of the term 'secular' was proposed during the deliberations of the Constituent Assembly (see K.T. Shah *CAD* VII: 815–16), there was no explicit mention of a secular state in the Constitution, until the Preamble was amended to include the term in 1976.

[26] See also Rev. Jerome D'Souza, *CAD* VII: 1059.

M. Ananthasayanam Ayyangar stated: 'I do not by the word 'secular' mean that we do not believe in any religion, and that we have nothing to do with it in our day to day life' (*CAD* VII: 881). Evidence of outright hostility to religion among advocates of a secular state in the Constituent Assembly is hard to come by.

Of the Constitution-makers who introduced secularism into India's political framework, the majority do not correspond to the description found in several critiques of secularism, that of a Westernized anti-religious elite displaying a naïve disdain of the strength towards religious belief in India. What then is the source of this powerful image? Closer examination reveals some hostility to religion in one strand of opinion in the Constituent Assembly. Modernist nationalists, as discussed earlier, identified a secular state, in a hopeful and erroneous move, with desired modernity, and saw religious belief and affiliation as vestiges of a pre-modern era, which processes of secularization would soon whittle away. Secularism, it was believed, would follow once processes such as modern education, the diffusion of science and industrialization got underway (Bilgrami 1998; Mahajan 1998). Nehru serves to exemplify this view in most accounts, and there is some supporting evidence in his speeches and writings.[27] However, it is important to note that processes of 'modernity' or secularization were *contingent* features associated with one conception of secularism in nationalist opinion: advocates of secularism in the Constituent Assembly were not all modernists, rationalists, or evangelists for a scientific temper. The preoccupation of the study of ideology with exemplary figures such as Nehru has meant that the significance of this strand of secularism in Indian political discourse has been overestimated. Criticisms of official secularism as ill-suited to India on account of its being anti-religious are as such off the mark.

---

[27] Railing against the tendency in his party that 'as if by saying that we are a secular State we have done something amazingly generous', Nehru said: 'We have only done something which every country does except a very few misguided and backward countries in the world' (*CAD* IX: 401). Instances of antipathy for religion can be found in Nehru's writings (see Madan 1998: 310). However, Nehru may not have seen secularization as an inexorable historical process that would erode traditional religion (Khilnani 2002). Nehru's concept of a secular state, while explicitly distancing itself from *traditional* religion, can be seen to reflect an ethical, even religious approach (Baird 1978).

Given that secularism did not by and large connote antipathy to religion for the Constitution-makers, does this suggest that the notion of the separation of religion and politics was absent from conceptions of the secular state? The view that secularism in India has not meant the separation of state and religion dominates the scholarly literature, both among critics of secularism, as well as its advocates. Dismissing secularism as 'an alien cultural ideology', Madan holds that there is no wall of separation in India, 'only the notion of neutrality or equidistance between the state and the religious identity of the people'. As a 'purely negative' strategy, this is 'impotent' (1998: 310, 313).[28] Others, more supportive of secularism, hold equally that 'it has never meant the separation of religion from politics' and therefore has been appropriated 'by communal parties and ideologies....' (Upadhyaya 1992: 851–2). Cossman and Kapur also suggest a contrast between a liberal democratic model of secularism based on a wall of separation approach on the one hand, and secularism as the equal respect of all religions (sarva dharma samabhava) on the other, that dominates legal and constitutional discourses in India (1996: 2621).

The view that Indian secularism departs radically from 'Western' separation of state and religion usually rests on the assumption that there is a *single* form of separation, typically identified with the complete dissociation of religion and state. Smith's classic text on Indian secularism, for instance, states that the concept of separation means 'simply that religion and the state function in two basically different areas of human activity, each with its own objectives and methods' (1963: 6). However, as the writings of Galanter (1998a [1965]: 254–67), Bhargava (1998: 493, 516), and Sen (1998: 457) on secularism have established, the separation of state and religion is not a single, simple doctrine. That state and religion should be separate does not, in itself, tell us how this should be accomplished. This could take the form of 'symmetric treatment' of different religions (*ibid.*) or what Bhargava terms a strategy of principled distance, where 'the state intervenes or refrains from interfering,

---

[28] Madan's critique of secularism is multi-faceted. He sees the notion of 'privatization of religion' as a late Christian idea, at odds with 'South Asia's major religious traditions—Buddhism, Hinduism, Islam, and Sikhism— [which] are totalizing in character...' (1998: 302, 319). As a strategy that is not 'rooted, full-blooded', the Indian policy of state secularism is 'feeble' (*ibid.*: 300). See also Larson 2001: 100.

depending on which of the two better promotes religious liberty and equality of citizenship' (1998: 515). Which variety of separation is preferred depends upon the wider theory of secularism (Bhargava 1998: 515), as well as values of the political system *other* than secularism (Sen 1998: 467).

Returning to the Constituent Assembly debates, we see that while secularism in most cases did not involve antagonism or even indifference to religion, it did include some forms of separation between state and religion. First, a secular state was taken to mean disestablishment, that is, the state would not have an official religion. A secular state was contrasted in political utterances both to a theocracy, and a religious state. While a clause explicitly stipulating disestablishment was considered during constitutional deliberations (Shiva Rao 1967 II: 87, 140, 174), disestablishment was eventually included indirectly in the Constitution, most notably in the form of fundamental rights prohibiting the state from extracting taxes for the promotion of any particular religion, stipulating that no religious instruction would be provided in educational institutions maintained wholly out of state funds, and proscribing compulsory attendance at religious instruction or worship in any educational institution recognized by the State or receiving aid out of State funds (Arts 27, 28).

A second conception of secularism as separation was that of state impartiality between different religions. A secular state implied that the state would not give preference to any particular religion; secularism here was identified with non-sectarianism. Ananthasayanam Ayyangar held: '[A secular state] only means that the State or the Government cannot aid one religion or give preference to one religion as against another. Therefore it is obliged to be absolutely secular in character, not that it has lost faith in all religions' (*CAD* VII: 881–2). Secularism as non-sectarianism or impartiality between religions was the conception most congenial to the temper of religious believers of different persuasions in the Constituent Assembly. Some pressed for measures such as the inclusion of the name of God in the Constitution on grounds that these were consistent with a secular state, because no particular God or religion was being favored for special attention (See H.V. Kamath and Pandit Maalviyau *CAD* X: 439–46). Secularism as non-sectarianism also underpinned proposals for allowing religious instruction in educational institutions funded partly or wholly by the state (H.V. Kamath, *CAD* VII: 873–4) and was advocated by the religious-minded of different faiths (see Madras Muslim League leader Mohamed Ismail Sahib's speech, *CAD* VII: 866–7).

Such usages might lead us to question whether state impartiality between religions really is a form of separation of state and religion, as it does not preclude non-discriminatory state support for *all* religions. As long as separation is not identified with the complete dissociation of the state from religion, however, some forms of non-discriminatory state support for religious institutions can be seen as consistent with separation, as implying, for instance, that state policy is not affected by the religious affiliations of institutions (on state support for educational institutions or hospitals irrespective of the religious denominations to which they are attached, see Sen 1998: 457). It is important also to note that proposals to align the state more closely with religion, favoured by religious believers of all persuasions, were rejected. No religious instruction was permitted in institutions maintained *wholly* out of state funds; neither would the Preamble have any reference to God (Chiriyankandath 2000: 19–20). Apart from a provision allowing ministers, parliamentarians, and judges the option of taking their oath of office in the name of God, the Indian Constitution makes no reference to God (Smith 1963: 127–8). To read constitutional secularism as state identification with *all* religions thus would be erroneous.

In addition to disestablishment and state impartiality between religions, a third conception of secularism as separation in the Constituent Assembly debates was that of the exclusion of religion from the political domain. In a secular state, the nationalist refrain went, there ought to be no 'mixing' of religion and politics: religion should be a 'personal matter' for citizens, restricted to their individual and associational private practices. Congresswoman Renuka Ray declaimed: 'Religion is a personal matter. Religious differences might have been exploited as a political expedient by the British, but there is no room for that in the India of today' (*CAD* V: 268).[29] The precise implications of the exclusion of religion from politics were rarely spelt out and varied among proponents.

[29] The common view that Gandhi was opposed to the separation of state and religion (Nandy 1998: 343) is misleading. Writing in the *Harijan* in 1942, Gandhi noted: 'We have suffered enough from state-aided religion and a state church...A Society or a group which depends partly or wholly on state aid for the existence of its religion does not deserve, or...does not have any religion worth the name' (q. Smith 1963: 149).

Was it applicable to the state alone, or to the wider public sphere? Did it require the de-politicization of religion, or its privatization? Which aspects of religion had to be excluded from politics—religious ideals, religious issues, religious political parties or religious organizations? Many disputes in the Constituent Assembly over the phrasing of rights to religious freedom and cultural and educational rights of religious minorities can be seen as disagreements over the precise scope of the exclusion of religion from politics. The strongest versions of the exclusion of religion from politics such as the privatization of religion were expectedly to be found among secular modernists in the Constituent Assembly. They pressed, among others, for the prohibition of religious instruction in educational institutions receiving any aid from the state (K.T. Shah, *CAD* VII: 868–70; Tajamul Husain, *CAD* VII: 871); the banning of all religious markers (Tajamul Husain, *CAD* VII: 818–9); prohibitions on the use of religious institutions for political purposes and the setting up of political organizations on a religious basis.[30] But the exclusion of religion from politics was not advocated by secular modernists alone. Given the belief that the colonial 'mixing of religion and politics' was responsible for Partition, several Hindu nationalists and Gandhians in the Constituent Assembly also espoused the view that religion had to be excised from the domain of the political.

To recapitulate, against dominant scholarly views that hold that to the extent that secularism has existed in the Indian polity, it has done so in a form distinct from the separation of state and religion, we have seen that several forms of separation of state and religion informed conceptualizations of the secular state in the Constituent Assembly. While Nehru is usually portrayed as the lone spokesman for secularism as separation of state from religion, or as emblematic of a tiny Westernized minority buffeted by a sea of faith, our analysis suggests that conceptions of secularism as separation were widely espoused in the Constituent Assembly by nationalists of varied ideological and political persuasions and all religious groups. These included secular modernists as well as those with strong religious attachments of different faiths.

---

[30] As Chiriyankandath (2000) notes, many diehard secular modernists were from religious minority backgrounds—K.T. Shah, who proposed (unsuccessfully) that the term secular be added to the Constitution, was a Jain, and Tajamul Husain, a Shia Muslim.

Secularism: Western Norms and Indian Idioms

I have so far argued that conceptions of secularism in India were similar to Western conceptions in that these involved notions of the separation of state and religion. I will now suggest that secularism as separation was favoured for similar reasons as in many Western countries, and often invoked liberal values.

Conceptions of secularism as separation in nationalist opinion noted above—those of disestablishment, state impartiality between religions, and the exclusion of religion from politics—appealed to a range of norms. Prominent among these were non-discrimination and equal citizenship for all individuals. The state had to distance itself from religion, it was argued, in order not to discriminate between its citizens on religious grounds, to treat all individuals as equals irrespective of the religion to which they belonged. Allaying apprehensions that a secular state would be anti-religious, Gandhian and Patel ally, K.M. Munshi, clarified:

> A secular state is used in contrast with a theocratic government or a religious state. It implies that citizenship is irrespective of religious belief, that every citizen, to whatever religion he may belong, is equal before the law... has equal civil rights, and equal opportunity to derive benefit from the state and to lead his own life and nothing more. (*CAD* VII: 1057)

K.T. Shah, a Jain secular modernist wanted the inclusion of a provision explicitly stipulating state neutrality in matters relating to religion: '...with the actual profession of faith or belief, the State should have no concern. Nor should it, by any action of it, give any indication that it is partial to one or the other. All classes of citizens should have the same treatment in matters mundane from the state...' (*CAD* VII: 816).

Several liberal values can be discerned in nationalist elaborations of the idea of a secular state. To start with, there was a concern with non-discrimination and equal citizenship construed individualistically. It was argued that the state had an obligation to treat its citizens as equals, not to discriminate between them on grounds of (religious) group membership. The further assumption, echoed in strands of contemporary liberalism, was that given a situation of religious pluralism and the importance of religion in people's lives, this commitment would be compromised if the state identified with or gave preference to any religion.

A state which was liberal in that it dealt with its citizens 'primarily as individuals and not as groups' (Smith 1963: 170), was apprehended here as a secular state.

The requirements of equal citizenship, however, were not the only considerations motivating nationalist conceptions of secularism as separation. Separation was regarded as a critical imperative, for as recent history had demonstrated only too well, 'mixing religion and politics' imperilled the nation. If conflicts about religious doctrines were played out in public institutions, the country would be torn apart. To save itself and to achieve the consolidation of the nation, the state had to keep clear of matters concerning religion. Secularism as separation of state and religion is sometimes rejected as alien to India on grounds that it is the product of the struggle for power between the church and the state specific to Western Christian contexts (Madan 1998). As scholars have noted, however, the historical emergence of secularism in Western countries was *also* the product of a 'struggle to make the state relatively independent of deeply conflicting religious groups' (Bhargava 1998: 497).[31] In this respect, the motivations for the adoption of secularism in India were similar to many Western countries.

These also included several liberal norms. Apart from equal rights for all individuals and state neutrality characteristic of contemporary liberalism, ideas of religious liberty for individuals and groups associated with older liberal traditions also informed nationalist articulations of secularism. Nationalists of diverse ideological hues—Gandhians, modernists, and Hindu nationalists—invoked liberal values in elaborations of a secular state.

At the same time, it is important to note that while committed to a liberal framework of rights and freedoms, nationalist opinion also departed from the standard liberal position in significant respects. Notably, *groups* as well as individuals were recognized as the subjects of rights and entitlements (Galanter 1998[1965]; Bajpai 1997; Mahajan 1998; Bhargava 2000).[32] In political speeches, there was an easy switch

---

[31] Western practice reflects both what Bhargava terms the religious strife model, as well as the church-state model of secularism (1998: 525–6). On the links between secularism and nation-building in the US, see Archer 2001: 278.

[32] Since the late 1920s, Congress policy documents reiterated a commitment to the protection of the culture, language and scripts of minorities. These included

between individuals and groups as entities to which a liberal regime of rights and associated norms of freedom, non-discrimination, and justice would apply. Seconding the Objectives Resolution, Purushottamdas Tandon stated: 'The Resolution...has equality as its underlying theme... we shall do justice to all communities and give full freedom in their social and religious affairs' (CAD I: 66–7).[33] While individual rights were more prominent in nationalist pronouncements, likely on account of their close links to national unity, the rights of groups to religious freedom and non-interference from the state were also often cited in articulations of secularism. This emphasis on the group was not a cultural predilection for the collective in a straightforward sense, but also reflected recent history where colonial practice had underscored the importance of state non-intervention in religion. Colonial policies of communal entitlements, and early nationalist views where communities were regarded as the units of the nation, supported the recognition of group rights.[34]

What was the role of India's religious traditions in nationalist conceptions of secularism? Hindu religious beliefs, it has been argued, are supportive of a secular state (Dr S. Radhakrishnan in Smith 1963: 147). Beliefs that although God may be called by different names, he is ultimately one; that all religions are true, because all are different ways of reaching the same God; that religion is ultimately a matter of personal realization, are conducive to the separation of state and religion. However, such beliefs also have limitations as a basis for a secular state. The view that all religions are ultimately true is itself a particular religious doctrine, not acceptable to followers of Islam, Christianity and other religions, who believe in the unique truth of their religions (Smith 1963:150). Moreover, while commonly regarded as contributing towards a social attitude of tolerance and 'live and let live' towards followers of different faiths, this view 'has given rise to an attitude of intolerance

---

notably the Nehru Report (1928), the Karachi Charter on Fundamental Rights of 1931, the Sapru Committee Report (1944). See Chandhoke 1999: 210–2.

[33] See also Vijayalakshmi Pandit, CAD II: 278; S. Radhakrishnan CAD II: 270.

[34] Until the 1920s, historians have argued, the nation was mostly envisioned as a composite of communities defined in religious, regional, and caste terms. The terms 'nation' and 'community' were often used interchangeably in English as well as Indian languages in the late nineteenth century (Pandey 1990: chs 6–7).

towards those who are convinced of the uniqueness of their faith and feel impelled to preach and propagate it' (q. Smith 1963: 151).[35]

While Hindu beliefs were rarely invoked explicitly in discussions of secularism, these can be discerned in elaborations of a secular state in two main forms. Hindu nationalists in the Congress sometimes portrayed the secular state as an outcome of attitudes of toleration and generosity towards other faiths among the majority Hindus, attitudes that derived, it was implicitly suggested, from the nature of Hindu religion, its unique capacities of openness and accommodation of diversity. The state in India was secular because the majority of the population was Hindu. Secularism as toleration of minorities was redolent of the superiority of Hindu religion and self-congratulation on the forbearance and self-restraint of Hindus; it implied 'that the numerical majority, the Hindus, would not use their power to give Hinduism a favoured place over other religions' (Embree 1990: 87). There was also a broader, cultural variant of this claim, wherein a secular state was embedded in the 'age old' values of Indian civilization of religious toleration. This view held that toleration of religious diversity was the Indian way of life, part of the country's ancient traditions, and found spokesmen among the religious-minded of all faiths. Both these versions occasionally accompanied conceptions of separation. Thus, for instance, state impartiality between religions and religious freedom were sometimes defended as representing a continuation of Indian or Hindu traditions of religious toleration. In contrast to conceptions where it was viewed as a corollary of the modern nation-state, the creation of a secular state here did not require the transcendence of a 'backward' past, but building upon the country's civilizational/Hindu traditions of the accommodation of religious diversity. National unity and the secular state were both based here on a common ancient heritage of toleration.

Notions of the tolerance of the majority community towards the minorities did not inform conceptions of a secular state alone. In

---

[35] Critics of secularism sometimes suggest that traditional religion offers superior resources for toleration than modern secularism does (Madan 1998: 316; Nandy 1998: 336–7). While exploring the resources that religion offers against extremism and violence is valuable, such support is likely to be based on heterodox interpretations that themselves rely on modern values. Moreover, religious traditions conducive to secularism or toleration are not *necessary* for a secular state—see, for instance, Archer 2001 on the US experience.

arguments in favour of minority safeguards, which we shall consider in Chapter 4, the theme of the tolerance and the generosity of the majority community appeared frequently, particularly after Partition, which was seen to obviate the political need for minority safeguards. Filial and feudal notions of duty informed notions of tolerance of the majority, explicitly or implicitly. The majority community was cast in the role of the responsible, easy-going, benevolent, and self-sacrificing older brother, indulgent and accommodating of even the excessive and unreasonable demands of his younger and weaker brothers, the minorities, as in this speech by a supporter of minority rights:

> ...the Hindu community who can be collectively described as the elder brother has in a generous mood conceded for the period of ten years... that they [Muslims] should get a reserved representation...to listen to what difficulties and complaints, apart from the justice or otherwise of these complaints, of the Muslim community [are]...No danger or harm can follow from this in the period of ten years if the elder brother listens to the grievances of the younger brother. These grievances and difficulties may be unreal or exaggerated, they may be due more to fear and suspicion rather than to any real reasons.... (Naziruddin Ahmad CAD V: 269–70)

There would be frequent elision between the majority community and the major party in arguments supporting minority safeguards, both preponderant numerically in the country and the Assembly respectively, both said to be generous beyond the demands of justice in accommodating the minorities. Such paternalist filial and feudal idioms meant that liberal ideals such as secularism drew their normative force in many instances from non-liberal cultural and historical idioms.

MINORITIES AND THE NATION

Thus far, I have identified the defining features of nationalist arguments over group rights. What did minority claims to special treatment in the Constituent Assembly debates look like? These reflected the strains of being caught in the midst of transition from a framework where they had enjoyed legitimacy, to one wherein they were suspect. Minority claims to preferential treatment in the Constituent Assembly exhibited a dual character: invoking a colonial vocabulary of group entitlement on the one hand, and increasingly seeking accommodation within the nationalist vocabulary, on the other.

In early discussions, the representatives of most groups claiming special provisions emphasized that the group was a minority of some kind. This appears to have been a response to the colonial institutional framework where groups regarded as 'minorities' were the chief beneficiaries of preferential treatment. So close was the identification of the term 'minority' with the notion of special treatment that even those opposed to the continuation of the colonial system of minority safeguards employed the same language to justify their stand. For instance, it was argued that the 'so-called minorities' were not the 'real minorities'. The latter were variously identified as 'the agriculturists', 'the rural people', 'the backward provinces', even 'the masses'. The claim was that these groups ought to receive special treatment, rather than the groups hitherto favoured by the British.[36]

The employment of the term 'minority' did not denote the numerical status of the group so much as the claim that the group was entitled to special treatment from the state. Indeed, the numerical status of a group was invoked most frequently to denote its numerical strength, rather than weakness, which made it a force to reckon with, and entitled it to safeguards over other, smaller groups.[37] Colonial policy had been based on the principles that important groups were entitled to representation, in proportion at least to their demographic share, or weighted to reflect their importance in the case of numerically tiny groups, such as the Anglo-Indians. References to the numerical strength of a group in minority claims served to indicate that the group constituted a significant element of Indian society, one therefore with a legitimate claim to representation, and that the extent of representation ought to be commensurate with its numerical proportions. Frequent complaints were voiced in the initial stages of the Assembly's deliberations when the composition of the various committees was being decided, in instances where a group's representation in a committee was not commensurate with its demographic share, that the group was being unjustly treated and denied its 'due' share

[36] N.G. Ranga, for instance, held: '...the real minorities are the masses of this country. These people are so depressed and oppressed and suppressed till now that they are not able to take advantage of the ordinary civil rights. These are the real minorities who need protection....' (CAD II: 280).

[37] A Scheduled Caste representative, for instance, argued: '...we are one-fifth of the population of the whole country. It is impossible for a democratic country to ignore one-fifth of its population' (CAD II: 285).

in comparison with other groups. The implicit claim was that justice demanded that important groups should receive representation in political bodies at least in proportion to their population.[38]

References to numerical strength were cited alongside other attributes regarded as supporting a group's claim to importance and eligibility for special treatment. These most commonly included the distinct cultural identity of a group and its socio-economic 'backwardness'. Minority claims were frequently competitive: the representatives of each group advanced reasons why their group was deserving of greater representation than any other on grounds that it was numerically superior, more 'backward' than others, or more distinct from the majority in its cultural practices.[39]

A central concern in the speeches of most representatives belonging to religious minority communities was the preservation of their distinct cultural identity in independent India. In the initial stages of the Assembly's deliberations, when the Muslim League was absent, this concern was mostly voiced by Christian and Sikh representatives. Rev. Jerome D'Souza expressed the apprehension that

> ...'absorption' in the sense of cultural or religious or any other absorption is something against which it is necessary for us to guard...the strength of this land will be based upon the strength of the individual members of the different communities. And they will not achieve their full strength unless they base themselves on convictions and ideals which are their very own. Cultural autonomy...even though it may appear in some sense as opposed to national unity, is still consistent with it. (*CAD* II: 296–7)[40]

The main threat to the cultural identity of religious minorities in this period was thought to stem from a drive for national unity, which it

---

[38] Smaller groups such as Anglo-Indians and Sikhs demanded weightage.

[39] Jaipal Singh, the most prominent tribal representative in the Constituent Assembly, complained about the representation given to his community in the Advisory Committee: 'Number for number, the Sikhs, the Christians, the Anglo-Indians, and the Parsis have been given more than is their due...whereas when we come to my people, the real and most ancient people of this country, the position is different' (*CAD* II: 337). See also S. Nagappa, *CAD* II: 344.

[40] Sardar Ujjal Singh asserted: '[The Sikhs] want their separate entity and position to be maintained and strengthened so that they may be able to contribute their full quota to the service of the country' (*CAD* I: 107).

was feared might lead to cultural homogenization. Several arguments were offered for why minority concerns regarding cultural autonomy were compatible with national unity. It was argued, for instance, that cultural uniformity was not necessary for national unity; that cultural autonomy was a prerequisite for national strength, as it was only through the retention of their own distinct cultures that members of these communities would be able to contribute effectively to the nation. The latter was redolent of early nationalist conceptions of the nation: until the 1930s, when communities rather than the individual citizen were regarded as the building blocks of the nation, the means of building up the nation was thought to be through the strengthening of these communities (Pandey 1990). Significantly though, the nation was now the accepted point of reference in relation to which minority claims had to establish their legitimacy. The cultural distinctness of a group was no longer sufficient in itself to qualify it for special treatment.

Most representatives of the Scheduled Castes also claimed minority status and political safeguards. Different claims to special provisions shared an emphasis on the social, political, and economic backwardness of Untouchables. Muniswamy Pillai (Congress) held: '... the Untouchables who form one-sixth of the population of this sub-continent are a minority community, because their social, political, and educational advancement is in a very low state' (CAD V: 202). Some representatives, particularly those from the Congress, were at pains to emphasize that Untouchables were culturally a part of the Hindu fold.[41] Others, less willing to identify themselves as Hindu, nevertheless sought to distinguish their claims from those of religious minorities. S. Nagappa, a close associate of Dr Ambedkar, argued: 'I do not claim that we are a religious minority or a racial minority. I claim that we are a political minority. We are a minority because we were not recognized all these days and we were not given our due share in the administration of the country' (CAD II: 284).[42] While claiming minority status, most Untouchable representatives were keen to distinguish themselves from

---

[41] See Dakshayani Velayudhan, CAD II: 343; also H.J. Khandekar, CAD II: 298–9. P.R. Thakur stated: 'We are no doubt a part and parcel of the great Hindu community. But our social status...is so very low that we do feel that we require adequate safeguards to be provided to us' (CAD I: 139).

[42] See also Dr Ambedkar's memorandum reprinted in Shiva Rao 1967 II: 109, 114.

religious minorities and the taint of separatism. The self-description 'political minority' reflected a concern regarding access to positions of political power.

Not all Untouchable representatives claimed political safeguards. Dakshayani Velayudhan (Congress), the only female Untouchable representative in the Constituent Assembly pleaded:

> ...Communalism, whether Harijan, Christian, Muslim or Sikh is opposed to nationalism. What we want is not all kinds of safeguards...I refuse to believe that seventy million Harijans are to be considered as a minority...what we want is the...immediate removal of our social disabilities. (CAD I: 152)[43]

As this speech indicates, the appellation 'minority' was closely associated with safeguards: representatives who renounced special treatment for their group, were also reluctant to claim minority status.

Although the term 'minority' continued to be used for Dalits in the Constituent Assembly, in official categorization, Untouchables were removed from the purview of the term. K.M. Munshi proposed an amendment that was adopted, defining the term 'minority' more narrowly to exclude the Scheduled Castes from its ambit, as well as deeming them a part of the Hindu community:

> ...so far as the Scheduled Castes are concerned, they are not minorities in the strict meaning of the term; Harijans are part and parcel of the Hindu community, and...safeguards are given to them to protect their rights only till they are completely absorbed in the Hindu community.... (CAD V: 227)

This move reflected both nationalist antipathy to the appellation 'minority' and a desire to restrict its usage, as well as anxiety about the separation of the Untouchables from the Hindu community that, it was feared their categorization as minorities would encourage. As noted earlier, whether Untouchables ought to be distinguished from the Hindu community for purposes of representation had been a sensitive point for nationalists

---

[43] See also CAD V: 264. Most Untouchable representatives, including those from the Congress, pressed for safeguards, although there were differences over the types of safeguards favoured. Congress Untouchables mostly advocated reserved seats in proportion to the population under joint electorates, whereas Ambedkar and his allies urged mechanisms that would allow the Untouchable electorate a greater voice in the choice of their representatives.

in the decades preceding independence, with Ambedkar and Gandhi emblematic of the adversarial positions in this debate.[44]

Another important group for whom claims for preferential treatment were made in the Constituent Assembly were tribal populations. Tribal provisions were considered separately by the Constituent Assembly from the rest of the minority safeguards and are outside the scope of the present study, but a brief consideration is in order. Tribal claims exhibited a similar dynamic to other minority claims, that of the persistence of older norms on the one hand, and adjustment to a new vocabulary on the other. The most prominent tribal representative in the Constituent Assembly, Oxford educated Olympian Jaipal Singh, an Anglican, demanded preferential treatment but disavowed the term 'minorities':

> I do not consider my people a minority...the Depressed Classes also consider themselves as Adibasis, the original inhabitants of this country. If you go on adding people like the exterior castes and others who are socially in no man's land, we are not a minority. In any case, we have prescriptive rights that no one dare deny. (*CAD* I: 144)

Some Untouchable representatives also cast their claims in terms of indigenity. Ambedkar associate S. Nagappa asserted: '...we the Harijans and Adibasis are the real sons of the soil...we ask [the Britisher] to quit because he is a foreigner...we have also a right to ask the Aryan, the migrator to go...the Mohammedan, the invader, to go out of this country' (*CAD* II: 284).[45]

While at first glance, these appear simply as assertions of the relative superiority of the claims of particular groups, on closer analysis we can discern an attempt to reposition such claims within the nationalist vocabulary. To begin with, the description of these groups as original

---

[44] Whereas Dr Ambedkar had asked for separate electorates for Untouchables in his 1947 memorandum to the Minorities Sub-Committee, this proposal was not seriously pressed during the Assembly's deliberations. Ambedkar's re-election to the Constituent Assembly on a Congress ticket (he had lost his seat during Partition), his subsequent key role in constitution-making as Chairman of the Drafting Committee, the inclusion in the Constitution of several of his key demands such as the removal of property qualifications for suffrage, reserved seats for Untouchables in proportion to their population in legislatures and public services, may all have contributed here.

[45] See also P.R. Thakur, *CAD* I: 140. On the discourse of indigenity among Dalits in colonial India, see Patankar and Omvedt, 1979: 417.

inhabitants served to distance such claims from religious minorities and, more generally, to suggest that the demand for special treatment did not rest on simply being a 'minority'. Further, the claim that a group was owed something by virtue of being the 'original inhabitant' of a land assumed full force within a *national*, as distinct from a colonial, framework. It was because the first title to the nation was held by the Untouchables and Tribals that caste-Hindus who had come to the nation later than these groups, and through their unjust dispossession, owed these groups special treatment. Tribal and Untouchable representatives would refer to a history of injustice and exploitation by Hindu society and invoke compensatory justice in favour of preferential treatment.[46]

Tribal claims for special treatment in this period manifested a dual character. On the one hand, these were distinctive among minority claims in their emphasis on the importance of land. Issues of cultural distinctness were bound up with land and special provisions were claimed in the form of the continuation of the system of separate land reserves instituted by the British (see Jaipal Singh, *CAD* III: 462–3). On the other hand, tribal representatives also demanded reserved quotas in the legislatures and the public services, on grounds that these were necessary in order to improve the abysmal social and economic conditions of the 'backward' tribes, and thereby facilitate greater *integration* of the tribes with the wider society. Jaipal Singh explained:

> ...Our standpoint is that there is a tremendous disparity in our social, economic and educational standards, and it is only by some statutory compulsion that we can come up to the general population level...We want to be treated like anybody else. In the past...we have been isolated and kept, as it were, in a zoo...Our point now is that you have got to mix with us. We are willing to mix with you, and it is for that reason... that we have insisted on a reservation of seats as far as the legislatures are concerned... (*CAD* V: 209)

In general terms, this illustrates a common characteristic of group claims: demands for 'self-government do not preclude claims based on temporary disadvantage' (Kymlicka 1995: 144). Preservation of distinctiveness is consistent with greater integration. In the context of Indian history, such arguments reflected minority attempts at greater accommodation

---

[46] Jaipal Singh held: 'I leave to the good sense of the House...that, at long last, they will right the injuries of six thousand years' (*CAD* II: 337). See also S. Nagappa, *CAD* II: 284.

with the nationalist vocabulary and its key concern of national unity. Political safeguards, it was argued, could serve an integrative role: reserved seats would reduce the huge disparities that had kept tribal populations separate from the wider society and thereby further national integration.

While the Constituent Assembly debates opened with the term 'minority' as the favoured designation to denote a group's entitlement to special treatment, by the close of these debates, the term 'backward' would increasingly be employed in this regard. The decline in the fortunes of the term 'minority' during the Constituent Assembly debates encapsulated the transformation that the regime of group preference underwent in its transition from colonial to independent India.

Conclusion

The dominant framework for the analysis of nationalist ideas in India has been colonial discourse analysis. Nationalism here is framed as the ideology of a bourgeoisie seeking to capture state power through an appeal to goals such as development and social justice, and is typically exemplified in the thought of key individuals such as Nehru (e.g., Chatterjee 1986). By contrast, this chapter has proposed that nationalist discourse be unpacked into its conceptual elements and mapped in the context of political debate. A conceptual approach to nationalist thought that draws upon the articulations of a range of nationalists, both eminent and less well known, allows for a better grasp of the internal complexity and ideological variations within nationalism. It enables more accurate comparisons of the extent to which nationalist ideology was similar to, or different from Western discourses than do what Bilgrami (1998: 380) terms 'omnibus categories' such as 'modernity' and 'Enlightenment rationality'. And finally, a conceptual account of nationalist ideology yields better information about the efficacy of ideas, of how and why certain ideas became dominant in debate and policy.

I have argued that nationalist discourse comprised a set of inter-related concepts, those of secularism, democracy, social justice, national unity and development, which were invoked by nationalists of different ideological hues in the Constituent Assembly. While nationalist discourse was by no means monolithic, on the question of special treatment for minority groups, the different strands of nationalist opinion broadly converged in opposition. Nationalist opinion in the Constituent Assembly usually spoke in a common, liberal voice against special provisions for groups. With its liberal and national aspects both aligned against minority safeguards, the ideological conditions for such provisions were unfavourable from the outset, an antipathy accentuated several times over by Partition.

While this takes us some way towards an ideological account of the changes to minority safeguards during constitution-making, our story is still incomplete. If nationalist opinion was hostile to group-differentiated rights, how did these survive in the case of 'backward classes'? Moreover, our examination of minority claims suggested that these sought to accommodate themselves to the nationalist vocabulary. So during constitution-making, not only did the *institutional* forms of minority rights change, the *parameters* of political debate were also transformed. It is to examine the difference in the standing of special provisions for 'backward classes' and those for religious minorities, and the shift in the parameters of political debate, that we now turn.

4

From Minority to Backward

The Nationalist Resolution
of the 'Minorities Question'

INTRODUCTION

This chapter argues that although generally opposed to special provisions for minority groups, nationalist opinion was not uniformly ill disposed towards these. In particular, arguments were available for preferential provisions for the 'backward classes'. This helps us better understand how special representation provisions in legislatures and services initially proposed for all minorities came to be restricted in the end mainly to the Scheduled Castes and Scheduled Tribes. Furthermore, as the deliberations of the Constituent Assembly proceeded, not only were minority provisions altered, claims for special treatment also came to be transformed. Both the grounds and the types of provisions advanced by advocates of group rights came to be aligned closer to the nationalist vocabulary.[1] Initially, as we saw, the status claimed for groups to denote their entitlement to special treatment was 'minority', so Dalits, for instance, sought to establish that they were a 'political' minority. By the end of the Assembly's deliberations, this had changed to 'backward', so Muslim representatives, for instance, now argued that religious minorities were also backward.

In other words, during the Constituent Assembly debates, and in part through the process of debating, the nationalist vocabulary

---

[1] Representatives from minority groups were the main, but not the sole, advocates of special rights for minorities. For instance, K.M. Munshi and Hriday Nath Kunzru spoke in favour of strong cultural rights for minorities in key debates.

expanded to become the new legitimating vocabulary of the polity. The Congress was not simply dominant in achieving its policy preferences with regard to group rights; it was also *hegemonic*, transforming the parameters of political debate. Although Congress hegemony is well-documented in its institutional aspects (e.g., Kothari 1964; Manor 1997), its ideological dimensions remain under-studied. These are usually referred to in broad-brush terms such as 'Nehruvian consensus' and 'statist developmentalism'. This chapter provides a detailed conceptual and empirical account of hegemony construction, in terms of the ascendancy of a normative vocabulary comprising secularism, democracy, justice, national unity, and development. At the start of the Assembly's deliberations, the Congress was dominant; it became hegemonic in part through the taming of group rights in accordance with its vision of the nation.

This argument is established through a close examination of debates in the Constituent Assembly over different institutional mechanisms for group rights. Political representation mechanisms were the single most important area of minority claims in the colonial period. Reservations in government employment would become the key area of preferential treatment in independent India. The incorporation in the Constitution of cultural and educational rights for minorities appears to counter the argument outlined above, namely, that 'backwardness' became the principal basis for group preference. Through a detailed analytical reconstruction of arguments in debates on separate electorates, proportional representation, job quotas, cultural and educational rights, this chapter shows how both institutional forms as well discourses of group rights were transformed. The first part of the chapter examines nationalist opinion; the second part focuses on minority claims.

THE NATIONALIST VOCABULARY AND POLICY OUTCOMES: POLITICAL SAFEGUARDS

Political Representation

The most contentious element of minority safeguards before the Constituent Assembly was that of special representation for minority groups. Separate electorates, different forms of proportional representation, and reserved quotas in legislatures in proportion to the population of the communities, were the chief mechanisms proposed for enabling minority representation in the legislature and the executive during the Assembly's deliberations.[2]

Conflicting Conceptions of Representation: The Case of Separate Electorates

The most extensive debate on separate electorates in the Constituent Assembly took place in August 1947, during discussions on the first report on Minority Rights. Although these had already been rejected by the Advisory Committee, Muslim League members advocated separate electorates for the report's proposal of reserved seats in legislatures for Muslims, Indian Christians, Scheduled Castes and Tribes in proportion to the population of these communities for a period of ten years. While proposals for separate electorates were, predictably, rejected in the Assembly,[3] a revealing discussion on separate electorates followed, centring on the concept of representation. Nationalist opinion opposed the conception of representation implicit in the claims of Muslim League representatives in each of its key aspects: that society was fundamentally divided on religious lines; that the interests relevant for representation derived from religious group membership; that the social identity of the representative was relevant to representation; and that the group ought to be the constituency for the election of representatives. The fault-lines between nationalists and Muslim League on separate electorates had been in the making for some time, and had been discernable at least since the 1930s (Shaikh 1989). Nationalists rejected the Muslim League's premise that there were deep and permanent cultural differences between communities. Society was not essentially and irrevocably divided on religious lines; instead, the presence of antagonistic religious difference was the product of British policy, and in particular, of colonial institutions of separate representation along religious lines. This quasi-empirical view regarding the nature of Indian society was accompanied by a particular normative vision of how the

---

[2] Different combinations of these mechanisms were proposed during the Constituent Assembly's deliberations. For instance, proportional representation was advocated in conjunction with reserved seats, as well as an alterative to legislative quotas.

[3] Separate electorates were eventually outlawed under the Indian Constitution.

nation's common good was 'constituted through the activities and institutions of political representation' (Williams 1998: 29).

First, against proponents of separate electorates, nationalists held that religious groups were not the relevant interests from the standpoint of representation. Different arguments were offered in this regard. In a secular state, it was argued, the substance of political decision-making had nothing to do with religion, so there was no need for the representation of religious groups. With regard to *political* issues, it was assumed that there were no significant differences in the interests of individuals along religious lines. Mahavir Tyagi argued:

> To give the right of suffrage to a section of the people on a religious basis is something which the world does not understand. After all, we do not come here to legislate about religions. We come here to legislate and make laws to see that peace is maintained in the country on a country-wide basis. It is not a question of...one or the other section being considered. It is the whole country which has to be taken into consideration when we legislate. So the idea of getting representation from religious sections is simply ridiculous. We have had it till now but we cannot continue it because the future constitution is not meant to be a constitution of religions. A State cannot be a confederation of so many religions or sects or groups. (*CAD* V: 218)[4]

Political representation involved deliberation on the common interests shared by all citizens, which were secular, rather than 'sectional' interests that were religious. The close association of secularism and national unity in the nationalist vocabulary is clearly evident here. Representation along religious lines simultaneously violated the separation of religion and state *and* was divisive of the nation.

Second, the social identity of representatives was not considered relevant to representation in nationalist opinion. Membership of a group, nationalists argued in contrast to proponents of separate electorates, was not necessary for the effective representation of a group's interests.[5] Different arguments were offered here. One concerned the

---

[4] See also Pandit G.B. Pant, *CAD* V: 223–4.

[5] The notion that only a person belonging to the group could adequately represent it was often incomprehensible from a nationalist standpoint. Ananthasayanam Ayyangar queried: '...Mr Pocker says "I want a good, honest representative". What is the definition of goodness? Goodness does not come by being a Muslim or a Hindu...' (*CAD* V: 216).

function of representation. In an important speech, Pandit G.B. Pant argued that while belonging to a group may have been relevant for the effective advocacy of a group's interests, such advocacy was the defining function of representation in a colonial framework where assemblies had primarily served an advisory function. Under a democratic framework where legislatures were decision-making bodies,

> ...it is not merely a question of advocacy now. It is a question of having an effective decisive voice in the affairs and in the deliberations of the Legislatures and the Parliament of this free country. Even if in an advisory capacity one were a very good advocate, he cannot be absolutely of any use...if the Judge whom he has to address does not appreciate his arguments...and there is no possibility of the Advocate ever becoming a Judge. (*CAD* V: 223)

A representative's group membership was relevant for colonial representation, whose function was to provide information about sections of the population to law-makers. It was not relevant in a democratic system, where representation was about collective deliberation and participation in law-making. A colonial vestige, the demand for separate electorates stemmed from a lack of recognition of the difference between an undemocratic and a democratic political system.

The changed function of representation in a democratic setting had implications not only for the identity of the representative, but also for the appropriate mechanism of election of representatives. In a democratic framework, it was argued, separate electorates would be harmful to minorities. Vallabhbhai Patel held:

> Assume that you have separate electorates on a communal basis. Will you ever find a place in any of the Ministries in the Provinces or the Centre?...You will exclude yourselves and remain perpetually in a minority. (*CAD* VIII: 350)[6]

---

[6] Arguing that separate electorates would be 'suicidal' for minorities, Pandit G.B. Pant held: 'The minorities if they are returned by separate electorates can never have any effective voice...will you be satisfied with the pitiable position of being no more than advocates—if advocates alone you wish to be—when your advocacy will be treated...with utter disregard and unconcern, which is bound to be the case when those who are the judges are not in any way answerable to your electorate?' (*CAD* V: 223)

Implicit in these nationalist arguments was a particular conception of democracy. Democracy was defined in terms of self-rule—freedom from rule by an external authority, and popular sovereignty—government by the people, where the people were the source of laws to which they were subject. This ideal in turn was embodied in the institutions of majoritarian parliamentary government, where government formation was based on a legislative majority, and the mechanism of decision-making was that of majority rule (Lijphart 1996). In contrast with the case for separate electorates, the assumption was that legislative majorities were temporary and issue-based, so religious or caste minorities, for instance, could be part of legislative majorities.[7] It was from the standpoint of this conception of democracy that separate electorates appeared as both undemocratic and harmful to minorities. They were undemocratic because separate electorates assumed that representatives were primarily advocates petitioning law-makers on behalf of a section of the populace, rather than the authority that made laws for the people as a whole. Separate electorates were harmful to minorities because it was felt they would isolate minority representatives from the main body of legislators, consolidating religious minorities into permanent legislative minorities, and the religious majority into a legislative majority. Weakening electoral links between the religious/legislative majority and the minority communities, separate electorates would give minority groups a voice in the legislature, while depriving them of any policy influence.

It is important to note that separate electorates were rendered undemocratic and harmful to minorities through a *particular* interpretation of democracy that foreclosed several other possibilities under which this would not be the case. As Mansbridge (2000) argues, if decision-making follows a deliberative rather than competitive model, then the advocacy of particular interests can, by bringing in conflicting perspectives, enhance the quality of democratic deliberation, and also offer increased influence on decision-making to minorities. Similarly,

---

[7] Several minority representatives opposed parliamentary democracy as unsuitable in India on account of the presence of permanent majorities and minorities. For instance, in 1947, Dr Ambedkar had argued that a British-style parliamentary executive 'rests on the premise that the majority is a political majority' and in India 'would result in permanently vesting executive power in a communal majority.' (Shiva Rao 1967 II: 102–3).

if democratic institutions were more consociational, with guaranteed representation for minority parties or groups in government, separate electorates would not detract from the policy influence of minorities.[8] These possibilities were available at the time: the Congress had professed a commitment to decision-making by consensus rather than majority rule for issues involving minorities; and consociational type of power-sharing mechanisms with minorities had been prominent in colonial representation (Wilkinson 2004: 103–8).

That these possibilities were foreclosed in the dominant nationalist interpretation of democracy had to do with the centrality of national unity and its antagonism to separate electorates in the nationalist scheme. As we saw in Chapter 3, separate electorates were considered inimical to national unity on several counts: as incompatible with the political integrity and stability of the country; as undermining social cohesion and the creation of a common national identity for all citizens. They were thought to do so by encouraging solidarity with one's religious group and strengthening minority group identities that were detrimental to national unity, and undermining the kind of social identity favoured by the nationalists—'the collective identity of being a citizen of independent India' (Dhandha 1998: 52). By contrast, it was argued that joint electorates would promote communication and trust across different groups, and identification with members of religious groups other than one's own. Ananthasayanam Ayyangar argued:

> ...I am a Hindu and if you allow me to represent you, I will come to you at least every four years. Similarly a Muslim can come to Hindus. Ultimately we will come together. This is possible only if we have joint electorates. If I do not come on his vote, if I am not his representative, what on earth is there to bind me to him?' (CAD V: 216)[9]

Significantly, most nationalist arguments against separate electorates were not directed against this mechanism alone, but special representation for minorities as such. How *any* form of special representation for religious minorities had a place in the nationalist vision

---

[8] Consociational institutions are not necessarily democratic and have exacerbated ethnic conflict in several contexts.

[9] Dr Ambedkar among others had put forward sophisticated arguments challenging the Indian nationalist view that separate electorates were necessarily antithetical to national unity (see Shiva Rao 1967 II: 110).

of the common good, remained unclear.[10] Proportional representation for elections to the Lower House of Parliament and the constitution of the Cabinet proposed by minority representatives in 1949 were dismissed as separate electorates under a new guise (Rohini Chaudhari, *CAD* VIII: 325–6); impracticable in an illiterate country (Sardar Patel, *CAD* VIII: 353); above all, a recipe for government instability and thereby a threat to civil peace (Dr Ambedkar, *CAD* VII: 1262). As Sridharan notes, alternative electoral systems to the first-past-the-post system, such as proportional representation were 'never seriously debated or even understood' by the Constitution-makers (2002: 355, 359). In the end, the view that national unity required a strong central government carried the day. Closing the debate, Dr Ambedkar held: '... whatever else the future government provides for, whether it relieves the people from the wants from which they are suffering now or not... it must maintain a stable government and maintain law and order'[11] (*CAD* VII: 1262).

Recasting Group Representation: Reserved Seats in Legislatures

It might be recalled that the Congress had endorsed legislative quotas for minorities under joint electorates in early deliberations. What were the grounds on which this mechanism for minority representation was endorsed in nationalist opinion? The first point of note is that reserved seats in legislatures for minorities were approved as 'temporary' provisions and as measures of 'compromise' or transition. In an ideal future, legislative quotas for minorities would no longer exist. When the Constituent Assembly accepted these provisions in August 1947, S. Radhakrishnan pressed for the inclusion of a caveat:

> ... It is our ideal to develop a homogenous democratic state—that is why we have provided for fundamental rights, we allow no discrimination in public employment, we say it is a secular State...we must declare our objective...and those devices which were hitherto employed to keep the different sections of society apart have to be scrapped...We have to

---

[10] Dr Ambedkar's opposition to proportional representation may have stemmed from the fact that PR did not offer minorities 'a definite quota' of representation (Sridharan 2002: 359).

[11] Supporters of a strong central government in the Constituent Assembly were ideologically diverse and included secular modernists such as Nehru and Ambedkar, as well as Hindu nationalists (see Singh 2006: 912–13).

> effect a compromise between the ideal we have in view and the actual
> conditions which have come down to us...[Let us] say that it is not
> our desire to maintain these minorities as minorities. The measures of
> compromise are transitional.... (*CAD* V: 283–4)[12]

The next point of note is that in the case of religious minorities, even
as temporary provisions, there was no *principled* defense in nationalist
opinion for reserved seats in legislatures. The most common argument
in their favour was that religious minorities needed time to adapt
from the colonial system where they had been accustomed to certain
privileges. When reserved seats for religious minorities were endorsed
by the Constituent Assembly in 1947, it was held that '[T]he idea of
accommodating the minorities even for ten years is not exactly in accord
with our principles' (Mahavir Tyagi, *CAD* V: 219). When reserved seats
in legislatures for religious minorities were withdrawn in 1949, Nehru
commended their abolition as 'a historic turn in our destiny', confessing
that he had never been convinced about the provision:

> Reluctantly we agreed to carry on with some measure of reservation...
> but always there was this doubt in our minds, namely, whether we had
> not shown weakness in dealing with a thing that was wrong...doing
> away with this reservation business is not only a good thing in itself ...It
> shows that we are really sincere about this business of having a secular
> democracy. (*CAD* VIII: 329, 332)

Like separate electorates, reserved seats too were opposed on
grounds of secularism, democracy, justice, development, and above all,
national unity. As in other cases, these notions were mutually reinforcing
and invoked by an ideologically diverse cross-section of nationalists.
Patel's letter accompanying the Advisory Committee report of 11 May
1949 withdrawing reserved seats stated: 'Although the abolition of
separate electorates had removed much of the poison from the body politic,
the reservation of seats for religious communities...did lead to a certain
degree of separatism and was to that extent contrary to the conception of
a secular democratic state' (*CAD* VIII: 311). The overriding concern with
national unity, and the belief that institutional recognition of religious
identities imperilled national unity, meant that reserved seats lacked a
secure basis in the nationalist vocabulary. While rejecting social difference

---

[12] See also Vallabhbhai Patel's speech in the House, introducing the first minority
report, *CAD* V: 199–200.

as a basis for representative institutions, nationalists made little advance towards fashioning an alternative justification for special representation for religious minorities.

How, in the light of this argument about the normative deficit of group representation in the nationalist vocabulary, do we make sense of the fact that reserved seats in legislatures were retained in the case of the Scheduled Castes and Tribes? Special representation in the case of these groups, I shall now argue, had a distinct basis in the nationalist vocabulary from religious minorities, and further, *this had little to do with representation as such.*

In nationalist arguments, the case for special treatment of Untouchables was constantly distinguished from that of religious minorities through an emphasis on their poverty and 'backwardness' (Bajpai 1997; Mahajan 1998: 122–4). What separated these groups from the majority was not so much religio-cultural difference, but socio-economic inequality, it was argued. Group representation aimed not at the recognition of group difference, but the rectification of 'backwardness'. Nehru held:

> Frankly I would like this proposal to go further and put an end to such reservations that still remain. But...I realise that in the present state of affairs in India that would not be a desirable thing to do...in regard to the Scheduled Castes...I do not look at it from the religious point of view or the caste point of view, but from the point of view that a backward group ought to be helped and I am glad that this reservation will also be limited to ten years. (*CAD* VIII: 331)

Here too, a convergence can be discerned between the Nehruvian developmental integration position and those who sought cultural assimilation: '...the Scheduled Castes have been given reservation not on grounds of religion at all; they form part and parcel of the Hindu community, and they have been given reservation apparently and clearly on grounds of their economic, social and educational backwardness' (Jagat Narain Lal, *CAD* VIII: 308).

As mechanisms for the 'upliftment' of 'backward sections', legislative quotas for the Scheduled Castes did have a place in the nationalist vision of the common good. Nationalist arguments are examined in greater detail below, but briefly, it was argued that reserved seats in legislatures would enable the economic and social advancement of these groups. This was considered desirable from the standpoint of social justice, national unity, and development. Intended to serve as 'a political form of affirmative action', 'a temporary measure on the way to a society where the need for special representation no longer exists' (Kymlicka 1995: 141), legislative quotas were seen as short-term and 'self-liquidating' (Galanter 1984; Mahajan 1998: 128–9). In the nationalist scheme, the envisaged role of special representation mechanisms was to diminish and not preserve group difference.[13] While Indian Constitution-makers did accommodate a group-based approach in some areas (Galanter 1998[1965] 241–2; Bhargava 2000: 38–9), insofar as legislative quotas were concerned, protecting group difference was not the object. Here, the ideal remained individualist egalitarian.

It is important to emphasize that even as temporary affirmative action measures, reserved seats for 'backward sections' were not defended in nationalist opinion as a means of *representing* the interests of these groups. That is, nationalists were not conceding here what they had rejected in the case of religious minorities: the relevance of the social identity of representatives for representation. There was, for instance, little recognition in nationalist arguments that on account of being historically marginalized, these groups had 'a distinctive *perspective* on matters of public policy' (Williams 1998: 6, emphasis in text) which merited representation, or that members of these groups were in a better position to understand and thereby represent these interests on account of their first-hand experience, better trust and communication with group members (Kymlicka 1995; Mansbridge 2000). Legislative quotas for Scheduled Castes were intended as one among several provisions for the amelioration of their social and economic disadvantage. The mechanisms whereby legislative quotas would contribute to this end were not detailed, but these pertained to representation only tangentially, to the extent of ensuring the inclusion of members of hitherto excluded groups (Mahajan 1998: 121).

While the case of Scheduled Tribes is outside the scope of this study, a few points are relevant here. First, unlike in the case of Untouchables, there was some acknowledgement in nationalist opinion

---

[13] For instance, Vallabhbhai Patel stated: '...the Scheduled Caste has to be effaced altogether from our society, and if it is to be effaced, those who have ceased to be untouchables and sit amongst us must forget that they are untouchables...We are now to begin again. So let us forget these sections and cross-sections and let us stand as one, and together' (*CAD* V: 272).

of a distinctive cultural identity in the case of Adivasis (Mahajan 1998: 130–1; Corbridge 2000: 68–9; McMillan 2005: 125–7). To be sure, some opposed special treatment for tribals, particularly proposals for Scheduled Areas, as separatist (see Biswanath Das *CAD* IX: 994–6). Nevertheless, nationalist opinion was accommodating of a measure of autonomy, albeit in tandem with greater integration.[14] This would be reflected in the policies eventually adopted—the constitutional provisions for the Scheduled Tribes have a dual character as scholars have noted, seeking to 'balance improvement of their condition and a degree of assimilation with preservation of their distinctiveness and a measure of autonomy' (Galanter 1984: 153). Second, as in the case of Dalits, insofar as legislative quotas were concerned, these were intended as an *integrative* mechanism and not as a means of recognizing and protecting the cultural distinctiveness of Adivasis. Dr Ambedkar, acute as always about institutional effects, saw reserved seats as counter-balancing 'the tendency towards segregation' in the policy of autonomous tribal councils, of 'cycles of participation' as 'a binding force, enabling both sections of the people to come together, influence each other through association and learn something from such contacts' (Shiva Rao 1968: 587). The institutional forms of political representation eventually adopted for Adivasis—reserved seats under joint electorates—were consonant with this integrationist aim. Third, as a developmentalist perspective dominated discussions of Adivasis, even protectionist policies such as those for tribal lands did not wholly pursue cultural preservation.[15] Rather, these sought to give

---

[14] Opposing Jaipal Singh's proposals for greater autonomy for tribal areas, K.M. Munshi said that the aim of the Drafting Committee's proposals was that isolated tribes 'should be absorbed in the national life of the country'. But he also wanted that the Scheduled Tribes 'be protected from the destructive impact of races possessing a higher and more aggressive culture and... encouraged to develop their own autonomous life' (q. Shiva Rao 1968: 582). The report on tribal areas by Gopinath Bardoloi, J.J.M. Nichols-Roy, R.N. Brahma, and A.V. Thakkar tread a similar line: '...what is required is evolution or growth on the old foundations.... the evolution should come as far as possible from the tribe itself but it is equally clear that contact with outside influences is necessary though not in a compelling way...it would not be desirable to permit any different system to be imposed from outside. The future of these hills now does not seem to lie in absorption...but in political and social amalgamation' (Shiva Rao 1967 III: 693–4).

[15] The committee reports on tribal areas read like colonial ethnographies of far-flung peoples and places, offering accounts of people's customs and habits,

Adivasi communities greater control over the pace and nature of cultural change.[16] Although there were references to the value of tribal ways of life, protecting the integrity of tribal cultures as such for its own sake was not defended in nationalist opinion: strong multicultural arguments are hard to find. Tribal land in some areas needed protection because of its importance in aboriginals' economic life. Progressive change in Adivasi cultures in the direction of greater integration with mainstream society was not ruled out: where tribals had successfully assimilated themselves with the local population, fewer protectionist policies applied. Third, and relatedly, cultural protection was articulated as an aim of special treatment mainly for areas where tribals formed a *majority*. For areas in which tribals were a *minority*, cultural protection was rarely admitted as a goal. Thus the case of tribals supports my argument that cultural difference as a criterion for the protection of minorities—defined by tribe, religion, caste (or indeed language)—remained under-supported in nationalist opinion. For purposes of legislative and employment quotas, tribals were treated as a minority and accommodated within an integrationist affirmative action framework. For purposes of land rights and tribal councils, tribals were treated as a (regional) *majority*, so some protection of cultural difference obtained.

Preference in Government Employment for the 'Backward Classes'

If the debate on group preference in the colonial period was dominated in the late colonial period by political representation, the most contentious area of special treatment in independent India has perhaps been reservations in government employment. This section examines the arguments offered in nationalist opinion for employment preference and the light these shed on why the Constitution came to include special provisions for the 'backward classes', but not religious minorities.

---

economic and political practices, mental capacities, climate, and terrain. See, for instance, the report by Gopinath Bardoloi, J.J.M. Nichols-Roy, R.N. Brahma, and A.V. Thakkar, in Shiva Rao 1967 III: 690.

[16] Safeguards for tribal lands were defended mainly on grounds that these tribal groups were a 'simple people', 'exploited with ease'; the 'sudden disruption' of their customs 'by exposure to the impact of a more complicated and sophisticated manner of life is capable of doing great harm' (Shiva Rao 1967 III: 774–5).

Secularism, National Unity, and a 'Casteless Society'

The debates on reserved posts in government employment for the 'backward classes' in the Constituent Assembly reveal a pattern similar to those on political representation. In nationalist opinion, quotas in the public services for these groups, while admissible in the short run, were regarded as undesirable in general. By and large, other methods of ameliorating backwardness, such as channelling more financial and educational resources towards disadvantaged groups, were considered preferable.

The general grounds of opposition to political safeguards were also invoked against reservation in the public services for Untouchables and Backward Tribes. Reservations were seen to undermine the commitment to secularism in several ways. From the standpoint of a secular state, the recognition of caste and tribe as categories of policy involved the mixing of ethnicity and politics. Reservations were also seen to involve departures from the equal treatment of all individuals irrespective of the community to which they belonged. In a typical criticism, it was held '... [This clause] will give rise to casteism and favouritism which should have nothing to do in a secular State' (Damodar Swarup Seth, *CAD* VII: 679). In terms of a secular society, reservations, it was felt, would strengthen caste identities and undermine progress towards 'a casteless and classless society', a popular nationalist slogan in this period.

Secularism was incompatible with caste both as a social hierarchy sanctioned by religion, as well as an identity group which was the focus of citizens' loyalties (Galanter 1984: 560). While the primary nationalist anxiety was about caste in its 'horizontal' aspect—the persistence of caste as a unit of affiliation—'vertical' and 'horizontal' aspects of caste were conflated in nationalist denunciations of casteism. Opposition to reservations as strengthening caste as an identity group could therefore draw legitimacy from the egalitarian critique of the caste system, even though reservations directly challenged caste as a hierarchical social order. Reservations were belittled as an ineffectual cure for the ills of 'backwardness':

> It is only a symptom of that evil [caste system] that all communities are not represented in the services in an equitable or just manner. To ask for representation, however, on class or caste basis in the services is to remedy the disease only superficially...we have got to cure the disease

from its very roots... [if] we recognise the principle that appointments should be made on the basis of castes and classes, let us think of where it would lead us....Our allegiance to the nation would become only secondary. Our primary allegiance would be to class or caste. This is an evil from which we have suffered so long, an evil that led to the partition of the country. (Raj Bahadur, *CAD* IX: 622–3)

In such criticisms of caste-based reservations, secularism was closely tied to national unity. Like other group preferential provisions, reservations in government employment for the lower castes were seen as damaging national unity in several related ways: by encouraging loyalties to caste groups, these undermined the emergence of secular citizen identities, social cohesion, and ultimately, the political integrity of the country. It was felt that because 'it is not easy to define precisely the term "backward", nor is it easy to find a suitable criterion for testing the backwardness of a community or class' (Damodar Swarup Seth, *CAD* VII: 679), reservations for 'backward classes' would make for an endless proliferation of groups claiming that they were 'backward', and thereby continual conflict and instability. As in the case of other group preferential provisions, nationalists of divergent ideological persuasions, majoritarian Hindus as well as modernist Nehruvians, converged on the view that caste quotas detracted from a secular state.

Merit, Justice, and Efficiency

There were also arguments directed more specifically against the policy of special treatment in government employment for the 'backward classes'. The most common objections here were cast in terms of merit, which invoked considerations both of justice and, more commonly, efficiency. Reservations for the 'backward classes' were held to be incompatible with rights to equality of opportunity. It was asserted: '...there can be only one of these two things—either there can be clear equal opportunity or special consideration' (*CAD* VII: 694). In criticisms of reservations, justice was identified with a regime of equality of opportunity construed as the removal of formal legal or quasi-legal barriers to the attainment of positions, such as the rules of the caste system that had prevented individuals of lower caste birth from having access to education and prestigious occupations. Equality of opportunity was construed here either in the form of basic non-discrimination on grounds of caste, religion, sex, or at most as implying careers open to talents where only academic merit mattered in recruitment.[17] Reservations detracted from merit because they implied that jobs would not be allocated on the basis of the qualities of individuals, but their *social* background: the appeal was to the meritocratic ideal of jobs being granted in accordance with the capabilities of individuals.[18]

The term 'merit' was identified with individualist justice against group claims, and thus employed even where the principle of merit as such was not at stake. Rev. Jerome D' Souza, for example, advocated that 'henceforth all kinds of special safeguards...to be given to backward groups, to be no longer on the basis of religion, but on the basis of individual merit, on considerations of individual deficiencies and needs...' (*CAD* VIII: 307). 'Individual merit' stood here not for the capabilities but the *disabilities* of individuals: preferential provisions, it was argued, ought to be distributed in accordance with the needs of individuals rather than their social group affiliation. A reservation policy based on need assessed individually, would be more just than one based on caste, and at the same time, more compatible with the requirements of secularism and national unity. Mahavir Tyagi urged: '...the landless laborers, the cobblers, or those...who do not get enough to live, should be given special reservations...in place of Scheduled Caste, the words "Scheduled Classes" be substituted so that we may not inadvertently perpetuate the communal slur on our Parliaments' (*CAD* VIII: 344–5).

A second merit-based objection to special consideration for the 'backward classes' in government jobs, and the dominant concern in this period, invoked considerations of efficiency. Selecting persons for jobs on the basis of their individual attributes rather than group affiliation, it was assumed, would make for a more efficient administration. Ananthasayanam Ayyangar held:

> ...the first requisite is that all appointments shall be made in the interests of public administration on merit and merit alone. But, having regard to the conditions of our country, there must be some provision in favour of those persons who...may not be able to come up to the mark...With regard to appointments which require enormous skill

[17] On the degrees and types of equality of opportunity, see Radcliffe-Richards 1998.

[18] On merit, desert, and justice, see Miller 1999. The relationship between desert and group preference is examined in greater detail in Chapter 6.

and capacity, certainly, these rules cannot be relaxed, because public interests demand otherwise. (*CAD* IX: 626)[19]

Considerations of efficiency are usually contrasted with those of justice. However, when reservations in government employment were opposed on merit-efficiency grounds, considerations of justice were not always absent. Administrative efficiency was sometimes seen as a means of realising just outcomes: justice here was construed in consequentialist terms of the realization of a more just state of affairs in the future. H.N. Kunzru noted:

> ... where important business of the State requiring knowledge and judgment has to be carried on from day to day, we should appoint people only on the ground of merit. We cannot appoint them merely on the ground that their appointment will give satisfaction to certain classes; for if that were done, the very classes that want an adequate share in the public services would be the first to suffer, for they have to gain more by the efficiency of the administration and the impartiality of the officers than the members of the more advanced classes. (*CAD* IX: 629)

Reservations for the 'backward classes' were thought to lead to a decline in institutional efficiency through their effects on the standards of performance of individuals. Reservations, it was felt, would lower incentives necessary for the development of skills and the achievement of excellence, diminishing motivation among non-Backward Class individuals excluded from reservations as well as those from the 'backward classes.' Thus, a common argument against reservation of government posts was that these would stigmatize and induce feelings of inferiority among the beneficiaries and stifle initiatives for the development of 'merit.'[20]

However, while employment quotas for the 'backward classes' were seen as detracting from key nationalist ideals, unlike in the case of religious minorities, there were also arguments in nationalist opinion in support of such provisions. Adapting Galanter's classification, three main types of arguments for preferential treatment can be distinguished: general welfare,

---

[19] Damodar Swarup Seth held that 'reservation of posts or appointments in services for the 'backward classes' means the very negation of efficiency and good government' (*CAD* VII: 679). See also Sardar Patel, *CAD* V: 200.

[20] See, for instance, Raj Bahadur, *CAD* IX: 623; Krishna Chandra Sharma, *CAD* VIII: 516. On the incentive justification for meritocracy, see Baker 1990: 57–8.

where such provisions are defended 'as a means to produce desired social outcomes'; individual fairness, where preferential treatment is viewed as 'an extension of the norms of equal treatment'; and group fairness, which 'emphasizes groups as the carriers of historic rights' and 'sees the present as an occasion to reckon accounts for past injustice' (1984: 552–4).[21] Broadly speaking, special treatment for 'backward classes' was defended in general welfare and group fairness types of arguments, in terms of social justice, national unity, and development.

Social Justice, National Unity, and Development: Consequentialist Arguments for Quotas

The most common nationalist arguments supporting preferential treatment for disadvantaged groups in the Constituent Assembly were consequentialist arguments: reservations were defended primarily as a means of moving collectively towards desired national goals, rather than as a matter of rights of individuals or groups. In one common argument, reservations for 'backward sections' were defended as contributing towards the creation of a more just society in the future, a society characterized by less stark socio-economic inequalities between groups. The appeal here was to the nationalist goal of social justice.[22] While detracting from justice considerations in the *present* such as equality of opportunity for all individuals, reservations would enable the realization of a more just society in the *future*, one characterized by greater equality overall, fewer disparities between 'backward' groups and the rest of the population.[23] How these would do so was not specified in any detail: it was assumed that reservation in the public services, as in the case of legislatures, would improve the socio-economic condition of the 'backward sections'

---

[21] In contrast with Galanter, I suggest that general welfare arguments can be of a consequentialist *justice* kind, with the achievement of a more just society as their goal; and that individuals as well as groups can be the units of welfare calculation.

[22] Social justice as part of Indian nationalist ideology was fed by several streams: Hindu social reform movements of the nineteenth century, Gandhian campaigns against Untouchability, Nehru's socialist rhetoric of development (Chatterjee 1986: 132–3, 155; Bhargava 2000: 35–6).

[23] Galanter terms these horizontal and vertical perspectives on equality (1984: 380). Horizontal and vertical equality can both, of course, consistently, be part of a case for preferential treatment.

mainly through their economic effects. 'Backwardness' was material in its source; quotas were one means among several others for reducing socio-economic disparities, inadequate in themselves for facilitating the material advancement of Untouchables and Adivasis.[24] Nevertheless, by positing social justice as a national goal and admitting the need for group-targeted mechanisms for this purpose, a basis was created in the nationalist vocabulary for quotas for the 'backward classes'.[25]

The most common consequentialist argument in nationalist opinion in favour of reservations for the 'backward classes', however, invoked the goals of national unity and development. Reducing socio-economic disparities between groups was desired not so much for itself, but because it would further the integration of 'backward sections' with the rest of the population, on the one hand, and national development and progress, on the other. Their overriding importance in nationalist discourse of this period meant that national unity and development were invoked in nearly every claim for preferential treatment for the 'backward classes' in the Constituent Assembly. In the case of national unity, the assumption was that the 'backwardness' of Untouchables and Adivasis was hindering their integration with the rest of the population. Bringing these groups 'up to the level of the rest' in economic terms would mitigate the social gulf that separated them from the rest of the population: vertical levelling, it was assumed, would produce horizontal integration.

By 'uplifting' sections that were dragging the nation down and inhibiting its progress, reservations would also further national development. As the growth and equity aspects of development were fused together, social justice and its mechanisms such as quotas could draw legitimacy from the national goal of development. 'Catching up' with the industrialized Western world, overcoming national backwardness, required reservations to boost the 'backward' sections in the short run; such measures were in the interest of the nation as a whole:

[24] This justification left reservations open to the criticism that these were not the most effective means for tackling 'backwardness'. For instance, Brajeshwar Prasad argued: '...by giving them a few seats here and there, their economic condition and their educational level will in no way be improved' (*CAD* IX: 663–4).

[25] As Mahajan points out, in discussing the Scheduled Castes, the Constitution-makers 'gave a positive content to the notion of social equality', going beyond assertions of 'the equality of all individuals, irrespective of their social attributes' (1998: 118).

'They need and must be given, for sometime to come at any rate, special treatment in regard to education...to opportunity for employment and in many other cases where...their present backwardness is only a hindrance to the rapid development of the country...' (K.T. Shah, *CAD* VII: 655). The existence of 'backward groups' was a symptom and a reminder of India's own 'backwardness', the gulf that separated it from advanced Western countries, the club of powerful nations to which it wanted to belong. Nationalist discourse often employed physiological metaphors of disease to characterize the 'backward' and 'backwardness', which was portrayed as an aberrant, disfiguring condition which the nation had to overcome in order to regain its health.[26] Here, the Indian nationalist view of sub-national groups as part of the whole supported reservations for the 'backward'—the health of the nation demanded special attention to its ailing parts:

> ...we must do all we can to bring them up to the general level, and it is a real necessity as much in our interests as in theirs that the gap should be bridged. The strength of the chain is measured by the weakest link of it and so until every link is fully revitalized, we will not have a healthy body. (*CAD* II: 312)

Located within a discourse of development, 'backwardness' was conceived primarily in economic terms, although with associated political and moral dimensions (Zachariah 2005).

The register of such developmental arguments was one of paternalistic benevolence (Jayal 1999): 'backward sections' were cast as objects of compassionate and philanthropic action on their behalf, rather than as agents of their own improvement. 'Backwardness' would be ameliorated by a state led by an enlightened elite, the 'we' implicitly was the upper echelons of Indian society. In its role as the director of the project of development, the postcolonial state, as scholars have noted, assumed a stance that was very similar to its colonial predecessor, that of guardian and protector of 'weaker groups' (Chatterjee 1995: 218), which served to legitimize the nationalist elite as the leaders of society, rescuing the 'masses' from backwardness. '[A]ctive participation' of the masses was 'hardly envisaged'; masses were 'materials to be moulded to a project of development as fulfilment of self-respect' of the nationalist elite

---

[26] On the antecedents of the conception of the national state as a body, and related notions of eugenics, see Zachariah 2005: 247–50.

(Zachariah 2005: 296–9). For our purposes, the relevant point is that framed within the goal of development, social justice and its instruments such as reservations were tinged with its characteristics. This was not a particularly democratic conception of social justice, in which participation by the 'weaker sections' played a central role in the overcoming of 'backwardness', but one that was designed and executed from 'above'.

Group Fairness: Compensation as Atonement

Although nationalist arguments for special treatment for the 'backward sections' mostly invoked desired national goals, there was nevertheless one significant fairness consideration. This was a group fairness or reparations argument (Galanter 1984: 554). The current disadvantages of Untouchables and Tribals, it was suggested, were the result of a history of oppression inflicted upon these groups by the upper castes. As such, reservations, while involving costs for members of the upper castes, were a form of compensation owed to these groups. The assumption was that the state would compensate for the history of upper-caste oppression of the lowest castes and tribes. Thakur Das Bhargava supported reservations for the 'backward classes': 'We ourselves are guilty of having brought them to this level. It is up to us to see that they are not left in the lurch and they advance with the other communities...' (CAD IX: 687).

Arguments for preferential provisions as compensation for past wrongs are regarded as weak for several reasons. One objection derives from the problem of how members of the current generation can be made to bear the costs of such provisions, when they were not the agents responsible for historical injustices.[27] In an important instance of the usage of indigenous cultural norms in political argument, Hindu beliefs regarding sin were invoked by some nationalists to make the claim that

---

[27] Even if this is accepted, there would still be a case for positive discrimination as compensation, on grounds that the current generation of upper castes have *benefited* from the historical exclusion of the lower castes from education and employment. On the problems of justifying quotas as compensation from the perspective of the victims of injustice, see Nagel 1979: 93; Rosenfeld 1991: 95. The contributions of past injustices to the creation of current inequalities are difficult to estimate and vary among individuals of the oppressed group. There are also problems with justifying group quotas on grounds of justice from the perspective of the wrongdoer. For discussions in the context of Indian debates, see Galanter 1984: 558; Mahajan 1998: 135–6.

the current generation of upper castes pay the costs for the actions of their forefathers. Thakur Das Bhargava described preferential provisions for 'backward classes' as '...an oath taken by the House...to see that within the coming years we will provide all the facilities which can be provided by the nation for expiating our past sins....' (CAD VIII: 946). [28] This line of argument also offered a way around another problem with the costs of quotas, namely, that these are unfairly distributed, and have to be borne by a few, relatively weaker members of the upper castes (Galanter 1984: 558). The invocation of Hindu beliefs regarding atonement allowed the issue of the distribution of costs within the upper castes to be blurred, as all its members could be presumed to bear responsibility for past injustices against the lower castes. In the compensation/atonement argument for quotas in nationalist discourse, the emphasis was not so much on the *rights* of the victims of injustice as the *duties* of the legatees of the wrongdoers. This was an argument made primarily by upper-caste Hindus, addressed to their caste brethren in the form of an appeal for self-reform and self-sacrifice. It affirmed their credentials as benevolent guardians of the 'weaker sections' of the nation, and served to underscore that Untouchables and Tribals were part of the Hindu community. Articulated in an idiom of atonement, preferential treatment was rendered as much an act of charity as a requirement of justice, pursued by a state that was implicitly identified with upper-caste Hindus. Although scholars have suggested that 'positive discrimination was not simply a form of *compensatory* justice' (Mahajan 1998: 135), the latter, our analysis suggests, clearly formed one of the arguments put forward by Constitution-makers in support of preferential treatment for the Scheduled Castes. Compensatory justice was a complementary subordinate principle to the dominant justification of positive discrimination, the goal of reducing group disparities. The idiom of atonement also legitimized transfers of valued resources such as government jobs towards disadvantaged groups and as such, aided the justification of special treatment.

While our analysis suggests that there were arguments in nationalist opinion in support of special treatment for Untouchables and Tribals, it is important to note that in each case, these were admitted as a temporary mechanism that would enable the realization of a state of affairs in

---

[28] Pandit G.B. Pant argued: '...we have to take particular care of the Depressed Classes...We have to atone for our omissions....' (CAD II: 332–3).

which differential treatment would no longer be necessary. Reservations in government employment, like legislative quotas, were intended as a means of reducing social disparities, and thereby group difference and not for protecting the social identity of beneficiary groups. Pressing for the inclusion of a clause in the Constitution setting limits to the duration of reservations in government employment as well to the groups to be included in the category 'backward classes', Hriday Nath Kunzru held:

> ...we should have a system that would not encourage fissiparous tendencies and under which it will not be to the interest of any class to claim that it is backward...the intention of the constitution [is] to remove all those conditions on account of which special protection is necessary...It was recognized that for the time being they were necessary, but... [protection] should be granted temporarily only, so that the population of the country might become fully integrated... (*CAD* VII: 681)

Thakur Das Bhargava noted: '...we should see to it that these classes do not continue in the category of 'backward classes' after they have come up to normal standards so that their backwardness is not crystallized or perpetuated' (*CAD* VIII: 946).

Like political representation, employment quotas for the 'backward classes' were sought to be firmly positioned within a regime of affirmative action, with integration of the beneficiary groups as the eventual aim. Other than the rectification of backwardness, no justification was available for job quotas. Although 'backwardness' was not defined, significant socio-economic disadvantage of designated groups was assumed; further, in this period 'backwardness' was regarded as attaching to Untouchables and Adivasis, but not to religious minorities.[29] Opposing an amendment moved by Sikh representatives that all minority groups receive special consideration in appointments to the public services as proposed in the first draft of the Constitution, Vallabhbhai Patel queried: 'After all, what is the Sikh community backward in? Is it backward in industry, or commerce or in anything?'[30] (*CAD* X: 249)

---

[29] The category 'backward classes' was not specified by the Constitution-makers, and its determination has been a subject of controversy in independent India. See Chapter 6 below.

[30] As per the demand of some Sikh representatives, the special provisions for Scheduled Castes with regard to reservation in the legislatures and services were extended to some 'backward' sections within the Sikh community, by classifying

To put it differently, while there was no place in the nationalist vision of the common good for the notion of group entitlements to a 'due share' of public posts, an alternative basis did exist for affirmative action for disadvantaged groups. Rejected as 'a general principle of governmental operation' (Galanter 1984: 363), quotas were admitted as a temporary affirmative action provision for Untouchables and Adivasis. These were defended on justice grounds of group fairness and in terms of national goals of integration and development. Arguments along these lines can be discerned in nationalist opinion from at least the 1920s, and these were further elaborated during the Constituent Assembly debates. No similar process of grounding in nationalist ideals can be discerned in the case of religious minorities. Employment quotas were not construed as a requirement of justice or development in dominant nationalist opinion, and were perceived as damaging to national unity. So although the first draft of the Constitution had included the provision that the claims of all minority groups would be taken into consideration in making appointments to the public services, unlike in the case of the 'backward classes', its inclusion was not accompanied by the fashioning of a corresponding normative basis in the nationalist vocabulary. As in the case of political representation, an analysis of arguments for reservation in the public services suggests that the retraction of the policy in the case of religious minorities was always a likely outcome.[31]

----

these sections in the list of Scheduled Castes. This was opposed by some Scheduled Caste representatives and only reluctantly accepted by the Congress leadership.

[31] Special provisions for the relatively advanced Anglo-Indian community in matters of recruitment to certain services might seem an aberration in the light of the foregoing account. Such provisions were in fact regarded as constituting a departure from the general principles of special treatment by dominant opinion in the House. See, for instance, Prof. Shibban Lal Saxena: '...these concessions are based on a principle which has not been followed anywhere else in the Constitution....' (CAD VIII: 938, also the statements of Thakur Das Bhargava, Mahavir Tyagi, and K.M. Munshi, CAD VIII: 939–41). These suggest that Anglo-Indian reservations were intended as an exceptional measure for a period of transition from the colonial system, and as an integrative rather than a protectionist mechanism. This, of course, does not explain why the exception was only made in the case of the Anglo-Indian community, why transitional, time-limited provisions were not instituted for Muslims and Sikhs. The nationalist elite's perceptions of the dangers of separatism in these cases, as well as political

The Nationalist Vocabulary and Policy Outcomes: Cultural and Educational Rights

So far, I have focussed on the case of political safeguards and argued that a reconstruction of nationalist arguments enables us to better understand their fortunes in the Constituent Assembly, in particular, the institution of quotas in the case of Untouchables and Tribals, but not religious minorities. Our characterization of the nationalist vocabulary of the previous chapter has been refined. While the nationalist vocabulary was hostile to political safeguards in general, social justice, national unity, and development were also construed as supporting temporary measures for the rectification of 'backwardness'. Nevertheless, the *ideal* with regard to political safeguards was still a largely individualist, difference-blind framework; groups were recognized as subjects of special rights for purposes of overcoming differences between them.

There was, however, one other type of minority provision not considered thus far. In the Indian Constitution, the cultural and educational rights of religious minorities are enshrined as justiciable fundamental rights, and assume the form of individual as well as group rights (see Chapter 2 above). How does this fit in with the argument that the amelioration of backwardness alone was recognized as a basis of special treatment in the nationalist vocabulary? Did the Constitution-makers elaborate grounds for special treatment for minority cultures in the area of *cultural* rights? I shall now argue that cultural rights too lacked a secure normative basis in the nationalist vocabulary. How secularism, justice, democracy, national unity, or development required special treatment for minorities in cultural matters was not spelt out. The gaps in their justificatory basis help us better understand the kinds of attenuation that minority cultural rights underwent during constitution-making. In contrast to 'backward' groups, where the duty of the state to render assistance was explicitly written into the Constitution, religious minorities were free to pursue culture at their own initiative without a constitutional *entitlement* to state assistance (although the state could

---

bargaining between minority and Congress leaders, also needs to be taken into account. Article 336 of the Indian Constitution relating to special provisions for the Anglo-Indian community in certain services postulated a reduction in the number of reserved posts every two years and a cessation of such reservation at the end of ten years; it ceased to operate in 1960 (Galanter 1984: 42).

offer support). Again, while Partition might have been a trigger for these changes, there were longer-term factors to do with the ideology of Indian nationalism that favoured this outcome.

The first point of note is that a substantial section of nationalists, comprising mostly Congressmen with Hindu leanings, opposed special cultural and educational rights for minorities on similar grounds to political safeguards. Secularism, for instance, was construed as implying that religious groups should not be recognized; justice as requiring the same rights for individuals belonging to majority and minority communities. As in the case of political safeguards, these conceptions were closely linked to national unity. Arguing for the restriction of educational rights to linguistic minorities, Damodar Swarup Seth held:

> ...in a secular state minorities based on religion or community should not be recognized. Besides...if these minorities are recognized and granted the right to establish and administer educational institutions of their own, it will not only block the way of national unity, so essential for a country of different faiths, as India is, but will also promote communalism, and narrow anti-national outlook as was the case hitherto, with disastrous results. (*CAD* VII: 899)[32]

Despite such opposition, however, fundamental rights in the Constitution would include cultural and educational rights for religious minorities. One way to account for this inclusion is to see it as the result of a political bargain. There is evidence in the Constituent Assembly debates to suggest that some sections of religious minorities, most notably among Christian representatives, may have given up claims to political safeguards in return for assurances that the religious, cultural and educational rights of minorities would receive adequate protection.[33]

[32] Pandit Thakur Das Bhargava proposed an amendment to extend the clause prohibiting discrimination against minorities in educational institutions, to all citizens, arguing that 'minority rights as such should not find any place' in a section on cultural and educational rights (*CAD* VII: 897–8).

[33] See Rev. Jerome D' Souza's speech supporting the withdrawal of reserved seats for religious minorities, *CAD* VII: 939–40. The right to practise and propagate religion had been made a fundamental right, against the opposition of hardline Hindu opinion within the Congress, at the insistence of Christian representatives who had held that propagation was an essential part of their religious tenet. For debates on the right to propagate religion, see *CAD* III: 488–503; *CAD* VII: 832–8. K.M. Munshi defended the right on grounds among others that the

While there may have been a trade-off between political and cultural safeguards among some proponents, importantly, such rights also found support within nationalist opinion. To begin with, as might be recalled from our discussion in Chapter 3, whereas secularism was construed as precluding the recognition of religious and cultural distinctions in the *political* arena, and thereby as incompatible with political safeguards for minorities, it was also seen to imply religious and cultural freedom for citizens. Indeed, in conceptions of secularism, the rights and freedoms of citizens to pursue religion and culture in their 'private' individual and associational capacity were regarded as the corollary of their exclusion from the political domain. Most nationalists held the pursuit of religion and the preservation of language and culture on the part of citizens of all communities to be legitimate goals.

Further, as noted earlier, in a departure from the standard liberal position, groups were recognized as subjects of rights and entitlements in nationalist opinion (Galanter 1998a [1965] 241; Mahajan 1998: 79–85, 103; Bhargava 2000: 38–9). While justice was construed as antithetical to special treatment in legislatures and employment, it was also seen to imply freedom for minorities in religious and cultural matters. Thus, for instance, it was held that individuals *and* groups should have the freedom to pursue their religion and develop their language and culture, or that justice demanded that no individual *or* group be subject to compulsion in matters of religion or language, rhetorical vacillations indicating that group rights were not considered antagonistic to individual rights in nationalist opinion. As such, the cultural rights of minorities did find some support from key nationalist ideals. While rejected as a ground for legislative or employment quotas, group difference was admitted as a basis for cultural and educational rights. That the cultural rights of minorities would survive in the Constitution, unlike political safeguards, is not surprising. However, as noted in Chapter 2, these would also undergo some attenuation during constitution-making, changes that are better understood through a closer examination of nationalist discourse.

Christian community had been 'nationalistic' in giving up the claim for legislative quotas.

To begin with, the accommodation of group rights existed uneasily with individual rights in nationalist opinion. The tension between individual and group rights ran through the debates on most provisions pertaining to religious and cultural rights, with the final form of several articles reflecting an uneasy compromise between the sometimes conflicting demands of the two (see Chapter 2). Nevertheless, the balance in nationalist opinion in this period tilted towards individual rights. Their close association with nation-building in this period appears to have been crucial here. The emphasis on individual rights meant that there were pressures to extend the cultural and educational rights of minorities to all citizens, and to qualify these in order to protect individuals within minority communities. So, on the one hand, against the wishes of individual rights advocates, a broad definition of the right to freedom of religion was adopted, encompassing the *practice* of religion; further, no justiciable provision for a uniform civil code was adopted. On the other hand, the right to religious freedom was not left unfettered: state intervention was permitted, for example, for reasons of upholding other fundamental rights such as those of non-discrimination and equality for all individuals.

Moreover, although nationalist opinion frequently reiterated a commitment to the rights of minorities in cultural matters, insofar as such rights involved special treatment for *minorities* over and above the rights enjoyed by *all* individuals and groups, their normative basis in the nationalist vocabulary remained unclear. The move from all groups having rights to pursue their culture, to the *special* cultural rights of minorities, was not articulated in nationalist opinion. Few reasons were offered in support of minority cultural rights. It was reiterated frequently that minorities would be guaranteed freedom in matters of religion, language, and culture, and protected from discrimination and interference from the state.[34] But how secularism, justice, national unity, and development, for instance, required special rights for minorities was not spelt out in nationalist pronouncements.

To put it differently, despite the fact that the cultural rights of minorities were consistent with some elements of the nationalist

---

[34] Since the 1931 Karachi resolution, Congress resolutions had included in their list of fundamental rights of citizens, guarantees for the protection of the culture, language, and scripts of religious minorities (see Zaidi 1984).

vocabulary, tensions remained with others, such as justice construed in individualist, difference-blind terms, as well as national unity. Unlike the case of 'backwardness', where such tensions were confronted and arguments offered for why its amelioration was desirable, few arguments were put forward by nationalists to suggest how the preservation of minority cultures formed part of their vision of the common good. As a basis for group-differentiated rights then, cultural difference, unlike 'backwardness', lacked an adequate basis in the nationalist vocabulary.

The justificatory deficit that remained for the protection of minority cultures was clearly evident in the debate over the article pertaining to the preservation of the distinct language, culture, and scripts of minorities. As noted in Chapter 2, the wording of this provision was modified by the Drafting Committee, a change opposed, among others, by several Muslim representatives as a diminution in the protection offered to minorities. The issue was raised in the context of the position of Urdu, the language associated with the Muslims of the United Provinces.[35] Z.H. Lari complained:

> ... [it implies] only that the minority...shall be entitled to conserve its own language...But the question is whether they will be entitled to use their own language in elementary education given at the *state* expense... the clause as it stands becomes innocuous...It states a truism: it is not a fundamental right at all. (*CAD* VII: 893–4)

A facility for a minority 'which is less than 50% was...made dependent upon the will of the majority' (*CAD* VII: 902).

In nationalist opinion, the desirability of children receiving primary education in their mother tongue was not denied; however the inclusion of a constitutional guarantee of state aid was opposed. Cultural rights of minorities were largely interpreted as *negative* liberties. The duties that these were seen to require of the state were limited to forbearance from interference, rather than also to protect or aid minority cultures.[36] Dr B.R. Ambedkar, Chairman of the Drafting Committee, noted that

---

[35] See especially the speeches of ZH Lari, *CAD* VII: 900–3; Begum Aizaz Rasul, *CAD* VII: 904. Stronger cultural rights for minorites were also advocated by Hindu representatives such as Pandit Hriday Nath Kunzru, *CAD* VII: 920–2. Eventually, advocates of Urdu such as Maulana Abul Kalam Azad and Z.H. Lari resigned in protest against its treatment (Wilkinson 2004: 121–2).

[36] On the multiple duties of avoidance, protection, and aid involved in the fulfilment of rights, see Shue 1980.

as per the constitutional article, there was '...no burden' cast upon the state. The 'only limitation that is imposed...is that if there is a cultural minority which wants to preserve its language, its script, and its culture, the State shall not by law impose upon it any other culture...' (CAD VII: 923). A more muscular rebuttal came from the UP Chief Minister Pandit G.B. Pant, responding to complaints about the status of Urdu in UP:

> ...where substantial numbers of such students are available, arrangements should be made; where the numbers are not substantial...we cannot incur such expenditure...Can anything be more equitable, can anything be more generous?...The fundamental right that we are adopting here...only gives *freedom* to the followers of a language which is different...to preserve their language. It does *not* *require* the government to make any special provision for them. But we have gone much beyond that, and we have given special *privileges*. (CAD VII: 916)

The right of minorities to preserve their language and script was thus construed as requiring mainly *negative* duties from the state of non-interference—the state would refrain from imposing on minorities a language other than their own, and allow minorities freedom to pursue their culture (Shue 1980; Mahajan 1998: 95). It was not seen as requiring positive action from the state to set up institutions to enable the preservation of minority cultures and languages. While the article did of course leave open the *possibility* of state aid for minority educational institutions, as the above speech suggests, such assistance was likely to be regarded as a concession that went beyond the requirements of the right, rather than a duty required for its fulfilment. That state aid was likely to be considered as such was indicative of the fact that the protection of minority cultures lacked an adequate justificatory basis in the nationalist vocabulary.[37] The form in which cultural safeguards were eventually incorporated in the Constitution was that minorities were free to promote their culture with the possibility, but not an entitlement, to assistance from the state.

---

[37] Dominant nationalist opinion on this question, as others of minority rights, was composed of ideologically dissimilar elements. For instance, liberals like Rajkumari Amrit Kaur argued that state assistance for minority educational institutions would be akin to the establishment of communal institutions (Shiva Rao 1967 II: 281).

Nationalist Vocabulary and Discursive Outcomes: Changing Bases of Minority Claims

I have thus far argued that the institutional forms of minority rights came to be realigned during constitution-making in accordance with the nationalist vocabulary. This, however, was only one aspect of the transformation of the regime of group preference in the transition from colonial rule. Minority claims for special treatment too came to be progressively recast during the course of the Constituent Assembly's deliberations. Whereas initially, these had relied on a colonial language of group entitlement, as the deliberations progressed, these increasingly invoked concepts from the nationalist vocabulary. In the process, a shared legitimating vocabulary was forged, one which was employed in arguments both for and against group rights. This was most starkly evident in the contrast between arguments and policies defended by minority representatives in the August 1947 debate on the first minority report, and those in the May 1949 debate on the revised report that withdrew political representation for minorities. The progressive adaptation of minority claims, however, is discernable in some form throughout the deliberations of the Constituent Assembly, in a range of debates on political representation, job reservations, and cultural rights.

Political Representation

The initial contrast between minority and nationalist claims is best illustrated by the case for separate electorates put forward by Muslim League representatives in the Assembly in August 1947.[38] Proposals for separate electorates typically advanced the following arguments. First, it was asserted that minority groups were a permanent feature of every human society, and not, as nationalist opinion claimed, largely a contrivance of colonial machinations and vested interests. There were fundamental and irreducible differences between communities, at least along lines of religion. To deny the existence of minority communities, B. Pocker Sahib Bahadur (Muslim League: Madras) declared, was going against the facts of human nature and having before us ideologies

---

[38] Claims for separate electorates were also put forward on behalf of Sikhs by the Akalis, and for Untouchables, by Dr Ambedkar in his 1947 Memorandum to the Minorities Sub-Committee.

that are impossible for realization. Human nature being what it is, there are bound to be minorities...' (*CAD* V: 211). Second, the fact that distinct minority communities existed along lines of religion meant that these differences had to be represented in political institutions. As the legislature made laws that affected all communities, it was 'necessary that in that legislature the needs of all communities should be ventilated' (*CAD* V: 213). To begin with, this was a claim that the entities relevant from the standpoint of representation were religious groups (Mahajan 1998: 102): the assumption was that the political interests of individuals derived from their religious group membership. Although bearing a superficial resemblance to the democratic idea that those affected by decisions should participate in their making, representation was not necessarily about popular participation in decision-making here.[39] Separate electorates had hitherto operated in a colonial framework of circumscribed democracy, where political participation was limited and legislative bodies played a largely advisory role rather than that of law-making, acting as sounding boards for various sections of Indian opinion (Shaikh 1989: 74–5).

Third, accompanying claims that distinct social groups had to be represented in legislatures was the assumption that group representation implied the presence of members of the group in legislative assemblies. This claim pertained to the *identity* of representatives: advocates of separate electorates assumed that the representatives elected would also belong to the group concerned.[40] As Shaikh (1989) observes for an earlier period, the underlying notion here was that of descriptive representation, where representation was seen to require a correspondence between the characteristics of the representative and those she represented.[41] Contrasts

[39] The demand for separate electorates had historically been driven by a concern to ensure that significant communities could put forward their concerns before the authorities that made the law, rather than one of deepening democratic participation by either the electorate or representatives. On the undemocratic origins of separate electorates, see, for instance, McMillan 2005: 23–4, 66.

[40] Strictly speaking, the mechanism of separate electorates does not require that representatives elected belong to beneficiary groups, only that the electorate be composed of group members.

[41] On descriptive representation in general, see Pitkin 1967; Phillips 1995. Drawing upon Pitkin's notion, Shaikh 1989 has contrasted the Muslim League's conception of descriptive representation that underpinned claims for separate

between descriptive and substantive representation are overstated: descriptive representation can be a means of enhancing the substantive representation of a group's interests in policy-making (Phillips 1995; Kymlicka 1995; Mansbridge 2000), and was advocated as such by Muslim League proponents of separate electorates. It was argued that the latter were necessary because only members of a group could properly understand, and thus adequately represent the needs of their group, particularly in the prevailing climate of distrust between communities:

> ...as matters stand at the present moment in this country, it will be very difficult for...non-Muslims to realize the actual needs and requirements of the Muslim community...even if a non-Muslim does his best to do what he can for the Muslim community...he will find it impossible to do so because he is not in a position to realize, understand, and appreciate the actual needs of members of that particular community, so long as he does not belong to that community.... (B Pocker Sahib Bahadur, *CAD* V: 213)

Fourth, most pertinently for the mechanism of separate electorates, it was argued that if minorities were to be represented, electoral constituencies had to be organized so that they could choose their representatives. On its own, the proposed safeguard of reserved seats under joint electorates would be an empty protection, facilitating the election of candidates favoured by the majority community or the ruling party:[42]

> ...the mere fact that a particular member belongs to a particular community is not a guarantee that his views represent the views of that particular community. That particular community, if at all it has to be

---

electorates with conventional liberal-democratic notions of representation, where the focus is not on the personal attributes of representatives as on the activity of representation. A contrast between Muslim and liberal democratic notions of representation is problematic for several reasons, including, for my purposes here, the fact that descriptive representation is not inherently undemocratic, nor opposed to substantive representation.

[42] Dr Ambedkar had voiced similar concerns in his Note on Minorities of 1947, arguing that reserved seats with joint electorates under the Poona Pact had resulted in 'a complete disenfranchisement of the Scheduled Castes'. He recommended separate electorates as a 'fool-proof and knave-proof method...to ensure real representation to the Scheduled Castes' (Shiva Rao 1967 II: 108–9). See also S. Nagappa's speech in support of his proposal that candidates for reserved seats poll at least 35 per cent from the Scheduled Castes in order to be declared elected (*CAD* V: 259–61).

represented, has got to elect the right man from among the members of that community. (B. Pocker Sahib Bahadur, *CAD* V: 213)[43]

In other words, for minority representation, it was necessary, but not sufficient, that the representative be a member of the minority community: to be a 'true representative', one who genuinely represented the views of the community, she had to be chosen by the community. An electoral link between the representative and the community she was supposed to represent was necessary 'to ensure the fidelity of...group representatives to their constituencies' (Williams 1998: 6). Separate electorates were defended as being the best mechanism for securing this end. Again, it is important to note that in the Muslim League's case for separate electorates, descriptive representation was considered necessary, but *not sufficient* for group representation. The case for separate electorates for Muslims went beyond the descriptive view that representation could be achieved simply by virtue of belonging to the same group and reflected a concern if not with accountability, then with something akin to it.

The demand for separate electorates reflected dissatisfaction among minority representatives with the Constitution-makers' proposals for legislative quotas, as not affording minorities an adequate voice in the election of their representatives. The decisive rejection of separate electorates in 1947 meant that minority dissatisfaction with reserved seats increasingly found other institutional forms. The grounds advanced by minority representatives in support of these mechanisms also moved closer to the nationalist framework.[44] This process was exemplified in demands for proportional representation, which gathered pace in 1948–9.[45] Initially, proportional representation was chiefly advocated to supplement reserved seats, and as a means of giving members of minority

---

[43] See also Chaudhari Khaliquzzaman, *CAD* V: 221–2.

[44] In the few instances in which separate electorates were advocated in the later stages of the Assembly's deliberations, their advocates increasingly invoked concepts from the nationalist vocabulary. See, for instance, Mohammed Ismail Sahib's speech of 25 May 1949 (*CAD* VIII: 277–9).

[45] This is not to suggest that nationalist hostility constitutes the sole explanation for the shift away from separate electorates to proportional representation. As far as the Muslims were concerned, Partition had left them scattered all over the country, creating an electoral disadvantage in a first-past-the-post system (Chaube 1973: 173).

groups a greater voice in the election of their representatives. Legislative quotas under joint electorates were regarded as an inadequate safeguard because the electoral disadvantage of minorities in mixed constituencies under a first-past-the-post system could not ensure that the person elected was a 'true' or 'real' representative of the community. Over time, there was a subtle shift in the case for proportional representation. It was increasingly favoured as an alternative to reserved seats in legislatures for minorities and advocated as a means of enabling greater representation of minority *political opinion* than obtained in a first-past-the-post electoral system.[46] Representation of minority *groups* in the legislatures, while desired, was now to be a by-product of the representation of minority political opinion.[47]

Various forms of proportional representation were advocated by minority representatives, for elections to the Lower House and the formation of the Cabinet, at different stages of the framing of the Con-stitution.[48] The arguments invoked in the case for proportional

[46] Phillips has criticized Pitkin's discussion for ignoring the distinction between these two kinds of proportionality, between the mapping of people and of opinion (1995: 49).

[47] For instance, in 1949, Prof. K.T. Shah argued in support of proportional representation that it 'is not intended so much to perpetuate communal minorities, as to reflect the various shades of political opinion which after all, should be reflected in your Legislature, if you desire to be really a democratic government....' (*CAD* VII: 1238). In a similar vein, Kazi Syed Karimuddin defended proportional representation as an alternative not just to separate electorates, but also reserved seats as it was 'not based on religious grounds' and applied 'to all minorities, political, religious or communal....' (*CAD* VII: 1234–5). By contrast, in August 1947, Kazi Syed Karimuddin had argued in support of K.T.M. Ibrahim Bahadur's amendment that a representative secure 33 per cent votes from his community: 'Reservation of seats is given for this purpose that [a representative] should represent a particular community. He should have the sentiments of his community in view...If a minimum number of votes from his community is not fixed...[e]ven a man of straw, or even a false convert will be able to defeat a genuine or real member of the community...the Muslim minority should be allowed to have a minimum number of voters from the community which will satisfy their political aspirations' (*CAD* V: 265).

[48] Whereas the electoral system in India for direct elections is a single member winner-take-all constituencies, in the case of the President and the upper chambers of legislative assemblies, where elections are indirect, proportional representation by the single transferable vote obtains (see Austin 1966: 153).

representation were substantially similar in the different forms advocated during the career of the Assembly.[49] Proportional representation was defended as the democratic solution to the democratic vice of 'tyranny of the majority'. At least three related arguments can be distinguished. First, it was argued that a first-past-the-post electoral system resulted, in effect, in the disenfranchisement of a large portion of the electorate. Proportional representation was more democratic, as it enabled a more adequate realization of the right of every individual in a democracy to be represented. Z.H. Lari (Muslim League), the most consistent supporter of proportional representation during the career of the Constituent Assembly, argued in the debate on the draft constitution in November 1948:

> The twin principles of democracy are that everybody has a right of representation and the majority has the right to govern...This is the significance of adult franchise but the method adopted really amounts to the disenfranchisement of 49 per cent of the voters...It is better for us to adopt this principle [proportional representation] which is more progressive in instinct and which is really democratic.... (CAD VII: 299)[50]

In such disenfranchisement claims, as Phillips notes, the democratic right of every individual to participate in the choosing of government is construed as 'an equal chance of voting for a winning candidate' (1995: 107). The contention is that unequal 'prospects of success' of individuals with respect to influencing electoral outcomes violate the equal political rights of individuals (Beitz 1989). As scholars have noted, the theoretical basis of this move is problematic: the principle of political equality is compatible with a range of institutional mechanisms which distribute opportunities for political influence, as well as actual political

---

[49] On the different institutional forms of PR advocated in the Constituent Assembly debates, see Sridharan 2002.

[50] Speaking in January 1949, Kazi Syed Karimuddin paraphrased Lord Acton: 'The one pervading evil of democracy is the tyranny of the majority that succeeds in carrying elections...[Proportional representation]...is also profoundly democratic for it increases the influence of thousands of those who would have no voice in the Government and it brings men more near an equality by so contriving that no vote shall be wasted and that every voter shall contribute to bring into Parliament a member of his own choice and opinion' (CAD VII: 1233). Z.H. Lari argued on similar lines in May 1949—see CAD VIII: 283.

influence, differently.[51] Egalitarian procedures regularly produce unequal results: inequalities in outcomes do not necessarily prove that procedural equality has been violated.

What is significant for our purposes here is that in the disenfranchisement argument, the case for minority representation was sought to be located within the nationalist framework. To begin with, the nationalist conception of democracy was invoked, with its norms of popular rule and political equality and procedures of universal adult franchise. Proportional representation, it was argued, was more democratic as it gave *more* people a voice in determining electoral outcomes, and ensured that *each* person had some share in the election of representatives. Further, minority representation was defended not on grounds that distinct social groups had a right to be represented in the legislature, as had been the case in arguments for separate electorates, but rather on grounds of equal *individual* rights. Finally, the identification of equal political rights of individuals with an equal chance of voting for a winning candidate meant that proponents of minority representation could portray their central concern, which was with electoral *outcomes*, as a matter concerning democratic *procedures*, in particular, the one-person-one-vote principle that formed the keystone of nationalist conceptions of democracy. The claim of disenfranchisement evoked the idea that procedural equality of the kind favoured in nationalist opinion was compromised when each person's vote did not contribute towards the election of a successful candidate.

The disenfranchisement argument regarding the democratic merits of proportional representation was closely intertwined with a second argument. Here too, proportional representation was favoured because it meant that each person's vote would count towards the election of a successful candidate. This, however, was considered more democratic not because it enabled each individual elect a person of their choice, but because it would result in assemblies that were more representative of the diversity of political opinion in society.[52] Democracy implied that

[51] As Phillips points out, the requirements of these concerns may conflict, so, for instance, 'in order to give people equal power over outcomes we have to weight their preferences unequally' (1995: 36). For a critique of the claim that individuals voting for candidates who do not win are disenfranchised, see Barry 1979; on the indeterminacy of political equality, see Beitz 1989.

[52] This distinction between the disenfranchisement and representativeness arguments draws upon Phillips 1995.

the legislature mirror the different shades of political opinion in society in proportion to their strength. Z.H. Lari noted in the debate on the minority report in May 1949:

> ...Those who have read the writings of Mill must have been impressed by his advocacy of the fundamental principle of democracy, that every political opinion must be represented in an assembly in proportion to its strength in the country...The entire thirty crores of people cannot come and deliberate here. Therefore, there is the device of sending representatives. But if you adopt a method by which only 51 percent of the people alone are represented in the legislature, it ceases to be the mirror of the nation...the question is, does the method of representation adopted by this House...implement the principles of democracy? (*CAD* VIII: 283)[53]

How, exactly, was an assembly that was more representative of the population, more democratic? One thought here was that representative democracy should be a replica of direct democracy, with the legislature reproducing 'the array of views held in the population at large' (Beitz 1989: 139).[54] Moreover, representativeness implied that majority and minority political opinion would be represented in proportion to their strength. In political speeches, the representativeness claim was thought to follow directly from the disenfranchisement argument. If the electoral system enabled a better realization of the individual's right to be represented, it was held, legislatures would be more representative of political opinion and thereby more democratic. However, while the principle of political equality was invoked in both the disenfranchisement and representativeness arguments, its implications in the two cases were distinct. As Phillips notes, political equality in the disenfranchisement argument implied that majority and minority preferences should have an *equal* chance of being adopted, and in the representativeness argument, that majority and minority preferences should be represented in proportion to their *strength* (1995: 107).

[53] See also D.H. Chandrasekharaiya's speech advocating proportional representation by single transferable vote for the election of Scheduled Caste representatives, *CAD* V: 274–5.

[54] Beitz criticizes this analogy between representative and direct democracy as obscuring the transition involved from 'small working assemblies' to legislatures of 'large, diverse populations' (1989: 139).

Importantly, like the disenfranchisement argument for proportional representation, the representativeness argument defended minority representation in terms of more individualist and proceduralist conceptions of democracy and representation. In contrast, with the case for separate electorates, these arguments did not assume that there were permanent and essential differences between religious groups; that the political choices of individuals derived from their religious group membership; that representatives had to belong to the group concerned; or that constituencies had to be defined along lines of religion. While desirable, the legislative representation of religious and other minorities was to be achieved by focusing not so much on the social identity of representatives, but on the procedure for electing them, a position much more congenial to nationalist opinion.

A third type of democratic argument held that proportional representation would mitigate the propensity within a parliamentary system for the concentration of power in one party. In a parliamentary democracy under a first-past-the post electoral system, it was argued, legislative majorities tended to act in disregard of opposing political views. By enabling the representation of minority opinion, proportional representation would save the parliamentary system from the undemocratic dispositions immanent within it, of disregarding dissenting views and the rights of individuals and minorities. Mahboob Ali Baig Sahib Bahadur, a prominent advocate of this line of argument in favour of proportional representation in the Constituent Assembly, argued in January 1949:

> ... [This] will enable peoples and parties in the country, who hold views different from the majority party, to be represented in the legislatures... Can you think of any parliamentary democracy where there is no opposition? Unless there is Opposition...the danger of its turning itself into a Fascist body is there.... (CAD VII: 1245)[55]

The mechanisms whereby the legislative representation of minority political opinion was thought to restrain legislative majorities were multiple—through a stronger Opposition, greater likelihood of coalition

[55] In the debate on the draft constitution in January 1949, Kazi Syed Karimuddin urged: '...where there is a heterogenous population, it is very necessary that we should have Coalition Governments. It will not be a bad thing that various representative elements should have to be consulted in forming a Ministry...' (CAD VII: 1234).

governments, necessitating more consultation with minority political opinion in government and policy formation.[56] What is conventionally regarded as a failing of proportional representation—government weakness and the susceptibility of policy-making to pressures from small political groups—was portrayed here as a strength. Again, it is significant that minority representation was defended here on democratic grounds, with democracy construed here, in line with nationalist opinion, in terms of the responsiveness of governments to popular opinion.

While I have focused so far on democratic arguments, the case for proportional representation pressed during 1948–9 also invoked other concepts from the nationalist vocabulary. It was argued that proportional representation would facilitate the representation of minorities without giving explicit recognition to religious and other ascriptive identities in the political realm. As such, unlike mechanisms such as separate electorates or reserved seats for religious minorities, proportional representation was consistent with secular principles: 'Without any spirit of communalism, representatives of political and communal minorities can be elected' (Kazi Syed Karimuddin, CAD VII: 1235).[57] As in nationalist opinion, conceptions of secularism and democracy were closely inter-linked. The recognition of majorities and minorities along religious lines in the political domain was seen to offend both secularism and democracy. Speaking in the debate on the draft constitution in January 1949, Prof. K.T. Shah argued:

> The possibility of securing varying shades of political opinion will give a chance, not only for minorities to be duly reflected in the Legislature of the country, but also for them to assert themselves, and to convert themselves into a majority, which, perhaps, those who might confuse Proportional Representation as synonymous with the possibility of communal representation would do well to consider. (CAD VII: 1238)

Proportional representation was also defended as strengthening national unity. A Parliament that was more representative of the different shades of opinion in society, it was suggested, would generate a stronger

---

[56] Several Muslim representatives put forward proposals that there be constitutional recognition of the Opposition, arguing that this was necessary as in the prevailing climate of opinion, criticizing the Congress party was perceived as tantamount to sedition. See, for instance, Z.H. Lari, CAD VIII: 158–61.

[57] See also Sardar Hukam Singh, CAD VII: 1250.

sense of belonging to the nation among minorities, and thereby enhance the stability of the state. In the face of the withdrawal of reserved seats for religious minorities in May 1949, Z.H. Lari urged:

> I concede that a minority must aspire to be an integral part of the nation...The minority must claim only such safeguards as are consistent with this aspiration...the adoption of this method is in the national interest and that for three reasons. 1. Parliament must be the mirror of the national mind: otherwise it will not have the respect which is due to it. 2. ...where national interest is preserved or is not jeopardized or imperilled it is necessary to consult minority opinion. If you do that it necessarily leads to consolidation of the State... 3. ...If you have proportional representation you will have an opposition in the House. You will have a party not on a communal basis but based on large national issues. (CAD VIII: 282–3, 286)

Finally, it was suggested that by encouraging the formation of political coalitions that cut across religious and other divisions, proportional representation would strengthen bonds of trust across communities and promote social cohesion.[58]

The case for proportional representation pressed in 1948–9 thus invoked the key concepts of the nationalist vocabulary, which were interpreted in ways that were similar to or compatible with nationalist conceptions. Support for proportional representation increased over time between 1947 and 1949 among minority representatives. Both the fact that proportional representation became the favoured institutional mechanism for minority representation, as well as the grounds on which it was defended, were indicative of how minority claims were being reformulated in forms more acceptable to nationalist opinion and in terms drawn from the nationalist vocabulary.[59]

[58] Speaking in the debate on the draft constitution in January 1949, Mohammed Ismail Sahib pleaded: 'It will make each group seek the franchise of other people. Therefore it would really work for unity rather than disunity' (CAD VII: 1224). For arguments supporting proportional representation as a mode of election for the President and the Council of States, and opposing proposals that the Cabinet be constituted by proportional representation, see, for instance, Dr B.R. Ambedkar, CAD VII: 1017, 1157–8.

[59] The withdrawal of reserved seats for religious minorities was supported by several minority representatives. Those who spoke in its favour in the debate in May 1949 included Begum Aizaz Rasul, Naziruddin Ahmed, Tajamul Husain, Col B.H. Zaidi, Muhammed Ismail Khan, H.C. Mookerjee,

Group Claims for Preference in Government Employment

Thus far, my account of the adaptation of group claims to nationalist discourse has focussed on demands for political representation for religious minorities. A similar pattern can be observed in the claims for 'backward class' preference in government jobs, which also invoked concepts from the nationalist vocabulary. While the latter were often construed in ways that were distinct from dominant nationalist opinion, as secularism, justice, national unity, and development came to be increasingly employed in group claims, a shared legitimating vocabulary was fashioned.

For instance, it was declared that special treatment in the case of Untouchables and Adivasis was not a concession but a requirement of justice, compensation that these groups were owed for a history of oppression. A group fairness type of justice argument, this was interwoven with the idiom of atonement found also in nationalist discourse. Speaking in August 1949, H.J. Khandekar asserted: '...reservation is being provided for us as a compensation for the atrocities we have suffered, and therefore I do not deem this provision as any great favour to us' (CAD IX: 666). Tribal representative Jaipal Singh declared: 'I do not come here to beg. It is for the majority community to atone for their sins of the last six thousand years' (CAD IX: 651). Unlike in Congress discourse, there was a greater emphasis here on compensation as a *right* of the historically oppressed rather than an act of generosity of upper castes. Yet, it is important to note that reservation was demanded here on justice grounds, and not as a matter of balancing the numbers of different social groups in the public services.

Backward Class representatives also defended preference in government jobs in consequentialist arguments, on justice grounds, for reducing socio-economic inequalities between groups, as well as in terms of the goals of national unity and development.[60] Secularism too was invoked:

Jerome D'Souza, R.K. Sidhwa, Frank Antony, and Sardar Sochet Singh. Some minority representatives who spoke against reserved seats endorsed proposals for proportional representation, including Sardar Hukam Singh and Maulana Hasrat Mohani.

[60] Prof. Yashwant Rai argued for representatives of the Scheduled Castes on public service commissions in August 1949: '...to give equal status to those communities which are backward and depressed and on whom injustice has been perpetrated for thousands of years and if you want to establish Indian unity, so

...the case of the Scheduled Caste is not pleaded on a matter of communalism...[but]...because they have been left in the lurch and due to their lack of social, economic and educational advancement ...it is not the object of any of the leaders of the Harijan community to perpetuate the communal bogey in this land for ever, but so long as they remain so backward in getting admission into the services, it is highly necessary that they must be given some protection. (V.I. Muniswamy Pillay, *CAD* VII: 689)

Reservations for the 'backward classes' were not 'communal' unlike those for religious minorities, it was asserted, implying that these did not have to do with the recognition of religion, or of group identity as such.

To be sure, strong advocates of 'backward class' reservations including Untouchable and Tribal representatives, also differed with nationalist opinion. Justice considerations of an individual fairness type were invoked in *support* of special treatment. One set of arguments pertained to the selection process. It was argued that the presence of members of the 'backward classes' in recruitment panels for the public services was necessary in order to prevent discrimination against candidates from these groups. Members of the upper castes dominated these services and their 'communal' consciousness meant that candidates from lower caste backgrounds were not treated fairly at the time of selection.[61] Nevertheless, it should be noted that the relevance of social identity for recruitment to the public service was defended here on grounds congenial to nationalist opinion, those of non-discrimination and fair treatment of individuals.[62]

---

that the country may progress....' (*CAD* IX: 619). See also Dr P.S. Deshmukh, *CAD* IX: 602–4.

[61] Yashwant Rai asked for '...representatives of the Harijans on the Federal Public Service Commission...so that they may watch over the interests of the candidates who apply...and prevent any injustice being done to Harijans' (*CAD* IX: 619). H.J. Khandekar noted that when Scheduled Caste candidates applied for '...certain Government posts, they are not selected for the posts because the people who select the candidates do not belong to that community or section... the scheduled caste people though they are well qualified do not get opportunity and fair treatment in the services' (*CAD* VII: 691).

[62] In the Advisory Committee, Dr Ambedkar argued for equality of opportunity *within* minority groups: 'Even among the members of the same minority there may be complaints of partiality, of provincial favouritism or personal favouritism ...Even among the minorities, we want equality of opportunity' (Shiva Rao

Another individual fairness consideration was that the existing criteria of selection for the public services were biased in favor of the upper castes. Criteria employed to select candidates it was argued, such as fluency in English or the importance attached to interview performance, where the candidate's deportment and grooming were important, placed members of 'backward classes' who were mostly rural and non-English speaking, at a disadvantage. Speaking in August 1949, S. Nagappa held:

> The questions are so silly that I think sometimes even the questioner does not know what the answer is. For instance, they may ask: "what is the distance between the sun and the moon?...Oh, you do not know how to tie a tie or wear a collar..." These are the things on which our candidates are examined...I would prefer to have a curriculum prescribed and text-books laid down for these people. There should not only be an oral examination, but some sort of written examination also. (CAD IX: 620)

Here, discrimination consisted not so much in the intent of selectors as in the design of selection procedures. While couched as an attack on merit, this argument implied that many of the criteria attached formally and informally to selection where 'backward class' candidates found themselves at a disadvantage, were not strictly speaking relevant to the job. Some of these were the result of the long monopoly that the upper castes had enjoyed over government employment that had meant, as Miller notes in a different context, that 'norms specific to those groups get attached to the jobs' (1999:193). While distinct from nationalist arguments, this consideration in support of special treatment relied upon notions of justice as non-discrimination between individuals that characterized nationalist opinion, and the view that the merit of individuals, rather

---

1967 II: 225). Speaking in 1948, Dr Ambedkar also held quotas to be an exception to the norm of equality of opportunity, which therefore had to be limited in scope:

> ...[if] we were to concede in full the demand of those communities who have not been so far employed in the public services to the fullest extent... we shall be completely destroying the first proposition upon which we are all agreed, namely, that there shall be equality of opportunity...if the reservation is to be consistent with [equality of opportunity] it must be confined to a minority of seats...unless you use some such qualifying phrase as 'backward' the exception made in favour of reservation will ultimately eat up the rule altogether. (CAD VII: 701–2)

than the attributes of the social groups to which they belonged, ought to determine selection.

Individual fairness considerations were also invoked in favour of preferential treatment in the context of educational inequalities, that is, pre-job discrimination. Dr P.S. Deshmukh, a prominent spokesman for the Other Backward Classes in the Constituent Assembly, argued in August 1949:

> Even today more than 85 percent of the people of India are without the facilities for education as they live in the villages, and we are asking these people to compete with people who have these facilities near by... It is like having a one mile race between two persons one of whom had already gone ahead half-a-mile, and another who had yet to start. That is quite unequal, unfair and unjust. (*CAD* IX: 601)[63]

The claim here was that formal equality of opportunity was unfair to members of 'backward classes' because of the cumulative and continuing effects of historical discrimination. Formal equality of opportunity was criticized from the standpoint of its own underlying norm of individual fairness. Unlike in nationalist arguments, where preferential treatment for the 'backward classes' was seen as detracting from equality of opportunity, albeit facilitating desired goals, here it was portrayed as a requirement of equality of opportunity. The underlying appeal was to the notion of *fair* equality of opportunity. In Rawls' classic formulation, fair equality of opportunity requires 'not merely that public offices and social positions be open in the formal sense, but that all should have a fair chance to attain them...' (2001: 43–4). It demands correction for disadvantages that derive from disparities in the social backgrounds of individuals, and therefore can justify unequal access to certain goods (Rosenfeld 1991: 28–9; Goldman 1979). As Galanter suggests, this argument for preferential treatment is compatible with the principle of merit, namely that individuals from different social backgrounds with similar capacities ought to have similar chances of employment. It recognizes the entitlement of members of 'backward classes' to special treatment as individuals, with their communal membership serving only to identify them as deserving beneficiaries; the entitlement does not vest in a communal group (Galanter 1984: 553). In other words, this line of

---

[63] See also H.J. Khandekar, *CAD* IX: 668.

argument too was compatible with the nationalist notions of justice as non-discrimination between individuals.

Finally, the arguments advanced by Untouchable representatives and other strong supporters of job reservations differed from nationalist arguments in their emphasis on the importance of positions in state power for the affirmation of equal status. S. Nagappa acclaimed the Objectives Resolution as giving 'us a scope and a chance and an opportunity to be equal, to *feel like equals...*' (CAD II: 284). The presence of Untouchables in state employment was desired as a marker of equal standing: government jobs were viewed in terms of their symbolic aspects, as conferring power and prestige through association, rather than material effects alone. Such claims reflected a concern not just with socio-economic advancement, but also with recognition of equal status.[64] Equal opportunity was construed in more demanding ways than in nationalist opinion, as requiring not just equal rights, but also state affirmation of the equal *worth* of members of historically denigrated groups. Nevertheless, here too, the underlying appeal was to the democratic ideal of political equality of all individuals espoused by nationalists: special treatment for the 'backward' was defended as an extension of the ideal of equal citizenship for all individuals.

The inclusion of groups apart from the Untouchables and Adivasis who were to be included within the category 'backward classes' was a subject of contention during the Constituent Assembly debates. Most Untouchable representatives, favoured a narrow interpretation of the term 'backward' that would render the Scheduled groups as the sole beneficiaries of quotas, whereas other lower caste representatives argued for a broader interpretation (see CAD VII: 686–92).[65]

---

[64] Chandrika Ram argued for quotas in the legislatures and services for OBCs: 'If a community, howsoever large it may be within a society and whatever pre-eminence it may have reached in the matter of its culture, does not possess political rights and has also no political representation...[it cannot] have the same status as the other communities in the eyes of the State' (CAD VII: 688).

[65] Quotas in the public services for OBCs were defended on grounds that their social and economic condition was similar to the Scheduled Castes, and that therefore, such provisions should logically be extended to Other Backward Classes. Guptanath Singh pressed for job preferences for agricultural, pastoral, and artisan communities: '...there are other sections in the country, whose

In addition to the arguments found in dominant nationalist opinion thus, those pressing for reservations for the 'backward classes' elaborated justice considerations of an individual fairness type well as democratic notions of equal worth of all citizens in support of special treatment. Nevertheless, as claims for preference in public appointments adapted or adopted nationalist premises, a *common* vocabulary was created, whose key concepts were deployed, and contested, among participants. Secularism, social justice, democracy, national unity, and development became the new currency of exchange in political debate.

In the initial deliberations of the Assembly, religious minority claims had focused on political representation policies. Relatively few arguments were advanced for special treatment in government employment. As the deliberations progressed, however, and the trend to limit special representation for religious minorities became evident, representatives increasingly turned their attention to job reservations. Several claims invoked ideals of justice as non-discrimination between individuals and secularism in support of preferential treatment in state jobs. Thus, for instance, statutory reservation for minorities was advocated to address recent discrimination against Muslim candidates in recruitment to the public services.[66] In the debate on the draft constitution in November 1948, Aziz Ahmad Khan urged:

> ...only those people require protection who have misgivings that...their rights will not be preserved...if as a matter of fact we are shaping this country in such a manner that there should not remain any difference, then it is necessary that there should not be any impediment that might create a feeling in the mind of an individual who has educational and citizenship qualifications that his claims are being ignored....I do not say that it is necessary to recruit 20 per cent Sikhs, 15 per cent Christians or 15 per cent Muslims in the public services of our country. (*CAD* VII: 682).

---

conditions are not better than the conditions of these friends, the Harijans and the Adibasis...' (*CAD* X: 240).

[66] In November 1948, Z.H. Lari pleaded: '...Take away the reservation from the Legislature and for God's sake give us reservation in the Services...If you peruse the results of the last twelve months there [United Provinces], hardly five percent of the Muslims have been taken in the services' (*CAD* VII: 300). On declining Muslim proportions in government jobs in the late 1940s, see Wilkinson 2005: 109–12.

Here, reservations in government employment were demanded not on grounds that groups were entitled to a due share of public posts, but rather on individualist, non-discrimination grounds that were consistent with the nationalist vocabulary.

Secularism was prominently invoked in arguments for the extension of preferences to 'backward' Sikhs. Speaking in August 1949, Sardar Hukam Singh queried: 'If reservation was denied to religious minorities and the Scheduled Castes were to get it for their backwardness then is there any justification to deny this concession to similar backward sections suffering from identical disabilities simply because they profess the Sikh religion? Would this be secularism?'(CAD X: 235).[67] Again, the appeal was to a key ideal from the nationalist vocabulary.

The most significant aspect of the shift in minority claims, however, was the emphasis now placed on 'backwardness'. It was argued that the religious minorities comprised people who were 'backward' and hence in need of reservations. Mohamed Ismail Sahib noted in November 1948:

> ...there are backward people among the non-majority people as well. The Christians are backward. As a matter of fact, they are not adequately represented in the services of the provinces. So also the Muslims, and also the Scheduled Castes.... (CAD VII: 693)

At the start of the Constituent Assembly debates, we saw that Untouchable advocates of special representation sought to establish that they were minorities. By the end of the Assembly's deliberations, religious minority representatives seeking reservations to establish that their members were 'backward'.

In the case of religious minorities, however, unlike that of the Scheduled Castes, the accommodation effected with the nationalist framework was partial. Often, the under-representation of a group in government employment was presented as sufficient to establish

[67] See also Sardar Sochet Singh, CAD VIII: 339–40. In deliberations on 14 October 1949, Sikh representatives made bitter speeches accusing the Congress of reneging on its commitments to minorities in withdrawing provisions for reserved seats in services and Minority Officers. See the statements of Sardar Bhopinder Singh Mann and Sardar Hukam Singh, CAD X: 253–60. In response, K.M. Munshi insisted that Sikh representatives had agreed to drop all other demands for special provisions in return for four groups within the Sikh community being included in the list of Scheduled Castes in the Punjab (CAD X: 261–2).

'backwardness'. Also, religious minority claims continued to invoke the earlier vocabulary of groups having a right to a 'due share' of representation that was *independent* of 'backwardness'. In the debate on the Draft Constitution in November 1948, Mohamed Ismail Sahib argued: 'When people feel that they are not adequately represented, they rightly feel that they must have due representation and then such a demand comes up...'(CAD VII: 693). The government should be able 'from time to time to make adequate arrangements in case *the claims of any particular group* are overlooked in public services' (Aziz Ahmad Khan, *CAD* VII: 682).[68] It was ambiguous in such speeches whether the 'claims' of minority groups appealed only to non-discrimination between individuals from minority and majority backgrounds, or also to the colonial notion that religious groups as such were entitled to a share of public posts, that we have seen was rejected by nationalists. Nationalists had not fashioned resources for preferential treatment on any grounds other than socio-economic disadvantage, and religious minorities were not regarded as 'backward sections' in this period. As such, religious minority claims had greater difficulty in accommodating themselves to the nationalist framework and continued to rely on the colonial rationale for group preference to a greater extent than those of the caste and tribal minorities.

Cultural Rights

Adaptation to the nationalist vocabulary can also be discerned in the case of claims to religious and cultural rights. In the debate on the civil code provision in November 1948, several Muslim League representatives put forward proposals to make religious personal laws immune from state interference. These were commonly defended, often by religious minded proponents of Muslim law, in terms of the nationalist ideal of secularism. A secular order, it was argued, was one in which citizens had *full* religious freedom, including the freedom to live by the tenets of their religious family laws. A secular state was excluded from the domain of religion and lacked the authority to intervene in matters regulated by it (see *CAD*

---

[68] Sardar Hukam Singh held in October 1949: '...if for the smooth working of the administration and for creating cordial relations between the different communities, the state decides on some adjustment in the services, then there should be no bar under the Constitution.....' (*CAD* X: 236).

VII: 540–6 and Chapter 3 above). Such arguments drew upon nationalist conceptions of secularism, but construed their implications differently. The separation of state and religion implied the exclusion not so much of *religion* from politics as of the *state* from the realm of religion; it connoted absolute group rights to religious freedom.

The conception of secularism implicit in the case in favour of Muslim personal law was more group-centred than dominant nationalist articulations. Mohamed Ismail argued:

> ...the right of a *group* or community of people to follow and adhere to its own personal law...is part of the way of life of those people who are following such laws; it is part of their religion and...of their culture. This secular State which we are trying to create should not do anything to interfere with the way of life and religion of the people. (*CAD* VII: 540)

State intervention in personal law was opposed here for violating the distinctive religious practices of a group, and the freedom of individuals to follow the practices of the group to which they belonged, rather than to choose in matters of religion. As noted by its nationalist opponents, there was no recognition that constitutional entrenchment of religious personal laws might restrict the freedom of individuals who might desire changes in these laws in the future, or not wish to be governed by a religious law at all.[69]

Another argument put forward by proponents of Muslim personal law cited grounds of liberty. Mohamed Ismail Sahib argued: 'The personal law of one community does not affect the other community...the freedom of following the personal law ought to be given to each community and it will not interfere with the rights of any other community' (*CAD* VII: 723). This was redolent of the familiar liberal principle that a liberty should not be curtailed unless it caused harm to others, or infringed anyone else's rights and pursuit of liberties. Again, as in the case of secularism, liberty was construed here in ways that were distinct from dominant nationalist opinion and less liberal. The harm in question was not to individuals, and the implicit contention was that the only relevant consideration for restricting religious freedom was the infringement of similar rights and

---

[69] M. Ananthasayanam Ayyangar, for instance, felt: '...if we make a provision here that the personal law shall not be interfered with, there will not be any right to the members of that community itself to modify that law' (*CAD* VII: 778).

liberties of other *communities*. Nevertheless, what is significant for our purposes here is that provisions of special concern for minorities were defended in a language of secularism and liberal freedoms characteristic of nationalist opinion of this period.

Claims for granting personal law immunity from state interference were rejected by the Constitution-makers, among others, on grounds that this would conflict with the state's obligation to enforce fundamental rights to equality and non-discrimination.[70] The reform of Hindu religious law loomed large on the political agenda in this period, particularly with regard to Untouchables and women.[71] However, the identification of secularism with absolute rights to religious freedom, was to remain in political discourse on group rights, and would become the bone of contention in the Shah Bano case.

Secularism was not always construed as precluding a role for the state in the domain of religion in minority claims. Madras Muslim League leader Mohamed Ismail pressed for religious instruction in educational institutions wholly funded by the state:

> ...It will be going against the spirit of the secular state if the state compels the students or pupils to study a religion to which they do not belong. But, if the pupils or their parents want that religious instruction should be given in the institutions in their own religion, then, it is not going against the secular nature of the State and the State will not be violating the neutrality which it has avowedly taken in the matter of religion. (*CAD* VII: 867)

This was, however, a lone voice: most minority representatives argued, in consonance with dominant nationalist opinion, that such instruction would be in contravention of the secular commitments of the state and

---

[70] Dr B.R. Ambedkar rejected proposals for the constitutional protection of religious personal law thus: 'The religious conceptions in this country are so vast that they cover every aspect of life, from birth to death. There is nothing which is not religion and if personal law is to be saved...in social matters we will come to a standstill...our social system...is...so full of inequalities, discriminations, and other things which conflict with our fundamental rights...It is, therefore quite impossible for anybody to conceive that the personal law shall be excluded from the jurisdiction of the State' (*CAD* VII: 781).

[71] K.M. Munshi argued: '[Many Hindus] feel that the personal law of inheritance, succession, etc. is really a part of their religion. If that were so, you can never give, for instance, equality to women. But you have already passed a Fundamental Right to that effect...' (*CAD* VII: 548).

should be left to the communities concerned (see the debate in December 1948, in particular, Kazi Syed Karimuddin, *CAD* VII: 880; Sardar Bhopinder Singh Man, *CAD* VII: 871 in December 1948).

Advocates of religious and cultural rights also sought accommodation with nationalist opinion in other ways. In keeping with nationalist opinion, it was argued that fundamental rights guaranteeing religious and cultural freedom for individuals and groups were sufficient; political safeguards were not necessary; and that political homogeneity was desirable. Jerome D'Souza's speech applauding the judicial protection offered to fundamental rights in December 1948 echoed nationalist sentiment on how minority claims ought to be accommodated in independent India:

> ....the desire of our country and of our leadership is to work for the political homogeneity of this vast country. Unfortunately that political homogeneity was threatened and to some extent destroyed by the need to give political safeguards to minorities. But remember those safeguards were asked...for the sake of religious and cultural and individual rights and not merely for the sake of political privileges or any emoluments which might come from them...[A]s long as these cultural and personal rights are safeguarded, we do not need any other political safeguard...the full and logical implications of what we are doing now is that a time should come when even the economic and other assistance to be given should not be based on the claims of classes as a whole but should be based upon the claims of the individual. (*CAD* VII: 939–40)

By the close of the deliberations of the Constituent Assembly, both opponents of group rights and its proponents contested a shared set of legitimating terms. Opponents argued that special provisions for minority groups were inappropriate in a secular democracy and would undermine national unity. Defenders of such policies in turn claimed that in a secular democracy, the rights of minorities had to be protected, and doing so would enhance national unity. At one level, the increasing adaptation of minority claims to the nationalist vocabulary simply reflected the power shift in this period—the reins of state power had passed from colonial to Congress hands, and the contours of political argument were recast accordingly, to better address the new wielders of power. At another level, the fact that the legitimating vocabulary of the polity came to be transformed suggests that the power shift in the transition from colonial rule took the form not simply of nationalist dominance, but of *hegemony*, not just numerical superiority, but the construction of a new ideological consensus.[72]

Conclusion

To recapitulate, while group preference in general was problematic in the liberal nationalist vocabulary, special treatment for cultural protection suffered from a greater justificatory deficit than that for rectifying socio-economic disadvantage. Its illegitimacy from the standpoint of nation-building was reinforced by liberal concerns for secularism and individual rights. Group-differentiated rights were legitimate only as temporary measures for rectifying 'backwardness', a condition that was associated with lower castes and tribals but not religious minorities in this period. That legislative and employment quotas for religious minorities were withdrawn, and cultural rights and reservations for 'backward classes' retained, but in a weak multicultural form is not surprising. To be sure, the long event of Partition, its impact on minority parties and numbers, the preferences of important personalities such as Nehru, Patel, and Ambedkar, favoured these policy outcomes. Nevertheless, it is significant that the institutional forms of group rights in the Indian Constitution were so consistent with the normative structure of the nationalist vocabulary.

There is, however, more to the story. Our analysis showed that constitution-making marked a shift not just in policies of minority rights, but also the parameters of political debate. As the deliberations of the Constituent Assembly unfolded, minority claims increasingly came to be aligned closer to the nationalist vocabulary, with secularism, democracy, social justice, national unity, and development invoked in claims for special treatment. These were often construed in ways that were different from, and more demanding than in nationalist opinion. Nevertheless, their increasing deployment meant that the nationalist vocabulary came to be translated during the Assembly's deliberations into a common framework for political debate on group rights. As such, both the institutional

[72] As discussed in Chapter 1 above, the usage of hegemony in this study is distinct from the Gramscian notion of the domination of one class or group over others (see Gramsci 1971: 5–12, 80, 161, 170, 263), and also from Laclau and Mouffe's (1985: 139) conceptualization of hegemony.

mechanisms of special treatment, and their normative basis, came to be recast during the Constituent Assembly debates in line with nationalist opinion. The Congress was not simply dominant, it was also hegemonic, transforming the conventions of political debate, a dimension of power that is missing from accounts of policy change.

The recasting of the framework of group rights at constitution-making has had important long-term, systemic implications. Its effects can be observed in the fact that all substantial extensions of quotas have been to groups designated as 'backward', as well as in the shape of group rights claims, where 'backward' has become the inclusive term to denote a group's eligibility to special treatment, just as 'minority' was in the late colonial period. The proliferation of claims for special treatment on 'backwardness' grounds indicates the relative strength of the weak multicultural position in the case of affirmative action for 'backward classes'. Since the Constitution was promulgated, the cultural rights of minorities have been augmented through legislative and judicial enactment (Mahajan 1998: 98). While their justificatory deficit has not prevented the extension of special treatment for religious minorities in cultural and religious matters, it has meant that state assistance for minority cultures has been seen as an act of generosity towards minorities, a discretionary concession rather than a requirement of rights to cultural protection. The influential critique by Hindu nationalists of 'minority appeasement'—that state assistance for minority cultures constitutes unjust favoritism, motivated by electoral considerations with little principled basis—is a symptom of the justificatory deficit of the weak multicultural position in the case of religious minorities.

As an explanation of the institutional and discursive outcomes with respect to group rights during constitution-making, our argument is necessarily incomplete. Ideas alone of course do not tell us all we need for explanation; like interests, ideational factors might only indicate broad tendencies, not whether these will be realized in any given instance. Nevertheless, as we have seen, ideas matter for accounts of policy change, both as *conditions* that facilitate particular institutional outcomes, and as discursive *outcomes* that accompany policy change.[73]

---

[73] An adequate appreciation of the explanatory power of ideas requires us to consider their role both as causes and as outcomes of policy change (see, for instance, Horowitz 1989).

In terms of the justification of group rights in a liberal democratic framework, Indian nationalism's long historical engagement with minority claims seems to have produced relatively modest conceptual innovation. True, unlike many of their peers, Indian nationalists espoused secularism and democracy that even in their dominant liberal individualist conceptions offered some protections to minorities. Group rights to cultural autonomy were admitted. And in recognizing that injustices were patterned along group lines, positing social justice as a goal and linking it to national unity, a basis was created for group-differentiated rights in the form of affirmative action. As scholars have noted, Indian Constitution-makers were in advance of liberal political theory and practice of their time, elaborating an egalitarian liberal framework which gave a substantive content to the notion of individual equality, emphasizing not just values of individual rights, but also social justice (Mahajan 1998: 119; Bhargava 2000: 36). The ideal, nevertheless, remained individualist egalitarian: a case for state support for the preservation of distinct minority cultures was not articulated in dominant nationalist opinion. Conceptions of secularism and justice sought ultimately to transcend ethnicity; conceptions of democracy remained largely majoritarian; conceptions of national identity and development accorded little recognition to minority cultures (or, indeed, cultural identity as such). To read this solely in terms of bad faith or prejudice against minorities would be too narrow: both its liberal and national aspects weighed against the elaboration of multicultural arguments within Indian nationalism; ardent liberals were among the staunchest opponents of minority rights. In this, Indian liberals were similar to their counterparts elsewhere: post-Second World War liberalism was individualist and colour-blind (Kymlicka 1989). This, together with the context of Partition, was not conducive to the elaboration of strong multicultural arguments.

In sharp contrast to their containment during constitution-making, the late 1980s heralded an expansion of group-differentiated rights. It is to an appraisal of arguments over differential treatment in this very different era that we now turn.

Part Two

The Moment of Crisis

Preferential Policies—1986, 1990

The late 1980s saw key changes in policies of group rights. The Muslim Women (Protection of Rights on Divorce) Act, 1986, exempted Muslims from the provisions of the Criminal Procedure Code. In 1990, the government announced the extension of quotas in government employment to a large new group of Other Backward Classes (OBCs), as per the recommendations of the Mandal Commission Report (1980). The Shah Bano and Mandal debates as these are better known, brought issues of group-differentiated rights to the national spotlight. Conventionally, these are regarded as part of separate trajectories pertaining to minority rights and reservations for 'backward classes'. When viewed alongside each other, as part of the career of group rights in India, Shah Bano and Mandal suggest that the late 1980s marked a moment of crisis in the constitutional resolution of differential treatment. Changes had, of course, been effected to group rights in the intervening period: religious rights of communities and educational rights of minorities had been augmented through legislative amendment and judicial interpretation (Parashar 1992; Mahajan 1998: 98–101; Agnes 2005); educational and employment quotas for 'backward classes' had expanded substantially in several states (Galanter 1984; Jaffrelot 2003). In the late 1980s, however, the cumulative effect of these piece-meal adjustments was registered as a crisis and a 'paradigm shift' in the national framework of group rights. The constitutional resolution came to be decisively reopened, and group-differentiated rights have since steadily expanded.

Part I argued that the recasting of the policy framework on group rights during constitution-making was accompanied by discursive changes, specifically a shift in the normative vocabulary of politics.

Part II investigates whether this holds in the case of group rights debates of the late 1980s. Did the normative vocabulary of secularism, democracy, social justice, national unity, and development continue to frame political debate? If so, were there changes in the dominant *meanings* of these concepts? And finally, can discursive continuity and shift shed new light on policy changes in group rights and the larger political shift of this period? The late 1980s marked a key turning point in the history of post-Independence India (Menon and Nigam 2007). With the 1989 election, the dominance of the Congress party decisively ended and an era of coalition governments began (Yadav 1999). While it had lost power at the state level previously, after 1989, the Congress had to cede power to other political actors at the national level, notably the Hindu nationalist Bharatiya Janata Party (BJP) and lower caste-based parties. More broadly, the period since the 1980s is associated with the rise of identity politics of caste and religion in India. In existing literature, the momentous changes in the political landscape are thought to represent a comparably radical break at the discursive level. These are characterized variously as the collapse of the Nehruvian consensus (Menon and Nigam 2007); a radical redefinition of the idea of group equality (Mahajan 1998: 152–4); the ascendance of India's vernacular traditions over a liberal democratic vocabulary (Yadav 1999: 2397); a critique of the 'normative values of modernity' (Chatterjee 2004: 41; Larson 1993: 74).

Part II offers a critical appraisal of such assessments. It shows that while there were discursive changes, their extent and forms have been largely misdiagnosed. Through a careful analytical reconstruction of arguments in the parliamentary debates on Shah Bano and Mandal, I argue that while significant shifts did occur in the normative vocabulary of political discourse, there were also substantial continuities. The Nehruvian consensus came to be renegotiated but not entirely repudiated. Religion and caste inserted themselves into the public political domain, but relied substantially on the normative (and of course, institutional) resources of liberal democracy to do so. Vernacular 'political society' used the modernist vocabulary of rights and justice to ascend to state power. Changes can indeed be discerned in the dominant *norms* that corresponded to the policy and political shifts of the period. Nevertheless, the legitimating vocabulary of the polity survived, a legacy of Congress hegemony.

Secularism, the key legitimating concept in the Shah Bano debate (1986), is the lens through which political arguments over exemptions for Muslim law are analysed in Chapter 5. Social justice, the principal legitimating concept in the Mandal debate (1990), is the focus for the analysis of arguments over employment quotas for OBCs in Chapter 6. These two concepts became emblematic of the political shift of this period: the dethroning of the Congress was associated with the critique of secularism by the Hindu nationalist BJP, and the advocacy of social justice by lower caste-based parties.

5

Secularism and Muslim Personal Law

The Shah Bano Debate, 1986

Introduction

The Shah Bano case (1985–6) encapsulated a range of issues: questions of sex equality and the role of the state; minority rights in a democracy; the place of religion in a secular order; the jurisdiction of courts and parliaments in the sphere of religious law.[1] In public debate, the Shah Bano case was identified with the Indian state's preferential treatment of minority cultures. In Part I, we saw that the Constitution-makers had declined to include special protections for Muslim personal law. By contrast, in the Shah Bano case, the Parliament was promulgating a law explicitly exempting Muslims from provisions of the Criminal Procedure Code, overruling a Supreme Court judgement. This was a shift to stronger multicultural policies, which granted Muslims greater self-governance in the arena of family laws, strengthening group autonomy vis-à-vis the state.[2] I have argued that the preservation of a distinct cultural identity for minority groups had a weak basis in the nationalist vocabulary during the

[1] A substantial scholarly literature exists on the Shah Bano case. For analyses of political discourse, see, in particular, Jayal 1999: ch. 3; Parashar 1992: ch. 4; Pathak and Sunder Rajan 1989; Hasan 1998; Das 1994. The Shah Bano case is also discussed in political theory debates as a key instance of conflict between minority rights and gender justice; see, for instance, Shachar 1998; Spinner-Halev 2001; Eisenberg 2005.

[2] On the distinction between strong and weak multiculturalism, and a defence of the latter in the context of state recognition of religious personal laws, see, for instance, Shachar 1998: 287. For a defence of stronger multiculturalism for the protection of the personal laws of *minority* groups, see Spinner-Halev 2001.

Constituent Assembly debates, and that this conforms to the institutional forms of provisions for religious minorities in the Indian Constitution. Does the expansion of special provisions for religious minorities suggest that a stronger normative basis was now available for the protection of minority cultures in the prevailing vocabulary?

Secularism serves as the prism through which changes in the normative vocabulary will be examined. In terms of the career of secularism in India, the Shah Bano case is usually regarded as a watershed. This claim will be critically evaluated through a close conceptual analysis of the parliamentary debate. I will show that notions of secularism espoused by the ruling Congress party were indeed altered in a manner conducive to special exemptions for Muslim personal law. Secularism was elaborated in Congress discourse primarily in terms of equal respect for all religions and minority rights, rather than the dominant terms of the Constituent Assembly debates, those of the exclusion of religion from the political domain. So construed, secularism was supportive of exemptions for religious minorities: the policy shift was accompanied by a discursive change that was favourable to this outcome.

However, this discursive change is less radical than commonly supposed. Notions of separation of state and religion were not abandoned in Congress discourse. Moreover, competing conceptions of secularism remained salient in political debate: unlike in the late 1940s, the legitimating vocabulary *as a whole* was not altered. Common assessments of secularism in India often move between the many distinct strands and connotations of secularism at play in political discourse without distinguishing between them. These have also relied on an overstated contrast between a 'Western' model of separation between state and religion and a distinctively 'Indian' model of equal respect for all religions. The notion of equal respect for all religions, however, has manifestly involved some forms of separation between religion and state and invoked several so-called Western liberal–democratic notions.[3] The proposal of a legitimating vocabulary comprising a constellation of concepts yields more precise assessments of discursive continuities and shifts with regard to secularism and its relationship to minority rights. It also sheds new light on the defining political shift of the late 1980s—the decline of Congress dominance and the rise of the BJP.

[3] See Chapter 3 above, for a discussion of the literature in this area.

This chapter is divided into six sections. The first section presents a brief historical background of the Shah Bano case and the question of religious personal law in India. The second and third sections unpack the discourse of secularism in the Shah Bano debate to establish whether secularism was construed differently from the Constituent Assembly debates, and if so, in what respects. The fourth and fifth sections examine the shifts in conceptions of secularism in relation to other concepts of the vocabulary, those of democracy and national unity. The final section assesses the continuities and shifts in the legitimating vocabulary on minority rights in the Shah Bano debate, and suggests wider implications for our understanding of policy and political change.

The Shah Bano Case and Religious Personal Law: A Brief Historical Background

The Shah Bano case involved a claim for maintenance filed by a divorced Muslim woman, Shah Bano.[4] Her husband, Mohammed Ahmed Khan petitioned the Supreme Court against a High Court order that directed him to pay maintenance to his divorced wife under section 125 of the Criminal Procedure Code, 1973. He argued that under Muslim personal law, he was not required to pay maintenance to his divorced wife after a certain period (*iddat*, roughly three months). As he had paid the *mehr* (dower) amount, section 127 of the Criminal Procedure Code absolved him from any further obligation with regard to maintenance.[5] The landmark Supreme Court judgement in *Mohammed Ahmed Khan vs*

---

[4] For more details, see Engineer 1987: 8–14; Parashar 1992: 189; Jayal 1999: 112–22.

[5] The relevant portion of Section 125 of the Code of Criminal Procedure deals with the right of maintenance where 'any person having sufficient means neglects or refuses to maintain his wife unable to maintain herself'. In 1973, the scope of the term 'wife' was expanded to include an ex-wife or divorced woman who has not remarried. But in response to some Muslim concerns, a caveat was added [Section 127 (3) (b)], enabling a magistrate to cancel an order made under Section 125 in favour of a divorced woman if she had received the whole sum payable on divorce 'under any customary or personal law' (Agnes 2005: 123; Parashar 1992: 164–8). Section 125 was popular among Hindu and Muslim women seeking maintenance (Mukhopadhyaya 1994: 117).

Shah Bano rejected the appellant's claims.[6] The judgement stated that 'the religion professed by the parties or the state of the personal law by which they are governed cannot have any repercussion on the applicability of such laws [that is Section 125]'[7]. The provisions of the Criminal Procedure code applied to all citizens irrespective of their religion; and it was emphasized that 'Section 125 overrides the personal law, if there is any conflict between the two' (Engineer 1987: 27).[8] Further, controversially, the judges also undertook to bolster their position by invoking Muslim Law and the Qur'an to show that there was no conflict between Islamic law and Section 125 of the Criminal Procedure Code, and to rebuke the legislature for its lack of initiative with regard to a uniform civil code for all citizens (*ibid.*: 33).[9]

This judgement unleashed what has been described as the biggest agitation launched by Muslims in post-Independence India (Engineer 1987: 1).[10] The Muslim Personal Law Board led attempts to mobilize the Muslim community against what it condemned as the Supreme Court's

[6] The Shah Bano judgement is regarded as 'the most important...instance of the Supreme Court's attempt to interpret Islamic scripture...'(Mehta 2005: 74).

[7] *Mohd Ahmed Khan vs Shah Bano Begum AIR* 1985 SC 945, reprinted in Engineer 1987: 25. Prior to the Supreme Court decision, lower courts, and a High Court had upheld Shah Bano's claim.

[8] Section 127 (3) (b) it was argued did not exempt a Muslim from Section 125 as *mehr* was not an amount 'payable "on divorce"' (q. Engineer 1987: 30).

[9] The judgement quoted verses from the Qur'an that it said 'leave no doubt that the Qur'an imposes an obligation on the Muslim husband to make provision for or to provide maintenance to the divorced wife' (q. Engineer 1987: 30). Previous Supreme Court decisions (*Bai Tahira vs Ali Hussain Fideali Chotthea AIR* 1979 SC 362 and *Fuzlunbi vs K. Khadil Vali AIR* 1980 SC 1730) had not engaged Islamic law and thereby avoided controversy (Agnes 2005: 123–4; see also Hasan 2005: 358); for a different view, see Mehta 2005: 85–6, who holds that these cases represented an unstable legal resolution.

[10] For Muslim mobilization against the judgement, see Engineer 1987: 12–13. Hasan notes that a striking aspect of the movement involving the *Jamaat-i-Islami, Jamaiyat-al-ulema* and the All India Muslim Personal Law Board was 'the unity displayed by the principal protagonists of religious identity, who were otherwise opposed to each other on fundamental doctrinal matters' (1989: 46). However, several prominent Muslim academics, lawyers and journalists also petitioned the government in favour of the judgement's stance of upholding of the right of divorced Muslim women to claim maintenance (Engineer 1987: 215–21; Hasan 1989: 47).

'interference' in Muslim Personal Law and its assumption of the right to interpret the Qur'an (*ibid*.: 9).[11] A substantial section of Muslim opinion perceived the judgement and the demand for a uniform civil code as a threat to the religious identity of Muslims and an attempt at assimilation.[12] The Congress government's initial response was one of qualified support for the Supreme Court judgement.[13] However, in a move widely perceived as capitulation to conservative Muslim opinion in a situation characterized by growing Muslim mobilization and electoral defeats for the ruling party, the government reversed its stance, and brought forward the Muslim Women (Protection of Rights on Divorce) Bill 1986, overriding the judgement.[14] The Bill itself was criticized as hastily drafted and pushed through Parliament, and attacked by women's organisations and in the English language national press as detrimental to the rights of women.[15] It was 'projected as the most glaring instance of the defeat of the principle of gender justice for the Indian woman, as well as the defeat of secular principles within the Indian polity' (Agnes 2005: 129). The critics of the

[11] Shah Bano herself later rejected the Supreme Court judgement in her favour as contrary to the Qur'an and urged the government to revoke it, pressing for a guarantee that 'no interference would ever be attempted in future' with Muslim personal law ('Shah Bano's Open Letter to Muslims', reprinted in Engineer 1987: 211). She is reported to have said 'If the majority of the community thinks it is wrong, how can one individual be correct?' (q. Kozlowski 1993: 87).

[12] Syed Shahabuddin (Janata Party), a leading voice against the judgement, noted: 'Ours is not a communal fight. It only amounts to resisting the inexorable process of assimilation. We want to keep our religious identity at all costs' (q. Khory 1993:125–6).

[13] Minister of State for Home Affairs Arif Mohammed Khan made a speech in Parliament in support of the judgement and against exemptions for Muslim law. He later resigned from the government in protest at the reversal of its stand (Hasan 1989: 47–8).

[14] The Congress party's loss of a series of by-elections, including one to a prominent critic of the Supreme Court judgement Syed Shahabuddin, and the prospect of further electoral defeats in the 1985–6 state assembly elections, are widely seen to have motivated its reversal of position (Hasan 1989: 48; Agnes 2005: 115, 125).

[15] The Bill was regarded as reflecting 'the point of view of only the conservative Muslims' (Parashar 1992: 177), with the government as having 'exaggerated the strength of the conservative opposition', and allowed 'the Ulama to appropriate the task of defining the over-arching concerns and interests of Muslims' (Agnes 2005: 126; see also Hasan 2005).

Bill ranged across the entire political spectrum, with Left groups and Hindu right-wing organizations alike aligning themselves against the Bill on grounds of gender justice. In the parliamentary debate, the positions of representatives largely followed the lines of party political affiliation. Congress members and those belonging to Indian Union Muslim League supported the Bill; those belonging to the Janata Party, Telugu Desam and the Communist Party of India, the Communist Party of India (Marxist), and the Bharatiya Janata Party opposed it, with the Janata Party allowing its members a free vote on the issue.[16]

This then constituted the immediate backdrop for the parliamentary debate that is the focus of this chapter. The Shah Bano case is regarded as an instance of preferential treatment of religious minorities; some more information is needed on the history of religious personal laws in India to understand why this is the case. While all Indian citizens are governed by a common criminal law, in matters of family law pertaining to marriage, divorce, succession, adoption, guardianship, and maintenance, members of four major religious communities, Hindu, Muslim, Christian, and Parsi, are governed by their respective religious laws.[17] These religious laws are also state-made in the sense that modern state institutions, mainly legislatures and courts, have been responsible for the codification of these laws out of a diversity of religious practices and their application to discrete communities.[18] In India and elsewhere, personal laws have both historically facilitated the consolidation of religious groups, and come to be an important component of their identities.[19] Across different

[16] Janata Party member Syed Shahabuddin was one of the most prominent supporters of the Bill. The Lok Sabha passed the Bill on 6 May 1986, the Rajya Sabha, on 9 May 1986, and the President gave his assent on 19 May 1986, bringing the act into operation.

[17] The extent to which these laws are grounded in religion is both disputed and variable across communities.

[18] Modern state law and courts in India, colonial and postcolonial, have given much 'greater reality' to the ideas that Muslims are one community and 'adhere strictly to a single body of law' (Kozlowski 1993: 77), thereby furthering the project of Muslim reformers to remould diverse Muslims into a single community. On the main statues for Muslim personal law in India, the Shariat Act 1937, and the Dissolution of Muslim Marriages Act 1939, see, for instance, Mahmood 1983.

[19] On Muslim personal law and Muslim identity in India, see, for instance, Minault 1982; Hasan 1989. On the centrality of family law for the construction of group

traditions of religious personal law, women typically have fewer rights than men in analogous situations.[20] Proponents of women's rights have thus argued that the burden of the protection of group identity is borne disproportionately by women, and frequently clashed with advocates of group autonomy.[21]

In India, the demarcation of a sphere of 'personal' law dates back to the late eighteenth century when East India Company administrators sought to exempt parts of religious law pertaining to matters such as family law, caste and religious endowments, from the purview of their regulatory action, apparently on grounds that these were an aspect of the religion of their subjects (Derrett 1963: 232–4; Parasher 1992: 62; Larson 2001: 5). The special status of personal law was to remain an enduring feature of British policy through the different phases of colonial rule, even as the state took some steps towards the codification and reform of these laws (Jayal 1999: 105–6). The independent Indian state thus inherited a situation where personal laws 'were not outside the purview of the State legal system...yet there was some ambiguity about its legislative powers vis-à-vis religious personal laws' (Parashar 1992: 76). The Constitution-makers, as we saw in Part I, did not resolve this ambiguity. On the one hand, the commitment of the state to equality was envisaged as requiring the reform of religious laws, particularly Hindu law with respect to Untouchables and women. On the other hand, the Constitution-makers did not introduce a right to a uniform civil code, implicitly recognizing the existence of a plurality of personal laws; further, group rights to religious freedom were instituted.

The identification in public debate of religious personal laws with minority preference in India derives from the fact that while the post-Independence Indian state has undertaken reforms in Hindu law, it has

---

boundaries in Israel see, for instance, Shachar 1998: 292–3, who distinguishes between the demarcating and distributive functions of family law and argues for restricting the authority of religion to the former.

[20] On sex inequalities in Hindu, Muslim, and Christian personal laws in India and their judicial interpretations, see, for instance, Mackinnon 2005: 269; on sex inequalities in decisions of rabbinical courts in Israel, see Shachar 1998: 301.

[21] Several studies have highlighted the role of women as emblems of community identity and sites for contention over tradition in India. See, for instance, Sangari and Vaid 1989: 12, and in the context of the Shah Bano debate, Pathak and Sunder Rajan 1989; Mukhopadhyay 1994.

largely adopted a stance of non-intervention vis-à-vis the personal laws of minority communities.[22] In 1955–6, Parliament passed the Hindu Code Acts that resulted in substantial reform in Hindu law; Galanter notes that Hindu social arrangements were 'for the first time moved entirely within the ambit of legislative regulation' (1989: 29). These were passed in the teeth of Opposition from conservative Hindus in the Congress. Their objection that the reform of Hindu law alone was discriminatory was countered by assurances that this was a step towards the eventual institution of a uniform civil code (Parashar 1992: 164). Whether the Hindu Code was indeed a step towards the secularization of law is debatable.[23] As Agnes (2005) notes, in post-Independence India, the broad trend has been away from the secularization of family law.[24]

With regard to minorities, the 'standard in India has been not to introduce any change with respect to the rights and privileges...unless there is substantial support for change within the minority community itself...' (Larson 2001: 8). Thus, during the reform of the Criminal Procedure Code 1973, which sought to extend the maintenance

[22] India's Parliament has been more non-interventionist than its courts (see Jayal 1999). Less intervention in the personal law of minority religions relative to the majority has also characterized state practice in other countries, notably Israel (see Spinner-Halev 2001: 101–2).

[23] The Hindu Code Acts grouped various customary practices, rituals, castes, and sects under the label 'Hindu', removed Hindus from the purview of various secular and uniform provisions, conferred tax benefits upon Hindu coparcenaries, and as such constituted a departure from the declared goal of the secularization and homogenization of family law through a uniform civil code (Agnes 2005: 113–15; see also Kishwar 1994: 2158). Sikhs, Buddhists, and Jains were included under the legal description of 'Hindu'. On how the reform of Hinduism by state institutions for the inclusion of untouchables has also served to create a more unified Hindu identity, see Galanter 1989; Mehta 2005.

[24] The only exception is the Special Marriage Act 1954, which allowed civil marriage without exit from religion. Although an enabling rather than compulsory legislation, the Special Marriage Act was opposed by conservative Hindu, Muslim, and Christian opinion at the time. As Agnes documents, its provisions subordinating personal laws have been whittled down over time. Notably, the privileges of Hindu male coparcenaries were protected through an amendment to the Act in 1972, and the choice earlier available to Hindus to be governed by a secular law of succession, removed (2005: 115–19). Viewed in this context, the Shah Bano legislation appears as one more instance of retreat from the secularization of family law in India.

obligations of husbands to include divorced wives, the government yielded to demands that Muslims be exempted and included an opt-out clause which became the hub of controversy in the Shah Bano case (Parasher 1992: ch. 4). By the time the Shah Bano controversy erupted in 1985, there had been a long history, colonial and postcolonial, whereby personal laws were seen as a key component of community identity. Post-Independence, the Indian state had undertaken some regulatory action with respect to Hindu law, but refrained from exercising such powers in the case of minorities. One of the main consequences of the enactment of the Muslim Women (Protection of Rights on Divorce) legislation was to turn the sense that minorities were receiving preferential treatment on this issue, into a politically effective critique of 'minority appeasement' by the Hindu Right.

SECULARISM AND THE SEPARATION OF STATE AND RELIGION

To what extent were conceptions of secularism in the parliamentary debate on the Muslim Women (Protection of Rights on Divorce) Bill 1986 different from those encountered in the Constituent Assembly? The impression on a first reading of the parliamentary debate in the Shah Bano case is one of the persistence of the legitimating vocabulary. For all the changes in the landscape of Indian politics in the intervening period, the appearance of political rhetoric of the mid-1980s is remarkably similar to that of the late 1940s. The normative terms identified as constitutive of the legitimating vocabulary on minority rights in the Constituent Assembly, those of secularism, democracy, justice, national unity, and development, continued to frame political arguments in the Shah Bano case.[25] These were employed together and interdependently, by representatives of all ideological and political persuasions, Left modernizers, Hindu nationalists, conservative Muslims alike, in claims both commending and denouncing the proposed legislation.

[25] Thus, for instance, Mostafa Bin Quasem (CPI-M) opposed the Bill: '...every Indian, whether he is Hindu or a Parsi or a Christian or a Muslim or belongs to any other religion, who is committed to the ideal of secularism, to the...principle of equality, principle of justice and has genuine aspirations for national unity and integrity, has a duty and responsibility to oppose this Bill' (*Rajya Sabha Debates*, henceforth *RSD*, 1986 col. 303).

We have seen, however, that these normative terms designated an array of interrelated concepts and idea-units, that there were competing conceptions of these concepts, and that a range of norms underpinned these conceptions. Are the conceptions of secularism in the Shah Bano debate then similar to those in the Constituent Assembly? At first glance, the connotations of secularism in the Shah Bano parliamentary debate do seem substantially altered in at least one important respect: they appear to have little to do with the separation of state from religion. Instead, the Parliament was promulgating an Act explicitly based on religious law and pronouncing an authoritative version of the law. The Act was further defended by government spokesmen as based on a correct understanding of religious law. The Law Minister introduced the Bill thus:

> We have spent eight months of wide study and research...for the purpose of appreciating what according to Muslim law is the obligation of the husband of a divorced woman...I have taken the trouble of studying every text of the Muslim law to see that that definition accords with Muslim understanding of the matter...what we have put in the Bill reflects the proper personal law of Muslims... [26]

Islamic laws and customs were frequently cited in the speeches of both advocates and opponents of the Bill in order to establish or challenge its merits. Supporters from the Congress and Muslim League often sought to show how, contrary to popular perception, Muslim law was progressive with regard to women. Opponents from the Janata and Left parties frequently emphasized their respect for Islam and contended that the Bill, in addition to being undesirable in other respects, was also un-Islamic. Most participants assumed the religious basis of Muslim personal law.

Did the Shah Bano debate, then, register a radical shift in the meaning of secularism, in that it was no longer conceptualized in terms of the separation between state and religion in the 1980s, as it had been in the late 1940s? As noted earlier, legislatures and courts in postcolonial India have arbitrated extensively in the religious affairs of Hindus. Further, in reforming Hinduism, legislatures and courts have often sought to claim that their decisions are based on Hindu law, or that they are not contrary to such laws, and have invoked the authority of religious texts to do so. In

---

[26] *Lok Sabha Debates* (henceforth *LSD*) 1986 cols 313–14, 321–2. Eduardo Faleiro, a prominent Congress spokesman defended the Bill as '...but a statement of the law as contained in the Islamic law....' (*LSD* 1986 col. 348).

some instances, this has involved pronouncing on what the essential aspects of Hindu religion are (Galanter 1998b; Chatterjee 1998; Mehta 2005).[27] In the case of minority religions as well, state legislatures have authorized versions of religious laws and state courts have administered these laws. The separation of state and religion in the sense of the prohibition of any contact whatsoever between the two has not characterized the practice of Indian state institutions at any point, and the Shah Bano debate does not, therefore, constitute a departure in this sense.

It might be argued, however, that the shift in secularism in the Shah Bano case reflects a departure not from separation so broadly conceived, but from the *particular* conception of separation which dominated during the Constituent Assembly debates, namely that of the exclusion of religion from the political domain. The most common elaboration of secularism in the Shah Bano debate was that of equal respect for all religions. The imperatives of equal citizenship, or the dangers of mixing religion and politics, which had been central to the elaboration of secularism in the Constituent Assembly debates, seem scarcely evident here.

Closer examination nevertheless reveals that these concerns had not disappeared altogether from the political discourse on secularism in the 1980s, but rather, were now mostly to be found in Opposition criticisms of the Bill. K.P. Unnikrishnan (Congress S) declaimed that the Bill marked a moment of infamy in the history of India's sovereign Parliament,

> for it makes a mockery of all underlying concepts and premises of our secular Constitution rooted in equality of citizens and equality before law and secularism...our inheritance from the Constitution and freedom struggle...sought secularization of law and let there be no compromise on secularization of law. We cannot encourage a perspective that people should be compartmentalized. But today, you have surrendered

[27] The most cited instance in this regard is the 1966 Satsang case (*Sastri Yagnapurushdasji vs Muldas Bhundardas Vaishya*) involving the opening up of Hindu temples to Untouchables. The court ruled Satsangis were Hindus and (thereby subject to temple-entry legislation), with the judgement engaging extensively with what was, and what was not, 'true' Hinduism. For a more detailed discussion and other examples, see Galanter 1998b [1971]; Chatterjee 1998; Mehta 2005. As scholars have noted, after Independence, state involvement in the regulation of religious practices of Hindus has increased (Chatterjee 1998). Indian legislatures and courts, in contrast to their American counterparts, have sought to reform religious tradition from *within*, in the process often defining 'what the proper practice of a particular religion requires' (Mehta 2005: 59).

to those dark forces which insist on expansive jurisdiction of religion
and that too medieval religion.... (*LSD* 1986 cols 432–6)

As the above speech indicates, several of the defining features of nationalist
conceptions of secularism in the Constituent Assembly debates continued
to characterize notions of secularism in the Shah Bano debate. These
included, most notably, the elaboration of secularism in terms of equal
citizenship for individuals; its close proximity to national unity; and its
defence as 'modern'. The Bill was considered anti-secular because it was
seen as violating the guarantees of equality before the law and non-
discrimination between individuals on grounds of religion, as embodied
in the fundamental rights of the Constitution. Several Opposition
MPs put forward motions that the Bill be ruled out of consideration as
unconstitutional on these grounds.[28] Muslim women, it was contended,
had the same status—that of citizens—as other women: to deprive them
of the protection of a law available to other citizens was discriminatory.
Secularism was seen as requiring the *same* laws for individuals belonging
to all religions, an assumption which had also characterized Congress
arguments against minority safeguards in the Constituent Assembly
debates. The further claim in the Opposition's case against the Bill was
that *differences* in the rights of women belonging to different religious
groups worsened the inequalities to which Muslim women were subject.
These two claims were usually run together in political arguments against
the Bill, and were encapsulated in the concern for the fate of the Muslim
woman, subjugated by her menfolk, in dire straits economically, and
denied the access that her sisters from other religious communities had to
the Criminal Procedure Code. The government legislation was castigated
for promoting two types of inequalities—differences in the rights of
women depending upon the religious group to which they belonged; and
the subordination of women to men, which religious law was thought to
entrench. The central implicit claim in the Opposition's case was that the
two kinds of inequalities were linked: religious discrimination worsened
sexual discrimination. Formal equality—treating likes alike—was the
means for achieving social equality here. The opposite of equality was
difference (MacKinnon 2005: 264); there were no worries here that the
symmetrical treatment of differently placed groups would reinforce the

---

[28] The Constitutional articles commonly cited were Article 14 on equal protection
of laws and Article 15 on non-discrimination on grounds of sex and religion.

dominant group (Nussbaum 2005: 121). That differential treatment was construed as unequal and unjust meant that a concern for legal uniformity against minority preference, like that of the Hindu Right BJP, could draw legitimacy from gender equality. Through the Shah Bano debate, the BJP was able to assume the moral high ground as liberal defenders of women's rights against oppressive Muslim tradition (Cossman and Kapur 1996; Hasan 1998).

As in the Constituent Assembly debates, secularism construed as equal treatment of all individuals was closely linked to national unity. The exemption of Muslims from provisions of the Criminal Procedure Code was regarded as simultaneously conflicting with the state's obligation to treat all individuals as equals irrespective of the religion to which they belonged, *and* as hindering national unity, perpetuating divisions among citizens along religious lines. Several Muslim members from Opposition parties were vocal critics of the Bill. Saifuddin Ahmad (Asom Gana Parishad) declaimed:

> ...we as Muslims...are Indians first, and then we are Muslims. We must get the benefit as the other people...Section 125 will be applicable to all the other communities except Muslims...Is this not discrimination in the eye of law? ...the leaders propagate unity, integrity and solidarity, and in practice you are backing out. You are separating us from the mainstream of the community. (*LSD* 1986 col. 410)[29]

The Bill was frequently characterized by its opponents as 'communal': the sense in which 'communalism' was invoked here was similar to the Constituent Assembly debates, as simultaneously anti-secular (as it mixed religion and politics) and anti-national (as it divided the citizenry on religious group lines). In such claims, as in the Constituent Assembly debates, there were multiple links between secularism and national unity. Secularism was defined in terms of equal citizenship rights, and these were construed individualistically (rather than, for instance, in terms of each group having an equal right to follow its religious practices), as well as implying the same rights for all individuals regardless of their

---

[29] See also L.K. Advani (BJP) (*RSD* 1986 col. 237). Close links between secularism and national unity also characterized the wider public debate, where 'those for the judgement were labelled 'progressive'...To be progressive, modern, secular was also to be a nationalist and in favour of national integration...the opposing camp was [projected as] anti-national and against national integration' (Mukhopadhaya 1994: 114; see also Agnes 2005: 124).

religious affiliation, because this was seen as a requirement of *national unity*. Secularism, so conceived, was considered as the basis for national unity both in an instrumental sense, as the means for integrating people from diverse religious groups, as well as in a constitutive sense, as the defining aspect of national identity. As in the Constituent Assembly debates, where secularism was supported by conservative Hindus and modernizing socialists in the Congress alike, its close relationship to national unity meant that secularism was advocated by an ideologically disparate group of parliamentarians. Only now, these belonged to a range of parties outside the Congress—the Left parties and the Hindu Right BJP.

Finally, secularism as the exclusion of religion and politics espoused by the Opposition in the Shah Bano debate was similar to Congress conceptions in the Constituent Assembly in that secularism was still cast as 'modern', and thereby desirable. The Opposition cast itself as the 'secular' and 'progressive' force against a Bill that was 'reactionary', 'medieval', and 'barbaric'. Claiming that he spoke for 'the entire secular and progressive forces of the country' against the Bill, Mostafa Bin Quasem (CPI-M) declared:

> History will not forgive this present Government. You have worked against a positive movement in our history. It is a movement towards emancipation of the Muslim women of our country. Instead of making a positive contribution thereto you have deliberately brought this Bill thereby subjecting them to 7th century primitivism. (*RSD* 1986 col. 311)

This line of criticism mocked Prime Minister Rajiv Gandhi's slogan of the time, of taking India into the twenty-first century (See P. Kolandaivelu of the AIADMK, *LSD* 1986 col. 400). The inflection of secularism with connotations of 'modern' and 'progressive' indicated that it was still seen as part of the state's 'modernizing agenda' (Jayal 1999), where the state assumed responsibility for socio-religious reform. While altered in some respects, most notably in the fact that there was no longer the confidence among the 'modernists' of the 1980s that state-led modernization could subdue religion over time, this strand continued to inform conceptions of secularism in political discourse over minority rights.

So did the Shah Bano debate mark a radical shift in the career of secularism not on account of the fact that the Parliament was promulgating an Act based on religious law, nor that the dominant conception of secularism in the Constituent Assembly debates—the exclusion of religion from politics—had dropped out of political discourse, but, rather, in the fact that the *Congress* had abandoned this conception of secularism? Secularism was mainly elaborated in Congress discourse in the Shah Bano debate as equal respect for all religions, which was construed primarily in terms of state deference to religion and protection of the rights of minorities. Insofar as Congress pronouncements on secularism in the Constituent Assembly debates had emphasized the exclusion of religion from the political domain for national unity and equal citizenship rights, this *did* represent a shift away from its earlier position. This move would render secularism more hospitable to special treatment for minority cultures than had been the case in the Constituent Assembly debates. Nevertheless, the changed connotations of secularism in Congress discourse continued to embrace some forms of separation of state and religion.

Secularism and Rights: Religious Freedom and Minority Rights

What exactly did the notion of 'equal respect for all religions', the dominant interpretation of secularism in Congress discourse in the Shah Bano debate, imply? To take some examples, prominent Congress spokesman Eduardo Faleiro declared: '...[in] a truly secular state in a multi-religious society, it is the paramount duty to *equally respect* all religions and give equal respect and protection to all laws, including personal laws, which are based on the religious tenets...' (*LSD* 1986 col. 343). Another Congressman asserted: '...the real definition [of secularism]...is that we show equal respect to all religions. The State has no religion. But the state is governed by this Constitution which guarantees *full protection* to all the minorities, which guarantees them their faith, their profession, their religion and their culture' (Jagan Nath Kaushal, *LSD* 1986 col. 408).

The first point to note here is that in response to the Opposition's criticism that in promulgating the legislation the Congress was abandoning its commitment to secularism, Congress spokesmen and supporters of the Bill from other parties contended that secularism *itself* required the 'protection' of Muslim personal law. They did so not by contending that the same criteria employed by Opposition representatives in the elaboration of secularism could be used to designate their action, in other words, not by disputing what Skinner has termed in a different context, the 'range of reference' of the term (1988: 113–14), but rather, by proposing somewhat different criteria for the application of the term secularism. These criteria, however, included the notion that the state would not identify with any religion: as such, not only was the term secularism invoked by opposing sides in this debate, secularism continued to be a shared legitimating concept, even as advocates of the legislation disagreed with its opponents about the correct *meaning* of secularism.

It is often contended in scholarly and political debate that there is an Indian model of secularism as equal respect for all religions that is radically distinct from the Western separation of state from religion.[30] In the Shah Bano debate, for instance, K.C. Pant (Congress) explained: 'The fact of the matter is that our people are religious...we cannot change it. We have to take that into account. And therefore respect for all religions becomes the bedrock of our secularism not merely separation of religion from State. That is the difference from the *western* concept....' (*LSD* 1986 cols 389–90). However, as discussed in Chapter 3, the contrast between an Indian equal respect for all religions and Western separation of state from religion is overstated. Articulations of equal respect for all religions in the Shah Bano debate clearly encompassed some forms of separation of state and religion. These included the view that the state did not identify with any religion, and that there was no privileged status for the religion of the majority. Separation was also significantly invoked in the elaboration of equal respect in the Shah Bano debate in the form of the requirement of state non-intervention in religion. Cabinet Minister Arjun Singh expounded on the meaning of secularism: 'I can only give a common sense approach which means that the State does not practice any religion, the State does not promote any religion and the State does not interfere in any religion. Every citizen is free to practice his own faith, his own religion and his own belief' (*LSD* 1986 col. 403).[31] It might be

---

[30] Cossman and Kapur, for instance, argue that two very different conceptions of secularism have 'competed for ideological dominance' in India since independence: separation from religion, seen as the Western model of secularism; and equal respect for all religions, identified with the Indian model (1996: 2621).

[31] See also P. Shiv Shankar, Minister for Commerce (*RSD* 1986 col. 316); Syed Shahabuddin (*LSD* 1986 col. 503). Of course, the state *was* clearly interfering in religion in the sense of authorizing a particular version of Muslim law, bringing

recalled that secularism had been construed as implying separation in a similar sense in the speeches of Muslim League advocates of state non-intervention in religious personal law in the Constituent Assembly.[32] While this continued to be the favoured line of argument of the advocates of personal law in the Shah Bano debate, the difference was that these now belonged to the Congress party.

Secularism as equal respect for all religions in the speeches of advocates of the government legislation was characterized primarily in terms of rights to religious freedom *of groups*. Congresswoman Rajendra Kumari Bajpai stated: 'The principle of secularism which we have adopted in our country does not recognise any uniform religion for the state. The people of different religions live here and all of them have been granted the right to follow their own religion, customs and marriage rituals' (*LSD* 1986 col. 426).[33] This was distinct from the notion of secularism underpinning opposition to the Bill in the Shah Bano debate, as well as earlier Congress conceptions of secularism, which had emphasized the equal citizenship rights of individuals irrespective of their religion.

Contrary to criticisms of the legislation as departing from the separation of religion and state, it is important to note that the Bill was not defended here in terms of the *intrinsic* correctness of a religious doctrine. In promulgating a legislation based on Islamic law, the Government was not accepting the notion of 'the divine immutability of the Shariat' or even that of 'the religious sanctity of personal law' (Hasan 1998: 75–6). Rather, the legislation was defended on grounds that the government had to defer to the wishes of most Muslims with regard to their personal law, a

------

the latter under the interpretive control of state courts (Chatterjee 1998). As Agnes notes, the 1986 Act imposed obligations on Waqf board and family members that were not imposed by the Shariat and to this extent 'modified the rules of the Shariat and overruled the theory of its immutability' (2005: 126).

[32] While similar, the Congress position in the Shah Bano debate was *not* identical to the position of Muslim League advocates of personal law in the Constituent Assembly. Congress representatives in the Shah Bano debate emphasized religious freedom for individuals as well as groups. Unlike Muslim League representatives in the Constituent Assembly, the Congress was not saying that governments lacked the authority to intervene in the reform of religious law because it was divinely ordained. Group autonomy in religion was asserted in this case through an exercise of parliamentary sovereignty, a fact that was noted in the debate.

[33] See also the speech of Ebrahim Sulaiman Sait, Muslim League member and one of the chief advocates of the Bill (*LSD* 1986 cols 492–3).

deference that was dictated by the rights to religious freedom in a secular state. In these respects at least, Congress discourse on secularism in the Shah Bano debate did not depart from notions of separation of state and religion.

There were, nevertheless, other departures in dominant conceptions of secularism in Congress discourse relative to the Constituent Assembly debates.[34] With the right to religious freedom of groups becoming the pre-eminent criterion of secularism, important changes ensued. First, religious freedom was no longer circumscribed by equal citizenship rights for individuals, as had been the case in the Constituent Assembly debates.[35] It was now contended that secularism implied *full* religious freedom for groups.[36] The elaboration of equal respect for all religions in terms of unconstrained rights to religious freedom for groups was crucial in enabling secularism's embrace of religion witnessed in this debate. For it meant that the views of the members of the religious community, rather than those of the state, would be decisive in determining the scope of religion. As such, if Muslims felt that personal law was a part of their religion, then secularism as 'full' rights to religious freedom dictated state non-interference in Muslim personal law. It might be recalled that similar arguments put forward by the Muslim League had been rejected by the Congress in the Constituent Assembly as incompatible with the equality of individuals.

Second, with equal citizenship rights for individuals demoted relative to rights to religious freedom of groups, legal pluralism achieved greater acceptance. Rejecting Opposition claims that the Bill was unconstitutional, Law Minister A.K. Sen explained:

[34] For a contrary view, see, for instance, Hasan who notes that arguments in the Shah Bano debate 'reveal a strong continuity in terms of Congress party discourse in the 1940s, 1950s, and 1980s' (1998: 75).

[35] The constitutional right to religious freedom is subject, among others, to fundamental rights to equality and non-discrimination of all individuals. Criticizing the Bill as anti-Constitutional, K.P. Unnikrishnan argued: '...[T]he concept of *absolute* freedom of religion [has been] introduced to subvert the Constitution' (*LSD* 1986 col. 377). See also Saifuddin Chowdhary (CPI-M), (*LSD* 1986 col. 362).

[36] See, for instance, K.C. Pant, (*LSD* 1986 col. 389). Ebrahim Sulaiman Sait stated: '...secularism...is full freedom to live according to one's own religion and not interfere with Shariat religion' (*LSD* 1986 col. 494).

...dead uniformity is not the prescription of the Constitution. What is prescribed is that if equals are treated unequally or unequals are treated equally, then it will lead to an infringement of the equality clause...if Muslim divorced women are treated on a different basis from other divorced women, it cannot be called a case of discrimination. (*RSD* 1986 cols 273–4)

The legislation did not violate formal equality: the case of Muslim women *was* different, so treating them differently in law was not tantamount to discrimination. Congress representatives frequently criticized Opposition members for being concerned about uniformity rather than equality. In the Congress position relative to the Constituent Assembly debates, there was a shift away from the standard liberal views that individual rights be unaffected by group membership: equal individual rights were no longer seen as requiring the same rights for all individuals of different religions. Further, the differential treatment of Muslim women, it was contended, would not disadvantage women, but rather advance gender equality: while treating Muslim women differently, the legislation would improve upon the provision available to women under the Criminal Procedure Code on divorce.[37] The primacy of respect for the rights to religious freedom, however, meant that this was not a central concern.

Unlike the Constituent Assembly debates, there were few worries in Congress discourse of any conflict between group rights to freedom of religion expansively construed, and the rights of individuals. In the Constituent Assembly, Congress representatives had notably argued that the protection of religious personal laws would contravene the right to equality for all citizens and the reform of iniquitous religious practices that discriminated against women and Untouchables. Also, it was felt that group rights to religious freedom could conflict with the religious freedom of individuals: state recognition of personal laws would detract from the freedoms of *individuals* who did not wish to be governed by community law (see Chapter 3 above).[38] In Congress discourse on secularism in the Shah Bano debate, the normative emphasis had shifted

[37] For instance, several Congress speeches alluded to the progressive character of Muslim personal law in its construal of marriage as a contract.
[38] On how the state helps groups limit individual freedom by granting religious groups the right to govern family law, see Spinner-Halev 2001: 103, and in the Indian context, Ahmed 2008.

from the individual to the group.[39] Equal respect for all religions meant that all *groups* had equal rights to religious freedom, that minority groups had as much right to pursue and preserve their religion as the majority—there would be no imposition in religious matters upon minorities.[40] That this might conflict with the entitlement of all individuals to equal respect was not now articulated in Congress discourse.

While arguments in support of the legislation underscored that all groups had equal rights to religious freedom, given that the state had undertaken reform of Hindu law in the 1950s, the rights to religious freedom were in effect being interpreted differently here in the case of majority and minority communities.[41] Opposition representatives queried whether the state would be willing to countenance outlawed practices such as *sati*, child-marriage, and Untouchability, as these were an integral part of Hindu religion. Did rights to religious freedom imply that these practices were outside the ambit of state regulation? (see, for instance, Kanak Mukherjee, *RSD* 1986 col. 321). As noted earlier, secularism as equal respect for all religions was construed by the Hindu nationalist BJP to imply that all groups should have the *same* rights—symmetrical treatment of different religious groups—and thereby as precluding

[39] While debates in political theory have tended to contrast individual and group claims, scholars of religion paint a more nuanced picture of a tension between different notions of individuality (for example, between a substantive or contextualized notion of individual/citizen and a formal or abstract notion—see Larson 1993).

[40] As Nussbaum points out, *all* groups do not enjoy equal respect under the Indian system of personal law—minorities other than Muslims, Christians, and Parsis do not have their religious laws protected in the same way. Also, minority sects within each religion are not treated as equals—religious personal law mostly reflects the practices of the dominant sect within each religion (2005: 127).

[41] Chatterjee notes that the reform of Hindu law in the 1950s created 'a serious anomaly in the notion of equal citizenship', a fact noted not only by the Hindu Right but also by progressive opinion. Socialist leader JB Kriplani argued:

> ...If they [Members of Parliament] single out the Hindu community for their reforming zeal, they cannot escape the charge of being communalists in the sense that they favour the Hindu community and are indifferent to the good of the Muslim community or the Catholic community... Whether the marriage bill favours the Hindu community or places it at a disadvantage, both ways it becomes a communal measure. (q. Chatterjee 1998: 361)

special treatment for minorities. How was equal respect for all religions in Congress discourse construed as *asymmetric* interpretation of rights to religious freedom in the case of majority and minority communities?

The first point of note here is that in addition to rights of religious freedom of groups, secularism in Congress discourse invoked another criterion, that of the rights of minorities. In most speeches, the legislation was defended on grounds that secularism implied equal respect for all religions *and* respect for the rights for minorities. The latter in turn implied deference to the wishes of Muslims with regard to their religion and, thereby, non-intervention in their personal law. By introducing the Bill, it was argued:

> ...whatever the Government has done is to assert its secular character. What the Government has done is to assert the rights of minorities...as and when any reform is necessary it will be minorities themselves...that will come forward and move for them. The government will not. That is...the cardinal approach of a secular State in a multi-religious society anywhere. (*LSD* 1986 cols 345–6)[42]

It was this sense of the secular, as connoting solicitousness of minority rights, which informed commendations of the Bill: 'This Bill will remove the fear created among the Muslim minority as a result of the judgement in the...Shah Bano case. Once again they will be convinced that the Congress is a secular party and firmly stand by it' (Abida Ahmed, *LSD* 1986 col. 420). Here, 'communal' primarily connoted antipathy to minority rights; as such, the BJP was communal.

While the identification of secularism with the rights of minorities takes us some way towards understanding how rights to religious freedom were interpreted differently in the case of majority and minority communities, it does not tell us what the *grounds* for the differential treatment of minority groups were. Indeed, the move from all groups having equal rights to religious freedom, to (some) religious minorities having in effect greater freedom from state regulation, was not one that was elaborated in Congress discourse. As we have seen, the standard of formal equality was put forward by the Law Minister—since the case of Muslim women was different, differential treatment was legitimate. But why, *normatively* speaking, were Muslims different? Why did the state seek to 'draw lines of lines of difference where society drew them'

---

[42] See also *LSD* 1986 col. 389; Jagan Nath Kaushal, *LSD* 1986 col. 405.

(MacKinnon 2005: 262), when it had expressly sought *not* to do so in 1950? As the history of racial segregation and women's rights suggests, differential treatment under a regime of formal equality can perpetuate injustice and subordination (*ibid.*): racial segregation was justified in the United States under the Equal Protection Clause on grounds that treating Blacks differently was consistent with equality. This has been a powerful consideration in favour of the symmetrical treatment of individuals advocated by twentieth-century liberals (Kymlicka 1989). How was its departure from the standard liberal position rendered consistent with equality in Congress discourse in the Shah Bano debate?

While few clear answers appear in the parliamentary debate, the differential treatment of Muslims can be justified in normative terms on at least the following, overlapping, equality grounds. First, it could be argued that as a minority, Muslims faced a greater threat to the integrity of their religion than the majority Hindus, whose practices were inevitably supported by the state and society (Nussbaum 2005).[43] Hence, equal respect for Muslim citizens required that the community be given greater control over personal law that was central to its identity. Second, a case could be made for special treatment on grounds that Muslims were a subordinated or oppressed group in Indian society and so deserved greater cultural autonomy. In a context where Muslim individuals suffered violations to their right to life and liberty, reduced economic opportunities and discrimination by public and private institutions, the imposition of personal law reform on Muslims would compound these injustices (Spinner-Halev 2001: 86).[44] A third argument could be that Indian state institutions are not representative of Muslims and other minorities as they are of the majority Hindus (Mehta 2005). The 'so-called reforms in Hindu laws' were an instance not so much of 'a secular state imposing reform on a religion, but the Hindu community, through its representatives, interpreting the

---

[43] As Nussbaum notes, 'In any modern secular society, the so-called secular norms that prevail are typically those that derive from a majority religious tradition' (2005: 115).
[44] Spinner-Halev notes that in contexts of group oppression in which the state is implicated, the 'normal liberal model' needs to be questioned: 'avoiding the injustice of imposing reform on oppressed groups' can be more important than 'avoiding the injustice of discrimination against women' (2001: 86, 95).

requirements of their own religion anew' (*ibid.*: 78).[45] Equal treatment of Muslims demands that the community be accorded a similar space for 'exercising collective self-determination over their religious understandings as Hindus have' (*ibid.*: 78–9); hence greater autonomy from state-led reform. Although this last argument was hinted at by advocates of the legislation as we shall see, by and large, there was little attempt to go beyond abstract formal notions of equality: substantive, contextual notions of equality that could justify differential treatment of Muslims were not elaborated.[46]

Nevertheless, unlike in the Constituent Assembly debates, some discursive moves towards fashioning a justification for special treatment of religious minorities on justice grounds can be discerned. Notably, the elaboration of secularism in terms of rights to religious freedom was inflected by an idiom of protection in ways that rendered it more favourable to preferential treatment of religious minorities. In the Constituent Assembly debates, the language of protection of 'weaker sections' had been used largely to refer to 'backward classes'. Now, religious minorities were also included in the category of 'weaker sections' to whom the state owed a duty of protection.[47] Here was an implicit acknowledgement that Muslims were in some sense a subordinate group. But *how* exactly religious minorities were a disadvantaged group remained unclear. Unlike in the case of other 'weaker sections', such as women and lower castes, where the language of protection supplemented justice arguments, the links between secularism as solicitude for religious minorities and justice were not elaborated in Congress discourse. The employment of an idiom of protection in the case of religious minorities both served as a bridge

---

[45] As scholars have noted, the ideology of the Constitution and key institutions such as the Supreme Court and legislatures 'has been significantly forged by the preoccupations of modern Hindu social and religious reform' (Mehta 2005: 73); see also Galanter (1998b: 280).

[46] Indian parliaments and courts have elaborated substantive equality justifications for differential treatment in several contexts, notably preferential provisions for lower castes, but not that of religious personal law (MacKinnon 2005: 266–70).

[47] Frank Anthony, an Anglo-Indian representative who had been a prominent member of the Constituent Assembly, declared: '...there is no doubt about it that most of the minorities... have looked to the Congress party to protect us and...the Muslims today, if they feel that it is a Koranic injunction...then the Government has not only an option but a duty to see that this Bill is passed' (*LSD* 1986 col. 395).

for the gap in the justification of preferential provisions, enabling the move from equal respect for all religions to special treatment for minority religions, as well as an indicator of its presence.

The interweaving of the idiom of protection with that of rights in the Shah Bano debate facilitated exemptions for Muslim personal law in other respects. It eased the tension between individual and group rights, while subtly shifting the balance in favour of the latter. As 'weaker sections' reliant on state protection, women and minority groups were drawn together and placed on par, the potential antagonism between their rights erased by the state's overarching solicitude.[48] The rendition of rights in a language of protection and respect also enabled special provisions for religious minorities to draw upon a range of normative sources. It did not presuppose specific subjects and reasons in virtue of which respect or protection was due: thus, for instance, protection could be owed, at the same time, by the government to its citizens; to a minority community; to a minority faith or to a particular aspect of it, such as personal law. The basis of this protection was similarly indeterminate: it could be owed simultaneously on account of respect for liberal rights and religious freedoms; in pursuit of a liberal welfarist ideal wherein the protection of 'weaker sections' was in the interests of social good; in order to honour historical promises made to minorities; or on account of respect for an Indian tradition of religious toleration.[49] So secularism as protection of religious minorities could seem to be loosely supported by a wide range of normative sources, without needing more detailed elaboration that would reveal areas of conflict.

Rendered in the language of protection, notions of rights were inflected by idioms drawn from paternalistic historical and cultural traditions favourable to preferential provisions for religious minorities. These included filial and feudal duties to protect weaker members and colonial liberal paternalism. The infusion of the language of rights by such norms was a pervasive feature of this debate, informing not just the defence of the legislation, but also opposition to it. While the opponents of the legislation cast themselves as protectors of women's rights, there was

---

[48] On the discourse of protection in the Shah Bano debate, see Pathak and Sunder Rajan 1989: 565–70; on the convergence of this discourse in the case of women and minorities, see Jayal 1999: 137–8. On how rights-based approaches cast disputes in terms irreconcilable values, see Eisenberg 2005.

[49] See, for instance, Eduardo Faleiro, *LSD* 1986 cols 344–5.

'little assertion of maintenance as a woman's right' in the parliamentary debate (Jayal 1999: 137).[50] Rather, maintenance was defended as a means of protecting women from destitution, and the legislation was castigated for departing from Indian traditions of 'chivalry', and 'tender care' towards the fairer sex (Suresh Kalmadi, *RSD* 1986 col. 255). With regard to religious minorities, the stance of guardianship, it may be recalled, had been a key legitimizing ideology of the colonial state. It belonged, however, within a framework where people were subjects granted privileges at the discretion of the state rather than citizens entitled to rights. One of the consequences of the intermeshing of the idioms of protection and rights was to undermine the status of rights as universal prerogatives of citizenship, and to render these akin to gifts bestowed upon subjects by a benevolent government, affording the state much greater room for manoeuvre with regard to the rights of particular sections of the population.[51] The rhetoric of protection of 'weaker sections' thus did not offer a strong basis for the protection of Muslim personal law as a multicultural *right*. It did, nevertheless, recognize that minorities were in an unequal position vis-à-vis the majority, and so deserving of special help.

SECULARISM, DEMOCRACY, AND REPRESENTATION

So far we have focussed how the values constitutive of secularism, those of rights to religious freedom and equality, were interpreted in Congress discourse. In terms of my argument, changes in conceptions of secularism should also be reflected in its relationships with other concepts of the legitimating vocabulary. Closer examination of the parliamentary debate suggests that the recasting of secularism in Congress discourse was indeed supported by shifts in notions of democracy and representation.[52]

[50] The Criminal Procedure Code from which Muslims were sought to be exempted was a colonial legislation in origin and substance, whose concern was 'not with individual rights, but rather with vagrancy as a threat to public order' (Das 1994: 128).

[51] Women's rights, for instance, were defended thus: '...the Criminal Procedure Code is a gift of Mrs Gandhi to the nation...what Madam Gandhi wanted to give to the poor and the destitute women, that kind of right is being taken away by the son' (P. Kolandeivelu, *LSD* 1986 col. 398–9).

[52] This account focuses on the intersection of conceptions of secularism and democracy in Congress discourse. For an analysis of the different democratic arguments in the Shah Bano debate, see Jayal 1999: ch. 3.

It was argued variously by Congress representatives in support of the legislation, that Muslims constituted a *large* section of the population; that an overwhelming *majority* of Muslims regarded personal law to be an integral aspect of religion and considered the Supreme Court judgement an affront to their religion; that it was only a small *minority* of Muslims who supported the judgement (see, for instance, Nawal Kishore Sharma *LSD* 1986 col. 414; M. Kadharsha, *RSD* 1986 col. 229); that if a majority of Muslims held this view, the government was obliged to defer to their opinion; and that this was what the government was doing in bringing forward the legislation to overrule the judgement. The Law Minister's speech defended the Bill thus:

> ...the Government could not be possibly blind to this apprehension on behalf of the *largest* minority community in India...So far as Muslims are concerned, are we to be governed by what *they* think should be their personal law, or are we to be governed by the feelings of those who think that secularism demands that everybody must be tarred with the same brush? I can appreciate the high spirit and rather liberal approach that many of the...members on the other side belonging to the minority of Muslims have. But the government cannot ignore the voice of the *vast majority* of the Muslims. (*LSD* 1986 col. 313)[53]

The government's promulgation of legislation overriding the Supreme Court judgement, an exercise of parliamentary sovereignty, was defended here on democratic grounds. A (democratic) government had an obligation to listen to popular opinion; it could not ignore the strongly expressed wishes of a large section of its constituents. Deference to Muslim opinion on personal law was supported here by the democratic norm of popular rule. In accordance with the democratic procedure of majority decision-making, the wishes of Muslims were identified here with the preferences of the majority in the community. Ostensibly, then, conceptions of democracy in Congress discourse in the Shah Bano debate reflected several continuities with those in the Constituent Assembly debates. Democracy was identified with the norms of popular sovereignty, the institutions of representative parliamentary government, and the procedures of majority rule within the constraints of a framework of rights. Muslim personal law was upheld in this case through an explicit assertion of parliamentary sovereignty.[54]

---

[53] See also K.C. Pant, *LSD* 1986 col. 388.
[54] See, for instance, Syed Shahabuddin *LSD* 1986 col. 503; Jayal 1999: 127–8.

Further, contrary to criticisms of the legislation as departing from secularism as separation of religion and state, the government was not necessarily accepting either that Muslim personal law was an essential aspect of religion, or that religion/Islamic doctrine ought to dictate maintenance provisions, but only that a majority of Muslims believed this to be the case, and that the principles of secularism and democracy therefore required that the government defer to the sentiments of the Muslim majority. By implication, if majority Muslim opinion *changed* and no longer favoured religious law in family matters, the government would rescind exemptions for Muslims.[55] In other words, Congress representatives were not making a case for the preservation of Muslim culture and identity as such: this was not a strong argument for the protection of minority cultures.

Nevertheless, there were deeper differences relative to Congress position in the Constituent Assembly debates. As in the case of secularism, the emphasis in conceptions of democracy was not on the rights of individuals, but on those of minority *groups*. More importantly, however, shifts can be discerned in the conception of representation implicit in political claims. To begin with, while decisions pertaining to minorities had also been defended in the Constituent Assembly on grounds that they had the consent of the majority in the groups concerned, the Congress then had shown lesser deference to the expressed *preferences* of minorities. Special representation provisions for minorities were opposed by the Congress as harmful to minority interests. By contrast, in the Shah Bano debate, Congress leaders suggested that the stated wishes of Muslims were the most important consideration. This stance of deference to the internal beliefs of a community had historical roots both in the colonial state's policy of non-intervention in the religious affairs of its subjects, as well as early Congress reassurances to minorities, which had affirmed that policy decisions on religious or communal issues would not be made without the consent of the group concerned (see Chapter 2 above). Some Opposition representatives criticized the government's reluctance to

---

[55] Little attempt was made by the government to ascertain the opinion among Muslims as a whole regarding the importance of divorce and maintenance provisions in Muslim law for community identity (Eisenberg 2005: 268). The views of a conservative clergy were accepted as representing the majority opinion in the community—see Agnes 2005: 126; Parashar 1992: 177; Hasan 1994.

distinguish between the current preferences and enduring interests of Muslims, and to override the former, seeing in this an abdication by the state of the role claimed for it by national movement leaders, that of a social reformer of oppressive traditions. K.P. Unnikrishnan quoted loosely from Tocqueville:

> When occasions present themselves in which the interests of the people are at variance with their inclinations, it is the duty of persons whom they have appointed to be the guardians of those interests to withstand the temporary delusions, in order to give them time and opportunity for cool and sedate reflection.... (*LSD* 1986 col. 438)

The Congress, it was suggested, was retreating from its earlier stance of the representative as trustee, acting as the guardian of the interests of those they represented, in favour of that of the delegate who executed their wishes (Pitkin 1967). This, however, reflected less of a general shift in the comprehension of the role of representatives in Congress discourse, than one relative to *Muslims*.

Second, conceptions of representation in Congress discourse in the Shah Bano debate also differed from those in the Constituent Assembly in terms of whether the group affiliation of representatives was relevant to representation. In Chapter 4, we saw that nationalists of the late 1940s robustly rejected descriptive representation claims put forward by Muslim League members, the notion that only a Muslim could represent Muslims. Now, there was a tacit recognition of descriptive representation: the speeches of several Congress members implicitly invoked the notion that representatives *belonging* to the Muslim community most accurately represented Muslim views on the issue of personal law (Jayal 1999: 128–33). The Law Minister stated: 'It was our duty to ascertain the views of the Muslims on their personal law and in that matter their voice would be more dominant than the voice of those who tend to speak for them until they get their proxy' (*LSD* 1986 col. 315).

Opposition members termed the claim 'astonishing' (*LSD* 1986 col. 434). When forced out of the realm of allusion and confronted explicitly, descriptive representation was still deemed illegitimate, albeit mainly by opponents of the government legislation. The association of descriptive representation with separate electorates, and of separate electorates with 'communalism', remained in political discourse. Madhu Dandavate, leader of the Janata Party and one of the most vocal opponents of the Bill, admonished:

I take it for granted that there are no separate electorates, and that it
will be a bad day in the country when the Muslim representatives are
elected by the Muslims, Hindu representatives by the Hindus and the
Christian representatives by the Christians...Each one of you, even
when you belong to the minority community...whether you belong to
the Congress party or the Opposition, you are elected not on the vote
of one religious community, but on the vote of Indians in this country
on the basis of adult franchise...I am proud of the secular heritage of
this country.... (*LSD* 1986 col. 377)[56]

Secularism here was equated with the disregard of religious community
affiliations in the political domain—the dominant connotation of
secularism in Congress discourse in the Constituent Assembly debates,
which now mainly informed Opposition members' criticisms of the Bill
as anti-secular.

A third crucial respect in which conceptions of representation in
Congress speeches in the Shah Bano debate were altered pertained to
the nature of group difference. In the Constituent Assembly debates as
discussed in Chapter 4, the Congress' rejection of special representation
provisions for minorities had relied on the notion that there were no
fundamental differences between religious groups. In the Shah Bano
debate, by contrast, the case for deference to Muslim understandings
assumed that there *were* significant differences between communities—
numerous references can be found in political speeches as to how Muslims
differed in their understanding of marriage, divorce and maintenance—
questions that Congress representatives in the Constituent Assembly
had argued were irrelevant to public policy making. The Law Minister,
A.K. Sen, defended the legislation thus:

We must look at it from the point of view of Muslims, and not from the
point of view which according to *us* should be there, because you must
sit on the Muslim chair and view the matter from the Muslim chair
and then try to find out what is the law which governs the Muslims and
which according to *them* is not merely a law of man's making but a law
ordained by God.... (*LSD* 1986 col. 314)[57]

Scholars have remarked upon the 'them' and 'us' rhetoric that featured
in Congress discourse in the Shah Bano debate (Hasan 1998: 76;

[56] See also Saifuddin Chowdhary (CPI-M), *LSD* 1986 col. 318.
[57] K.C. Pant noted: 'You and I may have our own views but we cannot deny this
perception of the Muslims' (*LSD* 1986 col. 388).

Jayal 1999). As the above quote illustrates, there was a subtle elision between the government/major party and the Hindu community, with the legislative majority identified with the permanent religious majority, the Hindus (Hasan 1998: 76–7). This, too, marked a departure from the Constituent Assembly debates, where the rejection of special representation provisions for minorities had relied on the contention that there were no *permanent* majorities and minorities in legislatures, only issue-based ones. In the Shah Bano debate, it was argued that minority communities had to be treated differently from the majority community—their personal law, for instance, had to be 'protected', whereas the state could undertake the reform of religious laws of the Hindus—because the latter, it was assumed, were doing the legislating. While the government could claim to know and act in the interests of Hindus, and thereby reform Hindu personal law, it could not do so in the case of Muslims, and had to rely on their expressed preferences. The case for preferential treatment of Muslim law in Congress discourse rested on an implicit identification of state institutions with the Hindu community (Jayal 1999: 125–7).

Does this suggest that now there was little difference between the Congress and Hindu nationalists? While Congress rhetoric did exhibit a rightward shift in the 1980s (Hasan 1994; Manor 1997), its position on minority rights was more complex. In claiming that the Parliament could not act for Muslims as it could for Hindus, Congress representatives were also accepting that they had *reduced* authority in relation to the Muslim community. In the Shah Bano case, in contrast with the BJP, the Congress implicitly acknowledged that majority and minority religions occupied different positions in relation to state institutions and so merited different treatment.[58] This was not a majoritarian argument, but rather one in which democratic authority was limited by minority rights. The standard liberal secular narrative that 'the state ought to have the authority of regulating religious principles for the purpose of justice, regardless of religion' (Mehta 2005: 79) was qualified here by recognition of the unequal positions of majority and minority groups vis-à-vis the state. Substantive equality arguments for minority rights were not elaborated, but a beginning in this direction can be discerned.

---

[58] Muslim majority states such as Egypt have been able to effect changes in Muslim personal law without much controversy (Spinner-Halev 2001: 102).

According greater autonomy to religious communities, however, in practice has often meant giving more power to conservative male religious leaders to define community rules, usually to the detriment of gender equality. From a substantive equality standpoint, the demands of rectifying group injustice and gender injustice can pull in opposite directions (MacKinnon 2005: 276): exemptions for personal laws that increase the autonomy of subordinate groups can also serve to institutionalize male dominance. One way out of this dilemma that theorists have suggested is for the interpretation of personal laws to be handed over to 'democratically accountable representatives' of minority communities (Chatterjee 1998; Spinner-Halev 2001: 108). This addresses the problem of who has the authority to interpret religious law, and can enhance group autonomy, allowing communities to 'debate questions important to their own identity on their own terms' (Mehta 2005: 83).[59] But state action in the Shah Bano debate did little to advance the cause of democratic self-determination among Muslims. Instead, the government's mode of consulting Muslim opinion 'bolstered the existing power structure of the community, accepted the clergy as the sole spokesmen of the community', and resulted in strengthening the position of the 'orthodox sections of the ulema' (Hasan 2005: 367–8; see also Agnes 2005: 126).[60] While avoiding group oppression, government action in the Shah Bano case thus did not advance gender equality or democratic self-determination among Muslims. Reasons for the reduced authority of state institutions to intervene in the case of minorities were not elaborated, leaving the impression of unjust minority favouritism. And in recognizing conservative Ulemas as the voice of the community, the government's policy reinforced stereotypes of Muslims as illiberal and obscurantist, preparing favourable ideological ground for the rise of the Hindu Right.

[59] Minority assemblies can also offer a forum for the negotiation of the content of the community identity 'through a continuous and democratic process of self-representation' (Chatterjee 1998: 377), and increase the likelihood of reform of personal laws (Spinner-Halev 2001: 110–11).

[60] Hasan notes that the ulema have since 'refused to move even an inch forward' on reforming personal laws, and that the question of who has the authority to determine matters regulated by personal law is more important for Muslim religious and political leaders, than for Muslim women (2005: 368, 364–5).

Secularism, National Unity, and Uses of the Past

Does the fact that secularism in the Shah Bano debate was construed as consonant with special treatment for religious minorities suggest that national unity was no longer tied to secularism in Congress discourse, as was the case in the Constituent Assembly? Closer examination suggests that national unity remained central to elaborations of secularism; however, its *requirements* were now construed differently, and conceptions of secularism were recast accordingly.

In many political arguments for special exemptions for Muslim law in terms of secularism, the ultimate appeal was to the value of national unity.[61] Congress Minister Dinesh Singh explained, 'The Congress party has always stood for the rights of the minorities—not because it has been regarded as a kind of privileged community but because it is essential for the unity and integrity of the country' (*LSD* 1986 col. 396). Secularism construed as equal respect for all religions was related to national unity in several ways. *Instrumentally*, secularism was thought to help with a range of national unity concerns, of which state stability and the maintenance of civil peace were the most prominent. Minority discontent, warned Arun Nehru, Minister of State for Internal Security, could 'develop into a law and order situation and this is one problem which no police force...can solve satisfactorily' (*LSD* 1986 col. 411). Given the threats to national unity from terrorism and religious fundamentalism, the accommodation of minority fears about their religious identity was imperative. This, it was argued, would contribute to greater identification of minorities with the nation (national loyalty); better relations between Hindus and Muslims (social cohesion), thereby mitigate threats to political stability.[62]

---

[61] On the centrality of national unity concerns in the Shah Bano debate, see Parashar 1992; Hasan 1998: 83. These do not, however, examine the links of national unity and secularism.

[62] K.C. Pant explained: '...the need for unity and integration at this time, the need to bring the communities closer at a time when fundamentalism was growing all around us...we should be more sensitive and being more sensitive, we should be more tolerant' (*LSD* 1986 col. 392). The All India Muslim Personal Law Board had advised the government that 'it would be unwise and against the interests of national unity' to arouse minority fears and apprehensions (*Statesman*, 27 October 1985, q. Hasan 1989: 46).

Secularism construed as equal respect for all religions was also defended instrumentally in terms of national unity as the platform on which diverse religious groups had historically been brought together as part of the national freedom struggle and Indian nationhood forged. The history of the Indian nation thus validated secularism and its associated ideals, such as the protection of minorities. According to Congress Minister Arjun Singh:

> This broad polity was evolved...during the freedom struggle...we were facing a mighty imperialist power and the leaders of this nation, in trying to forge a broad front against this imperial power, took into account the complexities of the Indian societies...brought everyone, of every persuasion, every faith...into that great and grand alliance for freedom. That force ultimately was able to subjugate the imperialist which is...ample testimony to their correct approach in unifying the nation.... (*LSD* 1986 cols 402–3)

It may be recalled that in Congress discourse in the Constituent Assembly debates, the recognition of religious difference in politics had been considered antithetical to national unity. Secularism was then construed as the disregard of religion as far as the rights of individuals were concerned. During the Shah Bano debate, the non-recognition of religious difference was seen as the greater threat to national unity. Secularism thus came to be recast in terms of 'full' freedom of religion for minorities, including the freedom to live by their personal laws.[63]

One crucial factor in this alteration in Congress conceptions of secularism was a changed sense of *state capability*. In sharp contrast to the heroic sense of state capacity that had characterized the Constituent Assembly debates, in this period, we witness parliamentarians cutting across party lines concurring that state-led reforms in themselves would be ineffectual.[64] This loss of faith in the abilities of the state to effect change did not pertain to religion alone, but was part of a wider disillusionment

---

[63] The primacy of national unity was another respect in which conceptions of secularism in Congress discourse in the Shah Bano debate differed from those advanced by Muslim League representatives in the Constituent Assembly.

[64] Madhu Dandavate (Janata Party), a prominent critic of the Bill, noted:'...if any reform is to be brought about, it will not be brought about merely by Statute...' (*LSD* 1986 col. 381). K.C. Pant (Congress), a supporter of the Bill, held: 'We cannot depend only upon the law for reforms. The society has to be ready for reform. The well-springs of that reform have to come from within...' (*LSD* 1986 col. 387).

in the 1980s with the role of the state in the economy and society. When
the state had been seen as all-powerful, a people divided by religion
were to be knit into a nation through the state's containment of religion
and community affiliations. Conceptions of secularism corresponded
to this. In the 1980s, by contrast, when there was far less confidence in
the capacity of the state to impose its will on society, national unity was
seen to require greater accommodation of religion (Varshney 1993; Jayal
1999). The contours of secularism came to be remoulded accordingly.

Secularism was also linked *constitutively* to national unity. The
argument that secularism as equal respect for all religions constituted the
basis on which the Congress had historically fashioned national unity,
was here taken a step further. Secularism conceived as non-intervention
in minority religious law was portrayed as an extension of traditions of
cultural diversity that had characterized India from antiquity:

> ...minorities in India, specially the largest minority group, the
> Muslims, because of peculiar historical circumstances...must not feel
> apprehensive about their future because India for thousands of years
> has been the biggest melting pot of faith, of religion and of races; and
> they have all lived together and they have maintained their faith. There
> have never been any attempts to throttle them or assimilate them;
> possibly that concept has been alien to Indian culture and...way of life
> and...thought.... (*LSD* 1986 col. 356)

As in the late 1940s, Indian identity was articulated in Congress
discourse in the Shah Bano debate as a secular identity. Only now, this
was seen to consist not so much in the disregard of the religious identity
of individuals, but rather, its recognition by the state. Whereas in the
Constituent Assembly, religious pluralism had been a key motivation for
the adoption of a secular state, in Shah Bano, it came to be *identified* with
secularism: secularism meant the preservation of religious and cultural
diversity. This in turn was now defended as the defining characteristic
of Indian history and philosophy. A.K. Sen, expounded on the meaning
of secularism:

> ...the Constitution sets up a secular democracy...not in the way of the
> uniformity of the grave, it sets up a fine mosaic where each community
> has its own part to play, its own culture to show and its own...
> philosophy to flower. That is Indian secularism...It flourishes on an
> acknowledgement of the different cultures of the various communities
> and religions which have come to stay in this great country...If we start
> on a fine mosaic and try to draw one single pattern all over the country,

then we shall be playing absolutely against the very foundation of our philosophy.... (*LSD* 1986 col. 516)[65]

Secularism was also related to national unity analogically: a secular state that respected religious diversity was akin to Indian civilization that had protected different religions. Thus while secularism continued to be closely linked to national unity in Congress discourse in the Shah Bano debate, there was a subtle redefinition of *how* Indian identity was secular. This involved, most notably, a de-emphasis on the modernizing ambitions of secularism of the late 1940s that had sought the restriction of the sphere of religion, and an emphasis on so-called traditional Indian values of the toleration of religious diversity. In Chapter 3, we saw that the close links between secularism and national unity meant that several traditionalists had espoused modernist notions of the exclusion of religion from politics in the Constituent Assembly debates. In the Shah Bano debated by contrast, the close links between national unity and secularism construed as the accommodation of religious diversity, meant that modernists now invoked Indian tradition in their defence of secularism.

It was in the arguments put forward by Opposition representatives *against* special provisions for Muslim personal law that secularism was linked to national unity instrumentally, constitutively and analogically, in ways similar to Congress discourse of the Constituent Assembly debates. Opposition representatives emphasized non-discrimination between citizens as the basis of Indian unity.[66] National unity remained central in the elaboration of secularism in both Congress and Opposition discourse (Hasan 1998: 72–83); the two disagreed, however, about its requirements, and on national identity, resulting in different conceptions of secularism.

In the changed notions of national unity and secularism in Congress discourse, a retelling of the story of secularism in Indian nationalism was crucial. In the Constituent Assembly debates, it might be recalled, 'history' was seen to demonstrate that the recognition of religion in politics was a threat to national unity. In the new narrative, it was not the exclusion of religion from politics, but its *accommodation* through equal respect for all religions that was portrayed as the basis of Indian unity. Through a

---

[65] See also H.R. Bharadwaj, *LSD* 1986 col. 476.

[66] See Sukomal Sen (CPI-M), *RSD* 1986 col. 271; P. Kolandaivelu (AIADMK) *LSD* 1986 col. 401.

reinterpretation of the history of the Congress party, the freedom struggle and of constitution-making itself, a continuous historical narrative was constructed of Congress support for non-intervention in the religious personal law of minorities. This involved a selective presentation of the views of the Constitution-makers, to which Congress policies in post-Independence India were then seamlessly linked.[67] The current policy of Congress leaders was portrayed as an exercise in restoring a long-standing position that had been upset by the Supreme Court judgement.[68]

In parenthesis, it should be noted that appeals to the past to legitimate positions were an important feature of political arguments, with the speeches of both Congress and Opposition spokesmen invoking the past in various forms—as policy precedent, the freedom struggle, the Constitution, political leaders regarded as national heroes—in support of their positions. While a detailed examination of the uses of the past as an ideological strategy is outside the scope of this study, some brief considerations are in order. First, the past was often invoked as *precedent* to establish that the current position had a respectable historical lineage and did not constitute a radical departure from an established stance. The main ideological purpose served by such invocations of the past was to counter charges that the legislation was motivated by political expediency. Congress Minister Arjun Singh defended the government's decision as a continuation of the secular traditions of the Congress party:

> ...the origins of secularism in the manner in which it is understood, and the origin of those considerations which this Bill seems to take into account should be traced, not after the Bill was introduced...the Constitution itself says that the rights of the minorities in each respect, their faith and all other matters, will be fully protected and that is the consideration for bringing forward this Bill. (*LSD* 1986 col. 403)

A second noteworthy aspect of invocations of the past was the consecration of the Constitution, the freedom struggle, and the 'founding fathers' as the fount of legitimacy for all political action. The very fact that special provisions for minority groups were enshrined in the Constitution and espoused by venerated leaders such as Gandhi and Nehru was seen to

---

[67] See the Law Minister's speech, *LSD* 1986 cols 311–12.

[68] Congress speeches during the reform of the Criminal Procedure Code in 1973 frequently cited. See, in particular, Ram Niwas Mirdha, *LSD* 1986 col. 444; also Nawal Kishore Sharma, *LSD* 1986 col. 413.

confer normative legitimacy, precluding the need for further justification. Such appeals to the past served to legitimize the government's decision by providing it with a long lineage, and by bestowing upon it some of the authority of the Constitution, and the aura of 'disinterested selflessness' associated with national heroes and the freedom struggle (Morris-Jones 1963: 280; see *LSD* 1986 col. 389). Congress representatives were the most prone to this form of appeal to the past, as they could pose as the direct heirs of the freedom struggle: the history of the nation was told as the history of the Congress party and secularism belonged to this history. However, Opposition representatives also frequently relied on this mode of historical validation, condemning the Bill as a break with these traditions of the Constitution and the national movement (see K.P. Unnikrishnan, *LSD* 1986 cols 432–6). In such appeals to the past, involving conflicting interpretations of the histories of the Constitution and the freedom struggle, the historicity of the events cited was often dubious and not germane. The discursive form of such appeals to 'history' resembled that of modern political myths (Bhattacharya 1993). As in the case of popular myths, present action was viewed as a repetition of past action stretching back to the antiquity, and past heroes served as exemplars governing its conduct. The legitimization of political conduct involved establishing a long lineage and continuity with the actions of past heroes and depreciating any element of novelty. Prof. K.K. Tewary, a vocal Congress spokesman, declaimed:

> We, the Congressmen have inherited the long established traditions of the Congress, and the efforts of the Indian nation to consolidate itself and to put faith into the people of diverse faiths in this land...The question of Muslims in India...is an article of faith with Indian National Congress; and those who have inherited the mantle of Mahatma Gandhi, Pandit Jawaharlal Nehru, Indira Gandhi, they cannot resile from the commitment.... (*LSD* 1986 cols 353, 355–6)

The changes in the narrative of the past, in the requirements of national unity and correspondingly, in conceptions of secularism made Congress discourse more hospitable to special provisions for religious minorities than had been the case in the Constituent Assembly debates. Rendering exemptions for Muslims consistent with secularism and national unity was, however, achieved, at the cost of reinforcing Hindu values in political discourse. The implanting of secularism and religious freedom in the values of 'Indian civilization' and 'Indian philosophy', although often espoused by followers of all faiths, has served as a conduit for the 'unstated norms of the Hindu majority' (Cossman and Kapur 1996: 2616). It has meant that secularism, while supportive of minority rights, is redolent of Hindu superiority and self-congratulation on the forbearance and generosity of Hindus, as reflected in the following speech:

> Ours is a democratic country and secularism is its sheet anchor... In comparison with the other countries, we have practised these things in a very liberal way since time immemorial...in the Ramayana... Ravana was the ruler of Lanka and demons were ruling there, but even Vibhishana had the freedom to plant tulsi in his house and recite the name of Lord Rama, why should we also not give them such freedom when the Congress has been struggling for ensuring security and the welfare of the minorities and the women since its inception? (Krishna Sahi, *LSD* 1986 cols 439–40)

Assimilation, it was argued, went against the grain of Indian/Hindu culture. As this speech illustrates, examples from Hindu myths and epics were invoked to make the case that Congress policy represented a continuation of the age-old civilizational traditions of the country. The lives of characters in Hindu myths were humanized and used as *historical* evidence—the 'evidential value' of the lives cited from Hindu epics was the same as historical instances of protection of minorities.[69] The harnessing to a historical narrative of characters and episodes from myths that existed, in a sense, outside history, lent hallowed historical depth to claims of Indian/Hindu traditions of toleration. More pertinently for our argument here, Hindu self-congratulation over their superior 'liberal' credentials (Hasan 1998: 79) could slip easily into a sense of Hindu superiority vis-à-vis other religions as less open-minded, as well as a grievance against special treatment of minorities, as exploiting Hindu generosity. These were recurrent themes in the discourse of the Hindu Right in this period.

Further, while the protection of Muslim law was justified as a continuation of Indian traditions, earlier modernizing goals were not entirely abandoned in Congress discourse. Rather, many speeches implied that such goals were held in abeyance until Muslims displayed a readiness for reform. The eventual goal was still the reform of religious personal

---

[69] Chatterjee notes that '[M]yth, history and the contemporary—all become part of the same chronological sequence...' (1995: 80); see also Bhattacharya 1993; Guha 1997.

laws, even a common civil code, only Congress and Indian traditions of secularism meant that this would not be *imposed* on unwilling minorities. Eduardo Faleiro observed:

> The country undoubtedly faces a threat to its unity. We have too many religions...too many divisive forces...the leaders of different communities must voluntarily...evolve a common system of law which will satisfy everybody and which will strengthen the unity of this country because we are Indians beyond and above being either Hindus or Christians or Parsis...there is no point in...asking the Government to bring this because it is against...genuine secularism. (*LSD* 1986 cols 346–7)

The Congress, it was suggested, differed from the Opposition not so much in terms of the desired objective of a common civil code, but the means of achieving it. For effective change to occur, imposition by the state would be counter-productive: the initiative for reform of personal law must come from religious communities. State non-intervention in minority personal laws was defended as the pragmatic yet principled approach grounded in Congress as well as Indian tradition.[70] This was essentially a consequentialist argument in favour of state non-intervention: the claim was not that forced reform of minority laws would be unjust or even understandably resisted as an attack on minority identity.[71] In some Congress speeches, this was defended as the stance of the state towards the religious affairs of *all* communities and not just minorities. Thus, it was argued that the state undertook the reform of Hindu law in the 1950s as this had the consent of the Hindu community. The implicit claim often was that Muslims who had not consented to such reform yet, were less 'advanced' than the Hindus.[72] Here then was one account

---

[70] Dinesh Singh explained: '...if this Bill serves to create greater confidence among the minority and the majority, we would have served the cause of the Directive Principles of the Constitution to bring about a common civil law' (*LSD* 1986 col. 398); see also Arjun Singh, *LSD* 1986 col. 404.

[71] Justice and consequentialist reasons for state non-intervention in minority personal law might be distinct '...since groups may wrongly feel aggrieved, making the consequences of imposing reform harmful because of this mistaken perception' (Spinner-Halev 2001: 97).

[72] K.C. Pant, averred: 'We cannot depend only on the law for reforms. Society has to be ready for reform...In Hindu society this process has been going on for decades. It had begun a hundred years ago. As a result of that and the efforts of so many tall leaders of this country the Hindu society has been able to regenerate itself' (*The Telegraph*, 15 May 1988, q. Hasan 1989: 49. See also P. Shiv Shankar,

of why Muslims ought to be treated differently by the state—because they were culturally 'backward' and therefore needed more time to reach desired standards.

Although Hindu nationalist themes are clearly discernable in Congress discourse, important differences remained relative to the Hindu Right. In Congress discourse, as we have seen, equal respect for all religions emphasized the rights to religious freedom of *minorities*, and an asymmetrical interpretation of equal respect for all religions. In the appeal to Indian tradition, toleration and religious freedom were not *explicitly* identified with Hindu religion and the emphasis was on unity through *diversity*. Nevertheless, given that the slide from Indian to Hindu values was easily made, Indian tradition could not provide a secure basis for special provisions for religious minorities; it could not prevent these from being viewed as a burden on the tolerance of Hindus. As such, while the discursive shifts in national unity in Congress discourse favoured special treatment of Muslims, these did so at the cost of expanding the ideological space for Hindu nationalism.

THE LEGITIMATING VOCABULARY ON GROUP RIGHTS: CONTINUITIES AND SHIFTS

What does our analysis of secularism in the Shah Bano debate suggest for the legitimating vocabulary on minority rights? First, the normative terms of the vocabulary identified in the Constituent Assembly debates (1946–9) continued to frame political debate on minority rights in the Shah Bano debate (1986). Secularism, democracy, rights, equality, national unity, and development were invoked in political arguments both for and against special provisions for minorities. Further, the connotations of each of these normative terms drew upon a common pool or idea environment comprising all the concepts of the legitimating vocabulary. Both proponents and opponents of the legislation, 'traditionalist' supporters of Muslim law as much as 'modernist' advocates of gender justice, defended their positions on grounds of secularism.

RSD 1986 cols 315–19). As Chatterjee observes, the differential treatment of majority and minority communities with respect personal law is often justified in India through a 'pragmatic argument' that there is 'a certain lag in the readiness of the different communities to accept reforms...' (Chatterjee 1998: 362).

In both cases, secularism was linked to the other concepts of the legitimating vocabulary through constitutive, instrumental and analogical relationships. Thus, for instance, in Congress discourse, secularism construed as equal respect for all religions was linked to national unity instrumentally, as the means for securing political stability in the present and building a multi-religious national movement in the past, as well as constitutively, as India's identity was defined in terms of ancient traditions of accommodation of religious diversity. Hence, as a frame whose normative terms defined the parameters within which debate on minority preference was conducted among ideologically and politically opposed representatives, and whose constitutive elements were elaborated in relation to each other, the legitimating vocabulary on minority rights identified in the Constituent Assembly debates, endured in the Shah Bano debate.

Like in the Constituent Assembly debates, in the Shah Bano case too, the key concepts of the legitimating vocabulary both drew upon Western liberal values, and at the same time, were inflected by the particular history of minority rights in India and indigenous cultural idioms. Thus, liberal values such as equality before the law, non-discrimination, religious freedom, individual rights, and constitutional rights informed elaborations of secularism. These were used by an ideologically diverse set of parliamentarians, with 'modernist' Congressmen and 'traditionalist' Muslim League representatives alike employing a language of rights to defend religious freedom. Values from different liberal traditions were in evidence in political debate, with individualist liberal rights intertwined with utilitarian considerations about welfare and the social good. With regard to the common contrast between Indian and Western secularism, we saw that equal respect for all religions as elaborated by the Congress and other proponents of the legislation in the Shah Bano debate invoked liberal and democratic values, and involved notions of separation of state and religion. At the same time, my analysis also showed that indigenous cultural and historical idioms were interwoven into the legitimating vocabulary. Thus, for instance, religious freedom was portrayed both as a constitutional right and as an essential value of Indian civilization.[73]

---

[73] Religious freedom, of course, is not only a Western liberal value: long-standing traditions of religious freedom exist in non-Western religious, social, and political practice.

Rights, in many instances, were construed less as entitlements of individuals, than as gifts of a benevolent authority to 'weaker sections' such as minorities and women.[74] Appeals to traditions of toleration of diverse cultures and the protection of 'weaker sections' were indicative of indigenous cultural norms as well as historical legacies of the colonial state. Congress discourse in the Shah Bano debate was less committed to standard individualist difference-blind liberalism than it had been in the Constituent Assembly debates of the late 1940s. It showed a greater willingness to take group identity into account in order to rectify inequalities and thus represented a move towards an egalitarian liberal justification of minority rights, although this was not developed.

Relative to the late 1940s, Congress discourse registered important shifts. In the Constituent Assembly debates, it may be recalled, the key concepts of the legitimating vocabulary were construed in ways that were hostile to special provisions for religious minorities. In the Shah Bano case, by contrast, special exemptions for Muslim personal law were rendered consonant with, and indeed a requirement of, the key legitimating ideals. Secularism was construed as equal respect for all religions and protection of minorities; rights, in terms of group and minority rights to religious freedom, rather than the earlier emphasis on the rights of individuals to equal citizenship; and national unity, as requiring the accommodation of religious diversity, rather than the disregard of religion. These were supported by the extension to religious minorities of the paternalist idiom of the duty of the state to protect 'weaker sections', earlier applied only to 'backward' Untouchable and tribal groups.

A conceptual analysis of political discourse nevertheless suggests that while shifts have indeed occurred, these are subtler than is commonly thought. Secularism in Congress discourse was still closely tied to national unity, only, the latter's requirements were now construed differently, in terms of religious freedom for groups, rather than equal rights of individuals. In terms of our framework, the mechanism whereby the changed connotations of secularism were brought about involved a substitution in the positions of religious freedom and equal citizenship in relation to secularism, with the latter moving to a peripheral position

---

[74] On paternalism in relation to gender in this debate, see Pathak and Sunder Rajan 1989; Das 1994.

from one adjacent to secularism. Sweeping claims regarding discursive shifts in this period are thus overstated.

Does the fact that Congress discourse in the Shah Bano debate was hospitable to Muslim personal law suggest that a foundation had been established in the normative vocabulary for special provisions for the protection of minority cultures, now that the shadow of Partition had receded? Our analysis suggests several reasons for caution. Whereas the discursive shifts of the Congress narrowed the justificatory deficit for preferential policies for minority protection, important gaps remained. With secularism, for instance, it remained unclear how, normatively speaking, the transition was made from all groups having equal rights to religious freedom, to the differential interpretation of rights to religious freedom in the case of majority and minority religious communities. Substantive equality arguments for preferential treatment of religious minorities in terms, for instance, of minority cultural protection, self-determination or group oppression remained under-articulated.[75] Similarly, in the case of national unity, whereas the preservation of cultural diversity was portrayed in Congress discourse as the distinguishing feature of India's eternal way of life, why this was valuable apart from the continuation of tradition was not argued for— why *this* Indian tradition was a good thing, when several others had been jettisoned, remained unclear. The long-term objective remained, as in the Constituent Assembly debates, that of national unity through a common legal framework for all citizens. No robust multicultural arguments were offered for the preservation of cultural diversity: that the protection of minority cultures could enhance the range of options available to *all* citizens, for example (Raz 1986) was not articulated in Congress opinion. Insofar as some advance was made towards the justification of special treatment of religious minorities, these relied on notions of individual or group disadvantage, and not the value of cultural diversity per se. With both equality and freedom-based arguments for preferential provisions for minority cultures remaining deficient, special provisions for religious minorities would continue to suffer from a justificatory deficit.

To turn to policy and political changes of the period, our analysis of discursive continuity and shift suggests, first, that the contending sides

---

[75] Notable elaborations in the political theory literature include Kymlicka 1989, 1995; Young 1990; Spinner-Halev 2001.

in the Shah Bano case were divided not just by electoral competition
and policy preferences, but also differences over the meanings of key
legitimating concepts. In particular, differences over the interpretation of
secularism defined the contending positions in the Shah Bano debate. In
the terms of my analysis, these can be understood in terms of differences
in the *arrangement* of concepts in relation to each other. For proponents
of the legislation, the propinquity of secularism to rights of religious
freedom meant that it was construed as antagonistic to state intervention
in religious laws. In the case of its opponents, secularism's proximity to
equal rights for individuals meant that it was construed as requiring such
intervention. Second, the policy shift towards stronger multicultural
provisions was accompanied by discursive shifts that were conducive
to this outcome. Secularism was reinterpreted in Congress opinion in
ways that rendered it more hospitable to special treatment for religious
minorities. At the same time, we saw that the discursive shift of the
Congress did not provide a secure basis for reconciling legal pluralism
and national unity, for establishing Muslim religious law over common
secular laws. That subsequent judicial decisions on Muslim personal law
have continued to urge a common code on national unity grounds, and
interpreted the legislation so that the maintenance granted to women is
similar to what they would obtain under the Criminal Procedure Code,[76]
is not surprising.[77]

[76] In an important decision, the Supreme Court in *Daniel Latifi* vs *Union of
India* interpreted the Muslim Women's Act so that the maintenance granted
to a divorced Muslim woman would be as much as would be offered under the
Criminal Procedure Code, bringing 'personal laws in line with equality and justice'
(Hasan 2005: 359). In other interpretations of the Muslim Women's Act by lower
courts, judges have awarded more generous divorce settlements than the small
allowance which women can claim under the section 125 Criminal Procedure
Code, relying upon 'the Preamble which proclaimed that the aim of the Act is to
protect the rights of Muslim women' (Agnes 2005: 127). However, the Act has not
necessarily meant a net improvement in the economic rights of divorced Muslim
women. Husbands have used the Act to appeal against settlements awarded by
lower courts, 'making the litigation process far more cumbersome and ambiguous
for Muslim women' (Agnes 2005: 128). Many Muslim women continue to invoke
the Criminal Procedure Code (Hasan 2005).
[77] In the 1995 Sarla Mudgal case, for instance, the Supreme Court judgement
noted that in 'the Indian Republic, there was to be only one nation—the Indian

In terms of the major political shift of the late 1980s—the decline of Congress dominance—our analysis suggests, to begin with, that this decline took the form not just of changes to electoral and party politics, but also to political ideology. While the Congress in the Shah Bano debate was able to change policy in its desired direction, in contrast with the Constituent Assembly debates, it was unable to reconfigure the legitimating vocabulary of the polity in accordance with its preferred interpretation. There was now far greater disagreement over the meanings of the key legitimating concepts, and no clear *reigning* set of public norms: competing conceptions of secularism remained entrenched throughout the debate, coalescing around two distinct poles. This was an indicator of a *loss of hegemony*, discernable in the lineaments of ideological contest in legislative debate. But the legacy of earlier Congress hegemony endured, notably in the form of the shared terms of the legitimating vocabulary in the Shah Bano debate, legacy of the ideological consensus forged at the time of constitution-making.

Not only was the Congress unable to persuade its opponents in the Shah Bano debate, the conception of secularism it advocated *itself* lacked legitimacy.[78] The discursive shift of the Congress, as we have seen, was accomplished by downgrading the criterion that had been central to the elaboration of secularism in the Constituent Assembly, equal citizenship rights for individuals. Opposition representatives, however, described the government policy as anti-secular by invoking this very criterion, and portraying the Congress in the Shah Bano debate as abandoning its previous, principled position. Paraphrasing Skinner from a different context, to the extent that the Congress' defence of Muslim personal law in the Shah Bano debate was perceived as relying on a *distinct* conception of secularism that marked a shift from the positions of venerated Constitution-makers, rather than a simply a new case that could be accommodated within their meaning, both the interpretation of secularism advanced by the Congress and, by extension, the special treatment of Muslim law, lacked legitimacy (Skinner 1988: 111, 115).

This, in turn, meant that the discursive shift of the Congress created a favourable ideological climate for the growth of the Hindu Right. The

---

nation—and no community could claim to remain a separate entity on the basis of religion' (q. Menon and Nigam 2007: 47).

[78] This understanding of ideological failure draws upon Skinner 1988: 126–8.

Shah Bano case has been regarded as a pivotal moment in the rise of
the Hindu nationalist BJP. Hasan, for instance, notes that the debate
'was particularly important in developing a critique of secularism, and
it played a crucial role in the de-legitimation of the Congress party
and its displacement from the centre of Indian politics' (1998: 72, 82).
Why, however, was the Congress most vulnerable to criticisms from
the BJP in the Shah Bano case, rather than, for instance, from the Left
parties who also opposed it in this case, and why was it most susceptible
with regard to *secularism*? A conceptual analysis of political discourse
provides the following clues. First, it may be recalled that national
unity was the pre-eminent consideration in Congress discourse, and
its realization through a common civil code for all citizens remained
the (deferred) aspiration. Within the terms of its own position, then,
the Congress was susceptible to the criticism that it was conciliating
minorities at the *cost* of the nation. The pursuit of this goal was delayed
mainly, it appeared, on proximate pragmatic grounds: justice based
arguments for exemptions for Muslims remained underdeveloped in
Congress discourse. The case for the accommodation of minorities
relied largely upon secularism interpreted in terms of Indian/Hindu
practices of toleration. The BJP was the chief advocate of the pre-
eminence of national unity over all other values; as well as the main
critic of minority rights as obstructing a uniform civil code for the
achievement of national unity.[79] Importantly, the BJP was also the chief
advocate of Indian/Hindu tradition as the basis of national identity.
It was thus ideally placed to mount the critique of Congress policy
as 'minority appeasement', a slogan which simultaneously appealed to
the sense that minorities were being conciliated for reasons that went
beyond justice, at the cost of the nation, and through an abuse of the
tolerance of Hindus.

Significantly, the critique of the Congress by the BJP after Shah
Bano did not assume the form of an attack on its commitment to
national unity, but to *secularism*, with Congress secularism mocked
as 'pseudo-secularism'. Contrary to influential opinion, in the Shah
Bano debate, the BJP did not reject secularism, or contend that
secularism should have yielded to other values such as gender justice

---

[79] In the arguments of Left representatives against the government bill, national
unity considerations were not prominent.

or national integration.[80] Rather, it projected itself as the upholder of 'real' secularism, challenging the Congress' claim to be secular.[81] The effectiveness of the BJP's strategy of discrediting Congress secularism as pseudo-secularism can be better understood if we recall that Congress' interpretation of secularism in the Shah Bano debate, as requiring special provisions for religious minorities, was seen as marking a shift from its earlier elaboration of secularism in terms of the equal rights for all individuals irrespective of religion. By manoeuvring itself into a position on secularism *similar* to that occupied by Congress in the Constituent Assembly debates, the BJP could portray itself as the champion of true secularism that emphasized the irrelevance of religion for rights. Hindu nationalism could thus appear 'as a principled modernist critic' of Islamic fundamentalism in contrast with the Congress's 'pseudo-secularism' of 'preaching tolerance for religious obscurantism and bigotry' (Chatterjee 1998: 347).[82] While the subsequent displacement of the Congress by the BJP as the largest national political party in the 1990s represented a major shift in the Indian polity, the ideological ground for this had existed in earlier Indian nationalist discourse, and was reinforced in important respects by the Congress' discursive shift in the Shah Bano debate. As such, the rise of the Hindu Right did not represent the reassertion of religion or India's indigenous traditions over modernist liberal democratic ideals.

Does it follow from this, as some scholars have suggested, that secularism and liberal democracy more broadly, are inextricably tied to a homogenizing nation-state and inadequate for dealing with the challenge of Hindu nationalism? Chatterjee has argued that 'respect for cultural

[80] Thus, for instance, Hasan notes that the 'Hindu Right's strategy attempted to dismiss cultural diversity by setting the equal treatment of all women in opposition to secularism' (1998: 80–2).

[81] As Chatterjee notes, in Hindu nationalism, 'the term "secular" is not itself made a target of attack... "anti-secular demands"... are not crucial to [its]...political thrust, or... public appeal' (1998: 347).

[82] The positions were not *identical*: the Congress, it may be recalled, had not interpreted equal citizenship rights in individualistic terms alone, and had supported cultural and educational rights for minorities. In Congress discourse, however, the latter had remained under-defended, and difference-blind equality in individual rights had dominated. See Chapters 3, and 4 above.

diversity [is]...impossible to articulate...in the unitary rationalism of the language of rights...there is no viable way out of this problem within the given contours of liberal democratic theory...' (1998: 365). A conceptual analysis of political discourse, however, suggests that secularism is a complex ideal that can assume multiple forms and relate to national unity in different ways, not a single monolithic ideology *necessarily* committed to symmetrical treatment of all individuals or embedded within a unitary homogenizing nation-state. Pessimism about liberal democratic ideals that characterizes influential strands of postcolonial studies derives from an unduly narrow understanding of their resources, and their identification with Western colonialism. Attention to the actual historical forms of liberal democratic ideas in postcolonial contexts, however, suggests several permutations are possible. While secularism and liberal rights can be hostile to cultural diversity, these can also accommodate group-differentiated rights. This was hinted at, but not developed in Congress discourse in the Shah Bano debate, suggesting perhaps the limits of political imagination, and the continuing hold of an unduly narrow understanding of the requirements of national unity. The main alternative to secularism advocated by some, the resources for toleration in Indian tradition (Nandy 1998), can veer easily into support for the majority Hindu religion. It may well be that in the complex area of religious personal law, democratic self-determination by religious communities is the best way forward (Chatterjee 1998; Mehta 2005); however, secularism also offers resources for the justification of special provisions for minority religions, whose elaboration by Indian policy-makers is still awaited.

6

Social Justice and Quotas in Government Jobs for Other Backward Classes

The Mandal Debate, 1990

INTRODUCTION

The 1990 Mandal debate heralded a new phase in the career of preferential treatment in India. National quotas in government employment, hitherto limited to the Scheduled Castes and Scheduled Tribes, were extended for the first time to the larger, more amorphous category of Other Backward Classes[1]. Quotas have since steadily expanded, notably in higher educational institutions for the OBCs. Like the Shah Bano case, the 1990 Mandal debate also represented a political watershed: lower caste-based political parties would henceforth be a significant force in Indian politics, signalling the end of Congress hegemony.

According to my argument, major policy and political change should be accompanied by shifts in the legitimating vocabulary. What were the discursive changes associated with the expansion of preferential treatment to the OBCs? Usually, the 1990s are characterized in terms of the resurgence of identity politics and the retreat of the liberal democratic values of post-Independence elites. Caste, which like religion had sought

[1] The 1990 Mandal debate was not the first instance of expansion of employment quotas in independent India. Quotas had been granted to groups designated as 'backward' (mainly caste and communal groups) in most Indian states—for details, see Galanter 1984, particularly ch. 6. Mandal, however, saw the consolidation and extension for the first time at the *national* level, of the ad hoc and irregular trajectory of expansion in state-level policies, and in this sense marked a paradigm-shift.

to be banished from the public realm by Nehruvian modernists, returned with a vengeance to the political centre-stage (Menon and Nigam 2007: 19). The advocacy of quotas in terms of parity of presence of different social groups marked, it is held a radical break from the constitutional basis of preferential treatment (Mahajan 1998).

Through a detailed analytical interpretation of arguments in the 1990 parliamentary debate, I show that dominant understandings of the respects in which Mandal represented a new departure need to be refined. The 1990 Mandal debate, most significantly, signalled the ascendance of social justice as a legitimating norm in its own right. This marked an important shift in justifications of affirmative action in India. Nevertheless, underneath the rhetoric of a 'share of state power' for the OBCs, the shift in the normative basis of group preference inaugurated by the Constitution-makers, towards ameliorating *disadvantage* rather than maintaining *distinctness*, survived. While claims for OBC quotas emphasized social rather than economic equality, these were substantially social justice arguments: in justificatory terms, these did not represent a triumph of identity.

Justifications for OBC quotas in Janata Dal discourse nevertheless differed from Congress arguments for preferential treatment for disadvantaged groups in the Constituent Assembly debates in important ways. In the Mandal rhetoric of social justice, in terms of my proposal of the legitimating vocabulary, the older nationalist ideal of equality was redefined by linking equality closely to democracy, and distancing it from national unity. This represented a substantial and distinctive ideological position, contrary to a common view that lower caste politics of the 1990s is simply populist, lacking in 'an overarching ideological framework' (Vora 2004: 289). Like political rhetoric more generally, the discourse of social justice of the 1990s is usually understood in terms of the self-interested behaviour of politicians, driven by electoral calculations of 'vote bank' politics, or group interest. Instrumental or identity concerns, however, do not suffice for an adequate understanding of discourses of social justice. A reconstruction of the arguments implicit in political rhetoric furnishes materials for better explanations of policies of preferential treatment and the politics of lower caste-based parties in India. It also illuminates important areas of tension in the political theory literature such as the relationship of social equality and social justice; merit and affirmative action.

Quotas for OBCs in Government Jobs: Some Historical Aspects

Galanter notes two main species of usage of 'backward classes': (a) an inclusive usage to designate all those who need special treatment (including Scheduled Castes and Tribes), and (b) caste groups above the Untouchables, the so-called OBCs of contemporary debates (1984: 159). Although the term 'backward classes' had been in use since the late 19th century, at Independence, it had not acquired a definite set of referents at the all-India level.[2] In the princely states of Kolhapur and Mysore, which had established preferential treatment for 'backward classes' in the early twentieth century, as well as the Bombay and Madras presidencies, the term was well known. However, 'backward classes' was used in its broad sense in some contexts and narrower usage in others. The term OBC acquired currency at the time of Independence as a designation for the non Scheduled Caste and Scheduled Tribe 'backward'. Constitution-makers recognized the category, but declined to specify which groups were to be included within it, despite being pressed on this score.[3] Nevertheless, it was clearly envisaged that 'backward groups' other than Dalits and Adivasis were eligible for preferential provisions and that caste and communal criteria might play a role in the identification of these groups.

The key issue that has dominated policy debates regarding preference for the OBCs in independent India concerns the

---

[2] Jaffrelot traces its earliest usage to the Madras administration's policies of preference for the under-educated in the 1870s (2003: 214). On the antecedents of reservations for 'backward classes' in the colonial period, see Chapter 2 above; also Singh 1982; Bayly 2000; Mendelsohn and Vicziany 1998.

[3] Dr B.R. Ambedkar, for instance, stated: '...we have left it to be determined by each local Government. A backward community is a community which is backward in the opinion of the Government' (CAD VII: 702). In contrast to the OBCs, the Scheduled Castes and Scheduled Tribes have had a more stable set of referents. Constitutional articles pertaining to the OBCs (referred to as socially and educationally 'backward classes' in the Constitution) notably include Articles 15 (4), (5) and 16(4), which qualify non-discrimination and equality of opportunity, permitting special provisions for 'backward classes' in employment and other areas; and Article 340, which permits the President to appoint a Backward Classes Commission to 'investigate the conditions of socially and educationally "backward classes"'.

identification of these groups.[4] Would OBCs be castes and communal groupings, or identified by economic and occupational criteria? An attempt to centralize policy with regard to the OBCs was undertaken in 1953, when the First Backward Classes Commission, popularly known as the Kaka Kalelkar Commission after its chairman, was set up to determine national standards and a central list of 'backward classes'. The Commission submitted its report in 1955, listing about 32 per cent of the then population as backward, identified mainly on the basis of caste.[5] Although the Kalelkar Report recommended reservations for the OBCs, and Kalelkar himself equivocated on the issue (Khan 2008: 217, 221), he eventually concluded that it would have been preferable to determine criteria of backwardness on principles other than caste, virtually repudiating the work of the Commission.[6] The Central government was

[4] For the identification of 'backward classes' and the criteria of backwardness favoured by higher courts, see Galanter 1984; also Witten 1983. The judiciary has also played a key role in establishing numerical limits on reservations. In *Balaji vs Mysore* (1963), the Supreme Court established a ceiling of 50 per cent for educational quotas.

[5] The Commission travelled the country for over two years, receiving more than 3000 petitions, conducting nearly six thousand interviews. It produced a list of 2,399 'backward castes' (de Zwart 2000). The report's recommendations included quotas in government service of 25 per cent in Class I, 33.5 per cent in Class II, and 40 per cent in Classes III and IV; 70 per cent reservation in medical, scientific, and technical colleges. Galanter notes that the Commission used caste in two ways: as the *units* or groups of classification (to whom general criteria of 'backwardness' pertaining to occupation, education, representation in government service would apply), and a caste's position in the social hierarchy as a *criterion* of backwardness (1984: 170). As a criterion for determining 'backwardness', official policies towards 'backward classes', as well as Scheduled Castes, have historically assumed a correlation between the position of a caste in the ritual hierarchy and the secular condition of its members (Dushkin 1972: 168).

[6] In his dissent, Kalelkar regretted that 'the result of our inquiry is that caste consciousness, caste loyalties and caste aspirations, have increased throughout the country'; 'the dangers to the solidarity of the country' needed to be considered; 'group investigation is repugnant to the spirit of democracy'; and since 'the nation has decided to establish a classless and casteless society', 'backwardness should be studied from the point of view of the individual and, at the most, that of a family. Any other unit will lead to caste or class aggrandisement' (Kalelkar Report 1956: xiii, xiv). However, in other places, Kalelkar also defended the consideration of caste in the determination of 'backwardness', and the report itself discusses caste

unenthusiastic about the report, with the Home Minister criticizing the emphasis on caste as separatist, and its recommendations were never implemented (Galanter 1984: 173). From the 1960s onwards, attempts at national listing and policy were abandoned, and reservation policy for OBCs became a matter for state governments (ibid.: 176). Most states set up their own Backward Classes Commissions and instituted reservations in public services and educational institutions under state control.[7] For all the variations in state patterns, caste and communal groups remained the main units for identifying the 'backward' (ibid.: 181–5; Jaffrelot 2003: 238–53). These were employed in conjunction with income, education and other criteria by state level commissions, in some cases to distinguish between 'backward' and the 'more backward' groups (Galanter 1984: 181–5; de Zwart 2000).[8]

The attempt at formulating a national policy for preferential treatment for the OBCs was revived when a Janata coalition government assumed power in 1977.[9] A Second Backward Classes Commission (known as the Mandal Commission after its Chairman, BP Mandal) was instituted in 1978. The Commission reported in 1980, placing

---

at length, arguing in favour of OBC reservations. It notes, for instance, that '[U]nless the services are manned by a fair proportion of the candidates belonging to backward class groups, they will not inspire confidence' which is necessary for the 'administrative machinery...[to]...become an instrument to implement the policy of a Welfare State' (ibid.: 137).

[7] Jaffrelot 2003 contrasts northern states (including UP, Bihar, MP, Rajasthan, West Bengal, Orissa) with Southern states (Karnataka, Tamil Nadu, Kerala, and Andhra Pradesh) that instituted reservation policies earlier, with Western states of Maharashtra and Gujarat reflecting an intermediate pattern.

[8] Distinctions within the 'backward class' category predate Independence. The Madras Communal Government Order of 1947 distinguished 'Forward non-Brahmin Hindus' from 'Backward non-Brahmin Hindus'. Claims for 'most backward caste' status have been made to Backward Class commissions on behalf of several caste groups, notably Vanniyars in Tamil Nadu, lower ranking Vokkalingas and Lingayats in Karnataka, Kurmis and Koeris in Bihar (de Zwart 2000).

[9] The Janata Party's social base and ideological leanings supported extension of quotas to the OBCs. Its 1977 manifesto had promised to pursue the recommendations of the Kalekar report (Galanter 1984: 186–7; Jaffrelot 2003: ch. 8).

52 per cent of the country's population in the OBC category.[10] Its recommendations included employment and higher education quotas of 27 per cent for the 'backward classes', in keeping with the Supreme Court's ruling that overall quotas not exceed 50 per cent. By the time the Mandal Commission submitted its report, however, there was a Congress government at the Centre, and while the report was discussed in Parliament on a few occasions in the 1980s and broadly endorsed, it remained in cold storage for ten years. The 1989 general election brought to power another Janata coalition government whose manifesto included a commitment to the implementation of the Mandal Report.[11] On 7 August 1990, the Prime Minister V.P. Singh announced the implementation of the recommendation of 27 per cent quotas in government employment for OBCs. Internecine conflict within the ruling coalition was thought to motivate the timing of the announcement, which attracted massive student protests and excoriating condemnation in the English language print media, with several prominent academics taking sides in the public debate on the issue.[12] The government decision was stayed pending a Supreme Court verdict regarding its constitutionality; employment quotas for OBCs were eventually implemented after being upheld by the Court in 1992.[13]

[10] This included 3,743 castes. As no caste-wise census figures are available after 1931, these figures are disputed. Most current estimates put the number of OBCs at around 40 per cent.

[11] For details of the political background to the government's decision see Jaffrelot 2003: ch. 10.

[12] These included eminent sociologists such as M.N. Srinivas, Andre Beteille, and Veena Das. *India Today* led the attack in the English language press, comparing the government's policy with South African apartheid. Strident criticism was also voiced in the columns of the *The Times of India*, *Indian Express*, and *Hindustan Times*. Some 63 students died in self-immolation protests (Jaffrelot 2003: 344–7).

[13] *Indra Sawhney and others* vs *the Union of India* (1992). While endorsing caste-based OBC quotas, the decision also offered many concessions to its opponents. It broadly affirmed the 50 per cent limit on quotas, disallowed quotas in promotions and highly specialized posts, emphasized the need for rigour in the identification of beneficiaries, and most influentially, mandated the exclusion of a 'creamy layer' of socially advanced persons/sections from Other Backward Classes (Dhavan 2008: 180–4; Dudley Jenkins 2003: 148–55). Several of the Supreme Court's restrictions on quotas were reversed by Parliament through

The broad party positions on quotas for the OBCs in the parliamentary debate in 1990 on the government's decision were as follows.[14] The Janata Dal, the main party in the ruling National Front coalition, unreservedly championed quotas for the OBCs and opposed the use of economic criteria to exclude the better-off OBCs. It also supported quotas for religious minorities. Left parties such as CPI (M) and Forward Bloc were strong supporters of OBC quotas but favoured priority for poor 'backward' castes and in some cases, the inclusion of upper-caste poor. The Hindu nationalist Bharatiya Janata Party (BJP), an ally of the ruling Janata Dal, pressed for including upper-caste poor and excluding well-off OBCs. The party opposed the extension of reservation to religious minorities. The Congress party was ambivalent in its support for the government policy, favouring economic criteria to exclude the better-off among the OBCs, as well as the extension of quotas to the economically poor upper castes. Many in the Congress and the BJP disapproved of the policy, and the parties were associated in public opinion with opposition to OBC quotas to some extent. During the initial stages of the parliamentary debate on the government's decision, there was little outright opposition from any party to OBC quotas, leading the Prime Minister V.P. Singh to applaud the new 'consensus' (*LSD* 4.10.1990 col. 191). Opposition to the government's decision within Parliament became overt and gathered momentum in the later stages of the debate, strengthened by the hostile response of middle-class public opinion.

SOCIAL JUSTICE AND EQUALITY

Competing Conceptions of Social Justice: Social versus Economic Equality

Social justice was the key legitimating concept in political arguments above quotas for OBCs in the Mandal debate. Announcing the government's decision to implement the recommendations of the Mandal Commission report, the Prime Minister, V.P. Singh, termed it 'a momentous decision of social justice' (*RSD* 1990, col. 309).

---

constitutional amendments, including the 77th amendment (1995), 82nd and 83rd amendments (2000), and 93rd amendment (2000)—see Dhavan 2008.

[14] There were some shifts in the stance of all parties during the course of the debate.

Parties critical of the government decision were careful to preface
their objections with declarations of support for the cause of social
justice (See *RSD* 27.12.1990 col.276; *LSD* 5.9.1990 col. 418). Social
justice was not a recent semantic acquisition—the term appears in the
Indian Constitution and had been employed to refer to provisions for
disadvantaged groups in policy documents and debates.[15] Nevertheless,
its *prominence* in justifications of preferential treatment marked a new
departure. Social justice in the Mandal debate was elaborated mainly
in terms of equality, by both advocates and opponents of quotas: like
the debate on affirmative action in the United States, the reservations
debate in India is largely an 'intramural debate among partisans of
equality' (Rosenfeld 1991: 2).

The first striking aspect about arguments in favour of OBC quotas
in the 1990 Mandal debate relative to the Constituent Assembly debates,
is that these explicitly distanced themselves from concerns of material
equality and instead emphasized *social* equality.[16] Social justice connoted
that the inequalities that quotas sought to rectify were concerned not
so much with the distribution of wealth and income in society, but with
inequalities in social status and power. Janata Dal spokesmen repeatedly
emphasized that quotas in the bureaucracy were not a means of reducing
economic inequalities in society or of securing basic material needs. While
social inequalities were, of course, associated with economic inequalities,
so that the lower rungs of the caste hierarchy were characterized by both
economic and social disadvantages, improving economic well-being was
regarded as incidental to the aim of quotas. Ram Awadhesh Singh, a
prominent advocate of OBC quotas, argued:

[15] The Kalelkar Report, for instance, contains numerous references to social
justice, used to denote special treatment for 'weaker sections', including the OBCs.
When the report was discussed in Parliament in 1965, however, the government
spokesman opposed the use of caste criteria as 'contrary to the first principle of
social justice' in their unfairness to the other poor (Galanter 1984: 178).

[16] In theoretical discussions of equality, a distinction is commonly drawn between
social equality, denoting equality of status, and distributive equality, concerning
the distribution of resources among individuals in a society (see Miller 1999:
231–3). In my usage, social equality is not regarded as independent of social
justice, but the distinction between equality of status and distributive equality
is maintained.

It is argued that is there not poverty among the upper castes, don't they
need a livelihood. This is not a struggle for livelihood. This is a struggle
for a share in state power...This is not an economic question. This is
a strange country. Here...respect (*izzat*) is not with wealth but with
caste; respect is enhanced when power is attached to it. (*RSD* 1990,
cols. 361–4, translation from Hindi)[17]

Second, while social inequalities were associated with economic
inequalities, so that the lower rungs of the caste hierarchy were
characterized by both economic and social disadvantages, these were not
viewed as a *consequence* of economic inequalities. Rather, the inequalities
of status that quotas sought to remedy were seen to derive from traditional
caste hierarchies that had historically excluded ritually inferior groups
from education and state power. Further, disparities in the representation
of upper and lower castes in government jobs and higher educational
institutions provided the main evidence for the social inequalities that
quotas sought to remedy, a point to which we shall return.

Third, social justice connoted that social *groups*, rather than individuals were the units of justice calculation and benefit allocation. Quotas
were intended for caste and communal groups included within the OBC
category as a whole, irrespective of the differences of socio-economic
circumstances within these groups. The assumption was that individuals
were disadvantaged on account of their group membership, and that the
latter must thus be taken into account in rectifying such disadvantages.
Proposals for excluding socially or economically advantaged individuals
from the OBCs, advanced mostly by Congress and BJP representatives,
were rejected by Prime Minister V.P. Singh as 'diluting' the purpose of
reservations: 'The rule is for the whole class and section...The rule is not
for individuals. When the whole section comes up to a certain level...we
will do away with it' (*RSD* 1990 col. 251). This construal of social justice
encapsulated several themes found in the thought of lower caste leaders
since the late nineteenth century—the emphasis on the denial of respect;
political power for undoing the effects of caste; and the advancement

---

[17] Hukumdeo Narayan Yadav, another Janata Dal spokesman, declared: 'It is not
a question of poverty, it is of self-respect' (*LSD* 1990 col. 409). The speeches of
supporters of OBC quotas often quoted at length from the Mandal Commission
Report. On the Indian socialist lineage of the Janata Dal's discourse of social
justice, see Jaffrelot 2003.

of the community as a whole, rather than of individuals within it.[18] Its recent antecedents were to be found in the thought of socialist Gandhian Dr Ram Manohar Lohia, an important influence for Janata leaders (Sheth 2002; Jaffrelot 2003).

Social justice in the discourse of advocates of OBC quotas thus connoted that *social disabilities* rather than economic deprivation were being singled out for rectification, that these disabilities were the consequence of *social hierarchies*, rather than economic arrangements, and that *social groups* rather than individuals were the relevant units from the standpoint of justice. Construing social justice in these terms had important political consequences: the entire group of OBCs and only the 'backward classes' could be identified as beneficiaries of quotas. For once quotas had as their primary aim the rectification of social inequalities deriving from ritual hierarchies, there was no need to exclude economically privileged OBCs, or to include economically disadvantaged sections of upper castes within the ambit of job quotas.

The construal of social justice in terms of social equality was characteristic of the pronouncements of the ruling Janata Dal and Left parties such as the CPI who were the staunchest advocates of OBC quotas. Despite their avowals to the contrary, however, there continued to be a strong presumption in political discourse of a link between quotas and economic disabilities. A variety of proposals based on economic criteria were put forward, with increasing frequency as the debate progressed, mainly by representatives from the Opposition Congress party, as well as the government's ally, the BJP. These demanded modifications in the government's policy, such as giving priority to the poor among the 'backward castes', stipulating means tests for 'backward caste' beneficiaries, and instituting quotas for economically weak sections among the upper castes. For instance, Congress spokesman S.S. Ahluwalia averred: 'Equity and fairplay demand that job reservations and other special measures for the 'backward classes' as a whole not be pre-empted by the richer or more privileged segments of 'backward classes'. It is equally essential that the poor and deprived of all sections of our people also be given equitable opportunities of

---

[18] Important theorists include Jyotiba Phule, Dr B.R. Ambedkar, and Ram Manohar Lohia—see O'Hanlon 1985; Omvedt 1994; Sheth 2002; Rodrigues 2005.

advancement' (*RSD* 1990 col. 45).[19] In proposals for giving priority to the poor among the OBCs, economic criteria were advocated to *supplement* caste membership, and there was no conflict between the two on the question of the identification of beneficiaries of quotas (see *RSD* 1990 col. 286).[20] In proposals to exclude those from economically privileged backgrounds, economic criteria such as means tests were proposed as a standard *independent* of, and potentially in conflict with, caste membership for the selection of beneficiaries. Implicit in most proposals that economic criteria be employed for the identification of beneficiaries of quotas was the sense that group membership was not always a reliable indicator of economic deprivation, and group-based quotas were unjust if this were the case.

What we find here is a distinct conception of social justice from that found in Janata Dal speeches.[21] Here, too, social justice was elaborated in terms of equality. Underlying criticisms of the government's reservation policy as unjust were principles such as basic needs, economic equality, and non-discrimination.[22] The government's proposal was seen as unjust because it did not target those most in need within the OBCs, and excluded the needy outside the OBCs: need was evaluated here in terms of economic criteria such as income, rather than in terms of recognition or status. The government's policy was also criticized as unjust on grounds that it would allow the already privileged to accumulate more and leave the position of those who had the least unchanged, thereby widening economic inequalities in society. Finally, the criticism of OBC reservations as unjust invoked the principle of non-discrimination.

[19] See also Congress President Rajiv Gandhi's speech, *LSD* 6.9. 1990 cols 487–90.

[20] Such suggestions were also mooted by supporters of the government's policy from Left parties. CPI(M) MP Somnath Chatterjee argued: '...when the kitty is small and the demand is large, one has to have some standard; and that can only be some economic standard or economic criterion' (*LSD* 1990, col. 474). On the general point, see also Mahajan 1998: 40.

[21] While these two conceptions of social justice represented the broad positions of advocates and critics of the government's quota policy, in practice, there was some overlap between these positions. For instance, Janata Dal representatives occasionally argued for quotas on grounds that the lower castes were deprived in material terms.

[22] This draws upon Baker 1990: 4–5.

If economic disadvantage was relevant for identifying beneficiaries of quotas, the exclusion of those similarly disadvantaged simply on account of their (upper) caste backgrounds seemed discriminatory and therefore unjust. Taken together, the principles of basic needs, economic equality, and non-discrimination demanded that quotas be directed to the economically deprived, and extended to all those who were similarly deprived, irrespective of their caste affiliation.

In contrast with the case in favour of OBC quotas, social justice was elaborated here in terms of economic, rather than social equality. This meant, to begin with, that the disadvantages that quotas sought to rectify concerned inequalities mainly in the distribution of economic resources and their consequences for the opportunities and life chances of individuals, rather than inequalities of status. In the pronouncements of Congress and BJP representatives, jobs in the bureaucracy were viewed less in terms of their implications for status and power, and more in terms of their economic aspects. Second, unlike in social equality arguments, the emphasis was not so much on historical discrimination as on current distributive inequalities. While it was accepted that these often overlapped with an inferior position in the ritual hierarchy, the implicit contention was that historical discrimination was neither a necessary nor a sufficient condition for economic deprivation. Third, unlike in the interpretation of social justice in terms of social equality in Janata Dal discourse, the units for the assessment of disadvantage or 'backwardness' were *individuals*, not groups. It was assumed that the individual or the family (assessed as unitary category), rather than the group, was the appropriate unit of justice calculation and thereby of benefit allocation.[23]

The main bone of contention here, of course, was the caste basis of the quota policy. Criticisms of the government's policy as 'casteist' attacked both the employment of caste groups as the units of justice calculations, as well as a caste's position in the ritual hierarchy as an

---

[23] Congress President Rajiv Gandhi's speech in the Lok Sabha criticized the government decision as seeking to benefit the well-off OBCs: '...when...you...take some affirmative action...you must accept that there are those people who perhaps though originally of a socially, educationally backward group, are today under no circumstances they can be described as socially and educationally backward... once an individual has risen above a certain level...does his family need it...?' (*LSD* 6.9.1990 cols 487–9).

indicator of disadvantage (Galanter 1984: 170; Dushkin 1972: 167). A caste-based reservation policy was unjust as it suffered from the shortcomings both of over-inclusion as well as under-inclusion: justice required that economically advantaged members of the OBCs be excluded, and economically deprived individuals from non-OBC groups be included within the purview of quotas.

Under-representation, Social Justice, and Democracy

So far, I have contrasted two conceptions of social justice in the Mandal debate, one that focused on status inequalities and another that emphasized economic inequalities. My characterization of social equality arguments as a type of social justice claim, however, can be challenged. Theorists of social justice have opined that social equality, the ideal of a society free from hierarchies, is 'freestanding and independent of justice' (Miller 1999: 239). Theorists of group rights in India have contended that quotas have been advocated in recent times simply as a means of rectifying inequalities in group representation, that group equality has been interpreted in ways that have little to do with concern for disadvantage (Mahajan 1998: 121, 152–4).

In the arguments of proponents of OBC quotas, justice was implicitly identified with a group's representation in an arena being roughly proportionate to its share of the population. It might be recalled that 'due representation' for significant social groups had been a recognized principle for the allocation of positions in the colonial regime of minority safeguards but had been rejected as a basis for special treatment by the Constitution-makers. Did the Mandal debate represent a resurrection of this older rationale for reservation, as a means of adjusting the inter-communal balance of power, and thereby, a break from the constitutional recasting of preferential treatment?

Nearly every political speech advocating quotas for a group cited its under-representation in the bureaucracy in support of its case. The statistics cited referred to the representation of group members as a percentage of the total number of administrative positions, or of positions at a particular level of the administration, in proportion to the demographic weight of the group, and relative to other groups, most notably the upper castes. The central normative claim here was that the under-representation of the group in the administration constituted an injustice. For instance, Janata Dal MP Hukumdeo Narayan Yadav argued: 'Eighty five per cent population of India live in villages but their representation in Indian Administrative Service is only 27 per cent. 15 per cent population of India live in urban areas but their representation...is 72 per cent. Now you tell us who are the looters and who are the sinners and who are the unjust people' (*LSD* 4.9.1990 cols. 410–11).[24]

Now while 'the under-representation of certain categories of people is often so stark that its injustice seems beyond question' (Phillips 1995: 21), the *general* claim that disproportional group presence in the administration represents an injustice can easily be challenged.[25] First, a group might be under-represented in the bureaucracy because the population in the group that has the education and skills for bureaucratic jobs is low compared to groups that are better represented in the bureaucracy. Under-representation here would result even in the absence of direct discrimination against the group. Second, the belief that a group's representation in the bureaucracy must approximate its demographic percentage seems to assume that people equally desire bureaucratic jobs. Members of different social groups, however, may differ in their disposition to seek bureaucratic jobs, because all cultures do not place an equal value on such jobs. In such a situation, disproportions in group-presence in the bureaucracy might reflect differences in preferences between social groups, rather than injustice.[26] Third, it might be argued that as the bureaucracy comprises mainly middle-class jobs, the social composition of the bureaucracy is going to mirror the demographic profile 'only if all major social groups are distributed equally, in proportional terms, along the social stratification system' (Rosenbloom 1977: 38–9). If this does not obtain, disproportional group representation in the bureaucracy would occur even in the absence of any discrimination against members of the group.

Each of these objections, however, can be countered from a standpoint of social justice. First, the lack of a pool of qualified candidates from a group, as well as the unequal distribution of groups along the

[24] A common claim was that the OBCs constituted 52 per cent of the population and only 4 per cent had Class I jobs. Similar claims were made regarding the under-representation of Muslims and women.

[25] This discussion draws Rosenbloom 1977; Phillips 1995; Gutmann and Thompson 1996.

[26] For an argument along these lines, see Barry 2001: 90–8.

stratification system, could indicate the absence of *fair* equality of opportunity in education and employment. Fair equality of opportunity
requires, in Rawls' well-known formulation, '[I]n all parts of society
there are to be roughly the same prospects of culture and achievement
for those similarly motivated and endowed' (2001: 43–4). On this, more
demanding version of equality of opportunity, the under-representation
of a group in the bureaucracy could constitute evidence of injustice even
in the absence of direct discrimination, for it would suggest that there
are inequalities in opportunities for education and training along group
lines. Second, there is the issue of adaptive preferences: as Sunstein notes,
people adapt their preferences to 'excessive limitations in opportunities or
unjust background conditions' (1991: 19). Members of culturally inferior
or economically disadvantaged groups might not aspire for prestigious
positions considered unattainable; they often lack the motivation
and confidence to seek such positions. In other words, differences in
preferences along group lines might themselves be the product of the
interaction of cultural and economic injustices, of 'injustices of recognition
and injustices of distribution' (Williams 1998: 17). Finally, as Anderson
reminds us, under-representation of a group in positions of wealth or
prestige undermines equality of opportunity by depriving its members
of favourable *social networks*. As these determine access to credit and
information, under-representation can signal inequalities of opportunities
for group members even in the absence of direct discrimination.[27] From a
social justice standpoint then, the under-representation of a group in the
bureaucracy, while not constitutive of injustice is likely to be indicative, of
it (Phillips 2004).

This was the type of move that advocates of OBC quotas in the
Mandal debate were making. Under-representation of lower castes,
it was asserted, was a feature not only of bureaucratic jobs, but also of
higher education—the statistics cited sought to make the case that the

---

[27] As Anderson notes, '[E]ven if whites did not discriminate, blacks would still
be excluded from many jobs due to their isolation from the predominantly
white social networks of communication and referral that regulate access to
mainstream opportunities (2002: 1202). In the context of the Mandal debate,
see, for instance, Balagopal 1990, and on the importance of informal channels
of connections in the allocation of jobs in the private sector and urban labour
markets in India, see, for instance, Thorat 2006: 2433; Ashwini Deshpande
2006: 2446.

higher one went up the educational ladder, the lower the representation of OBCs was. This, in turn, was thought to indicate massive disparities in educational opportunities between lower and upper castes.[28] Cultural differences in preferences did exist that prevented lower castes from seeking higher education and administrative jobs and meant that these groups predominated in agricultural and manual labour occupations. However, these were undesired differences, the result of stunted aspirations in a context where access to education and state power was denied to lower castes over several generations. Finally, while arguments for OBC quotas emphasized inequalities in status and power, these also presumed that there was considerable overlap of membership at the lower levels of caste and class hierarchies. Lower castes were predominantly lower *class* as a result, it was held, of historical discrimination. For instance, Somnath Chatterjee of the CPI (M) argued in favour of OBC quotas: 'We are against casteism, division of people on the basis of caste. But can we deny the historical fact, which is there that such people belonging to certain castes are today the most exploited, socially, educationally and also economically?' (*LSD* 5.9. 1990 col. 479) Caste, it was suggested, had both class and cultural effects that resulted in inequalities in opportunities for members of lower castes.[29]

[28] Most arguments for OBC quotas emphasized differences in educational access between lower and upper castes, i.e. pre-job discrimination. Compared to Dalits, there were fewer references to concentration in particular types of jobs (job discrimination). On these different types of discrimination in the Indian context, see, for instance, Ashwini Deshpande 2006: 2446.

[29] The Mandal Commission Report had sought to establish the low class status of the castes identified as OBCs using a system that assigned points for economic as well as social disadvantages, weighted in favour of the latter. Whereas my findings suggest that caste and socio-economic backwardness were linked at the discursive level, substantial empirical evidence also exists on the educational and economic disadvantages of lower castes. For data on the relationship between caste position and educational disadvantage based on the National Sample Survey Organization's 55th Round Survey (1999–2000), see, for instance, Deshpande and Yadav who conclude that caste 'is the single most important predictor of educational inequalities' and call for more empirical information about disadvantage in order to 'de-essentialize identity markers like caste or religion' (2006: 2420, 2424). On the relationship between caste and economic equalities, and how all indicators of disadvantage (such as monthly per capita expenditure, education, occupation, housing, poverty

The rhetoric of under-representation in claims for OBC quotas thus pressed at the distinction between direct or intentional discrimination, and structural inequalities along lines of group identity, which it was argued were the result of group-based discrimination. This was not a general claim regarding the injustice of under-representation: the argument was not that justice required proportionate representation for *all* groups in every arena (Philips 1995). Rather, the claim relied for its normative force on background beliefs regarding historical injustices to lower castes in terms of exclusion from prestigious education and employment, and their continuing effects, in terms of the patterning of *current* social, economic and political inequalities along lines of caste membership. While numerical disparities in the representation of groups were a politically potent symbol of injustice, the underlying normative claim was not primarily about the injustice of 'pictorial' inadequacy (Phillips 1995: 47; Kymlicka 1995: 141).

The claim that disproportionate representation in the bureaucracy was unjust sometimes took another form. Here, it was urged that the under-representation of the lower castes was undemocratic, and thereby unjust. Disproportionate group presence in the administration signified a denial of the equal right of each individual to participate in government. Quoting approvingly from the Mandal Commission Report, Indrajit Gupta, veteran parliamentarian from the Communist Party of India and one of the staunchest supporters of the government's decision, declaimed:

> In a democratic set-up, *every individual and community* has a legitimate right and aspiration to participate in ruling this country. Any situation which results in a near-denial of this *right* to nearly 52 per cent of the country's population needs to be urgently rectified....52 per cent of this population which we are talking about at present, is supposed to enjoy only 4.5 per cent of the top grade jobs. Is this not gross injustice? (*LSD* 6.9.1990 cols 478–9)[30]

Injustice in this case derived both from the fact that *rights* were violated, and because these rights were democratic, pertaining to participation in government.

---

ratios), are 'very clearly stratified by caste' see Ashwini Deshpande 2006: 2445; Thorat 2006: 2433.

[30] See also Chitta Basu, *LSD* 4.10.1990 cols 166–8.

Again, the general claim that disproportional representation in the administration signifies a denial of the equal right of each individual to participate in government is problematic. First, as scholars have argued, the principle of political equality is compatible with a range of institutional mechanisms; these may seek to equalize either opportunities for political influence or power over political outcomes, and the two may not coincide (Beitz 1989; Phillips 1995: 36). More generally, egalitarian procedures such as equal voting rights regularly produce unequal outcomes in terms, for instance, of the social composition of political assemblies. Group under-representation as such does not necessarily prove that the norm of political equality or some form of procedural equality has been violated. A second reason for scepticism towards the claim that disproportional group representation violates the equal right to participate in government relates to the distinction, emphasized most notably by Pitkin (1967) and Phillips (1995), between participation and representation. The notion of equality of presence is implicit in the idea of participation, as everyone can, in principle, participate, so that 'as applied to political participation, it might seem entirely appropriate that those who are most active should in some way mirror the composition of the population as a whole' (Phillips 1995: 34). The same, however, is not true of representation, which rests on the principle of the few representing the many: this is what distinguishes representative from direct democracy. While proportionate representation of all social groups may be justified, it does not automatically follow from an equal right to participate in politics (see Beitz 1989; Phillips 1995: 36; also Chapter 4 above). A third objection to the claim that the under-representation of a group in the bureaucracy violates an equal right to participate in politics stems from the fact that the bureaucracy is not a representative political institution. Throughout the 1990 Mandal debate, the bureaucracy was characterized in terms that rendered it indistinguishable from political assemblies—as a 'decision-making institution', 'institution of governance'. These characterizations facilitated the application of norms of political representation to bureaucratic recruitment. It might however be argued that group representation in the bureaucracy cannot be judged by the same criteria as political representation, indeed, that we ought not to be concerned with the social composition of the bureaucracy at all, because bureaucrats are not expected to perform a representative function, unlike those elected to political assemblies. The obligations of a civil servant,

Beteille notes, are different from that of a politician: '[T]o expect the civil servant to protect or promote the particular interests of his caste or community is to set him at odds with the basic requirement of his service' (1992: 75).

In response to these objections, it should be noted, first, that the claim that the under-representation of the lower castes violated their equal right to participate in politics was a variant of the argument from fair equality of opportunity discussed above. Disproportionate representation was seen as evidence that inequalities in opportunities persisted. As the arena where opportunities were unequal had to do with political decision-making, and the effect of the inequalities was to deprive a *majority* of the population of the opportunity to *participate* in the exercise of political power, under-representation was simultaneously, undemocratic. Second, it is important to recall that the equal right to participate in government plays an important *symbolic* role in democratic societies, that of affirming the equal status of all citizens: it has become 'an essential expression of the basic equality between members of each state' (Miller 1978: 19). When the under-representation of certain groups in arenas of state power occurs against a historical background of their exclusion on account of low status, it seems to imply, as Phillips (1995: 39) notes in another context, that members of these groups are inferior to others, less fit to govern than the rest. In the claim that the under-representation of the lower castes in the administration constituted a denial of the equal right to participate in politics, part of what was at issue was that the latter served to exemplify the ideal of equal status, and it was this sense of political equality that under-representation was thought to offend. CPI MP Indrajit Gupta quoted the following passage from the Mandal Commission Report:

> ...an essential part of the battle against social backwardness is to be fought in the minds of the backward people themselves. In India, the Government service has always been looked upon as a symbol of prestige and power. By increasing the representation of OBCs in Government services, we give them an immediate feeling of participation in the governance of this country...Even when no tangible benefits may flow to the community at large, the feeling that now it has its own man in the "corridors of power" acts as a morale booster. (*LSD* 6.9.1990 cols 477–8)

Further, *substantive* representation of the interests of lower castes in government was not the central issue: the claim was not that increased political representation of historically disadvantaged groups would ensure that their interests were more effectively advocated in, and considered by the administration. As Anderson points out, such representation might be advocated on the identity politics grounds that groups are irreducibly distinct, so that trans-group perspectives are impossible. It might also be defended on grounds of deliberative democracy, that the construction of more genuinely universal, trans-group perspectives that pay adequate regard to the interests of all, requires the presence in decision-making arenas of those whose perspectives are different (Anderson 2002: 1204–5). Neither of these claims were put forward by advocates of Mandal: their contention was not that the OBCs were a group with a distinct social identity or that the inclusion of OBCs would enhance the quality of democratic deliberation towards shared ends. In other words, the primary thrust of arguments in favour of OBC quotas in the Mandal case was not the inclusion of a distinctive point of view, from either an identity politics or a deliberative democracy standpoint.

Rather, in under-representation claims in the Mandal debate, the normative work done by democracy pertained primarily to the denial of equal opportunities to exercise political power and equal status and dignity. Against the contention that the benefits of representation are *merely* symbolic or psychological, it can be argued that these are substantive democratic goods.[31] The inclusion of members of hitherto denigrated groups affirms the equal dignity and worth of all citizens, which is a core democratic value, and enables the participation of citizens from diverse social groups on terms of equality, thereby furthering the realization of democratic political institutions. It was because the underlying concern in under-representation claims was less with representation in the sense of a distinctive point of view, and more with reversing the exclusion of lower castes from arenas of state power and the presumption that members of these groups were inferior, that the bureaucracy was cast as simply another political institution, with group presence in the administration treated as identical with representation in political assemblies.

---

[31] Lower caste parties have been criticized for focussing on 'symbolic and cosmetic changes' (Vora 2004: 282), such as the installation of statues of leaders, renaming public buildings and parks, instead of pursuing redistribution of material resources to their constituents. For an alternative interpretation, see Jaoul 2006.

Arguments in favour of OBC quotas thus relied substantially on familiar social justice notions of fair equality of opportunity, and democratic notions of participation and political equality. Defenders of OBC quotas departed from standard social justice arguments in maintaining that the caste hierarchy rather than the economic structure of society was the fundamental cause of inequalities of opportunities, and that social justice required the greater equalization of status, respect and power, and not just material goods.[32] Nevertheless, under-representation remained a short-hand for disadvantage: it was not considered sufficient in and of itself to establish a group's entitlement to preferential treatment, but was supported by background beliefs regarding the historical denial of equal opportunities and equal status to members of certain groups. Group representation in the Mandal debate was advocated not as a 'universal strategy' for achieving group equality in the case of *all* social groups as suggested (Mahajan 1998), but rather, as a means of promoting equality for *particular*, disadvantaged groups.[33] In this respect at least, the shift in the central normative basis of quotas inaugurated by the Constitution—from accommodating distinct communities to addressing socio-economic disadvantage—endured in the 1990 Mandal debate.

SOCIAL JUSTICE AND ARGUMENTS FOR QUOTAS

Notwithstanding important continuities, the advocacy of OBC quotas on grounds of social equality did exhibit new features relative to justifications for quotas in the Constituent Assembly. In the elaboration of social equality in Janata Dal discourse, earlier nationalist conceptions of equality were redefined along two broad lines. First, whereas in dominant nationalist opinion in the Constituent Assembly, quotas were seen as *detracting* from individual fairness type of equality considerations (equality of opportunity, merit), albeit acceptable as a means towards

---

[32] Scholars disagree about the extent to which social justice should concern itself with the distribution of status, respect and power. Jeff Spinner-Halev (1998), for instance, argues that self-respect as a basis for state policy is problematic as its bases are multiple and contradictory.

[33] The claim thus pertained not to 'microcosmic' but to 'selective' descriptive representation; on the distinction, see Mansbridge 2000.

desired national goals (see Chapter 4 above), in Janata Dal discourse, individual fairness considerations were interpreted as *consonant* with preferential treatment. Second, the earlier nationalist goal of reducing socio-economic disparities between groups underwent changes both in terms of how the goal of equalization was conceived, as well as the mechanism whereby quotas were thought to contribute to the realization of this goal. The empowerment of the disadvantaged would play a crucial role in both cases.

Adapting Galanter's (1984) classification, three main kinds of justice arguments for quotas can be discerned in Janata Dal discourse: compensatory justice, non-discrimination, and general welfare.[34] In the Mandal debate, compensatory justice considerations were rarely deployed as an independent argument for quotas; these were usually invoked to reinforce arguments from systematic group disadvantage. Janata Dal spokesmen did sometimes suggest that it was *because* past injustices against the lower castes had assumed the form of exclusion from institutions of state power, that justice now required that these groups be included in the bureaucracy through quotas.[35] However compensation and the related idiom of atonement for past sins was less prominent in the Mandal debate than in the Constituent Assembly debates. Several factors might have contributed here. In the Constituent Assembly, the case for quotas as compensation was addressed primarily to upper caste Hindus in the form of appeal for self-reform, or paternalistic, philanthropic concern for

---

[34] In contrast with Galanter's schema, where general welfare arguments necessarily have groups as their units of calculation and are not justice claims, my usage below admits the category of consequentialist justice arguments, which in turn can apply to both individuals and groups. A large philosophical–legal literature exists on compensatory justice, equal opportunity and social utility rationales for affirmative action, based mostly on the experience of the US. Key contributions can be found in Cohen, Nagel, and Scanlon 1977; Cahn 2002; LaFollette 2007.

[35] Janata Dal MP Ram Dhan quoted approvingly from the Kaka Kalelkar Report: "'Being convinced that the upper castes among the Hindus have to atone for the neglect of what they were guilty towards the lower classes, I was prepared to recommend that all special help should be given only to the backward classes...' "Even the poor and the deserving among the upper classes could be safely kept out from the benefit of this special help'" (*LSD* 5.9 1990 col. 444). Ram Vilas Paswan, Minister for Labour and Welfare, asserted: 'The Mandal Commission is washing off the sin that was committed earlier' (*LSD* 4.9.1990 col. 460).

underprivileged lower castes (Bajpai 1997). Also, compensatory justice appeared less powerful in the case of OBCs than Dalits: opponents of OBC quotas, for instance, often emphasize that these groups did not suffer the same oppression as Dalits and Adivasis. More pertinently for our purposes here, the case for OBC quotas relied predominantly on considerations of *social* justice rather than compensation.[36] Quotas were advocated as a requirement of social justice in individual fairness and general welfare types of arguments in the Mandal debate. Importantly, despite appearances, several arguments in favour of preferential treatment in government jobs invoked the principle of merit.

Equality as Individual Fairness and Quotas

In one type of argument for quotas, it was contended that individuals from lower caste backgrounds had historically been prevented from realizing positions commensurate with their talents by the caste system's exclusion of these groups from education and prestigious occupations (see Hukumdeo Narayan Yadav, *LSD* 4.9.1990 col. 406). Speeches cited examples from Hindu epics, such as the Ramayana and the Mahabharata, as historical evidence of how exceptionally gifted individuals from the lower castes had been forced to forsake the vocation suited to their skills and to accept instead the calling dictated by the caste of their birth.[37] The effects of this historical discrimination persisted, preventing lower caste individuals from making headway in the higher echelons of education and employment commensurate with their abilities and efforts, even after legal barriers to their access had been removed. The under-representation of OBCs in the administration was viewed here as evidence that policies of formal equality of opportunity, which had been in operation since

[36] Reparations do not in theory require that the victim group be disadvantaged in socio-economic terms, although in practice this has often been the case.

[37] The most frequently cited episode in political speeches was the legendary archer Eklavya's sacrifice of his thumb to his guru Drona from the Mahabharata. When deployed as historical evidence, examples from Hindu epics lent historical depth to political claims, in this case, to establish that the history of discrimination against the lower castes stretched back to antiquity. Examples from Hindu epics also had rhetorical appeal because of the audience's familiarity with these episodes and their quasi-religious status. These were deployed as historical evidence in arguments both for and against quotas.

Independence, were not sufficient for removing 'the cumulative effects of past discrimination' (Galanter 1984: 553). As such, departures from equal treatment in the form of quotas were required in order to make up for disadvantages faced by individuals from lower caste backgrounds that were the result of an unjust social system. The Prime Minister VP Singh challenged the critics of quotas:

> What is the merit of the system itself? That the section which has 52% of the population gets 12.55% in Government employment...in the power structure it is hardly 4.69. I want to challenge first the merit of the system itself before we question whether it is on merit that we reject this individual or that...a person or a family in this system is condemned to a social or economic order...In that what are a child's opportunities?...the present socio-economic system is such that it is adversely biased...against the weaker sections, then, asking [them] to compete equally with other sections which are better-off is something defective in the system itself...*treating unequals as equals is the greatest injustice*...Correction of this injustice is very important....(*RSD* 1990 cols 233–4)

Here, equality of opportunity was criticized from the standpoint of underlying norms of individual fairness. The notion of *fair* equality of opportunity discussed earlier was invoked: inasmuch as this requires the eradication of differences in the individuals' circumstances that are the product of social disadvantages, fair equality of opportunity can justify 'unequal allocations' of certain goods and thereby preferential treatment (Rosenfeld 1991: 28–9).[38] As Galanter points out, this argument for preferential treatment seeks to enable the hiring of individuals who would have been selected on merit grounds were it not for obstacles such as educational and social disadvantages that were the result of past discrimination. Preferential provisions are justified here as a temporary measure towards a society in which policies of equal treatment would be sufficient for non-discrimination (Galanter 1984: 553; Parekh and Mitra 1990: 100).[39] Importantly, unlike Congress nationalist arguments in the Constituent Assembly, where reservations were seen as undermining

---

[38] Although there are difficulties with group-based *quotas* from the standpoint of individual fairness—see Miller 1999.
[39] For a defence of quotas on grounds of non-discrimination, see Gutmann and Thompson 1996: 349–52; Harris and Narayan 2007.

equality of opportunity and unfair, proponents of Mandal often portrayed these as a requirement of equality of opportunity and fairness.[40]

While employment quotas are sometimes justified as one of the means of rectifying the unfairness in the competition for jobs on account of inequalities in *basic* opportunity goods such as income, health, and primary education, as Gutmann and Thompson note, the case for quotas on grounds of non-discrimination does not *depend* on the inadequacy of basic opportunity goods. Inequalities in education and employment are correlated and persist in a cyclical way across generations, and the requirement for many prestigious, highly paid jobs in society is success in higher education (Gutmann and Thompson 1996: 321). While advocates of OBC quotas often cited low levels of income, primary education, housing, and other basic goods among lower castes,[41] the case for preferential treatment on grounds of non-discrimination primarily focussed on breaking the cycle of inequalities in educational and employment opportunities associated with caste-based discrimination.

Equality as a Social Goal and Quotas

OBC quotas were also advocated in consequentialist justice arguments in the Mandal debate, as a means to the realization of a more just society in the future. What was the vision of a just society and how would quotas contribute to the realization of this goal? When quotas for

---

[40] Proponents of OBC quotas equivocated between rejecting equality of opportunity as antithetical to social justice on the one hand, and claiming equality of opportunity *properly* construed as a requirement of social justice, on the other. The Mandal Report, for instance, voices support mainly for equality of results, noting that '"Equality of opportunity" and "equality of treatment" places the weak and the strong on par and to that extent, it amounts to denial of social justice...'(1980: 67). In other places, however, it argues from an egalitarian conception of equality of opportunity (1980: 28).

[41] For instance, Hukumdeo Narayan Yadav declared: 'On one side you have built magnificent schools in Delhi where children of only high class people get education...On the other side are the children ...who get education in the schools which have no roofs and sit on the floor. You want to put both of them on the same footing in competitions. The true philosophy of education is that there should be same education for the son of a king or for a son of Scheduled Caste. If you have courage...put locks on all the private schools...' (*LSD* 1990 col. 411).

Untouchables and Tribals were introduced in the Indian Constitution in the late 1940s, the desired egalitarian goal had been conceived largely in terms of the reduction of *socio-economic disparities* between groups (see Chapter 4). The means whereby quotas in the bureaucracy would further this goal was through improvement of the material conditions of beneficiaries, although exactly how this would be achieved was not elaborated. By contrast, in Janata Dal discourse in the 1990 Mandal debate, a just society was construed as having fewer inequalities not only of economic resources, but also of status and power. The desired goal was defined as a society that was democratic as it was just, where the equal worth of all citizens was affirmed, and the distribution of power was more equal. Further, the mechanism whereby quotas were thought to facilitate this goal was not so much through improving the socio-economic conditions of beneficiaries, but by giving them political power. Thus, the empowerment of the disadvantaged was both a part of how the goal of equality was defined, as well as the favoured means for its realization. Elaborating on the rationale of quotas, the Prime Minister V.P. Singh said:

> it is not so much the issue of economic condition but of the power structure—the power structure which has crystallized in a social structure...Bureaucracy is a very important component of this whole power structure....It is not merely a question of...alleviating the economic conditions of our people...After all, if you take the strength of the whole of the Government employees as a proportion of the population, it will be 1% or 2%...We are under no illusion that this...will resolve the economic problems of the whole section of 52%...We consciously want to give them a position in the decision-making of the country, a share in the power structure. (*RSD* 1990 cols 232–3)

Precisely how the transfer of political power would bring about social transformation was not specified. It appeared to offer, at one stroke, symbolic benefits of respect and agency as well as enhanced employment and educational opportunities. What was clear was that political power for the underprivileged was envisaged as the main agency and motor for the creation of a just society, and was advocated as the solution for all injustices in society. Oppression—the deprivation of political power—was seen as the means through which all forms of injustice— social denigration and economic exploitation alike—operated. The key to the removal of injustice was placing the oppressed—the lower castes, the poor—in positions of political power. Responding to criticisms of quotas for the OBCs, the Prime Minister V.P. Singh proposed that additional quotas be instituted for the poor: 'Without giving power, a poor man cannot remove his poverty...Poverty is not only an economic problem, poverty is a political problem. Give political power and the poor will make their own way' (RSD 1990 col. 355, translation from Hindi).[42]

The centrality of the empowerment of the disadvantaged in Janata Dal discourse meant a diminution in the hitherto dominant *paternalist* tenor of welfarist arguments. Unlike in quota arguments in Congress opinion in the Constituent Assembly, 'backward sections' were not cast in the role of passive objects of benevolent state action, recipients of philanthropic initiatives directed at them, but were to be the agents of their own betterment. The emphasis on the centrality of political power was not a new theme: Janata Dal discourse was here drawing upon the ideological work of low caste leaders, parties, and movements dating back over a century. What was new in the 1990 Mandal debate was that this theme had moved from the periphery to the centre-ground of policy-making.

The ideological moves of Janata Dal discourse in the Mandal debate strengthened the case for quotas in the bureaucracy. Quotas were no longer seen as only one means among others, and ineffectual in themselves, for ameliorating the vast socio-economic disparities in society. Rather, quotas became the pre-eminent instrument of social justice, because political power for the 'backward' was now central both to how the desired goal of a just society was defined, as well as the process through which it was to be brought about. By affording representation to the OBCs in a key decision-making institution, quotas were *already* accomplishing a large part of their purpose. How this power was subsequently used, whether it contributed to the reduction of socio-economic inequalities, were separate issues; the case for quotas did not wholly depend on these.

Consequentialist justice arguments for OBC quotas in Janata Dal discourse in the Mandal debate marked an important shift in general welfare arguments for quotas in India in at least two respects. First, as

---

[42] V.P. Singh argued: '...If we want to bring changes in the society, we will have to bring changes in the bureaucracy also which is a decision making institution...We have to place the downtrodden in bureaucracy...' (LSD 6.9.1990 cols 535–6).

we have seen, the *literal* empowerment of the disadvantaged became fundamental to the characterization and realization of a just society. Second, social justice was extricated from the embrace of national unity that had characterized earlier Congress arguments on affirmative action. These respects are brought into sharp relief when Janata Dal discourse is counterposed to arguments advanced by representatives from parties more qualified in their support for OBC quotas. In one argument, prominent in the speeches of parliamentarians from the CPI (M), the desired goal was defined in terms of a society with fewer disparities in the distribution of socio-economic goods such as income, education, health, and nutrition. Political power was not of paramount importance here; quotas in the bureaucracy were valued not so much for ensuring the representation of disadvantaged groups, but for contributing thereby to the reduction of poverty and economic inequality. Greater representation of the OBCs in the bureaucracy was only one among numerous measures for tackling massive distributive inequalities in society, and unlike in Janata Dal discourse, was not seen as having any special efficacy. Insofar as quotas had little impact on the more fundamental material inequalities, these were an inadequate instrument of social justice, according to CPI (M) leader Somnath Chatterjee:

> it is essential that there has to be an all round economic development directed towards alleviating principally the economic distress, social backwardness, of these poor people in this country....this mere reservation will not solve the problem. It will be a good step, it will give them an impression that they will be participating more effectively in the governance of the country. (*LSD* 5.9. 1990 cols 483–4)

Another set of general welfare arguments for quotas, most prominent in the speeches of Congress and BJP representatives, emphasized the interests of the nation. The creation of a more just society, while desired here, was valued not so much in itself, as for its contribution to national unity and development: as such these were not consequentialist *justice* arguments. The respects in which the national good rationale differed from justifications for quotas in Janata Dal discourse is cogently articulated in the following speech by Congress Rajya Sabha MP Rajmohan Gandhi:

> After we attained Independence...the Government has rightly concentrated, on this section and the whole House has agreed that this section is largely backward and has suffered for such a long time...But the question is this: Are we supporting and sheltering that section

only for its own sake or are we supporting and sheltering that section so that it can find itself equal in relation to the other sections? These are two ways of looking at it. The third way of looking at it is to realize that we are sheltering and supporting that section which is a part because we want to strengthen the whole. Today, at this time, when our nation's unity is assailed from many quarters, it is all the more important that we are absolutely clear that we should strengthen and support a part because we want to preserve the unity and strength of the whole. (*RSD* 1990 col. 343)

Congress leader and former Prime Minister Rajiv Gandhi invoked national development:

> When we think of poverty and backwardness, it is not just a question of...a *social wrong* which has existed for many years. Today we need to harness all the energies of the nation...to compete with other countries. That can only be done if we harness all the resources of our people. That includes...the most backward, the poorest....(*LSD* 6.9.1990 cols 485–6)

This was the form that the older national development argument would increasingly assume in the era of economic liberalization: preferential treatment would make available for the market economy the talent hitherto wasted by the caste system and thereby further national progress. It might be recalled that national unity and development had been the *dominant* justifications of quotas when these were introduced in the Constitution in the late 1940s (Bajpai 1997). Quotas, nationalist opinion had contended, would not only enable the 'upliftment' of 'backward sections' but also their closer integration with the rest of the population, and national progress: India could not be a developed nation if large sections of its population remained 'backward'. By contrast, in Janata Dal discourse in the 1990 Mandal debate, the consequences of OBC quotas for national integration and development were marginal. Social justice was now a goal that was valued in its own right, the pre-eminent appeal in political argument.

Social Justice and Merit

Preferential treatment is commonly thought to conflict with the principle of merit, namely, that jobs be assigned to the best-qualified individual. Arguments for why jobs should be allocated on merit broadly divide into two categories: individual justice arguments, which claim that the best-qualified applicant deserves the job;[43] and utilitarian arguments, which hold that considerations of utility, in terms of the efficient performance of institutions, for instance, demand that the best qualified person be hired.[44] Merit-based objections to OBC quotas, while muted in the parliamentary debate, were influential in the wider public debate on Mandal. Advocates of OBC quotas in Parliament ostensibly attacked merit, but on closer examination, invoked its underlying principles in several instances.

One line of argument sought to redefine job requirements, and thereby what would count as a relevant qualification for a job (Dworkin 1986). Requirements for bureaucratic positions were redefined in line with preferred social outcomes, such as making the administration more responsive or better informed about the needs of disadvantaged groups. Once job requirements were recast in these ways, membership of a disadvantaged group could become a relevant qualification for positions in the bureaucracy (Gutmann and Thompson 1996; Miller 1999). Members of such groups could be seen as better-qualified for these jobs than non-members, because they served the social function of the job better, and quotas for 'backward classes' would no longer compromise merit, but enable the identification and hiring of the best qualified individuals for the job. The Prime Minister V.P. Singh argued:

> ...what we have in education is...scholastic merit in certain subjects. And that pertains to the individual—individual merit. But the basic lacuna... in the education system which gets reflected in the administrative system, is: what about the social merit of a person? Not how much knowledgeable he is, but how he relates to the other human beings...what is the criticism about the administration or bureaucracy today? Not that it is not knowledgeable or that it is mediocre...[but] that it does not care. A mother is a mother, not because she is an intellectual [but]...because she cares; and that is what people look for, in the administration. And if that be so, we will have to re-define what is administrative merit...to put

---

[43] See, for instance, Miller 1999. Several theorists disagree with the view that justice demands that jobs be allocated by merit, because, for instance, they reject the idea of desert (e.g., Rawls 2001 [1971]), or because they reject the huge differentials in material rewards and esteem that accompany meritocratic allocation of jobs (e.g., Nagel 1979).

[44] See Rosenfeld 1991: 98. As jobs are 'at least partly means of performing services for society' (Gutmann and Thompson 1996: 334), there remains an ineradicable utilitarian element in arguments for hiring by merit.

a social content into it...those who have gone through suffering, those who know the pinch...if they are in the administration, they will be more responsive....(*LSD* 1990 cols.194–5)

Here, merit-based objections to quotas were countered through a redefinition of the goals of the bureaucracy, and correspondingly, of the merit required for administrative positions. Against the contention that quotas would diminish the efficiency of the administration and undermine the quality of services, it was urged that preferential hiring of members of the 'backward classes' who understood the needs of disadvantaged groups better, would improve the performance of the bureaucracy.[45] In claims for quotas put forward by Janata Dal spokesmen, the social function of the bureaucracy was often defined expansively to include 'every consideration of social justice which could be used in favour of hiring members of disadvantaged groups' (Gutmann and Thompson 1996: 327–8), obscuring the potential conflict between merit and preferential treatment.

A second common merit argument in support of OBC quotas in Janata Dal discourse relied on considerations of desert. 'Merit' which was measured by performance in standard tests, it was argued, was the product of favourable educational and socio-economic circumstances.[46] Standard merit tests were not a good measure of the abilities or the efforts of these candidates: they over-represented the potential of candidates from privileged backgrounds and under-represented the potential of members of 'backward classes'. Quotas sought to compensate for inequalities in performance that were the product of unfair social circumstances, rather than differences in ability. This argument did not contest the notion that jobs ought to be awarded to those who deserved them on account of their abilities and efforts. Rather, it was argued that gifted individuals from lower caste backgrounds had historically been prevented from realizing positions commensurate with their talents by

[45] Although this was not an argument put forward by advocates of Mandal, it can be argued that members of excluded groups add value to the institution's democratic or educational goals. Here, the meritocratic standards are altered by goals such as integration or diversity—see Anderson 2002: 1215, 1247.

[46] In public debates on reservations in India and elsewhere, merit is usually equated with success in competitive examinations. For a critique, see, for instance, Galanter 1984: 555; Satish Deshpande 2006: 2443.

the caste system (see Hukumdeo Narayan Yadav, *LSD* 1990, col. 406).[47] Further, massive and inherited inequalities in economic, social, and educational opportunities persisted along caste lines, preventing individuals from the 'backward classes' from achieving results which corresponded to their abilities and efforts, so that their performance did not reflect their true deserts. This implied that a Backward Class candidate with a lower grade might deserve a job in preference to a general category candidate with a slightly higher grade on grounds of *merit*, as the former's grade predicted a better job performance than the latter's. It also implied that similar grades might be indicative of a difference in qualifications: identical grades might suggest, as Nagel observes that a candidate from a disadvantaged group is better qualified for the job than one from a privileged group as she 'had to overcome more severe obstacles to acquire those credentials' (1979: 91).[48] Janata Dal spokesman Jaipal Reddy held:

> Can merit be...assessed in a socio-educational vacuum? This question was put by a Supreme Court judge in *Vasant Kumar's* case and I would quote: 'Is not a child of the Scheduled Castes, Scheduled Tribes or Other Backward Classes, who has been brought up in an atmosphere of penury, illiteracy and anti-culture, who is looked down upon by tradition and society, who has no books and magazines to read at home, no radio to listen, no TV to watch, no one to help him with his homework, who goes to the nearest local board school and college, whose parents are either illiterate or so ignorant and ill-informed that he cannot even hope to seek their advice on any

[47] Compare Ram Manohar Lohia: '...contraction of opportunity and ability is a necessary accompaniment of caste...A new ideology must be adopted which is that abilities stem from opportunity....The narrowing selection of abilities must now be broadened over the whole, and that can only be done if...backward castes and groups are given preferential opportunities' (q. Sheth 2002: 124–6). In the 1990 Mandal debate, merit based criticisms of the caste system mostly invoked considerations of fairness. The economic inefficiency of caste discrimination in terms of the allocation of labour and overall growth is a theme that has gained prominence since the liberalization of the economy. In this, as in other areas, Dr Ambedkar's arguments anticipate recent debates.

[48] For criticisms of merit-based objections, and a defence of affirmative action in terms of equalizing opportunities, see also Harris and Narayan 2007, who argue that affirmative action is necessary for 'levelling the playing field' for groups facing ongoing institutional discrimination on account of class, race, gender, and disability.

matter of importance...has not this child got merit if he, with all his disadvantages, is able to secure the qualifying 40% or 50% of the marks at a competitive examination where the children of the upper classes who have all the advantages...and who have perhaps been specially coached for the examination may secure 70, 80 or even 90% of the marks? Surely, a child who has been able to jump so many hurdles may be expected to do better and better as he progresses in life.' (*RSD* 1990 cols 97–8)[49]

'Treating unequals equally is the greatest injustice' was a frequent refrain of the Prime Minister VP Singh in the Mandal debate. Such claims relied on the principle of fair equality of opportunity discussed earlier and defended quotas as a corrective to policies of equal opportunity in a context characterized by massive socio-economic inequalities.[50]

Merit-based objections to quotas were also countered in the Mandal debate through criticisms of the criteria of merit that informed standard tests and popular conceptions of merit. Thus, it was argued that selection procedures did not provide a level playing field, as criteria such as fluency in English or the importance attached to interview performance, placed members of 'backward classes' who were mostly rural and non-English speaking, at a disadvantage. While couched as an attack on merit, the underlying argument did not reject the principle of merit. Rather, it implied, as Miller (1999) has noted in another context, that many of the criteria attached formally or informally to administrative jobs, where Backward Class candidates found themselves at a disadvantage, were not, strictly speaking, relevant to the job, in the sense that the job could be carried out equally well without them. So modifying these criteria in order to facilitate the entry of more Backward Class candidates would not detract from the principle of merit. That criteria irrelevant to the job had

---

[49] For this line of argument, see also the Mandal Report, which notes that merit is 'largely a product of favourable environmental privileges and higher rating in an examination does not necessarily reflect higher intrinsic worth of the examinee' (1980: 67).

[50] While desert-based considerations suggest that hiring by merit may require some kinds of preferential treatment, these do not support more rigid mechanisms such as group quotas, which entail that a fixed number of positions in an institution be filled by members belonging to particular groups. The general problem here is one of justifying mechanisms that take the group as their unit of calculation from the standpoint of desert-based justice that is founded on claims of individuals (Miller 1999).

come to attach themselves to job qualifications was evidence of the existing significantly unmeritocratic order in which jobs tend to be reserved by informal means for particular categories of people, as a result of which norms specific to those groups get attached to the jobs' (Miller 1999: 193). Advocates of lower caste quotas in India have argued that criteria of merit such as proficiency in the English language and performance in examinations do not measure merit in terms of capacities most relevant for the performance of a job, and are biased towards the upper castes (see Ilaiah 2006: 2448).[51]

Speeches in favour of OBC quotas in the Mandal debate also attacked the historical associations of merit-based arguments. It was held, for instance, that the claim that Indians were not capable of self-government had been one of the main ideological props of British colonial rule.[52] Lower castes had been denied education and political power for centuries on grounds that they lacked 'merit'—the requisite capacities and skills. While such claims sought to discredit merit-based objections to quotas, they did so by attacking the unmeritocratic elements—racial superiority, hereditary privilege—of systems that claimed to be meritocratic—and in doing so, affirmed the principle of merit. Criticisms of the unmeritocratic aspects of systems that trumpet the cause of merit have been prominent in recent debates on reservations in the private sector, where jobs are commonly accessed through networks of family, kinship and caste (Guru 2005; Jodhka and Newman 2007).[53]

So far, I have sought to show that contrary to appearances, several arguments in favour of OBC quotas in the Mandal debate invoked principles of merit. This, however, is not to suggest that all arguments

[51] The understanding of merit in India, it is argued, is Brahmanical, based upon 'imported textbooks and mugged up reproduction', rather than measuring potential for innovation and productivity (Ilaiah 2006: 2448).

[52] Ram Dhan averred: 'As far as merit is concerned, history bears a testimony that so long as this country had the governance of the so-called meritocratic persons, it had to face foreign invasions and was subjugated...The Britishers used to say that Indians were an incompetent and inefficient lot. They thought that handing over the reins of power to Indians would bring catastrophic results to the people of that country' (*LSD* 5.9.1990 col. 445).

[53] That the private sector in India lacks an open and transparent system of hiring, relying extensively on the family and network connections, is also pointed out by many critics of OBC reservations—see, for instance, Beteille 2005; Gupta 2005.

for quotas in the Mandal debate sought only to protect merit. In general welfare arguments discussed above, quotas implied departures from policies of hiring the best qualified in order to promote desired social goals. Other arguments rejected the principle of merit more directly. For instance, it was argued that jobs were a training ground for skills, and hence ought to be awarded to those who were lacking in skills. Janata Dal MP Hukumdeo Narayan Yadav declared:

> You talk of qualifications and competition for getting jobs. This is like telling a person to learn swimming before he is allowed to jump into the swimming pool. If that is so, where will he learn the swimming?... Dr Lohia's philosophy was that whether such a person is competent or not, first he should be given a job. In due course of time, he will become competent for holding such a job...The people belonging to upper castes have behind them thousands years' old 'Sanskaras'. We have got no such 'Sanskaras'. (*LSD* 4.9. 1990 col.414)

This understanding of the social purposes served by bureaucratic jobs implied that the least qualified had the best claims on positions, and was at odds with the meritocratic view of hiring the best qualified person for the job. Implicit in such arguments was the assumption that given a fair chance, anyone could acquire the requisite qualifications: there could be no differentials of qualification arising from differences in talents and efforts between individuals, because there were no differences of ability that were not a consequence of unjust social arrangements. This view was indicative of the strong egalitarian tenor of arguments for quotas in the Mandal debate, where social justice was identified with promoting the claims of the disadvantaged, and not with 'protecting the claims of the most qualified' (Gutmann and Thompson 1996: 327–8). While the requirements of these two can clearly conflict, the arguments of the advocates of OBC quotas also illustrate that the normative underpinnings of policies of group preference and hiring by merit are closer than appearances suggest.

Social Justice and Democracy

We have noted that arguments in favour of OBC quotas in the Mandal debate reflected an increased reliance on democratic values, and a declining dependence upon national unity. In what respects did conceptions of social justice and democracy in Janata Dal discourse mark a shift from Congress discourse in the Constituent Assembly? In the Mandal debate, democracy was frequently employed interchangeably with social justice—indeed, these two were often so closely entwined in political claims as to seem indistinguishable.[54] It is nevertheless useful to keep democracy and social justice distinct for analytical purposes.

Speeches in support of OBC quotas frequently emphasized that these groups that comprised a *majority* of the population of the country had been excluded from institutions of state power. The latter were disproportionately peopled by individuals belonging to numerically small groups, such as the upper caste, the educated, or urban populations. Ram Awadhesh Singh declaimed:

> ...for centuries the *majority* peoples were forbidden to enter the state... and now the door has been opened for them. That state revolution happened and the people affected by the revolution are uneasy...because a *handful* of rich, upper caste people with English speaking skills had a monopoly over state power...over government service. (*RSD* 1990 col. 313, translation from Hindi)

Dalit leader Mayawati lambasted the critics of the government's policy:

> You are depriving the oppressed people of justice but...the total number of oppressed, backward and minorities in the country is 85 per cent...if 85 per cent of the people...stand for their rights, the handful of people cannot thrust their will on them. (*LSD* 1990, cols 185–6)[55]

At first glance, such claims appear to support the view that lower caste politics is simply a form of majoritarianism, the appeal to numbers, a form of muscle flexing. While this has undoubtedly been an element in lower caste claims, on closer examination, the contention that 'backward sections' also constituted a majority of the population bore some of the weight of establishing the *justice* of claims for quotas for these groups.

---

[54] Several political theorists also conflate democracy and social justice. Here, following Miller (1978), democracy refers to a form of government, and social justice, to questions regarding the distribution of social goods.

[55] This has been a long-standing theme in the pronouncements of lower caste leaders. Notably, in the 1960s, Ram Manohar Lohia had asserted that Dalits, 'backward castes', 'backward' Muslims and Christians, tribals, and women, together constituted 90 per cent of the country's population but held less than 10 per cent of posts in the country's government, industry, military, and professions. Lohia pressed for 60 per cent reservations for the majority backward sections. See Lohia 1964; Sheth 2002: 125; Vora 2004: 277.

First, in the claim that it was unjust to exclude the majority section of the population from institutions of governance, the underlying ideal of democracy invoked was popular rule. Democracy implied a form of government in which the people participated in decision-making—government *by* the people to use the common formulation, rule by the many, as opposed to rule by small elite. OBC quotas would increase access to participation in decision-making institutions for the major section of the population and were thereby democratically just.[56] Described as an institution of governance, the bureaucracy was rendered akin here to political assemblies, subject to the same participative criteria. Second, as noted earlier, the domination of political institutions by a privileged minority was considered unjust because it denied that those excluded possessed an *equal* capacity or qualification to rule (Phillips 1995: 17). OBC quotas would affirm the equal worth of persons historically considered inferior and were thereby democratically just. Janata Dal spokesmen frequently referred to the democratic significance of equal dignity and respect for 'backward classes' who had been subject to indignity and humiliation. Democratic ideals of participation and political equality were thus constitutive of notions of social justice. In contrast, in Congress nationalist arguments in the Constituent Assembly, social justice had mainly been construed in terms of economic redistribution and not explicitly linked to democracy.

In the Mandal debate, democracy was also linked *instrumentally* to social justice in the arguments of advocates of quotas. We noted previously that placing political power in the hands of the underprivileged was portrayed as the engine of social transformation, the means for the creation of a more equal society. Democratization of political institutions was thus envisaged as the means for bringing about social justice. A group's exclusion or under-representation in institutions of state power was seen here not so much as a *consequence* of unjust socio-economic inequalities but as its *cause*; increased representation of the group in state institutions was thus the appropriate remedy.[57] Prime Minister VP Singh noted:

[56] On how inclusion benefits all members of a group, and not just the direct beneficiaries, see Khan 2008: 228–9.

[57] For an elaboration of this point in the context of race and segregation in the US, see Anderson 2002: 1207.

...Only those who have been in power have availed of all the opportunities...Centuries ago the Aryan invaders defeated the Dravidian inhabitants of this country and established their supremacy and
today these people have remained downtrodden. It is *because* these
people never had a share in the power structure of the society... .
(*LSD* 6.9.1990 cols. 535–7)

Like in nationalist doctrines, a causal link was posited between democracy
and social justice. Those who had been denied political power had also,
as a direct result, suffered socio-economic deprivation; once political
power was restored to them, the marginalized would be able to effect an
improvement in their material circumstances.

Finally, social justice and democracy were also linked *analogically* in
the advocacy of quotas for the OBCs in the Mandal debate. Conceptions
of democracy and social justice drew upon the same fundamental
notion of equal human worth (Miller 1978). Social, political, and
to a large extent economic inequalities were related and thought to
derive from the same source. There was a general presumption against
inequality, which tended to be viewed as the product of injustice, and
as undemocratic. That conceptions of social justice and democracy were
analogous meant, for instance, that just as a regime of formal equality
of opportunity was not an adequate characterization of social justice,
fidelity to procedural equality was insufficient for democracy. In both
cases, the *outcomes* of procedures for the social composition of decision-
making institutions mattered. With their constitutive, causal and
analogical interlinkages, social justice and democracy were closely intertwined in Janata Dal speeches in the Mandal debate. This represented a
shift from nationalist discourse in the Constituent Assembly.

While a full analysis of conceptions of democracy in Janata Dal
discourse in the Mandal debate is outside the scope of the present study,
some brief points deserve mention. The implicit ideal of democracy in
the case for OBC quotas was some kind of *participative* democracy.[58]
We saw that social justice was defined partly in terms of empowerment
of the disadvantaged. The participative ideal meant that empowerment
was to be brought about through the *presence* of the disadvantaged in

---

[58] The Prime Minister V.P. Singh alluded to this explicitly: '...When we talk of
participative democracy, when we talk of decentralization, we forget one very
important structure, bureaucracy. How are you going to give them participative
powers?' (*RSD* 1990 col. 347)

political institutions. It also implied an expansive application of democratic norms, beyond popular assemblies, to all institutions of power—hence OBC quotas in the bureaucracy. Participative democracy denoted an anti-paternalist egalitarianism; it implied giving the disadvantaged control over decisions, rather than merely acting in their interests. This was a more substantial conception of democracy than articulated in Congress nationalist discourse in the Constituent Assembly, where democracy had been construed largely in liberal representative terms. In Indian politics, the 1990s are associated with the deepening of Indian democracy, reflected in the higher levels of political participation by lower castes (Yadav 1999). Our analysis suggests that this political trend also had a conceptual counterpart, in more participative *conceptions* of democracy: political discourse reflected, and shaped the defining political trend of the period.

The justification of quotas on grounds of democratic justice strengthened the case in their favour. Increasing the representation in public institutions of historically excluded groups was a desired goal in itself; the reduction of socio-economic inequalities would follow but was a separate matter. Unlike nationalist opinion in the Constituent Assembly, quotas were no longer one means among several others, ineffectual on their own for addressing economic inequalities in society. However, democratic justice arguments in the Mandal debate were weaker in other respects. An earlier generation of lower caste leaders, notably Dr B.R. Ambedkar and Dr Ram Manohar Lohia had defended preferential treatment on grounds that these would benefit all castes and advance a common good.[59] In the Mandal debate, by contrast, very few attempts were made by advocates of OBC quotas to show that democratic justice was in the interests of all social groups, majority lower castes and minority upper castes alike.[60] Also, the democratic values of participation and equal respect were not linked to the distributive goal of redressing economic disadvantage in any strong sense: little attention was devoted to how the democratization of public institutions would

[59] Ram Manohar Lohia wrote in the 1950s: 'A crusade to uplift the downgraded groups would revive also the high caste...set right frames and values which are today all askew' (q. Sheth 2002: 117).

[60] On this point, see also Khan, who nevertheless suggests that in emphasizing respect or dignity, the arguments of lower caste leaders in the Mandal debate 'hint at the universal benefit of living in an inclusive democracy' (2008: 231).

improve the socio-economic conditions of beneficiaries. As such, the case for OBC quotas remained vulnerable to the charge that its appeal to democracy was a form of majoritaranism or sectionalism on behalf of dominant lower castes; the potential for a more universal definition of democracy remained underdeveloped.[61]

Social Justice and National Unity

National unity and development, it might be recalled, had dominated debates on quotas in the Constituent Assembly of the 1950s. While nationalists were worried about the impact of group-differentiated rights on social cohesion, political integrity, and the construction of a secular developmental state, they had also articulated justifications for quotas in terms of the national good (Bajpai 1997). In the 1990 Mandal debate, by contrast, considerations of national integration and development were not prominent. These were voiced mainly by Congress and BJP representatives in opposition to OBC quotas. Reservations were criticized as socially divisive, and as inconsistent with national progress, out of step with the times. Development was now identified with the liberalization of the Indian economy and the information technology revolution, captured in Rajiv Gandhi's slogan of taking India into the twenty-first century (see Dinesh Singh, *LSD* 1990 cols 404–5). Professor Sourendra Bhattacharjee (Congress) asked, 'whether, on the threshold of the 21st century, we would be approaching the coming century with a caste and communal divide or look forward to building a modern and scientific society....' (*RSD* 9.8. 1990 col. 259). Congress spokesman Vasant Sathe castigated the government for dividing the country on caste lines:

> ...the people who participated in the freedom struggle...had said that our dream is to create a casteless society in this country...Manu in ancient times deformed our society by dividing the people on the basis of their birth...You are now trying to bring Manu through Mandal... .
> (*LSD* 5.9.1990 cols 458–60)[62]

---

[61] On some problems of identity politics arguments from democratic standpoints, see, for instance, Anderson 2003; in the context of Indian debates, see Mehta: 'the idea that all our disagreements can be traced to who we are...makes reasoned discussion and argument...almost impossible' (2006: 2425).

[62] This was a wider theme in English language public media—see, in particular, the coverage in *India Today*, 15 September 1990.

As in the Constituent Assembly, criticisms of the quotas as 'casteist' in the Mandal debate conflated vertical and horizontal aspects of caste. Congress concern with quotas as strengthening caste as a *community* of attachment drew legitimacy from the illegitimacy of caste as a hereditary *hierarchy*. This has been an enduring characteristic of Indian nationalist arguments.

While criticisms that OBC quotas were 'casteist' were partially countered by arguments that caste had to be taken into account to challenge social inequalities (see Moturu Hanumantha Rao, *RSD* 1990 col. 346), the belief that the recognition of caste would necessarily strengthen caste loyalties was not directly addressed. Instead, considerations were advanced for why OBC quotas were nevertheless consistent with national unity and development. In a few cases, older arguments persisted, with quotas defended as temporary mechanisms of uplift, the ultimate goal defined as a secular society that would no longer be characterized by caste and communal distinctions between citizens. The Prime Minister V.P. Singh argued: 'We are in full agreement that there has to be a society where these distinctions are not there. But at the same time, for bringing them up and levelling them up we have to take steps' (*RSD* 1990 col. 268). In a few cases, quotas were defended as advancing 'backward' sections and thereby furthering national progress[63]; however, unlike in nationalist discourse in the Constituent Assembly, this was not the main justification for quotas in Janata Dal discourse.

The diminished significance of national unity and development in Janata Dal discourse was not simply a matter of degree: it meant that certain *kinds* of arguments for quotas, which were earlier illicit, were now affirmed. Among the proponents of OBC quotas, we find few concerns of the kind that had dominated Congress discourse in the Constituent Assembly: that these would consolidate caste divisions, detract from a sense of belonging to a common nation, or fuel social conflict. In response to Congress criticisms that the government's decision had triggered strife and instability, it was asserted: 'When you take a measure which is far-reaching, which disturbs the balance...this is going to happen' (*RSD* 1990 col. 278). National unity here could be *overridden* in the interests of social

---

[63] Hukumdeo Yadav defended OBC quotas thus: 'If we are to take the country towards progress, the poor, oppressed...people of the society who have been exploited socially, economically...for centuries must be uplifted' (*LSD* 4.9.1990 col. 416).

justice. Janata Dal representatives demonstrated a greater willingness to tolerate costs for political stability and social cohesion that a commitment to social transformation might entail.

Occasionally, an attempt was made to suggest that while social justice might conflict with national unity in the short term, the two were in harmony over the long term.[64] This picked up on a long-standing theme in lower caste thought, prominently articulated by Lohia in the 1960s.[65] The oppression of lower castes was portrayed as the main reason for the political subjection of the country: social justice, it was argued, was a condition for national strength. Ram Awadhesh Singh cautioned:

> ...India has lost time and again when it was economically prosperous... The reason for the defeats was this that the majority section of society, the weak section...was kept excluded from participation in state power.
> (RSD 1990 cols 360–1, translation from Hindi)

This narrative of the Indian past differed from nationalist versions in that the culpability for national weakness was attributed to Brahmin dominance and lower caste oppression. Its iconography was also distinct: unlike Gandhi, Nehru, and other leaders associated with the national movement, the historical figures invoked in support of the government's policy by Janata Dal spokesmen were non-Brahmin and Dalit leaders such as Jyotiba Phule, Dr B.R. Ambedkar, Periyar Ramaswamy, and Dr Ram Manohar Lohia, largely opponents of the Congress.[66] The narrative drive here was provided by the struggles for the rights of Untouchables and lower castes rather than the ascendancy of the nation. Janata Dal representatives were claiming a heritage that had intersected

[64] 'Unless we take the risk...for the betterment of the society, after fifty years this country will not be strong' (RSD 1990 col. 278).

[65] Ram Manohar Lohia had noted: 'Caste means depriving people of their abilities and that is the most important reason why the Indian people are so backward and so often have been enslaved' (q. Sheth 2002: 125). For Nehru writing in the Discovery of India, too, India succumbed to external invasion time and again because of internal decay, 'the growing rigidity and exclusiveness of the Indian social structure as represented chiefly by the caste system' (q. Chatterjee 1986: 135).

[66] The Prime Minister V.P. Singh defended the government announcement as: 'the realization of the dream of Bharat Ratna Dr B.R. Ambedkar, of the great Periyar Ramaswamy and Dr Ram Manohar Lohia' (RSD 1990 col. 232). See also Ram Awadhesh Singh, RSD 1990 cols 367–8.

only sporadically and often contentiously with the national movement. Nevertheless, for all the differences between Congress and lower caste nationalist narratives, the Constitution remained a common touchstone of political legitimacy, invoked by advocates of OBC quotas, as well as their critics. The government's decision to grant quotas to the OBCs was introduced as a fulfilment of its obligations under the Constitution (see *RSD* 1990 cols 309–10).

Whereas in nationalist discourse in the Constituent Assembly, social justice often appeared as a means to national integration and development, in an interesting reversal, advocates of OBC quotas sought to harness national unity to the cause of social justice. Kashiram Rana defended OBC quotas thus:

> People belonging to backward classes are also Indians...Their blood is not different from other people...they have a right to live a good life, others who consider themselves of higher classes should make some sacrifices for their fellow brethren.... (*LSD* 6.9. 1990 col. 467)

Hukumdeo Yadav queried:

> Suppose one of your family members is ill at home and the doctor has advised him to take ghee, milk, fruits and vitamins but the well-off brothers insist on taking the food according to their share...Is such a person a brother or a cruel man? (*LSD* 4.9.1990 col. 414)

The case for preferential treatment for the OBCs here relied on notions of (national) community, which in turn was defined in terms of bonds of kinship. Defining citizenship in terms of the bonds of community simultaneously signalled the entitlement to equal consideration of all members *and* implied a degree of concern for fellow members that required sacrifices from the better-off for the worse-off (Baker 1990; Miller 1999). At one level, the contention was, to put it in Dworkin's terms, that the fundamental right of each individual to be treated as an equal was compatible with, and might under some circumstances require, unequal treatment. The status of (male) siblings within a family represented the moral equality of persons. At another level, casting the nation in terms of filial notions of community implied that better-off citizens should acquiesce in departures from equal treatment and bear the costs of preferential treatment for disadvantaged citizens, as they would for one of their family. Just as it was inhumane to insist on one's portion in the face of the greater needs of a sibling, so too it was inappropriate to insist upon one's (deserved or equal) share when

brethren were suffering from want.[67] In other words, the analogy between
the nation and the family facilitated the appropriation of national unity
for the cause of social justice. While this remained a marginal strand in
Janata Dal discourse, it illustrated how the bonds of nationality could be
put to the service of social justice.

Establishing the benefits of quotas for the nation was not a central
concern for the advocates of OBC quotas in the Mandal debate, unlike
for an earlier generation of lower caste leaders.[68] This marked a major
shift in the justification of preferential treatment. It strengthened the
case for quotas: the diminished import of national unity meant that
social justice was now valued in its own terms, and that considerations of
national unity had to yield to the demands of social justice. However, it
also meant that one powerful account of how preferential treatment for
the 'backward classes' served the common good was lost. Materials for
alternative accounts existed as we have seen, but their elaboration was
not often attempted by advocates of quotas in the Mandal debate: how
a more just society would benefit all citizens or realize a common good
remained unarticulated. As such, the advocacy of OBC quotas remained
susceptible to the charge that it was a sectional interest seeking power, its
appeal to social justice largely rhetorical.

The Legitimating Vocabulary on Group Rights: Continuities, Shifts, and Implications

Justifications of preferential treatment in the 1990 Mandal debate
reflected important changes relative to the Constituent Assembly debates.
In the latter, it might be recalled, quotas were regarded as detracting
from key nationalist values, albeit admissible as temporary, exceptional
provisions for the amelioration of socio-economic disparities of the
'backward'. In dominant nationalist opinion, secularism was construed
primarily in terms of the disregard of ascriptive distinctions in political
life; democracy, in individualist and proceduralist terms of the rights of

---

[67] As Miller (1999) suggests, the appeal of need as the appropriate criterion for
the distribution of benefits is enhanced when we conceive of the community in
solidaristic terms, as characterized by close ties between members.
[68] There were, of course, references to the national good in arguments put forward
by advocates of OBC quotas, but such appeals were rarely substantive.

individuals to participate in the choosing of representatives; justice and equality, predominantly in terms of equality of opportunity and non-discrimination between individuals; and national unity, as incompatible with a general policy of group preference. In the 1990 Mandal debate, the key concepts of the legitimating vocabulary were interpreted differently by Janata Dal representatives: democracy, for instance, was construed in participative terms and as implying a concern with outcomes relating to the social composition of assemblies; justice and equality, in terms of fair equality of opportunity and empowerment of the disadvantaged.

In terms of my proposal, these changed connotations can be understood in terms of a reconfiguration of the concepts of the legitimating vocabulary. Broadly speaking, if the key regulating relationship in Congress discourse in the Constituent Assembly was between secularism and national unity, in Janata Dal discourse in the Mandal debate, it was between justice and equality on the one hand, and democracy on the other. More specifically, the conceptual mechanism whereby the discursive shift was accomplished involved a relocation of equality in proximity to democracy on the one hand, and its distancing from national unity, on the other. The proximity of equality to national unity in nationalist opinion in the Constituent Assembly had meant that equality was construed as implying that all individuals would have the *same* rights irrespective of community, and the amelioration of socio-economic disparities that hindered the integration and development of the nation. In Janata Dal discourse in Mandal, the proximity of equality to democracy meant that equality was construed in terms of participation of the 'backward' in political power; its distancing from national unity meant that equality so conceived would be pursued even if it involved some costs to national unity. This was accompanied by changes in the register of the discourse on preferential treatment. Corresponding to close links between equality and democracy, the paternalist philanthropic idiom of 'protection' of 'weaker sections' that had been prominent in nationalist discourse in the Constituent Assembly debates, declined. Corresponding to the distancing of equality from national unity, organic metaphors of 'part' and 'whole', 'disease' and 'health' of the body politic, and of 'backwardness' as a blot on the face of the nation, were rarely in evidence.

While several commentators have noted the powerful resonance of the rhetoric of social justice, they have tended to misidentify where its novelty lies. Thus, for instance, in his influential account of the expansion of the participatory base of Indian democracy in the 1990s, Yadav notes: 'For the first time the neat arrangement of the borrowed high ideological spectrum was disturbed by homespun ideological fragments. The raw narratives of social justice...[made] it respectable to talk about caste in the public-political domain' (1999: 2397). My analysis, however, suggests that the ability of social justice to confer respectability on issues of caste equity derived not so much from its roots in 'homespun ideological fragments', as its creative appropriation of the 'high ideological spectrum'. We saw that in the Janata Dal's discourse of social justice, a justification was fashioned for OBC quotas in the administration through a redefinition of older nationalist goals. This involved not so much an importation of indigenous norms, as, in the terms of my proposal, a rearrangement of concepts in the prevailing vocabulary, principally bringing notions of democracy into closer alignment with those of equality. Indeed, it was because it built upon an existing normative vocabulary that the discourse of social justice *could* confer legitimacy on caste in politics (Skinner 1988).

A related influential tendency has been to see social justice as part of an indigenous vocabulary, radically opposed to the liberal democratic language of an English-speaking elite. Yadav, for instance, speaks of an 'alien vocabulary of liberal democracy' giving rise to 'two radically different languages of politics corresponding to the Bhasha/English divide. The former, a language of democratic rights and social justice, was deployed to win elections, while the latter, a language of macro-economic and bureaucratic management, guided the framing of policies' (1999: 2398). Lower caste politicians have often pressed their case in a vernacular idiom against an English-speaking political elite. But our analysis has shown that their arguments have drawn substantially upon liberal and democratic norms. The discourse of social justice employed by proponents of quotas invoked a range of values drawn from different liberal traditions. Rights-based liberal concerns regarding non-discrimination and equality of opportunity were intertwined with utilitarian considerations about welfare and the social good. Egalitarian liberal commitments to fair equality of opportunity were employed to critique proceduralist liberal concerns of formal equality of opportunity and merit. This is not to suggest that indigenous cultural and historical idioms were absent. For instance, occasionally arguments for OBC quotas on grounds of group fairness in the Mandal debate, like similar arguments in the Constituent Assembly, invoked the Hindu idiom of atonement for past sins. More generally, political discourse continued to reflect an easy traffic of themes between religious and filial domains on the one hand, and the public, political domain on the other, with filial idioms notably invoked to justify sacrifices on the part of upper castes for the benefit of their less-advantaged brethren. Nonetheless, the presence of liberal and democratic *values* in the Indian political discourse is more substantial and widely shared than is often portrayed to be the case, even as its spokesmen and language have become more vernacular.

Another respect in which the discursive shift represented by the ascendancy of social justice has been misdiagnosed is in the radical shift that this is thought to represent in justifications of reservations since constitution-making. The recasting of the normative basis of group preference during the Constituent Assembly debates, from cultural distinctness to 'backwardness', endured in the Mandal debate. This was reflected in the fact that quotas were now argued for exclusively within the frame of affirmative action, with all claimants seeking to establish that they were 'backward', much in the manner in which groups claiming preferential provisions during the Constituent Assembly debates had sought to establish their minority status. 'Backward' had become the *inclusive* term or the rhetorical shorthand to denote a group's eligibility to special treatment—claims for quotas for Muslims and women in the Mandal debate strove to demonstrate the 'backwardness' of their group.[69] The term 'minority' itself was now largely employed as an adjunct to the 'backward classes'; both were encapsulated within the broad category of 'weaker sections' of society. This characterized quota claims not just in government employment, but in legislative and educational arenas more generally.[70]

---

[69] For instance, Shamim Hashmi argued in favour of reservations for Muslims: '...the entire Muslim community is socially backward, is economically completely ruined and psychologically demoralized. For meeting these three points, we demand that you give reservation to the Muslim community as a whole' (*RSD* 1990 col. 244 translation from Hindi). Similarly, it was argued in favour of quotas for women that '...if you take all the communities right across the board...without any bar of religion, community or caste, it is the women of this country who are the most disadvantaged, who are the most backward, economically, socially, culturally...' (Jayanthi Natarajan, *RSD* 1990 col. 302).

[70] For example, the 1990s witnessed a revival of demands for legislative quotas for Muslims, and here too, it was the 'backwardness' of the group that was cited.

While 'backwardness' had become the sole basis for claiming quotas by the time of the Mandal case, it was by no means self-evident what 'backwardness' consisted in. Several criteria were invoked in political debate, including poverty and economic deprivation; educational disadvantage; low social status; a history of discrimination and oppression by dominant groups; under-representation in government employment and educational institutions (Galanter 1984). These could be related in different ways.[71] In practice, how one conceived of the interconnections between these criteria depended upon one's preferred set of beneficiaries. Much of the criticism of the government decision and the Mandal Report employed one criterion against another to make the case that there had been over-inclusion of advantaged groups and under-inclusion of the truly 'backward'. Criticisms of Mandal as 'casteist' obscured the fact that the Mandal debate actually registered a decline in the importance of the *ritual* disabilities of caste as criteria of 'backwardness'. Instead, the *secular* profile of a caste, involving criteria such as literacy, poverty, representation in education and administration, had gained ascendancy in descriptions of 'backwardness'.

Not only did all groups claiming job quotas do so on grounds of 'backwardness', contrary to influential opinion, the under-representation of a group in the administration was not considered sufficient for establishing disadvantage. Even in Janata Dal discourse, which asserted the rights of OBC groups to a 'share in state power', under-representation denoted inequalities of status and distributive injustice along group lines as we have seen. The contention that groups as such were entitled to a 'due share' of representation in public appointments, which had been common in the colonial period, was not in evidence in the Mandal debate. In these respects, the constitutional recasting of preferential treatment endured in the Mandal debate. Of course, there were significant changes: the nationalist ideal of equality was substantially redefined in the Janata Dal's rhetoric of social justice, in ways that were much more accommodating of group-differentiated rights. However, departures from the nationalist

---

Interviews with Minorities Commission chairperson, Prof. Tahir Mahmood, and leaders of Muslim organizations petitioning for legislative quotas, September 1999, New Delhi.

[71] Thus, for instance, educational deprivation could be regarded as a consequence of poverty, or as existing independently of it, a consequence of the historical exclusion of certain groups from access to education.

vocabulary are less radical than is often suggested. Underneath the Janata Dal rhetoric of the rights of groups to representation in the administration, the norms invoked often pertained to *individualist* justice type considerations. The defence of OBC quotas by the Janata Dal in terms of social justice in the Mandal debate continued to draw upon the pool of concepts comprising the legitimating vocabulary. And older concerns about caste-based quotas, as detracting from national unity and development, remained prominent in the pronouncements of Congress and BJP representatives.

The formulation of a legitimating vocabulary also enables a better grasp of policy difference and political change. In the Mandal debate, as in the Shah Bano case, the opposing positions on group-differentiated rights were divided not just by competition over power, but by differences over the interpretation of shared political ideals. In Janata Dal discourse, the proximity of social justice to democracy meant that conceptions emphasized empowerment and recognition, in contrast to notions of social justice in Congress discourse. For the Congress, the proximity of social justice to national unity meant that it favoured the extension of job quotas to economically disadvantaged upper castes, so as to accommodate all social groups.[72]

In the Constituent Assembly debates, we saw that the expansion of the nationalist vocabulary reflected the establishment of Congress hegemony. In the Mandal debate, the salience in political discourse of competing conceptions of social justice indicated that no single party was now hegemonic. The electoral decline of the Congress was mirrored in the shape of political discourse, in the fact that the Congress no longer set the terms of the debate on legitimating norms. The prominence of social justice and its close links with democracy in the Mandal debate reflected the rise of new political forces, lower caste-based parties such as the Janata Dal. Nevertheless, the Janata Dal too was unable to impose its conception of social justice on the polity as a whole: considerations of distributive equality remained significant in justifications of preferential treatment, as did national unity. In ideological terms, as much as electorally, the era of single party hegemony was over.

---

[72] Prof. C. Thakur of the Congress welcomed the announcement of 5–10 per cent reservation for the economically 'backward' thus: 'we all want a just society...we also want a socially cohesive society' (*RSD* 1990 col. 285).

What does this analysis of discursive continuities and shifts suggest for our understanding of policy shifts with respect to group-differentiated rights? The first aspect of note is that the advocacy of preferential treatment in terms of social justice in the 1990 Mandal debate provided a more robust basis for special treatment than had been available in the nationalist vocabulary during the Constituent Assembly debates. In Congress arguments in the Constituent Assembly, quotas were seen as involving the balancing of *competing* considerations to equality—as detracting from equality of opportunity and merit, albeit as contributing towards the reduction of social disparities. Their scope was consequently sought to be restricted. In Janata Dal discourse, by contrast, equality of opportunity and merit were construed as congruent with quotas for 'backward classes'; consequently, such a limitation was not required. Further, the redefinition of equality as a goal in terms of empowerment and recognition meant that quotas were no longer seen as one of several means *towards* possible future reduction of socio-economic disparities, but rather as *realizing* the empowerment of historically disadvantaged groups. Finally, the de-emphasis on national unity meant that quotas were acceptable on social justice grounds *even* if these involved some costs in terms of social cohesion. As such, the policy change involving the extension of quotas in government employment to a large new group of beneficiaries was accompanied by discursive shifts conducive to this outcome.

At the same time, internal tensions remained in the justification of quotas in terms of social justice in Janata Dal discourse. Fair equality of opportunity arguments relied heavily on the *class* effects of caste discrimination—inequalities in the distribution of socio-economic resources played an important role in the interpretation of equality of opportunity and merit as compatible with preferential treatment in Janata Dal discourse. Further, the goal of a more equal society was still seen to involve the reduction of socio-economic inequalities. As such, the Janata Dal remained vulnerable to criticisms on distributive grounds, to pressures for class-based refinements to the policy, notably the exclusion of well-off OBCs, as well as the inclusion of economically disadvantaged upper castes.[73] That the trend towards the enlargement of quotas has

---

[73] From a democratic justice standpoint, the exclusion of better-off members of a disadvantaged group can be undesirable. As Anderson argues, more

been accompanied by attempts to incorporate economic criteria in some form is not surprising. Most notably, the Supreme Court judgement on the Mandal case in 1992 upheld quotas for OBCs, but asked for the exclusion of economically well-off OBCs (the so called 'creamy layer').[74] The 'creamy layer' criterion is a key policy development, which attempts to bridge the tensions in the case for OBC quotas between caste/class and group/individual criteria. Importantly, this limitation has endured despite the expansion of the policy of preferential treatment for OBCs in other areas (Dhavan 2008).

What light does our account of continuities and shifts in discourses of group preference in the Mandal case shed on the key political development of the 1990s, the decline of Congress dominance? To begin with, my analysis supports the view that the rise of centre-left caste and regional parties needs to be seen as a significant contributing factor. These parties did not just undermine the electoral dominance of the Congress, they also challenged its ideological hegemony, putting forward distinctive conceptions of social justice and democracy. A puzzling feature of lower caste politics in India has been that the 'third front' political space that these parties occupy has become an established feature of the polity since the 1990s, despite the fact that the parties

---

privileged members of disadvantaged groups are 'in a better position to function successfully as agents of integration', with the latter construed as 'effective participation and interaction on terms of equality' by individuals from diverse social backgrounds 'in the shared spaces of civil society' (Anderson 2002: 1214, 1245; see also Weisskopf 2004).

[74] The judgement asked the Government of India to specify within four months 'the bases, applying the relevant and requisite socio-economic criteria to exclude socially advanced persons/sections (creamy layer) from Other Backward Classes (Dudley Jenkins 2003: 149). The Central government's criteria for identifying the 'creamy layer' in its office memorandum dated 8.9.1993 produced by the Prasad Committee included the children whose parents hold constitutional positions, Class I and Class II officers of the All-India Central and State services and equivalent posts in public sector undertakings and private employment, Colonel and above in the defence services, lawyers, doctors, financial consultants and other professionals, families owing irrigated land equal to more than 85 per cent of the state land ceiling laws, and parents having a gross annual income of Rs 100,000 or more (the income ceiling was raised to Rs 450,000 in 2008). Leading proposals for policy reform have also sought to combine caste and class criteria to address both group and individual disadvantage—see, for instance, Deshpande and Yadav 2006.

themselves have often been short-lived and prone to fragmentation.[75] Our analysis suggests the discursive shift exemplified by the Janata Dal's advocacy of social justice in the 1990 Mandal debate has carved out an ideological space for lower caste–based centre-left parties, which is *distinct* from the other major parties. That this arena has resisted absorption by the two other poles of Indian politics, the Congress and the BJP, is not surprising, given that *national unity* concerns that are central to both parties, occupy a peripheral position in their discourse of social justice.

At the same time, their ideological profile also offers clues as to why lower caste-based parties advocating social justice have been prone to fragmentation and less successful in becoming national, all-India parties. The vision of social justice they embody focuses overwhelmingly on caste, whose components vary regionally, with differences of interests not only *between* lower and upper castes, but also *within* 'backward' castes.[76] Contemporary advocates have rarely provided any substantial account of how social justice is a common good, in the interests of all social groups, although materials can be discerned in several claims.[77] With the uncoupling of social justice and national unity, one powerful account of how preferential treatment served the common good

---

[75] Splinter groups of the Janata Dal include Mulayam Singh's Samajwadi Party, Laloo Prasad Yadav's Rashtriya Lok Dal, Naveen Patnaik's Biju Janata Dal, Nitish Kumar's Janata Dal (U), and Ram Vilas Paswan's Lok Janshakti Party.

[76] These differences have led to political conflict between parties and movements representing OBCs and Dalits (e.g., Samajwadi Party and Bahujan Samaj Party in Uttar Pradesh); the relatively advanced and more 'backward' OBC castes (e.g., Yadavs and Kurmis in Bihar); and between different Dalit castes (e.g., Malas and Madigas in Andhra Pradesh). Many lower caste parties and movements are dominated by a single OBC or Dalit caste (e.g., the Rashtriya Lok Dal is dominated by Yadavs and the Bahujan Samaj Party, by Chamars). See Pai and Singh 1997; Vora 2004.

[77] Such arguments can take a variety of forms. It can, for instance, be argued that the inclusion of lower castes brings in additional relevant perspectives into decision-making and thereby enhances the quality of decisions, and, thereby democracy—see Anderson 2002. For a defence of preferential treatment in higher education in India as a means of integrating members of disadvantaged groups into the societal elite, see Weisskopf 2004. Elite integration, Weisskopf notes, can serve the general interest by providing the political system with greater legitimacy, and strengthen democratic institutions by widening participation.

provided by nationalists was lost; alternative accounts, in terms of society-wide benefits of social justice or democracy, were not elaborated in Janata Dal discourse. As such, the ideological resources of the kind fashioned in the Mandal debate provided a basis for the resilience of lower caste-based centre-left space in Indian politics, but not for the endurance of these parties or their expansion on an all-India scale. This, in turn, is commensurate with the shape of lower caste politics since the late 1990s, with the smaller or more 'backward' castes in North India, for instance, leaving OBC parties to form their own.[78] More empirical work is required to test these claims; nevertheless, my analysis suggests that ideological explanations offer a rich potential for advancing our understanding of lower caste politics.

Social justice has also been a central preoccupation in contemporary political theory. Among advocates of social justice, the focus has been on distributive equality—the distribution of economic resources among individuals in a society—which, in turn, has often been contrasted with social equality or equality of status (Miller 1999: 232). My findings support the strand of egalitarian scholarship that emphasizes continuities between distributive and social equality and underlines the significance of the latter for social justice (Young 1990; Phillips 1995; Wolff 1998; Anderson 1999; Fraser and Honneth 2003). As advocates of OBC quotas highlighted, inequalities of status, like distributive inequalities, can undermine equality of opportunity in education and employment. Further, the characterization of social equality as group-based needs qualification. Social equality arguments in the Mandal debate derived their normative force chiefly from the denial of equal opportunities and equal worth—to *individuals*; these did not affirm the normative significance of groups as such. Finally, social equality advocates in Indian debates have held that the distribution of respect and power in society are also concerns of social justice, not just the distribution of material goods. The extent to which the distribution of the democratic goods of respect and power are matters for social justice is a question that recent egalitarian scholarship has begun to address,

---

[78] As Jaffrelot documents, Yadavs occupied an overwhelming share of posts in state assemblies and governments in the administrations of Mulayam Singh Yadav and Laloo Prasad Yadav. This in turn lead to the exit of Kurmi leaders such as Nitish Kumar to form their own parties, and of voters from smaller OBC castes to support rival parties such as BSP and BJP (2003: 368–86).

although a full treatment is still awaited. At the same time, my findings also suggest that it is useful to retain the conceptual distinction between social and distributive equality, to hold these as distinct, albeit related ideals. Proponents of social equality in the Mandal debate differed from those who emphasized distributive inequalities in maintaining that the fundamental cause of unjust inequalities was the caste hierarchy and not so much the economic structure of society, and in emphasizing that social justice required the greater equalization of status, respect and power, as much as material goods. Difference in the significance accorded to social equality, among other factors, is likely to distinguish different philosophical and real-world theories of social justice.

Postscript: The Debate on Reservations for OBCs in Higher Education Institutions 2005–6 (Mandal II)

Since 1990, reservations debates in India have moved to new areas.[79] The broad direction of policy change has been one of expansion of affirmative action. In 2005–6, OBC quotas were proposed for institutions of higher education and legislation passed enabling reservations in the private sector.[80] In the wake of the recommendations of the Sachar Committee

---

[79] Reservations in the private sector appear in the election manifesto promises of both the major parties, the Congress and the BJP, from 2004. These have assumed significance since the economic liberalization of the 1990s, as a much higher proportion of desired jobs are now in the private sector.

[80] In 2005, the Constitution was amended to permit affirmative action in all educational institutions including private institutions not receiving aid from the state (Article 15.5, Constitution 93rd Amendment Act, 2005), overturning Supreme Court rulings that this was impermissible (notably, *PA Inamdar vs State of Maharashtra* 2005). In 2006, legislation was passed to institute quotas for SCs, STs and OBCs in all educational institutions aided directly or indirectly by the Central Government, including elite institutions such as the IITs, IIMs and AIIMS (Central Educational Institutions Reservation in Admission Act, 2006). It was envisaged that corresponding to the reservation quota, there would be an increase in the overall number of places in all institutions, to be implemented over a three-year period. The legislation excluded minority educational institutions as well as programmes of high specialization (Dhavan 2008). OBC quotas in higher education institutions were implemented following Supreme Court endorsement of supporting legislation (*Ashoka Thakur vs Union of India* 2008).

(2006) and the Ranganath Misra Commission (2007), educational and employment quotas for Muslims are under consideration.[81] What were the contours of the legitimating vocabulary in this era of expansion of preferential treatment? Were the discursive shifts identified in the Mandal case sustained? Some brief considerations are in order.

An examination of the 2005–6 parliamentary debates on OBC quotas in higher education suggests that the broad picture is one of consolidation and extension of the trends identified in the 1990 debate.[82] Social justice had established itself as a key legitimating value in its own right. Invoked in nearly every speech in the debate, parties competed with each other to claim social justice as part of their history. Significantly, justifications of quotas advanced by representatives from all political parties, Congress, the Left as well as regional and lower caste parties, relied largely on egalitarian notions of equality of opportunity.[83] Unlike the Constituent Assembly debates, and in sharp contrast to the wider public debate, there was virtually no opposition to quotas as detracting from equality of opportunity or merit. Instead, representatives voiced a keen awareness of the effects of environmental privileges enjoyed by the members of advanced upper caste families, the unfairness of a system of open competition in a society with massive disparities of income and education, and the small percentile differences that separated 'forward' and 'backward' caste candidates (*LSD* 21.12.2005).

---

[81] The Sachar Report (2006) found evidence of severe socio-economic disadvantage among Muslims and recommended a range of measures to improve access to education, employment, housing, credit, although it stopped short of recommending quotas. The Ranganath Misra Report (2007) proposed a 15 per cent minority quota in educational institutions and government employment, of which 10 per cent was earmarked for Muslims. It also recommended that benefits for Scheduled Castes, hitherto limited to Hindus, Sikhs, and Buddhists, be extended to all religious groups (notably Muslims and Christians). Both reports were commissioned by the UPA government elected in 2004, and have influential supporters in the current administration (Interviews 2009, New Delhi).

[82] On the specificities of higher education as a sector, see, for instance, Satish Deshpande 2006: 2440–1.

[83] See, for instance, Prof. Basudev Barman (CPI-M): 'in a society where equality of status and opportunity is not there and where glaring disparities in incomes exist and persist, there is no room for equality in any sense...treating unequals as equals is the greatest injustice and correction or elimination of this injustice is very important...' (*LSD* 2006).

Fair equality of opportunity had become the dominant justification for preferential treatment for the OBCs, and importantly, was now employed also by Congress representatives, in contrast to the 1990 Mandal debate. Compensatory arguments rarely made an appearance.[84] In terms of the centrality of social justice in political argument, the defence of preferential treatment as a requirement of equality of opportunity properly conceived, and as consistent with merit, the discursive shift observed in Janata Dal discourse in the 1990 Mandal debate endured, and indeed had expanded into a polity-wide shift.

Nevertheless, in the pronouncements of different political parties, this common vocabulary of social justice had different emphases. Thus while democracy and social justice were closely inter-linked in several speeches, democratic arguments about the participation of the disadvantaged in decision-making institutions were most prominent in the speeches of lower caste regional political parties, as were claims for reservations as a constitutional *right*.[85] Among Congress representatives, from different social backgrounds, a more paternalist tone of protection of 'weaker sections' was often in evidence.[86] An emphasis on economic deprivation was prominent in the pronouncements of representatives from Left parties.[87] Economic criteria continued to be pressed frequently for directing quotas towards the poorer sections of beneficiary groups, usually by Left and Congress representatives.[88] Demands for quotas within quotas were also

---

[84] When they did, compensatory arguments associated OBCs with Dalits and Adivasis. Prabodh Panda (CPI) noted: 'Why should there be reservation for the OBC?...Present generation is not responsible...but [they]...cannot disown the past...the injustice of our society...The Scheduled Castes and the Scheduled Tribes are like slaves of our country' (*LSD* 14.12.2006).

[85] The emphasis on reservations as a constitutional right, as Beteille (2005) points out, blurs the distinction between enabling provisions (employment and educational quotas) and mandatory provisions (legislative reservations).

[86] Janardhan Poojary, for instance, noted that Arjun Singh who belonged to the royal family was looking after the 'backward classes', and that the Nehru family had always protected the 'weaker sections' (*RSD* 18.12.2006).

[87] Prasanta Chatterjee (CPI-M), for instance, welcomed 'the step towards ensuring equality of access to higher education to a larger number of economically deprived students...Wider policy to change and alter the socio-economic system is...necessary' (*RSD* 18.12.2006).

[88] Prasanta Chatterjee (CPI-M) proposed that benefits should be targeted to the more deprived OBCs in the first instance, and for any unfilled quota positions

put forward to channel benefits to poorer sub-groups *within* the lower caste beneficiary groups.[89] These reflected the continuing hold both of economic criteria, and disadvantage more broadly defined, on claims for group representation. As in the 1990 debate, the under-representation of a group in higher education and other arenas was prominently invoked in quota claims, but it remained linked to disadvantage. All demands for quotas in higher educational institutions sought to establish the backwardness of the group. Such demands were increasingly voiced for Muslims, where the educational backwardness of the community identified by the Sachar report was emphasized.[90]

In relation to the 1990 Mandal debate, two features stand out. Social equality concerns were less prominent, and national unity and development were more often invoked in defence of preferential treatment. In part, this reflected the fact that it was the *Congress* party that was now leading the expansion of OBC quotas, rather than a lower caste-based party. With the significance it now accorded to social justice, and its move from non-discrimination to more egalitarian notions of equality of opportunity, the Congress had now *redefined* its position relative to the 1990 Mandal debate and, of course, since the 1950s. Further, while

---

to go to the 'creamy layer'. Dr P.C. Alexander (Independent) lamented that 'the really deserving poor backward class members will never get the benefit of this Bill' (*RSD* 2006). Academic interventions in reservations debates in higher education and the private sector have also favoured making 'the creamy layer' the 'last claimant' on reservation benefits and sought to take greater account of individual disadvantage in the design of affirmative action programmes (see Deshpande and Yadav 2006: 2420; Sheth 2005). On why relatively well-off sections of disadvantaged groups ('creamy layer') should *not* be excluded from higher education benefits, see Weisskopf 2004; Thorat 2006; Satish Deshpande 2006.

[89] Paramjit Kaur Gulshan (Shiromani Akali Dal) argued for reviving an earlier formula for subgroups of Scheduled Caste Sikhs: 'More than 50 per cent of the Scheduled Castes [in Punjab] belong to the 'Majhabi' and 'Balmiki' groups. Only 2 per cent Scheduled Castes are getting the benefit of reservation whereas several other subgroups are lagging far behind. They are the poorest of the poor and the most backward among the Scheduled Caste' (*LSD* 14.12.2006).

[90] Asaduddin Owaisi (AIMIM, an ally of the ruling UPA) noted that the Sachar Committee report 'clearly states the educational backwardness of the Muslim community... there are 39 per cent OBCs and 0.8 per cent Scheduled Caste in the Muslim community...how fair is it to deny the benefits of reservation on the basis of religion?...' (*LSD* 2006).

the Congress' core concern of national unity remained significant, this was now unequivocally interpreted as consistent with group preference. Indeed, Arjun Singh defended reservations as a legacy of the Congress-led freedom movement, that incorporated regional streams:

> the whole question of reservation started with the First Amendment of the Constitution which was moved by Pandit Jawaharlal Nehru which took into account all the movements which have ultimately contributed to the freedom of India...All those social movements, whether they were in the South or in Maharashtra or anywhere else, constitute a very powerful stream in our national ethos and therefore...[Pandit Nehru] was only taking note of what...ultimately helped us to achieve freedom... . (*LSD* 14.12.2006)

In this reinterpretation of the Congress history, Nehru's distaste of caste-based reservations at the time of constitution-making was papered over, the modernization narrative of overcoming divisive caste (as well as religious and linguistic) identities, invisible. Yoking together social justice and national unity reflected the Congress' traditional attempt to carry all sections of the population with it, and was reflected in the shape of the policy, which sought to institute quotas for OBCs by *increasing* the total number of places in higher education. A national integration rationale for quotas was also articulated by BJP leaders (see, for instance, Tapir Gao, *LSD* 14.12.2006).

Another shift relative to the 1990 Mandal debate was the renewed importance of national development in political discourse. That the benefits of India's high growth rates since the 1990s should be equitably shared among all sections of the population' was a common argument in support of OBC quotas. In some cases, where quotas were defended as distributing benefits of growth more widely, development was subordinated to the cause of social justice (see, for instance, Prof. Ramdass, *LSD* 14.12.2006). In other cases, the advancement of socially and educationally 'backward classes' itself was seen as 'vital not only in the interest of achieving...the object of an egalitarian society, but also in order that India may march forward along with other nations of the world' (Prof. Basudev Barman, *LSD* 21.12.2005). A few criticisms of OBC quotas as divisive and as inconsistent with a competitive market economy were voiced.[91] In most

---

[91] Industrialist Rahul Bajaj (Independent) opposed the Bill: 'in a globalized world of today, there are no entitlements. Everybody has to earn his place in the society. And if we have 50 per cent...entitlements and reservations...we are creating a

cases, however, national unity and development were construed as consistent with social justice.

In several respects—the renewed emphasis on material inequalities, development, and national unity—the Mandal debate of 2005–6 reflected characteristic themes of Congress discourse on preferential treatment. Did this then indicate the beginnings of a new Congress dominance, even hegemony, albeit with a different vocabulary? The evidence from legislative debates suggests otherwise. Not all parties shared the Congress' emphasis on the nation as the pre-eminent justificatory frame: unlike the late 1940s, the Congress was unable to reconfigure the orientation of political discourse as a whole. For lower caste and regional parties, social justice was the sole referent, with representatives from Southern parties claiming to be pioneers, delineating a history studded with Dravidian leaders that was distinct from, and often antagonistic to, the Congress.[92] Democratic and rights based considerations in defence of quotas were much more prominent in the pronouncements of lower caste and regional parties. As such, contending values remained entrenched in political discourse.

Were more universal justifications for affirmative action articulated in the 2006 debate? Apart from cursory references to national unity, there was little attempt in Congress discourse to elaborate arguments for how OBC quotas served a common good. Justifications of reservations in terms of national unity largely alluded to its instrumental role in integrating diverse social movements into a successful national movement. How reservations

---

society which does not learn to compete hard, and, does not want to compete with the rest of the world' (*RSD* 2006). Tathagatha Satpathy (Biju Janata Dal) lamented: '...Today, we are in a backward race, and we want to become more and more backward so that we get the benefits of this nation...If you say, on the one hand that there is no merit...on the other hand, you are saying globalization...we want to be competitive internationally...this is a very reactionary mindset, and I hope [we] will...think of the nation...of India's future; and not become caste-ridden, religion ridden, petty or small, but grow beyond all that...rise above personal greed and party interests' (*LSD* 14.12.2006).

[92] References to leaders of Dravidian movements were prominent in this debate. L. Ganesan (MDMK) noted: 'Reservation is not an end in itself; rather, it is only a means to an end. Social justice is the end. For this principle...our Thantai Periyar...suffered...When many of you people [had] never heard about social justice, our own Thanthai Periyar started the movement for social justice...' (*LSD* 14.12.2006). See also A. Krishnaswamy (DMK), *LSD* 21.12.2005; *LSD* 14.12.2006.

might contribute to the ideal of a democratically just society, and thereby benefit all citizens, for instance, was not articulated in Congress opinion.[93] Given that caste-based quotas were previously seen as detracting from national unity in Congress discourse, it was vulnerable to criticisms that educational quotas were simply a means of courting an electorally powerful constituency, for gaining OBC votes (Dhavan 2008).

Principled arguments for preferential treatment for disadvantaged groups in terms of the general interest remain under-developed in Indian political discourse.[94] Two arguments from the American experience are particularly relevant for India. The first stresses the educational value of diversity for democratic citizenship. As Nussbaum (2008) argues, in a plural country, effective citizenship requires an understanding of the variety of viewpoints and social backgrounds that compose the nation. Inclusion of under-represented groups through affirmative action provides individuals from *all* social groups the opportunity to broaden their horizons of experience in ways that make them better citizens. A second, related argument for affirmative action elaborated by Anderson (2002: 1195) highlights the role of integration in mainstream institutions, both for removing existing barriers to equal opportunity faced by disadvantaged groups, as well as creating a democratic civil society. Integrated institutions (schools, universities) teach individuals 'of different walks of life to learn to live together on terms of equality', which in turn '...is the indispensable social condition of democracy...' (*ibid*.: 1223). Drawing upon Anderson, Weisskopf (2004) has argued that the inclusion of members of under-represented groups in spheres such as higher education and prestigious jobs improves the democratic system overall—by increasing its

---

[93] For an exception, see Dr K. Keshava Rao (Congress): 'If you look into the NCERT reports...if you look into South Africa or any report in America, you will find that they vouchsafe for the fact that inclusiveness and trying to take the minority along will strengthen the quality of life, quality of education, and quality of the polity' (*RSD* 2006).

[94] Moves towards cross-national policy learning can be discerned in official discourse, for instance, in the Sachar Report's recommendations of an Equal Opportunity Commission and a Diversity Index that have been taken further in the Menon Report (2008), and the Kundu Report (2008); for an analysis, see Khaitan 2008. While these propose more universal institutional alternatives to group-based quotas, the benefits to society as a whole of increased opportunities for under-represented groups are not discussed.

legitimacy, bringing in a range of concerns into decision-making, enabling marginalized groups to exercise their rights and responsibilities as full citizens. Of course, affirmative action can also contribute to the general interest by improving economic efficiency—for instance, exposure to diverse backgrounds fosters skills required for success in the global marketplace, and improves performance in jobs that require knowledge of marginalized communities. Difficult questions remain about the groups that ought to be beneficiaries and the mechanisms for affirmative action, where progress depends on more empirical information, gathered, for instance, through social surveys designed for this purpose (Deshpande and Yadav 2006), and a caste-based census. Nevertheless, moving the debate beyond the well-worn grooves of reservations as a spoils system versus merit as privilege, towards consideration of the universal benefits of affirmative action is essential to make better sense of the contribution of affirmative action to democracy in India. As part of this, a reckoning of the role of reservations in the integration of elites of disadvantaged groups into mainstream institutions is a necessary step.

Conclusion

This book has focused on two critical junctures in the history of the post-Independence Indian state: the late 1940s, which saw a centralization of power, and the late 1980s, which marked a decentring of power. Thus far, scholars have focused on the institutional, social, and economic aspects of this structural change. In a new departure, this book has constructed an account of political change in India in terms of political ideology, focusing on constitutional and legislative debates over group-differentiated rights. Drawing upon the insights of liberal political theory, postcolonial theory and ideological analysis, through a detailed study of political arguments in three landmark debates on group rights (the Constituent Assembly debates of 1946–9, the Shah Bano debate of 1986, and the Mandal debate of 1990), this study has proposed a conceptual model. A legitimating vocabulary comprising a set of inter-linked concepts, those of secularism, democracy, social justice, national unity and development, has framed political debate on group rights in independent India. Political arguments, both for and against preferential policies, advanced from conflicting party and ideological positions, and in distinct periods in independent India, have invoked one or the other of the concepts from this vocabulary. Differences in approaches to these key normative concepts between participants in political debate, and changes in their dominant conceptions over time, can be understood in terms of the changing inter-linkages between these concepts and their relative priority in the legitimating vocabulary.

Seen through the lens of this legitimating vocabulary, political change in India appears in a new light. Constitution-making was associated with the centralization of political power and the containment of group-differentiated rights. By contrast, the Shah Bano and Mandal debates were associated with the decentralization of political power and the expansion of group rights. While detailing the changes to the legitimating vocabulary of debate that accompanied the shifts in the distribution of power in the polity, this study has also argued that, broadly speaking, *the ideational framework embodied in the Indian Constitution has endured.* Contrary to common opinion, the resurgence of identity politics and the expansion of group-differentiated rights does not mark a fundamental break with the Nehruvian left-liberal consensus, although it does involve a renegotiation of its terms. In other words, the ideological legacy of Congress hegemony of the late 1940s endures even after its institutional coordinates have shifted. In part, this attests to the resources that democratic and liberal principles offer for the justification of group rights. It also testifies to the importance of the *process* of debate in the refashioning of political norms. In conclusion, I will draw out some wider theoretical implications of this argument and identify some areas for future research.

Most broadly, this book shows that ideas and ideals matter; more narrowly, that the principles professed by politicians merit scholarly attention. Writings on the global South typically contrast the domain of stated norms and that of actual practice (e.g., Brass 1994; Chatterjee 2004). 'Lived reality', it is argued, inhabits a very different moral universe from the realm of 'paper' ideals. Following a different route, this book has made *stated* ideals in a postcolonial context its subject and considered the purchase that these offer for understanding 'real' politics. Moving away from a focus on key individuals, this study has highlighted the importance of legislative language and debate for an empirical study of ideology. It has explored the possibilities of a largely textual analysis of political rhetoric, which abstracts in the first instance from the contexts of use that dominate Marxisant and institutionalist accounts. Throughout, it has shown that the construction of ideology occurs not just in the writings of extraordinary individuals but also through practical engagement in policy-making, in routine practices of political debate. Under evanescent talk, enduring patterns of reasoning congeal, not fully comprehended by the politicians deploying rhetoric in expedient ways, which is, of course, why instrumentalist accounts of ideology are generally inadequate.

In epistemic terms, an analytical reconstruction of legislative rhetoric advances our understanding of politics in at least three ways that this book has explored. The first pertains to ideology as an explanatory factor. By illuminating legitimating norms, an analysis of political rhetoric improves our grasp of the conditions within which particular policy outcomes are brought about. The preceding chapters have shown how limitations affecting the scope of group rights during constitution-making in the late 1940s were facilitated by a dominant liberal nationalist vocabulary in which differentiated rights were regarded with suspicion. The repositioning of preferential policies at constitution-making, towards the amelioration of disadvantage rather than the recognition of cultural difference, remains influential. Notably, most claims for group-differentiated rights today, including those for religious minorities, overwhelmingly employ the language of 'backwardness', rather than the cultural distinctiveness invoked at the start of the Constituent Assembly debates. The causal effects of the change in the policy framework of group rights in 1950 for the transformation of the Indian political system since, is a promising subject for future idea-centric research.[1]

A second epistemic gain from a focus on legislative debate pertains to the *normative-conceptual coordinates* of political forces. The preceding chapters have detailed, among others, the conceptions of secularism and national unity associated with Congress dominance in the 1950s, and the very different conception of social justice associated with the rise of lower caste-based political parties in the 1990s. The expansion of group preference from the late 1980s was accompanied by a shift to more multi-cultural and egalitarian conceptions of secularism, democracy and social justice, as witnessed in the legislative debates on Shah Bano and Mandal. Unpacking macro-units of ideology, such as liberalism and nationalism into their conceptual components, offers not just a better grasp of ideo-logical architecture (Freeden 1996), but also more accurate assessments of discursive, and political change. Against sweeping appraisals of the fate of India's founding ideals ('secularism in India has failed' or that the 'Nehruvian consensus is dead'), this book has offered more nuanced assessments. The rise of a new politics of caste and religion since the 1980s represents discursive shifts in India's founding ideals, but not a radical break. This does, however, raise the question: what kind of change would constitute a fundamental break from the legitimating vocabulary of the Indian Constitution? Specification of criteria for systemic change is an important task for future work in this area.

---

[1] As Horowitz notes, the systemic effects of policy change are not sufficiently recognized (1989: 280–1).

A third respect in which a conceptual analysis of rhetoric advances our understanding of politics pertains to approaches to political hegemony. This book has shown that the structural shifts in political power in post-Independence India can be delineated through a largely textual reading of legislative debates, which remain a neglected source of empirical evidence for hegemony construction and breakdown. A new approach to the study of hegemony, that is theoretically distinct in eschewing the frame of class analysis of Marxisant approaches, and empirically grounded in legislative argument, has been indicated in this book. Further theoretical development of a more thoroughly ideational approach to hegemony, understood primarily as a political process whereby particular ideologies are translated into public norms for the polity as a whole, is also a key area for future work.

The legitimating vocabulary of the Indian polity, this book has shown, has been substantially democratic, as well as liberal in character. Liberal democratic norms, and not just institutions, have a significant presence in the Indian polity. In both liberal and postcolonial theory, the study of norms in postcolonial contexts is dominated by what might be described as a neo-orientalist fascination with 'indigenous' social forms of religion, caste, and tribe. Political ideologies typically accorded attention are Hindu nationalism and Islamic fundamentalism, the languages of caste, religion, and kinship. While political anthropologists are beginning to pay attention to democratic institutions such as elections, liberal and democratic ideologies remain under-studied in postcolonial contexts. Stepping into the breach, this book has shown that it is possible and profitable to construct an account of post-Independence India in terms of the career of liberal and democratic political norms. Their hybrid forms might offend purists of traditions, Western and Indian alike, but liberal and democratic values have been more sophisticated and influential in India than is commonly believed. A wide range of liberal norms have informed debate over group rights (e.g., secularism, equal citizenship, equality of opportunity); these have been invoked by politicians across the party political and ideological spectrum, followers of Gandhi, Ambedkar, and Lohia as much as Nehru, elite as well as subaltern spokesmen. Indian conceptions of secularism as equal respect for all religion have invoked notions of separation of state and religion; similarly vernacular conceptions of social justice have drawn upon egalitarian notions of fair equality of opportunity for all individuals and democratic notions of political equality. A rich potential thus exists for cross-cultural comparative research into liberal and democratic political norms, which would also benefit from more attention to indigenous traditions of political thought.

Does the Indian experience suggest that liberalism is fundamentally opposed to group-differentiated rights? Certainly, liberal ideas in India, as elsewhere, have been hostile to minority rights in some instances. As this study has shown, secularism and equal rights were construed as largely antithetical to strong multicultural rights during constitution-making. However, these have also been favourable to group-based rights in other cases: in the Shah Bano debate, secularism and national unity, and in the Mandal debate, equality of opportunity were construed as requiring special treatment. On closer examination, then, liberal ideologies in postcolonial contexts do not appear as monolithic blocs *necessarily* opposed to differentiated rights or inextricably embedded within a unitary homogenizing nation-state. Postcolonial theory needs a more nuanced palette for liberalism that does not dissolve it into macro-social processes such as capitalism and colonialism, or assimilate it into distinct phenomena to which it bears a contingent relationship, such as state centralization or unitary nationalism.

Recent scholarship has highlighted ideological continuities between Nehruvian secularism and Hindu nationalism (Chatterjee 1998; Hansen 1999). To some extent, this is corroborated by my study, which has shown ideological convergence between secular and Hindu nationalism. As we have seen, Hindu nationalism's capture of liberal ground as a result of the Shah Bano debate has a longer history, one that was clearly in evidence in the Constituent Assembly debates, the 'high water mark of liberal universalism' (Rudolph and Rudolph 2001: 47). At the same time, this book has also argued that these similarities should not be overstated. In the Constituent Assembly debates, for instance, secular nationalists, unlike Hindu nationalists, supported strong cultural and educational rights for minorities. In the Shah Bano debate, Congress representatives urged the differential treatment of minority religions, implicitly acknowledging that minorities and majorities were not equals *vis-a-vis* state institutions. Both represented modifications of standard liberal positions in egalitarian liberal directions. In recognizing the gaps that exist between ideals and realities, and the respects in which general laws need to take into account the social bases of inequality,

Indian politicians have on the whole been better social theorists than their European counterparts (Mahajan 1998; for France, see Laborde 2008).

Whereas postcolonial theorists have often argued for an alternative to liberal norms, this study has suggested that Indian policy-makers have not yet fully tapped the resources that liberal and democratic principles offer for the justification of group-differentiated rights. Differential treatment of minority personal law in India can be justified, for instance, on grounds of equal respect for all individuals, as minority religions are disadvantaged in relation to the majority religion; because the imposition of reform on subordinated groups compounds injustices (Spinner-Halev 2001); and as minorities are under-represented in state institutions, and so disadvantaged with regard to collective self-determination in religious matters, unlike Hindus (Mehta 2005). Similarly, quotas for disadvantaged caste or religious minorities in education and employment can be justified as a universal benefit, for instance, from the standpoint of democratic citizenship, as it offers individuals from different social backgrounds the opportunity to interact in ways that makes them better citizens (Nussbaum 2008), better equipped to live together on terms of equality (Anderson 2002); or as improving the overall legitimacy of the democratic system (Weisskopf 2004). In public reasoning in India, justifications for group-differentiated rights from universal standpoints of a common good are underdeveloped, a challenge that remains to be addressed by policy-makers and advocates alike.

Does liberalism suffice as a framework for comprehending and evaluating multiculturalism? My findings suggest, to begin with, that normative considerations other than the freedom and equality of individuals are likely to be significant in political debates on group rights in postcolonial contexts. In Indian debates, arguments based on national unity, economic development, democratic equality, and group justice have been common. The tendency of first-generation liberal multiculturalism to view all our moral intuitions and reasoning on group rights in terms of whether these detract from or deepen the realization of liberal principles, is unduly limiting. Moreover, the dominance of the liberal paradigm has meant that in analyses of group-differentiated rights, including this study, norms such as freedom and equality are cast overwhelmingly as *liberal* values. This has obscured the framing of these ideals within other traditions, for instance, socialism and republicanism, or religious thought, and the resources that these might offer for the justification of group rights.

The Indian case suggests that postcolonial contexts are an important site for the exploration of the limits of liberal multiculturalism, and the dilemmas of group-differentiated rights in general. In many postcolonial states in Asia and Africa, group rights pre-date individual rights and national consolidation. Colonial practice, as well as local traditions, both religious and secular, favoured communitarian forms. Questions that animate Western debates on multiculturalism regarding the appropriate norms and institutions for the accommodation of cultural diversity and historical group disadvantage, had to be addressed by policy-makers much earlier. At one level, this study of group preference in a postcolonial context suggests that the significance of nation-building for the justification of group-differentiated rights has been underestimated. The orientation of liberal values such as secularism or equality of opportunity, towards special treatment, has depended upon how the requirements of national unity and economic development are construed. Although revised liberal multiculturalism does locate minority rights in the context of nation-building (e.g., Kymlicka 1995, 2007), the close relationship between liberalism and nation-building in Western contexts remains under-appreciated. At another level, Indian debates suggest that it is fruitful to explore the possibility of 'postcolonial multiculturalism'. The structural similarities of the postcolonial situation—the simultaneous pursuit of nation-building, economic development, and liberal democratic institutions that were sequenced over a longer period in the history of Western Europe—make similar debates on group-differentiated rights likely, particularly a common emphasis on national integration and economic development. However, the very different histories of state formation and national movements, of ethnic demography and national identity, rule out one single pattern of 'postcolonial multiculturalism'. Indeed, the adequacy of the concept of multiculturalism for the characterization and evaluation of approaches to differential treatment in postcolonial contexts needs further investigation.

Finally, this study has suggested that it is productive to focus on liberalism as a political ideology rather than an abstract philosophy. It is at this level of analysis that the relationship of liberal principles to national projects of civic cohesion and economic development is most evident, as well as the asymmetric effects of these projects on different social groups. Engagement with liberal ideologies can illuminate unexamined assumptions and thereby advance normative liberal theory on multiculturalism. But it is also crucial for the kind of interpretive social science explored in this book, where the character of liberal democratic ideologies clarifies the process of policy and political change. Comparative interpretive theory, involving analyses of liberal and democratic ideas across different countries for explanatory purposes, is an important area for the future development of comparative political thought.

While this book has focused on structural change in the Indian polity, its findings also bear upon an important aspect of institutional *continuity*. For theorists of democratization, a key puzzle has been the survival of democratic institutions in India, despite their many limitations. In many respects, India remains a democracy mostly in an electoral sense. Notably, the rule of law is routinely breached, violence and discrimination against religious and caste minorities are common, often aided by state institutions such as the police. Large-scale poverty and economic inequality undercut the equality of political and civil rights. Nonetheless, democratic institutions (notably elections) endure, notwithstanding high levels of poverty, illiteracy, and ethno-linguistic diversity that obtain in India. What accounts for this? Existing explanations for democratic institutions in India include the colonial legacy of British-style parliamentary institutions; the nature of the Indian national movement and the Congress party; the pattern of ethnic cleavages; the democratic dispositions of India's early leadership (for an overview, see Varshney 1998). At least two important implications, however, follow from this study. First, as noted earlier, the ideational framework fashioned at the time of constitution-making has proved to be generally resilient. This suggests that democratic institutions in India are supported by a normative-conceptual framework that has endured, even as the meanings of its key terms have changed over time. That a broadly inclusive and flexible vocabulary of public reasoning supports the survival of democratic institutions is a hypothesis for future investigation suggested by this study. Accounts of stability in India tend to highlight the role of indigenous social forms such as caste and their supple adaptation to democratic politics. By contrast, this book suggests that India's modern traditions of public reasoning might also play a role in democratic stability. While the recent provenance of many public norms is Western, their adaptation to the Indian context, and sustenance as political ideals for over a century, in the context of a society that is predominantly illiberal and undemocratic, is an achievement of modern India, in particular, of its political institutions.

That the ideational framework of the polity has survived in India begs the further question: how has it done so? This brings us to the second respect in which this book illuminates the puzzle of Indian democracy. To begin with, it has shown that the *process* of public debate plays a crucial role in the consolidation of political norms. Even that which is insincerely, or confusedly articulated, becomes rooted through repeated articulation, in unaccustomed earth. Furthermore, as the preceding chapters demonstrate, political norms are also *recast* through public debate. For instance, the orientation of the legitimating vocabulary of the polity towards group-differentiated rights came to be substantially altered, from broad hostility in the late 1940s, to relative openness by the 1990s. The role of debate and discussion in the adaptation, internalization, and transformation of political norms is an important area for future research. In keeping with the recent literature on democratization, my contention here is that democratic institutions can be self-supporting, and generate conditions for their own continuation. Elections, for instance, create opportunities for negotiation, compromise, bargaining, and in doing so offer incentives to a range of different groups to follow the rules of the democratic game. One important and neglected mechanism in this regard is the process of open discussion itself, under-pinned by political and civil rights.[2] India's robust traditions of critical public debate, sustained by a free press, independent judiciary and vigilant civil society organizations, are regarded as an important asset for its democratic institutions. This study, however, suggests that the role of open critical public debate needs more systematic empirical investigation from those interested in explaining the endurance of democratic institutions than it has received so far. With regard to theoretical advance on democracy, as with multiculturalism, India remains diagnostically significant, its complex

---

[2] In a different context, Sen has termed this the 'constructive role of democracy in the formation of values and in the understanding of needs, rights and duties' (1999: 11). As he notes, India's argumentative tradition is important not just for the 'public expression' of values, but also 'the interactive formation of values' (2005: 14).

resolutions, an affirmation of the importance of normative eclecticism and practical compromise, however, open-ended and imperfect, over the receding certitudes of prescriptive theory.

Bibliography

Ahmed, Farrah (2008). 'The Effect of the Institutional Features of the Indian System of Personal Laws on Personal Religious Autonomy'. Unpublished M.Phil. thesis, University of Oxford.

Adeney, Katharine (2007). *Federalism and Ethnic Conflict Resolution in India and Pakistan*. Basingstoke: Macmillan.

Agnes, Flavia (2005). 'Law and Gender Inequality: The Politics of Women's Rights in India' in Mala Khullar (ed.), *Writing the Women's Movement: A Reader*, 113–30. New Delhi: Zubaan.

Aloysius, G. (1997). *Nationalism without a Nation in India*. New Delhi: Oxford University Press.

Anderson, Elizabeth (1999). 'What is the Point of Equality?', *Ethics*, 109 (2): 287–337.

____ (2002). 'Integration, Affirmative Action and Strict Scrutiny', *New York University Law Review*, 77: 1195–271.

____ (2003). 'Sen, Ethics and Democracy', *Feminist Economics*, 9 (2–3): 239–61.

Ansari, Iqbal (1999). 'Minorities and the Politics of Constitution Making in India' in D.L. Sheth and Gurpreet Mahajan (eds), *Minority Identities and the Nation State*, 113–37. New Delhi: Oxford University Press.

Appadurai, Arjun (1993). 'Number in the Colonial Imagination' in Carol A. Breckenridge and Peter van der Veer (eds), *Orientalism and the Postcolonial Predicament*, 314–39. Philadelphia: University of Pennsylvania Press.

Appiah, Kwame Antony (1997). 'Multicultural Misunderstanding', *New York Review of Books*, 44 (15): 30–6.

Archer, Robin (2001). 'Secularism and Sectarianism in India and the West: What are the Real Lessons of American History?', *Economy and Society*, 30 (3): 273–87.

Austin, Granville (1966). *The Indian Constitution: Cornerstone of a Nation*. Oxford: Clarendon Press.

Baird, Robert L. (1978). 'Religion and the Legitimation of Nehru's Concept of the Secular State' in B.L. Smith (ed.), *Religion and the Legitimation of Power in South Asia*, 73–87. Leiden: Brill.

Bajpai, Rochana (1997). 'Recognizing Minorities: Some Aspects of the Indian Constituent Assembly Debates, 1946–1949'. Unpublished M.Phil. thesis, University of Oxford.

_____ (2000). 'Constituent Assembly Debates and Minority Rights', *Economic and Political Weekly*, 35 (21–2): 1837–45.

_____ (2002). 'The Conceptual Vocabularies of Secularism and Minority Rights in India', *Journal of Political Ideologies*, 7 (2): 179–97.

_____ (2003). 'The Legitimating Vocabulary of Group Rights in Contemporary India'. Unpublished D.Phil. thesis, University of Oxford.

Baker, John (1990). *Arguing for Equality*. London: Verso.

Balagangadhara, S.N. (1994). *"The Heathen in his Blindness..." Asia, the West, and the Dynamic of Religion*. Leiden: Brill.

Balagopal, K. (1990). 'This Anti-Mandal Mania', *Economic and Political Weekly*, 25 (40): 2231–4.

Barrier, Gerald N. (1968). 'The Punjab Government and Communal Politics, 1870–1908', *The Journal of Asian Studies*, 27 (3): 523–39.

Barry, Brian (1979). 'Is Democracy Special?' in Peter Laslett and James Fishkin (eds), *Philosophy, Politics and Society*, 156–95. Oxford: Blackwell.

_____ (2001). *Culture and Equality: An Egalitarian Critique of Multiculturalism*. Cambridge: Polity Press.

Bayly, C.A. (1996). *Empire and Information: Intelligence Gathering and Social Communication in India, 1780–1870*. Cambridge: Cambridge University Press.

Bayly, Susan (2000). *Caste, Society and Politics in India from the Eighteenth Century to the Modern Age*. Cambridge: Cambridge University Press.

Beitz, Charles (1989). *Political Equality: An Essay in Democratic Theory*. Princeton, N.J.: Princeton University Press.

Benhabib, Seyla (2002). *The Claims of Culture: Equality and Diversity in the Global Era*. Princeton, N.J.: Princeton University Press.

Béteille, Andre (1992). *The Backward Classes in Contemporary India*. New Delhi: Oxford University Press.

_____ (2005). 'Matters of Right and of Policy', *Seminar*, 549.

Bevir, Mark and R.A.W. Rhodes (2002). 'Interpretive Theory' in David Marsh and Gerry Stoker (eds), *Theory and Methods in Political Science*, 131–52. Basingstoke: Palgrave.

Bhargava, Rajeev (1998). 'What is Secularism for?' in Rajeev Bhargava (ed.), *Secularism and Its Critics*, 486–542. New Delhi: Oxford University Press.

_____ (2000). 'Democratic Vision of a New Republic: India, 1950', in Francine Frankel, Zoya Hasan, Rajeev Bhargava and Balveer Arora (eds), *Transforming India: Social and Political Dynamics of Democracy*, 26–59. New Delhi: Oxford University Press.

Bhattacharya, Neeladri (1993). 'Myth, History and the Politics of Ramjanmabhumi', in Sarvepalli Gopal (ed.), *Anatomy of a Confrontation: Ayodhya and the Rise of Communal Politics in India*, 122–40. London: Zed Books Ltd.

Bilgrami, Akeel (1998). 'Secularism, Nationalism and Modernity', in Rajeev Bhargava (ed.), *Secularism and its Critics*, 380–417. New Delhi: Oxford University Press.

Blyth, Mark M. (1997). '"Any More Bright Ideas?" The Ideational Turn of Comparative Political Economy', *Comparative Politics*, 29 (2): 229–50.

Bose, Sugata and Ayesha Jalal (1999). *Modern South Asia: History, Culture, Political Economy*. New Delhi: Oxford University Press.

Bourdieu, Pierre (1977). *Outline of a Theory of Practice*. Cambridge: Cambridge University Press.

Brass, Paul (1994). *The Politics of India since Independence*, 2nd edition. Cambridge: Cambridge University Press.

Brasted, H.V. and C. Bridge (1994). 'The Transfer of Power in South Asia: A Historiographical Review', *South Asia*, 17 (1): 93–114.

Brown, Judith (1990). *Modern India: The Origins of an Asian Democracy*. Oxford: Oxford University Press.

Cahn, S.M. (ed.) (2002). *The Affirmative Action Debate*. New York and London: Routledge.

Chandhoke, Neera (1999). *Beyond Secularism: The Rights of Religious Minorities*. New Delhi: Oxford University Press.

Chandra, Kanchan (2004). *Why Ethnic Parties Succeed: Patronage and Ethnic Head Counts in India*. Cambridge: Cambridge University Press.

Chatterjee, Partha (1986). *Nationalist Thought and the Colonial World: A Derivative Discourse?* London: Zed Books Ltd.

——— (1995). *The Nation and Its Fragments: Colonial and Postcolonial Histories*. New Delhi: Oxford University Press.

——— (1998). 'Secularism and Tolerance' in Rajeev Bhargava (ed.), *Secularism and Its Critics*, 345–79. New Delhi: Oxford University Press.

——— (2004). *The Politics of the Governed: Reflections on Popular Politics in Most of the World*. New Delhi: Permanent Black.

Chaube, Shibani Kinkar (1973). *Constituent Assembly of India: Springboard of Revolution*. New Delhi: People's Publishing House.

Chiriyankandath, James (2000). 'Creating a Secular State in a Religious Country: The Debate in the Indian Constituent Assembly', *Commonwealth and Comparative Politics*, 38 (2): 1–24.

Cohen, Joshua (1989). 'Deliberation and Democratic Legitimacy' in Alan Hamlin and Philip Pettit (eds), *The Good Polity: Normative Analysis of the State*, 17–34. Oxford: Blackwell.

Bibliography 299

Cohen, Marshall, Thomas Nagel, and Tim Scanlon (eds) (1977). *Equality and Preferential Treatment*, Princeton, N.J.: Princeton University Press.

Cohn, Bernard (1987). *An Anthropologist Among the Historians and Other Essays*. New Delhi: Oxford University Press.

Constituent Assembly Debates (1950). *Constituent Assembly Debates: Official Report, 1946–1950*, 9 December 1946–24 January 1950, Vols I–XII. New Delhi: Government of India.

Corbridge, Stuart (2000). 'Competing Inequalities: The Scheduled Tribes and the Reservations System in India's Jharkhand', *The Journal of Asian Studies*, 59(1): 62–85.

Corbridge, Stuart and John Harriss (2000). *Reinventing India: Liberalization, Hindu Nationalism, and Popular Democracy*. Cambridge: Polity Press.

Cossman, Brenda and Ratna Kapur (1996). 'Secularism: Bench-Marked by Hindu Right', *Economic and Political Weekly*, 31 (38): 2613–30.

Coupland, Reginald (1968). *The Indian Problem 1833–1935*. London: Oxford University Press.

Dallmayr, Fred (2004). 'Beyond Monologue: For a Comparative Political Theory', *Perspectives in Politics*, 2 (2): 249–57.

Das, Veena (1994). 'Cultural Rights and the Definition of Community', in Oliver Mendelsohn and Upendra Baxi (eds), *The Rights of Subordinated People*, 117–58. New Delhi: Oxford University Press.

Derrett, John Duncan M. (1963). *Introduction to Modern Hindu Law*. Bombay: Oxford University Press.

Deshpande, Satish and Yogendra Yadav (2006). 'Redesigning Affirmative Action: Castes and Benefits in Higher Education', *Economic and Political Weekly*, 41 (24): 2419–24.

Deshpande, Satish (2006). 'Exclusive Inequalities: Merit, Caste and Discrimination in Indian Higher Education Today', *Economic and Political Weekly*, 41 (24): 2438–44.

Deshpande, Ashwini (2006). 'The Eternal Debate', *Economic and Political Weekly*, 41 (24): 2444–6.

De Zwart, Frank (2000). 'Practical Knowledge and Institutional Design in India's Affirmative Action Policy', *Anthropology Today*, 16 (2): 4–7.

Dhandha, Meena (1998). 'Justifications for Gender Quotas in Legislative Bodies: A Consideration of Identity and Representation', *Women's Philosophy Review*, 20: 44–62.

Dhavan, Rajeev (2008). *Reserved! How Parliament Debated Reservations: 1995–2007*. New Delhi: Rupa.

Dirks, Nicholas (2001). *Castes of Mind: Colonialism and the Making of Modern India*. Princeton, N.J.: Princeton University Press.

Dudley Jenkins, Laura (2003). *Identity and Identification in India: Defining the Disadvantaged*. London and New York: Routledge.

Dushkin, Lelah (1972). 'Scheduled Caste Politics' in J. Michael Mahar (ed.), *The Untouchables in Contemporary India*, 165–226. Tucson: University of Arizona Press.

Dworkin, Ronald (1986). *A Matter of Principle*. Oxford: Clarendon Press.

Eisenberg, Avigail (2005). 'Identity and Liberal Politics: The Problem of Minorities within Minorities' in Avigail Eisenberg and Jeff Spinner-Halev (eds), *Minorities within Minorities: Equality, Rights and Diversity*, 249–70. Cambridge: Cambridge University Press.

Embree, Ainslee (1990). *Utopias in Conflict: Religion and Nationalism in Modern India*. Berkeley and Los Angeles: University of California Press.

Engineer, Asghar Ali (ed.) (1987). *The Shah Bano Controversy*. Bombay: Orient Longman.

Farr, James (1989). 'Understanding Conceptual Change Politically' in Terence Ball, James Farr, and Russell L. Hanson (eds), *Political Innovation and Conceptual Change* 24–49. Cambridge: Cambridge University Press.

Foucault, Michel (1980). *Power/Knowledge: Selected Interviews and Other Writings, 1972–1977* (edited by Colin Gordon). New York: Pantheon Books.

Fraser, Nancy (1997). *Justice Interruptus: Critical Reflections on the "Post Socialist" Condition*. New York: Routledge.

Fraser Nancy and Axel Honneth (2003). *Redistribution or Recognition? A Philosophical Exchange*. New York: Verso.

Freeden, Michael (1996). *Ideologies and Political Theory: A Conceptual Approach*. Oxford: Oxford University Press.

Freeden, Michael. (2007). 'The Comparative Study of Political Thinking', *Journal of Political Ideologies*, 12 (1): 1–9.

Galanter, Marc (1984). *Competing Equalities, Law and the Backward Classes in India*. New Delhi: Oxford University Press.

_____ (1989). *Law and Society in Modern India*. New Delhi: Oxford University Press.

_____ (1998a) [1965]. 'Secularism, East and West', reprinted in Rajeev Bhargava (ed.), *Secularism and Its Critics*, 234–67. New Delhi: Oxford University Press.

_____ (1998b) [1971]. 'Hinduism, Secularism and the Indian Judiciary', reprinted in Rajeev Bhargava (ed.), *Secularism and Its Critics*, 268–91. New Delhi: Oxford University Press.

Geertz, Clifford (1973). *The Interpretation of Cultures: Selected Essays*. New York: Basic Books.

Gofas, Andreas and Colin Hay (2008). 'Causal, Constitutive or Constitutively Causal? The Explanatory Status of Ideas in Post-positivist Political Analysis', paper presented at the annual meeting of the *American Political Science Association*, Boston.

Goldman, Alan (1979). *Justice and Reverse Discrimination*. Princeton, N.J.: Princeton University Press.

Gooptu, Nandini (2001). *The Politics of the Urban Poor in Early Twentieth-Century India*. Cambridge: Cambridge University Press.

Gopal, Sarvepalli (1988). 'Nehru and the Minorities', *Economic and Political Weekly*, 23 (45/47): 45–7.

Gramsci, Antonio (1971). *Selections from the Prison Notebooks of Antonio Gramsci* edited and translated by Quintin Hoare and Geoffrey Nowell Smith. London: Lawrence & Wishart.

Guha, Ramachandra (2007). *India after Gandhi: The History of the World's Largest Democracy*. New Delhi: Picador India.

Guha, Ranajit (1997). *Dominance without Hegemony: History and Power in Colonial India*. Cambridge, Mass.: Harvard University Press.

Gupta Dipankar (2005). 'Limits of Reservations', *Seminar*, 549.

Gupta, S.K. (1985). *The Scheduled Castes in Modern Indian Politics: Their Emergence as a Political Power*. New Delhi: Munshiram Manoharlal.

Guru, Gopal (2005). 'Corporate Class and Its "Veil of Ignorance"', *Seminar*, 549.

Gutmann, Amy and Dennis Thompson (1996). *Democracy and Disagreement*. Cambridge, Mass.: The Belknap Press of Harvard University Press.

Gwyer, Maurice and A. Appadorai (1957). *Speeches and Documents on the Indian Constitution*. Bombay: Oxford University Press.

Habermas, Jurgen (1998). *The Inclusion of the Other: Studies in Political Theory*. Cambridge: Polity Press.

Hansen, Thomas Blom (1999). *The Saffron Wave: Democracy and Hindu Nationalism in Modern India*. New Delhi: Oxford University Press.

Harris, Luke Charles and Uma Narayan (2007). 'Affirmative Action as Equalizing Opportunity: Challenging the Myth of "Preferential Treatment"' in Hugh LaFollette (ed.), *Ethics in Practice, An Anthology*, 448–59. Malden, M.A.: Blackwell.

Hasan, Zoya (1989). 'Minority Identity, Muslim Women Bill Campaign and the Political Process', *Economic and Political Weekly*, 24 (1): 44–50.

——— (1998). 'Gender Politics, Legal Reform, and the Muslim Community in India' in Patricia Jeffrey and Amrita Basu (eds), *Appropriating Gender: Women's Activism and Politicized Religion in South Asia*, 71–88. New York: Routledge.

——— (2005). 'Governance and Reform of Personal Law in India' in Indira Jaising (ed.), *Men's Laws Women's Lives: A Constitutional Perspective on Religion, Common Law and Culture in South Asia*, 353–73. New Delhi: Women Unlimited.

Horowitz, Donald (1989). 'Cause and Consequence in Public Policy Theory: Ethnic Policy and System Transformation in Malaysia', *Policy Sciences*, 22 (3–4): 249–87.

Ilaiah, Kancha (2006). 'Merit of Reservations', *Economic and Political Weekly*, 41 (24): 2447–9.

Imam, Mohammed (ed.) (1972). *Minorities and the Law*. Bombay: N.M. Tripathi.

Indian Round Table Conference (1931). *Indian Round Table Conference 12th November, 1930–19th January, 1931: Proceedings*. London: H.M. Stationery Office.

Jaffrelot, Christophe (2003). *India's Silent Revolution*. London: C. Hurst & Co.

_____ (2004). 'Composite Culture is Not Multiculturalism: A Study of the Indian Constituent Assembly Debates' in Ashutosh Varshney (ed.), *India and the Politics of Developing Countries: Essays in Memory of Myron Weiner*, 126–49. New Delhi and London: Sage.

Jalal, Ayesha (1985). *The Sole Spokesman: Jinnah, the Muslim League and the Demand for Pakistan*. Cambridge: Cambridge University Press.

Jaoul, Nicolas (2006). 'Learning the Use of Symbolic Means: Dalits, Ambedkar Statues and the State in Uttar Pradesh', *Contributions to Indian Sociology*, 40 (2): 175–207.

Jayal, Niraja Gopal (1999). *Democracy and the State: Welfare, Secularism, and Development in India*. New Delhi: Oxford University Press.

Jha, Shefali (2002). 'Secularism in the Constituent Assembly Debates, 1946–1950', *Economic and Political Weekly*, 37 (30): 3175–80.

Jodhka, Surinder S. and Katherine Newman (2007). 'In the Name of Globalization: Meritocracy, Productivity and the Hidden Language of Caste', *Economic and Political Weekly*, 42 (41): 4125–32.

Kalelkar Commission (1956). *Report of the Backward Classes Commission*. New Delhi: Government of India.

Kaviraj, Sudipta (1992). 'The Imaginary Institution of India' in Partha Chatterjee and Gyanendra Pandey (eds), *Subaltern Studies VII*, 1–39. New Delhi: Oxford University Press.

_____ (1994). 'On the Structure of Nationalist Discourse' in T.V. Satyamurthy (ed.), *State and Nation in Context of Social Change*, 298–333. New Delhi: Oxford University Press.

Khaitan, Tarunabh (2008). 'Transcending Reservations: A Paradigm Shift in the Debate on Equality', *Economic and Political Weekly*, 43 (38): 8–12.

Khan, Omar (2008). 'Justifications of Preferential Treatment in India', Unpublished D.Phil thesis, University of Oxford.

Khilnani, Sunil (1997). *The Idea of India*. London: Hamish Hamilton.

_____ (2002), 'Nehru's Faith', *Economic and Political Weekly*, 37 (48): 4793–99.

Khory, Kavita R. (1993). 'The Shah Bano Case: Some Political Implications' in Robert D. Baird (ed.), *Religion and Law in Independent India*, 149–65. New Delhi: Manohar.

Kishwar, Madhu (1994). 'Codified Hindu Law: Myth and Reality', *Economic and Political Weekly*, 29 (33): 2145–61.

Kooiman, Dick (1997). 'The Strength of Numbers: Enumerating Communities in India's Princely States', *South Asia*, 20 (1): 81–98.

Kothari, Rajni (1964). 'The Congress "System" in India', *Asian Survey*, 4 (12): 1161–73.

Kozlowski, Gregory C. (1993). 'Muslim Personal Law and Political Identity in Independent India' in Robert D. Baird (ed.), *Religion and Law in Independent India*, 103–20. New Delhi: Manohar.

Krishna, K.B. (1939). *The Problem of Minorities in India or Communal Representation in India*. London: G. Allen and Unwin.

Kukathas, Chandran (1992). 'Are There Any Cultural Rights?', *Political Theory*, 20 (1): 107–39.

Kumar, Ravinder (1985). 'Gandhi, Ambedkar and the Poona Pact, 1932', *South Asia: Journal of South Asian Studies*, 8 (1): 87–101.

—— (1987). 'Introduction' in A.K. Gupta (ed.), *Myth and Reality: The Struggle for Freedom in India, 1945–1947*, xiii–xxviii. New Delhi: Manohar.

Kymlicka, Will (1989). *Liberalism, Community and Culture*. Oxford: Clarendon Press.

—— (1995). *Multicultural Citizenship, A Liberal Theory of Minority Rights*. Oxford: Clarendon Press.

—— (2001). *Politics in the Vernacular*. Oxford: Oxford University Press.

—— (2007). *Multicultural Odysseys: Navigating the New International Politics of Diversity*. Oxford: Oxford University Press.

Kymlicka, Will and W. Norman (eds) (2000). *Citizenship in Diverse Societies*. Oxford: Oxford University Press.

Laborde, Cecile (2008). *Critical Republicanism: The Hijab Controversy and Political Philosophy*. Oxford: Oxford University Press.

Laclau, Ernesto and Chantal Mouffe (1985). *Hegemony and Socialist Strategy: Towards a Radical Democratic Politics*. London: Verso.

LaFollette, Hugh (ed.) (2007). *Ethics in Practice: An Anthology*. Malden, M.A.: Blackwell.

Larson, Gerald (1993). 'Mandal, Mandir, Masjid: The Citizen as an Endangered Species in Independent India' in Robert D. Baird (ed.), *Religion and Law in Independent India*, 87–102. New Delhi: Manohar.

—— (2001). *Religion and Personal Law in Secular India: A Call to Judgment*. Bloomington: Indiana University Press.

Lijphart, Arendt (1996). 'The Puzzle of Indian Democracy: A Consociational Interpretation', *The American Political Science Review*, 90 (2): 258–68.

Lohia, Rammanohar (1964). *The Caste System*. Hyderabad: Navahind.

Lok Sabha Debates (1986). *Parliamentary Debates, Official Report*. New Delhi: Lok Sabha Secretariat.

_____ (1990), *Parliamentary Debates, Official Report*. New Delhi: Lok Sabha Secretariat.

_____ (2006). *Parliamentary Debates, Official Report*. New Delhi: Lok Sabha Secretariat.

MacKinnon, Catherine A. (2005). 'Sex Equality and "Personal Laws" under the Constitution of India' in Indira Jaising (ed.), *Men's Laws Women's Lives: A Constitutional Perspective on Religion, Common Law and Culture in South Asia*, 259–85. New Delhi: Women Unlimited.

Madan, T.N. (1998). 'Secularism in its Place' in Rajeev Bhargava (ed.), *Secularism and Its Critics*, 297–320. New Delhi: Oxford University Press.

Mahajan, Gurpreet (1998). *Identities and Rights: Aspects of Liberal Democracy in India*. New Delhi: Oxford University Press.

Mahmood, Tahir (1991). *Minorities and the State at the Indian Law*. New Delhi: Sterling.

_____ (1983). *Muslim Personal Law: Role of the State in the Indian Subcontinent*. Nagpur: All India Reporter.

Mandal Commission Report (1991) [1980]. *Reservations for Backward Classes: Mandal Commission Report of the Backward Classes Commission 1980*. New Delhi: Akalank Publications.

Manor, James (1997). 'Parties and the Party System' in Partha Chatterjee (ed.), *State and Politics in India*, 92–124. New Delhi: Oxford University Press.

Mansbridge, Jane (2000). 'What Does A Representative Do? Descriptive Representation in Communicative Settings of Distrust, Uncrystallized Interests, and Historically Denigrated Status', in Will Kymlicka and Wayne Norman (eds), *Citizenship in Diverse Societies*, 99–123. Oxford: Oxford University Press.

Margalit, Avishai and Joseph Raz (1990). 'National Self Determination', *The Journal of Philosophy*, 87 (9): 439–61.

McMillan, Alistair (2005). *Standing at the Margins: Representation and Electoral Reservations in India*. New Delhi: Oxford University Press.

Mehta, Pratap Bhanu (2005). 'Reason, Tradition, Authority: Religion and the Indian State' in Indira Jaising (ed.), *Men's Laws Women's Lives: A Constitutional Perspective on Religion, Common Law and Culture in South Asia*, 56–86. New Delhi: Women Unlimited.

_____ (2006). 'Democracy, Disagreement and Merit', *Economic and Political Weekly*, 41 (24): 2425–7.

Mendelsohn, Oliver and Marika Vicziany (1998). *The Untouchables: Subordination, Poverty and the State in India*. Cambridge: Cambridge University Press.

Menon, Nivedita and Aditya Nigam (2007). *Power and Contestation: India since 1989*. Hyderabad: Orient Longman.

Miller, David (1978). 'Democracy and Social Justice', *British Journal of Political Science*, 8 (1): 1–19.

_____ (1999). *Principles of Social Justice*. Cambridge, Mass.: Harvard University Press.

Minault, Gail (1982). *The Khilafat Movement: Religious Symbolism and Political Mobilization in India*. New York: Columbia University Press.

Modood, Tariq (2007). *Multiculturalism*. Cambridge: Polity Press.

Morris-Jones, W.H. (1963). 'India's Political Idioms' in C.H. Philips (ed.), *Politics and Society in India*, 133–54. London: G. Allen & Unwin.

Mukhopadhyay, Maitrayee (1994). 'Between Community and State: The Question of Women's Rights and Personal Laws' in Zoya Hasan (ed.), *Forging Identities: Gender, Communities, and the State*, 108–29. Boulder, Co.: Westview Press.

Munshi, K.M. (1967). *Pilgrimage to Freedom*. Bombay: Bharatiya Vidya Bhavan.

Nandy, Ashis (1998). 'The Politics of Secularism and the Recovery of Religious Tolerance' in Rajeev Bhargava (ed.), *Secularism and Its Critics*, 321–44. New Delhi: Oxford University Press.

Nagel, Thomas (1979). *Mortal Questions*. Cambridge: Cambridge University Press.

Nehru, Jawaharlal (1946). *Discovery of India*. Calcutta: Signet Press.

Nussbaum, Martha C. (2005). 'Religion, Culture and Sex Equality' in Indira Jaising (ed.), *Men's Laws Women's Lives: A Constitutional Perspective on Religion, Common Law and Culture in South Asia*. 109–37. New Delhi: Women Unlimited.

_____ (2008). 'Affirmative Action and the Goals of Higher Education', paper presented at conference on Affirmative Action in Higher Education in India, the United States and South Africa, New Delhi, March 19–21.

O'Hanlon, Rosalind (1985). *Caste, Conflict, and Ideology*. Cambridge: Cambridge University Press.

Okin, Susan Moller (1999). 'Is Multiculturalism Bad for Women?' in Joshua Cohen, Matthew Howard, and Martha C. Nussbaum (eds), *Is Multiculturalism Bad for Women?* Princeton N.J.: Princeton University Press.

Omvedt, Gail (1994). *Dalits and the Democratic Revolution: Dr Ambedkar and the Dalit Movement in Colonial India*. New Delhi: Sage.

Owen, Hugh (1972). 'Negotiating the Lucknow Pact', *Journal of Asian Studies*, 31 (3): 561–87.

Pai, Sudha and Jagpal Singh (1997). 'Politicization of Dalits and Most Backward Castes', *Economic and Political Weekly*, 32 (23): 1356–61.

Pandey, Gyanendra (1990). *The Construction of Communalism in Colonial North India*. New Delhi: Oxford University Press.

Pantham, Thomas (1997). 'Indian Secularism and its Critics: Some Reflections', *The Review of Politics*, 59 (3): 523–40.

Parashar, Archana (1992). *Women and Family Law Reform in India*. New Delhi: Sage.

Parekh, Bhikhu (1989). *Colonialism, Tradition and Reform: An Analysis of Gandhi's Political Discourse*. New Delhi and London: Sage.

_____ (2000). *Rethinking Multiculturalism: Cultural Diversity and Political Theory*. Basingstoke: Macmillan.

Parekh, Bhikhu and Subrata Mitra (1990). 'The Logic of Anti-Reservation Discourse in India' in S.K. Mitra (ed.), *Politics of Positive Discrimination: A Cross National Perspective*, 91–109. Bombay: Popular Prakashan.

Patankar Bharat and Gail Omvedt (1979). 'The Dalit Liberation Movement in the Colonial Period', *Economic and Political Weekly*, 14 (7–8): 409–24.

Pathak, Zakia and Rajeswari Sunder Rajan (1989). 'Shah Bano', *Signs*, 14 (3): 558–82.

Phillips, Anne (1995). *The Politics of Presence*. Oxford: Clarendon Press.

_____ (2004). 'Defending Equality of Outcome', *Journal of Political Philosophy*, 12 (1): 1–19.

_____ (2007). *Multiculturalism without Culture*. Princeton, N.J.: Princeton University Press.

Philips, C.H. (1962). *The Evolution of India and Pakistan, 1858 to 1947: Select Documents*. London: Oxford University Press.

Pitkin, Hanna (1967). *The Concept of Representation*. Berkeley: University of California Press.

Rabinow, Paul and William Sullivan (1987). *Interpretive Social Science: A Second Look*. Berkeley and Los Angeles: University of California Press.

Radcliffe-Richards, Janet (1998). 'Equality of Opportunity' in Andrew Mason (ed.), *Ideals of Equality*, 52–78. Oxford: Blackwell.

Rajya Sabha Debates (1986). *Parliamentary Debates: Official Report*. New Delhi: Lok Sabha Secreteriat.

_____ (1990). *Parliamentary Debates: Official Report*. New Delhi: Lok Sabha Secreteriat.

_____ (2006). *Parliamentary Debates: Official Report*. New Delhi: Lok Sabha Secreteriat.

Rawls, John (1971). *A Theory of Justice*. Cambridge, Mass.: The Belknap Press of Harvard University Press.

_____ (2001). *Justice as Fairness: A Restatement*. Cambridge, Mass.: The Belknap Press of Harvard University Press.

Raz, Joseph (1994). *Ethics in the Public Domain: Essays in the Morality of Law and Politics*. Oxford: Clarendon Press.

Retzlaff, Ralph (1963). 'The Problem of Communal Minorities in the Drafting of the Indian Constitution' in R.N. Spann (ed.), *Constitutionalism in Asia*, 55–73. Bombay: Asia Publishing House.

Rodrigues, Valerian (2005). 'Ambedkar on Preferential Treatment', *Seminar*, 549.

Rosenbloom, D.H. (1977). *Federal Equal Employment Opportunity: Politics and Public Personnel Administration*. New York: Praeger Publishers.

Rosenfeld, Michel (1991). *Affirmative Action and Justice: A Philosophical and Constitutional Inquiry*. New Haven: Yale University Press.

Roy, Srirupa (2007). *Beyond Belief: India and the Politics of Postcolonial Nationalism*. Durham: Duke University Press.

Rudolph, Susanne H. and Lloyd I. Rudolph (1987). *In Pursuit of Lakshmi: The Political Economy of the Indian State*. Bombay: Orient Longman.

———— (2001). 'Living with Difference in India: Legal Pluralism and Legal Universalism in Historical Context' in Gerald Larson (ed.), *Religion and Personal Law in Secular India*, 36–65. Bloomington and Indianapolis: Indiana University Press.

Rueschemeyer, Dietrich (2006). 'Why and How Ideas Matter' in Robert Goodin and Charles Tilly (eds), *The Oxford Handbook of Contextual Political Analysis*, 227–51. Oxford: Oxford University Press.

Sachar Committee Report (2006). *Social, Economic and Educational Status of the Muslim Community in India: A Report*. New Delhi: Government of India.

Sangari, Kumkum and Sudesh Vaid (1989). *Recasting Women: Essays in Colonial History*. New Delhi: Kali for Women.

Sarkar, Sumit (1983). *Modern India: 1885–1947*. Delhi: Macmillan.

———— (1997). *Writing Social History*. New Delhi: Oxford University Press.

———— (2001). 'Indian Democracy: The Historical Inheritance' in Atul Kohli (ed.), *The Success of India's Democracy*, 23–46. Cambridge: Cambridge University Press.

Seal, Anil (1968). *The Emergence of Indian Nationalism: Competition and Collaboration in the Later Nineteenth Century*. London: Cambridge University Press.

Sen, Amartya (1998). 'Secularism and Its Discontents' in Rajeev Bhargava (ed.), *Secularism and Its Critics*, 454–85. New Delhi: Oxford University Press.

———— (1999). 'Democracy as a Universal Value', *Journal of Democracy*, 10 (3): 3–17.

———— (2005). *The Argumentative Indian: Writings on Indian History, Culture and Identity*. London: Penguin.

Sen, D. (1940). *The Problem of Minorities*. Calcutta: University of Calcutta.

Shachar, Ayelet (1998). 'Group Identity and Women's Rights in Family Law: The Perils of Multicultural Accommodation', *Journal of Political Philosophy*, 6 (3): 285–305.

Shaikh, Farzana (1989). *Community and Consensus in Islam: Muslim Representation in Colonial India, 1860–1947*. Cambridge: Cambridge University Press.

Sheth D.L. (1999). 'The Nation-State and Minority Rights' in D.L. Sheth and Gurpreet Mahajan (eds), *Minority Identities and the Nation State*, 18–37. New Delhi: Oxford University Press.

———— (2002). 'Ram Manohar Lohia on Caste in Indian Politics', in Ghanshyam Shah (ed.), *Caste and Democratic Politics in India*, 108–33. New Delhi: Permanent Black.

———— (2005) 'Considerations for a Policy Framework', *Seminar*, 549.

Shiva Rao, B. (1967). *The Framing of India's Constitution: Select Documents*, Vols I–IV. Delhi: Indian Institute of Public Administration.

———— (1968). *The Framing of India's Constitution: A Study*. Delhi: Indian Institute of Public Administration.

Shue, Henry (1980). *Basic Rights: Subsistence, Affluence, and U.S. Foreign Policy*. Princeton, N.J.: Princeton University Press.

Singh, Parmanand (1982). *Equality, Reservation and Discrimination in India, A Constitutional Study of Scheduled Castes, Scheduled Tribes, and Other Backward Classes*. Delhi: Deep and Deep.

Singh, Pritam (2006). 'Hindu Bias in India's "Secular" Constitution: Probing Flaws in the Instruments of Governance', *Third World Quarterly*, 26 (6): 909–26.

Skinner, Quentin (1988). 'Some Problems in the Analysis of Political Thought and Action' in James Tully (ed.), *Meaning and Context: Quentin Skinner and his Critics*, 97–118. Cambridge: Polity Press.

———— (2002). *Visions of Politics, Volume I Regarding Method*. Cambridge: Cambridge University Press.

Smith, Donald Eugene (1958). *Nehru and Democracy: The Political Thought of an Asian Democrat*. Calcutta: Orient Longman.

———— (1963). *India as a Secular State*. Princeton, N.J.: Princeton University Press.

Spinner-Halev, Jeff (2001). 'Feminism, Multicultural Oppression, and the State', *Ethics*, 112 (1): 84–113.

Sridharan, E. (2002). 'The Origins of the Electoral System: Rules, Representation, and Power-Sharing in India's Democracy' in Zoya Hasan and R. Sudarshan (eds), *India's Living Constitution, Ideas, Practices, Controversies*, 344–69. New Delhi: Permanent Black.

Sunstein, Cass (1991). 'Preferences and Politics', *Philosophy and Public Affairs*, 20 (1): 3–34.

Swift, Adam (2001). 'Politics v Philosophy', *Prospect*, August–September.

Taylor, Charles (1985). *Philosophy and the Human Sciences: Philosophical Papers* 2. Cambridge: Cambridge University Press.

_____ (1992). 'The Politics of Recognition', in Arny Gutmann (ed.), *Multiculturalism and the Politics of Recognition*, 25–73. Princeton, N.J.: Princeton University Press.

Thorat, Sukhdeo (2006).'Paying the Social Debt', *Economic and Political Weekly*, 41 (24): 2432–5.

Upadhyaya, Prakash Chandra (1992).'The Politics of Indian Secularism', *Modern Asian Studies*, 26 (4): 815–53.

Van Dyke, Vernon (1995). 'The Individual, the State, and Ethnic Communities in Political Theory', in Will Kymlicka (ed.), *The Rights of Minority Cultures*, 31–56. Oxford: Clarendon Press.

Varshney, Ashutosh (1993). 'Contested Meanings: India's National Identity, Hindu Nationalism, and the Politics of Anxiety', *Daedalus*, 122 (3), 227–61.

_____ (1998).'Why Democracy Survives', *Journal of Democracy*, 9 (3):36–50.

Vora, Rajendra (2004). 'Decline of Caste Majoritarianism in Indian Politics' in Rajendra Vora and Suhas Palshiker (eds), *Indian Democracy: Meanings and Practices*, 271–97. New Delhi and London: Sage.

Wadhwa, K.K. (1975). *Minority Safeguards in India: Constitutional Provisions and their Implementation*. Delhi: Thomson Press.

Washbrook, David (1999). 'The Rhetoric of Democracy and Development in Late Colonial India' in Sugata Bose and Ayesha Jalal (eds), *Nationalism, Democracy and Development: State and Politics in India*, 36–49. New Delhi: Oxford University Press.

Weiner, Myron (1997). 'India's Minorities: Who Are They? What Do They Want?' in Partha Chatterjee (ed.), *State and Politics in India*, 459–95. New Delhi: Oxford University Press.

Weisskopf, Thomas (2004). *Affirmative Action in the United States and India: A Comparative Perspective*. Routledge: New York.

Wendt, Alexander (1998). 'On Constitution and Causation in International Relations', *Review of International Studies*, 24 (5): 101–18.

Wilkinson, Steven (2004). *Votes and Violence: Electoral Competition and Ethnic Riots in India*. Cambridge: Cambridge University Press.

Williams, Melissa (1998). *Voice, Trust and Memory: Marginalised Groups and the Failings of Liberal Representation*. Princeton, N.J.: Princeton University Press.

Witten, Samuel (1983). 'Compensatory Discrimination in India: Affirmative Action as a Means of Combatting Class Inequality', *Columbia Journal of Transnational Law*, 21 (2): 353–88.

Wolff, Jonathan (1998). 'Fairness, Respect and Egalitarian Ethos', *Philosophy and Public Affairs*, 27 (2): 97–122.

Yadav, Yogendra (1999). 'Electoral Politics in the Time of Change: India's Third Electoral System, 1989–99', *Economic and Political Weekly*, 34 (34&35): 2393–9.

Young, Iris Marion (1990). *Justice and the Politics of Difference*. Princeton, N.J.: Princeton University Press.

Zachariah, Benjamin (2005). *Developing India: An Intellectual and Social History, c. 1930–50*. New Delhi: Oxford University Press.

Zaidi, A.M. (1984). *Congress and the Minorities: A Study of Congress Policy towards Minorities during the Last 100 Years*. New Delhi: Indian Institute of Applied Political Research.

Zelliot, Eleanor (1988). 'Congress and the Untouchables, 1917–1950' in Richard Sisson and Stanley A. Wolpert (eds), *Congress and Indian Nationalism: The Pre-Independence Phase*, 182–98. Berkeley: University of California Press.

Index